Chinese Families Upside Down

China Studies

PUBLISHED FOR THE INSTITUTE FOR CHINESE
STUDIES, UNIVERSITY OF OXFORD

Series Editor

Rana Mitter, *University of Oxford*

VOLUME 42

The titles published in this series are listed at *brill.com/chs*

Chinese Families Upside Down

*Intergenerational Dynamics and
Neo-Familism in the Early 21st Century*

Edited by

Yunxiang Yan

BRILL

LEIDEN | BOSTON

Library of Congress Cataloging-in-Publication Data

Names: Yan, Yunxiang, 1954- editor.
Title: Chinese families upside down : intergenerational dynamics and
  neo-familism in the early 21st century / edited by Yunxiang Yan.
Description: Boston : BRILL, 2021. | Series: China studies, 1570-1344 ; 42 |
  Includes bibliographical references and index. | Summary: "This book offers
  the first systematic account of how intergenerational dependence is
  redefining the Chinese family. The authors make a collective effort
  to go beyond the conventional model of filial piety to explore the rich,
  nuanced, and often unexpected new intergenerational dynamics.
  The book is an essential read for scholars and students of China studies
  in particular and for those who are interested in the present-day family
  and kinship in general"– Provided by publisher.
Identifiers: LCCN 2020056532 (print) | LCCN 2020056533 (ebook) |
  ISBN 9789004450226 (hardback) | ISBN 9789004450233 (ebook)
Subjects: LCSH: Families–China–History–21st century. |
  Intergenerational relations–China–History–21st century.
Classification: LCC HQ684 .C4754 2021 (print) | LCC HQ684 (ebook) |
  DDC 306.85095109/05–dc23
LC record available at https://lccn.loc.gov/2020056532
LC ebook record available at https://lccn.loc.gov/2020056533

Typeface for the Latin, Greek, and Cyrillic scripts: "Brill". See and download: brill.com/brill-typeface.

ISSN 1570-1344
ISBN 978-90-04-45022-6 (hardback)
ISBN 978-90-04-45023-3 (e-book)

Copyright 2021 by the authors. Published by Koninklijke Brill NV, Leiden, The Netherlands.
Koninklijke Brill NV incorporates the imprints Brill, Brill Hes & De Graaf, Brill Nijhoff, Brill Rodopi,
Brill Sense, Hotei Publishing, mentis Verlag, Verlag Ferdinand Schöningh and Wilhelm Fink Verlag.
Koninklijke Brill NV reserves the right to protect this publication against unauthorized use. Requests for
re-use and/or translations must be addressed to Koninklijke Brill NV via brill.com or copyright.com.

This book is printed on acid-free paper and produced in a sustainable manner.

*In honor of James L. Watson and Rubie Watson for
their enduring contributions to the study of Chinese family and kinship*

Contents

Acknowledgements IX
List of Figures XI
Notes on Contributors XII

1 Introduction: The Inverted Family, Post-Patriarchal Intergenerationality and Neo-Familism 1
  Yunxiang Yan

2 "We Do": Parental Involvement in the Marriages of Urban Sons and Daughters 31
  Deborah S. Davis

3 The "Leftover" Majority: Why Urban Men and Women Born under China's One-Child Policy Remain Unmarried through Age 27 55
  Vanessa L. Fong, Greene Ko, Cong Zhang, and Sung won Kim

4 United in Suffering: Rural Grandparents and the Intergenerational Contributions of Care 76
  Erin Thomason

5 Floating Grandparents: Rethinking Family Obligation and Intergenerational Support 103
  Xiaoying Qi

6 Families Under (Peer) Pressure: Self-Advocacy and Ambivalence among Women in Collective Dance Groups 123
  Claudia Huang

7 Intimate Power: Intergenerational Cooperation and Conflicts in Childrearing among Urban Families 143
  Suowei Xiao

8 Losing an Only Child: Parental Grief among China's *Shidu* Parents 176
  Lihong Shi

VIII

9   The Chinese Proto Neo-Family Configuration: A Historical
    Ethnography   194
    William Jankowiak

10 The Statist Model of Family Policy Making   223
    Yunxiang Yan

11 Three Discourses on Neo-Familism   253
    Yunxiang Yan

    Index   275

Acknowledgements

This volume grew out of the two-day conference entitled "The Rise of Neo-Familism in China: Reflections on Anti-Traditionalism in the May Fourth Movement on Its 100th Anniversary," held at the University of California, Los Angeles, on May 3–4, 2019. The paper presenters at the conference were (in alphabetical order) Vanessa Fong, Sarah Friedman, Becky Hsu, Claudia Huang, William Jankowiak, Jun Jing, Tianshu Pan, Lihong Shi, Charles Stafford, Erin Thomason, Wei Wei, Yunxiang Yan, Kuang-Hui Yeh, and Xiang Zou. Deborah Davis, James L. Watson, and Rubie Watson read all the papers before the conference and played key roles as discussants during the session.

At the end of the conference, we participated in a group discussion on publication plans, deciding the central theme of the edited volume would be neo-familism from the perspective of intergenerational dependence. To produce a well-focused and cohesive volume, I took pains to reduce the final volume to six papers. The eight other excellent papers are certainly worthy of being published in professional journals; nevertheless, it is a great loss to have had to omit them from this final volume. I want to take this opportunity to thank Sarah Friedman, Becky Hsu, Jun Jing, Tianshu Pan, Charles Stafford, Wei Wei, Kuang-Hui Yeh, and Xiang Zou again for their invaluable contributions to the conference. To cover some important topics, I reached out to Deborah Davis, Xiaoying Qi, and Suiwei Xiao and they graciously responded by submitting contributions after the conference, for which I am most grateful. I also owe a special thanks to Deborah Davis, William Jankowiak, Charles Stafford, James L. Watson, and Rubie Watson for their insights, experiences, and wisdom while walking me through the process of editing this book, and to Dr. Li Tian, of Anhui University, China, for his untiring and generous help on my research project on Chinese neo-familism.

Chapter 5 by Xiaoying Qi and Chapter 7 by Suowei Xiao are revised versions of articles previously published in *International Sociology* 33:6 (2018) and *The Journal of Chinese Sociology* 3:18 (2016), respectively.

The 2019 conference and the subsequent work in preparing the present volume were generously supported by funding from UCLA's Asia Pacific Center, Office of Interdisciplinary & Cross Campus Affairs, Division of Social Science, Division of Humanities, and private donors. I am very grateful to Director Min Zhou, Vice-Provost Timothy Brewer, Dean Darnell Hunt, Dean David Schaberg, Mr. and Mrs. Howard Lee, Ms. Jenny Cheng, and Professor Emerita Agnes Lin. I would also like to thank Ms. Esther Jou at the UCLA Center of

Chinese Studies for administrative support during the conference and during the subsequent process of editing this volume.

All of us benefited greatly from the two anonymous reviewers for Brill, whose detailed and insightful comments guided us through the revision process and helped us to strengthen the final product. As in nearly all of my published works, Ms. Nancy Hearst edited all the chapters in this volume and transformed our writing to a higher level. I also owe special thanks to senior editor Qin Higley and associate editor Elizabeth You at Brill Academic Publishers and book series editor Rana Mitter for their help.

With the support of all the authors and other paper presenters at the 2019 conference, I respectfully dedicate this book to James J. Watson and Rubie Watson.

Yunxiang Yan
Los Angeles, August 2020

Figures

2.1 Number of Shanghai marriages and divorces, 1980–2017   40
2.2 Where divorce cases are granted, 1978–2017   50
3.1 Marital status of male survey respondents (n=202) in 2014–15   59
3.2 Marital status of female survey respondents (n=204) in 2014–15   59

Notes on Contributors

Deborah S. Davis
is Professor Emerita of Sociology at Yale University and Distinguished Visiting Professor at Fudan University in Shanghai. She is the author of many articles and books, including *Long Lives: Chinese Elderly and the Communist Revolution* (1991), *Creating Wealth and Poverty in Postsocialist China* (2009), and *Wives, Husbands, and Lovers: Marriage and Sexuality in Hong Kong, Taiwan, and Urban China* (co-edited with Sara K. Friedman, 2014).

Vanessa L. Fong
is Olin Professor in Asian Studies and Professor of Anthropology at Amherst College. She is interested in how the experiences of a partly transnational cohort of Chinese only-children and their families shed light on anthropological, sociological, and psychological theories. Her research focuses on a cohort of youth born under China's one-child policy between 1979 and 1986. Since 1998, she has been engaged in a longitudinal project that will follow this cohort and their children throughout the course of their lives. She is the author of *Only Hope: Coming of Age Under China's One-Child Policy* (2004) and *Paradise Redefined: Transnational Chinese Students and the Quest for Flexible Citizenship in the Developed World* (2011).

Claudia Huang
is Assistant Professor of Human Development at California State University, Long Beach. She has conducted fieldwork in Chengdu, Sichuan, where she was born and raised before immigrating to the United States as a child. Her research interests include aging and retirement, intergenerational dynamics, and state-society relations.

Sung won Kim
is Assistant Professor of Comparative Education at Yonsei University at the Department of Education, Seoul, South Korea. Her research interests include comparative perspectives on education in China, and she has published in journals such as *Comparative Education Review, The China Journal,* and *Review of Educational Research.*

Greene Ko
is pursuing a bachelor's degree in Sociology and Law, Jurisprudence, and Social Thought at Amherst College.

NOTES ON CONTRIBUTORS

William Jankowiak

is Professor of Anthropology, University of Nevada, Las Vegas. He has authored over 115 academic and professional publications, including *Sex, Death, and Hierarchy in a Chinese City: An Anthropological Account* (1993) and *Family Life in China* (co-authored with Robert L. Moore, 2017). He is the editor of *Romantic Passion: A Universal Experience?* (1995), *Intimacies: Between Love and Sex Across Cultures* (2008), and *Stimulating Trade: Drugs, Labor and Expansion* (2003) (with Dan Bradburd).

Xiaoying Qi

is Associate Professor in Sociology, Australian Catholic University. She has published articles in leading internationally refereed journals, including *American Journal of Cultural Sociology, British Journal of Sociology, International Sociology, Journal for the Theory of Social Behaviour, Journal of Sociology*, and *Sociology*. She is the author of *Globalized Knowledge Flows and Chinese Social Theory* (2014) and *Remaking Families in Contemporary China*.

Lihong Shi

is Associate Professor of Anthropology at Case Western Reserve University. She studies reproductive politics and family and gender relations, particularly reproductive choice and family change under China's birth-control policy. She examines an emerging reproductive choice in rural China where a large number of couples have decided to have only one daughter, even though the modified policy allows them to have a second child. By delving into the socioeconomic factors contributing to this drastic reproductive decision, she looks at significant changes that are occurring within Chinese families. She is the author of *Choosing Daughters: Family Change in Rural China* (2017).

Erin Thomason

is Assistant Professor in the Department of Chinese Studies at Xi'an Jiaotong-Liverpool University (XJTLU), China. She is a cultural and psychological anthropologist specializing in rural China. Her ongoing research considers how economic development and changes in family structure impact subjective experiences and assessments of well-being. Her book-in-progress explores how multigenerational families in rural China solve ethical problems of care.

Suowei Xiao

earned her Ph.D. in Sociology at University of California, Berkeley, and is Associate Professor at the School of Sociology, Beijing Normal University. She is the author of *Desire and Dignity: Class, Gender, and Intimacy in Transitional*

China (2018) and a number of articles on gender, intergenerational relations, family change, and class formation.

Yunxiang Yan

is Professor of Anthropology, University of California, Los Angeles, and Adjunct Professor in School of Social Development and Public Policy, Fudan University. He is the author of *The Flow of Gifts: Reciprocity and Social Networks in a Chinese Village, Private Life under Socialism: Love, Intimacy, and Family Change in a Chinese Village, 1949–1999* and *The Individualization of Chinese Society*. His research interests include family and kinship, social change, the individual and individualization, and the anthropology of moralities.

Cong Zhang

is an Assistant Professor of Social Development and Public Policy at Fudan University. Her research interest is mainly on gender, parenting, grandparenting, families and kinship in China. Her publications have appeared in *China Quarterly, Journal of Marriage and Family* and *Journal of Family Studies*.

CHAPTER 1

Introduction

The Inverted Family, Post-Patriarchal Intergenerationality and Neo-Familism

Yunxiang Yan

On the traditional Ghost Festival day in 1997, I sat with a group of men at the central intersection of Xiajia village, watching the villagers chat on their way to and from the family graveyards. Suddenly, Uncle Lu, a 74-year-old man, called out my name and challenged me to recount in a few words the most important social changes in the village. Having caught me unprepared, he went on to comment that there had really been only two social changes during the previous five decades. One is "the grandfather is turned into the grandson" (爷爷变孙子), and the other is "the women have gone up to the sky" (妇女上了天). The former refers to the loss of parental authority and power and the rise of youth autonomy. In this context, the kinship terms "grandfather" and "grandson" connote different positions of status and power; the grandson is said to refer to a powerless person. The latter is derived from the Communist slogan "women uphold half of the sky" and is meant to complain that the status of women had improved dramatically (Yan 2003:98–99).

The above paragraph is from my book *Private Life under Socialism*. When I was trying to organize various ideas for the present chapter, the magisterial and witty Uncle Lu literally showed up in my dream one night and inspired me. What Uncle Lu said on that occasion vividly captured a national trend of family change wherein the generational and gender axes of patriarchy have been transformed and in many cases even inverted. This trend continued in the subsequent decades but, intriguingly, it had not led to the ascent of nuclear family and individualism, despite of the advance of market economy and increase of social mobility in rural and urban areas alike (Jankowiak and Moore 2017; Santos and Harrell 2017; Yan 2018). Instead, the ad hoc and flexible multigenerational household has become the most popular form of family configuration, and intergenerational dependence, especially downward intergenerational transfer and grandparenting, emerged as a key strategy of family life by the early 21st century (Brandtstädter and Santos 2009). During the same time, the importance of intimacy and emotionality between adult children and their parents has significantly increased (Bregnbæk 2016; Evans 2008; and

© YUNXIANG YAN, 2021 | DOI:10.1163/9789004450233_002

Yan 2016, 2018). The new saliency of the vertical relationship between elderly parents and adult children has at least equipoised the triumph of the horizontal husband-wife relationship that I observed in the late 1990s (Yan 1997).

In a broader and comparative perspective, the Chinese case bears some resemblance to recent family changes in Euro-American societies. The dominance of the nuclear family has been in constant decline in the United States since the 1970s while concurrently the relationship between older parents and their adult children has gained saliency. This is so much the case that Vern L. Bengtson claimed at the turn of the new century: "For many Americans, multigenerational bonds are becoming more important than nuclear family ties for well-being and support over the course of their lives" (2001: 5). Bengtson's intergenerational solidarity model (Bengtson and Roberts 1991) has enabled many scholars to identify the affective and instrumental functions of intergenerational relationships in family life in the United States, the UK, Germany, France, Italy, Spain, Norway, Sweden, and other Western societies (Dykstra and Fokkema 2010; Silverstein et al. 2010; Steinbach 2008). Other sociological studies have also revealed that grandparenting and multigenerational families are on the rise in Europe and the United States (Cherlin and Seltzer 2014; Di Gessa et al. 2016; and Swartz 2009). One thus wonders why the global triumph of the nuclear family predicted by William J. Goode (1962) was only a short-lived victory in Euro-American societies and why intergenerational dependence and solidarity regained saliency throughout the world in the early 21st century (Cherlin 2012).

Beyond the similarities with family life on the surface level, there are also visible differences in the macro factors that resulted in such a seemingly global convergence. Take the American case as an example. The declining importance of the nuclear family and the concurrent complexity of household configuration are primarily caused by the separation of sexual intimacy, marriage, and childbearing (Cherlin 2004), the trinity that used to be locked together for the stability of both the traditional patriarchal family and the modern nuclear family. Consequently, cohabitation, divorce and single parenthood, remarriage and step-parenthood, childbearing outside of wedlock, same-sex union/marriages and new reproductive technologies have produced a diversity of family forms and kinship ties (Cherlin and Seltzer 2014; Levine 2008). Together with the ultra-low fertility rate, these can be attributed to the modern pursuit of individual autonomy and self-fulfillment as described in the theory of a second demographic transition (Lesthaeghe 2010). Yet, in my view, feminism and the world feminist movements played equally important roles in breaking the patriarchal spell of both the traditional family and the breadwinner-homemaker model of the nuclear family.

INTRODUCTION   3

On the other side of the coin, the increase in multigenerational families is closely tied to the practical challenges faced by single-parents, unmarried parents, divorced parents, or singles who have been pushed out by the job market by the younger generations who had to seek sanctuary from their parents in one way or another. In other words, the multigenerational family is likely the last resort of some Americans instead of an ideal form that everyone aspires to pursue (see e.g. Cherlin 2006; and Nelson 2006). It is therefore also a reflection of the rapid increase in social inequality during the past several decades (Cherlin and Seltzer 2014; and Swartz 2009). A study of children living in extended families shows a clear racial divide: fifty-seven percent of African American children and thirty-five percent of Hispanic children ever lived in an extended family, while the percentage of White children is a much lower twenty percent. Social-economic status makes a huge difference too. Forty-seven percent of children whose parents did not finish high school lived in an extended family for some time, while only seventeen percent of children whose parents had a bachelor's degree did so (Cross 2018). The ideal family form for middle-class Americans seems to remain intact, with the key ingredients of parents and children, dual incomes, home ownership, and the spirit of the whole (nuclear) family fighting together to achieve its goals. As long as they can afford to pursue this family ideal, most American couples will do so without burdening their own parents, as shown in the longitudinal study of thirty-two middle-class families in Los Angeles (Ochs and Kremer-Sadlik 2013).

The Chinese case diverges from the American case on both counts. By the early 21st Century, neither the deinstitutionalization of marriage nor the decoupling of marriage and childbearing are occurring in China (Davis and Friedman 2014a), and the legitimacy of individual autonomy and self-fulfillment remains dubious as individualism has long been understood as egotism (Yan 2021). More importantly, grandparenting and the multigenerational family configuration constitute a nationwide, across-the-board family change, regardless of the social and economic status of the involved parents and grandparents. It is a family strategy not only for people in the lower rungs of the society but also for middle-class couples to move up to a higher level or at least to avoid falling down the social ladder. For affective or ethical reasons, many families at the top of the social pyramid also adopt a multigenerational family configuration to showcase filial piety. In other words, while individualism is one of the catalysts for the return of complexity in Euro-American families, the driving force for a similar trend in China is the partial return of familism, or, as I call it, neo-familism.

Structural factors contributing to the new saliency of intergenerational relationships in Euro-American societies similarly established the premises for family change in the Chinese case as well; chief among them are the competitive and precarious job market, the ever-growing gap of social inequality, the increase in various sorts of social risks, and the decrease in the provision of social welfare within the larger context of the state-led market economy and the individualization of Chinese society (Yan 2010, 2012). What sets the China case apart from the risk societies in Europe and the United States is the decisive influence of the party-state on the Chinese family in terms of macro-level social engineering, family policy making, and ideological control, which have tipped the same set of structural factors in favor of the party-state and have shifted more burdens to the family institution and Chinese individuals, as shown in my research elsewhere (Yan 2018 and 2021) and in Chapters 10 and 11 of the present volume.

Building on existing scholarship and based on the latest field research, the present volume offers the first systematic account of the newly emerging intergenerational dynamics in light of the perspective of post-patriarchal intergenerationality (more on this below). Our point of departure is that the former family script has been challenged and modified as new ethical norms and behavioral patterns have been created. The notion of filial piety, which used to govern intergenerational relations, has been reinterpreted in novel ways, the foci of the experiential meanings of family life have shifted from ancestors to grandchildren, intergenerational intimacy has emerged as a new bonding mechanism, and new patterns of intergenerational support have developed due to the flexible structural configuration of the multigenerational household (Choi and Luo 2016; Yan 2016, 2018; and Zhang 2017). Consequently, what constitute a good grandparent, a good parent, or a good child have been redefined, and this requires attempts to make sense of the new family script and the new behavioral patterns across generational lines. While fully aware of the continuing male dominance in Chinese culture and the gendered aspects of all social relations, the authors of the present volume make a collective effort to explore what has occurred in terms of the patterns of intergenerational dynamics in Chinese family life in the early twenty-first century.

In the following pages, I first review the social conditions for the intergenerational interactions that have resulted in an inverted generational hierarchy in the post-Mao era. In the second section I develop the notion of post-patriarchal intergenerationality and then use it to examine the new patterns of intergenerational interactions and intersections. I argue that this new conceptual tool is necessary to capture the nuanced but radical changes in intergenerational dynamics, such as inverted transfers of resources, flipped power relations, and signs of generational inequalities. In the third section I contextualize post-patriarchal intergenerationality in the rise of neo-familism and highlight the

INTRODUCTION 5

main features of neo-familism as social practice (the discourse of neo-familism will be explored in Chapter 11 by Yan). The last section of this introduction offers a sketch of subsequent chapters in the volume, each of which speaks to the post-patriarchy intergenerational dynamics and neo-familism in Chinese family life, albeit from very different perspectives.

1 The Inverted Family

The patriarchal family in traditional Chinese culture features an elaborate hierarchical system wherein individuals were classified and ranked by generation, age, and gender. Power, prestige, and privilege, as well as the flow of material resources, were allocated to individuals according to their hierarchical positions. Among these rankings, the generational hierarchy was the principal category that defined what a patriarchal family was and how it functioned (Baker 1979; Fei 1997 [1942]). The inversion of the generational hierarchy therefore defined the inverted family.

The most widely recognized indicator of the inverted generational hierarchy is the constant decline of parental authority and power and the parallel increase in youth autonomy and freedom in both urban and rural Chinese families. This trend actually began in the 1950s, and by the 1980s it had developed further in the cities than in the countryside (Parish and Whyte 1978; Davis and Harrell 1993; Yan 2003). It has continued in both urban and rural China during the subsequent four decades (see the chapters in Brandtstädter and Santos 2009; Davis and Friedman 2014b; Jankowiak and Moore 2016; Santos and Harrell 2017; Shen 2013). During the reform era, decollectivization, rural-urban migration, and marketization empowered the young in a number of ways, and at the same time, they have further weakened parental power in the countryside. Driven by the ever-expanding consumerism, the skyrocketing housing market, and the increasingly competitive job market, young urban adults have been forced to rely on parental support for both marriage and child-rearing, yet they still enjoy autonomy and choice in terms of their life style. Due to the legacy of Maoist socialism, most urban parents had sufficient resources, such as state-subsidized housing and pensions, to help their adult children but, intriguingly, regardless of the parents' resources available to their children, few parents could regain their lost authority and power. In my empirical study of parent-driven divorce among urban youth, for example, a large number of urban youth willingly relied on their parents to handle their divorces in terms of the legal and financial settlement because they were free to choose a new spouse and could count on parental support for their second marriage (Yan 2015). By the early twenty-first century, the continued decline of parental authority and power was accompanied by the increased dependence of adult children on their parents; this trend became particularly common in many former rural areas because of the rapid absorption of millions of rural residents into the cities as part of the urbanization process (Yan 2016).

But gaining both power and support from their parents does not, however, make the generation of adult children a take-all winner because they too must forgo their personal desires and pursuit of self-development for the sake of their own child or children. This is the second feature of the inverted family, whereby the child (or children) of the third generation have become the locus of family life and the single most important reason for intergenerational solidarity and mutual dependence. Care, attention, emotional attachment, and material resources all flow downward to the third generation through selfless efforts by the grandparents and parents in each family, a trend that elsewhere I refer to as descending familism (Yan 2016). The practice of descending familism has also shifted the experiential meaning of life from glorifying the ancestors to enabling the grandchildren, a complete inversion of the previous order in family values.

State-sponsored ideological attacks and political campaigns against ancestor worship in popular religion have not only eliminated the ancestors from people's daily lives but have also brought to an end the Chinese pursuit of eternity. Without the ritual worship of their ancestors, few individuals in the early twenty-first century still believe in an afterlife. With the elimination of ancestor worship, Chinese parents are now forced to focus their spiritual and emotional devotion on to their child or children, so much so that they regard their child or children as an extension of themselves (see Chapter 8 by Shi). As a result, at the level of their spiritual and emotional lives, the more the parents become involved in the lives of their adult children, the more they feel that the two generations are fused together into an integrated whole. The decline of public life during the post-Mao era and the mandatory retirement age (55 for women and 60 for men) have further narrowed the spiritual world of older parents (see Chapter 6 by Huang), leaving their adult children as the only possible hub for their emotional and spiritual attachments. This is why the grandchild is such an irresistible attraction for the love, care and support of their grandparents. Needless to say, the new focus on the grandchild pushes the development of the inverted family to a new stage, whereby, as described by Uncle Lu, "the grandfather is turned into the grandson.

A third feature of the inverted hierarchy across generational lines (and by extension the inverted family) is simply the reverse ratio of elders to young adults and children due to the declining fertility rate and the increasing life expectancy

INTRODUCTION   7

during the past several decades. Life expectancy at birth was 45.6 years for females and 42.2 for males in 1950; by 1980 the two indicators had increased to 69.3 years for females and 66.4 years for males. Meanwhile, the total fertility rate dropped from 5.8 children per family in 1950 to 2.3 children in 1980. China has completed its first demographic transition within thirty years, a remarkable overachievement, as noted by Wang Feng (2011). Translating this achievement to everyday family life, it means that by the end of the 1970s there were already fewer children than adults (parents and grandparents combined) in most families.

Imposition of the one-child policy in 1980 accelerated this ongoing demographic transition, radically reducing the number of children per family, especially among urban families. As a result, as early as the 1990s the singleton child had become known as the "precious little emperor." The continuing decline of fertility since then has further increased the importance of children. Paternal and maternal grandparents, whose life expectancy has also increased, treasure their grandchildren so much so that parental indulgence of the little emperors pales in comparison. The inverted intergenerational hierarchy is a reflection of the inverted pyramid in the demographic structure and the social consequence of the one-child policy, which has become increasingly common among rural families during the last fifteen to twenty years as a growing number of rural youth choose to have fewer children, or even one singleton child (Shi 2017).

The most telling example in this connection is the 4-2-1 pattern of intergenerational relations whereby a married couple of two singletons has one child and four parents/parents-in-law, dubbed the double-singleton family (双独家庭) among Chinese sociologists and demographers. Given that the one-child policy was strictly implemented during the 1980s and the early 1990s in urban China, the largest cohort of singletons entered the stage of marriage and child-bearing age after 2005 and it peaked around 2015. A number of sociologists and demographers estimate that the peak of the double-singleton family formation will be between 2020 and 2040, when 35–40 percent of urban families will consist of the 4-2-1 structure of intergenerational relations (Ding and Wu 2009; Feng 2015; and Guo et al. 2002).

In addition to state family-planning policies that turned the demographic structure of the family upside down, labor migration in particular and increased social mobility in general have had an equally profound impact on intergenerational relations. Despite the ideological attacks on the patriarchal family and the political campaigns against patriliny in the early 1950s, rural collectivization, the urban work-unit system, and the household registration system that legally banned rural-urban migration had the counter-effects of sustaining certain elements of the traditional family, including the close proximity of the generations in their working, living, and residential arrangements

(Davis-Friedmann 1991; Parish and Whyte 1978; Whyte 2005; Whyte and Parish 1984). Starting from the mid-1980s, the state began to relax its tight control over labor migration, allowing villagers to seek temporary jobs in the cities (as so-called "migrant workers"). The registered number of migrant workers reached 4.8 million in 1986 but jumped to 30 million in 1989, representing the first tidal wave of labor migration that attracted the attention of the central government and led to a number of policies aiming to bring it under control. In subsequent decades, the cities were flooded with even more rural laborers, whose population reached 100 million in 1997 and 247 million in 2015. More than 65 percent of the domestic migrants were born after 1980 and more than 70 percent consider themselves to be part of the urban population, even though the majority have yet to be granted an urban residency status by the local governments (N. Zhang 2018).

The flip-side of the increasingly large floating population (or 流动人口 as they are called in China) is the separation of generations, which takes several forms. The most common is the left-behind phenomenon (Chapter 4 by Thomason), referring to the elderly grandparents and young children who are forced to stay put in their rural villages while the able-bodied parents in their family seek temporary jobs in the cities. The prolonged separation of parents and children results in a skipped-generation family whereby the grandparents live with and care for the grandchildren and the middle generation of parents works in the cities. To remedy various problems associated with the left-behind phenomenon, an increasing number of migrants have begun to bring their young children with them to the cities, and when they cannot handle work and childcare at the same time, they move their elderly parents to the cities as well, leading to a new pattern of "floating grandparents" (Chapter 5 by Qi).

Regardless of whether grandparents are left-behind or floating around, the previous order of intergenerational relations has been interrupted, Among those left-behind, for example, grandparents assume extra responsibilities when the middle generation in a multi-generational household is absent for most of the time, and they often find themselves inadequate to substitute for the role of the parents, not only in terms of providing care but also in terms of socialization. Yet their positions become even more difficult and more vulnerable when they are uprooted from their rural home communities and become temporary caregivers in their adult children's home in the cities. In either case, they and their adult children must adjust their behavioral patterns to meet the new challenges so that they can collaborate closely to create the best possible opportunities for the third generation, which brings us to the fourth characteristic of the inverted family, that is, new patterns of conflict, especially across generation lines.

The gradual yet constant development of self-awareness and individual desires in family life from the proto-inverted family of the 1980s (see Chapter 9 by Jankowiak) to the much stronger yet still ongoing trend of individualization at the turn of the twenty-first century (Shen 2013; and Yan 2010) has posed the most serious internal challenge to traditional familism, contributing to disorder in the family and resulting in the previous ranking order of generational relations being turned upside down. The contradiction between individual happiness and family prosperity/continuity constitutes a major thread of neo-familism (Yan 2018; Chapter 6 by Huang). Consequently, an increasing number of individuals have begun to be proactive in making choices about how they want to live their family lives. Prolonged co-residence with parents and delayed marriage seem to work well for some young men and women (Chapter 3 by Fong *et al*), whereas some parents are determined to intervene in the married life of their adult children when they sense that something is not quite right (Yan 2015). It is therefore much more difficult to pinpoint an across-the-board pattern of intimacy, influence, authority and power in intergenerational relations. When the family is turned upside down, most conflicts in the intergenerational relationship are reflected in a variety of contradictions, such as dependence vs. independence, care vs. intimacy, and so forth.

Last but not the least, the inverted family is also a product of state policy-making. The Chinese state played a decisive role in triggering the initial family-transformation process in the 1950s and thereafter it enacted family policies that were either multidirectional or self-contradictory. The abiding thread, however, has been to make the family institution best serve the interests of the nation-state, a statist model of family policies that I explore in Chapter 10. Under this model, revolutionizing the family to establish and consolidate the political legitimacy of the party-state and to carry out the socialist transformation stand out as the core mission of the majority of family policies from 1950 to the late 1970s. The 1950 Marriage Law, and a number of accompanying regulations and policies, implemented in the context of the full-blown planned economy and the radical CCP ideology, undermined parental authority and power.

However, there are also state policies and regulations that reinforced intergenerational dependence and patrilocal residence. During the early stage of the economic reforms (1980 to the mid-1990s), the party-state regulated the family through various pragmatic policies in order to carry out the national project of the four modernizations. Chief among these policies was the one-child policy that sought a radical reduction in the national birth rate. The challenge of urban unemployment and social mobility compelled the party-state to promulgate family policies that were in the best interests of the nation-state, especially when the party-state had to deal with pressing issues such as the return to the urban areas of the sent-down youth (see Chen 2015) or the influx of rural-urban migrants. Beginning in the late 1990s, the state shifted the responsibilities of social welfare provision to the family institution and, consequently, issued policies and launched ideological campaigns to strengthen the family for the construction of a harmonious society. Filial piety, a cornerstone of Confucian ethics and traditional familism, was recalibrated as part of the socialist core values and intergenerational solidarity was promoted through new laws and government policies. What remains clearly unchanged among state family policies from 1949 to the present, however, is the statist model (see more detailed discussion in Chapter 10 of the present volume). The state has indeed made pragmatic concessions and arrangements to deal with the family institution, such as regulating intergenerational relations, but all of these must serve the interests and ultimate goals of the state. In this connection, the inverted family is best viewed as the result of both planned and unexpected consequences of state family policies.

Admittedly, the image of an inverted generational hierarchy, or a family being turned upside down, is derived from the perspective of those who grew up under the former family script, such as Uncle Lu who was born in the late 1920s and socialized under traditional patriarchal culture. In contrast, for Chinese youth who were born after the radical one-child policy of 1980, the inverted Chinese family is the normality in their daily lives. In a similar vein, to what extent patriarchal power in intergenerational relations has declined or has been retained only makes sense to those who are familiar with the former family script and lived through the former patterns of family life. The younger generations born in the 1980s and 1990s are often clueless about this hierarchy and about such power relations as they have grown up with tremendous space and freedom to negotiate with their parents and grandparents every aspect of family life. Nowadays, the intergenerational relationship between young adults and their parents and/or grandparents has become a working relationship wherein the involved individuals must constantly and consistently work on it so that they can benefit from it. This brings us to the notion of post-patriarchal intergenerationality.

2   Post-Patriarchal Intergenerationality

As Santos and Harrell lucidly delineate (2017), in the classic sense patriarchy refers to the prestige and power of the senior generation over the junior generation, which is institutionalized through patrilineal descent, patrilocal post-marital residence, and patriarchal ideology and practice in family life.

INTRODUCTION   11

Expanded by feminist theory, patriarchy in a broader sense is also manifested in the gender axis of power and inequality, that is, male dominance in both the public and private spheres. Based on an extensive review of the existing scholarship as well as new research findings, Santos and Harrell contend that Chinese society has moved away from the classic type of patriarchy because the generational axis of prestige and power has been "weakened in some ways, flipped in others, and twisted its lineality in still others." (2017:32) However, although the patriarchy of male dominance has been transformed, it still remains intact (see the chapters in Santos and Harrell 2017).

Focusing on new developments in the generational axis of patriarchy and building on the scholarly consensus, I propose the notion of post-patriarchal intergenerationality as a new conceptual tool to deepen our understanding of Chinese family life. With respect to the dominance of the senior generation, Chinese family life has arrived at a post-patriarchal era, yet the significance of intergenerational relations has not been altered. On the contrary, because of the decline of patrilineality, patrilocal residence and patriarchal religiosity (i.e., ancestor worship), a new type of multigenerational family, with flexible residential patterns and financial arrangements, has emerged as the dominant household configuration. This form operates by new, often contested, ethical norms and behavioral patterns that cannot be fully understood in terms of conventional conceptual tools such as filial piety. As will be shown below, post-patriarchal intergenerationality captures these new developments and meanings of intergenerational dynamics in the era of post-patriarchal family and kinship.

In part, I have been inspired by the early discussions on intergenerational geography, primarily among British social geographers. Hopkins and Pain (2007) advocate a relational approach to study age groups, proposing intergenerationality, intersectionality, and life course as the key conceptual tools and calling for a relational geography of age that examines the elderly and the children in relation to each other. In their responses to critiques from Horton and Kraftl (2008), Hopkins and Pain reconfirm that they regard "intergenerationality as both a descriptive tool and part of a broader apparatus for explaining social and cultural processes and phenomena" because it "helps to dismantle rigid categories such as childhood and old age, exposing their porosity and cultural specificity while being open to the same critiques" (Hopkins and Pain 2008: 289–90; see also Vanderbeck 2017 for an overview of the relevant scholarship on the geography of intergenerational relations).

The novel attempt by Hopkins and Pain shifts the exclusive focus on a particular age group in cultural geography, such as the elderly, to relations between two age groups, such as the elderly and their adult children. This has always been the case in anthropological studies on the Chinese family and thus can hardly be considered particularly new. What inspired me, however, is to consider intergenerationality as a conceptual tool to describe actual changes in family life as well as to theorize new patterns of intergenerational interactions. Here the saliency of intergenerational interactions, as opposed to intergenerational relations, is the defining feature of intergenerationality. To take a closer look, the notion of post-patriarchal intergenerationality consists of the following advantages.

First of all, intergenerationality is a neutral term that has no preconceived meanings and thus may widen our vision. Most studies of intergenerational relations in Chinese family life employ the notion of filial piety, which, as a cornerstone of Confucianism and Chinese familism, presumes the senior generation's moral authority, social prestige, and political-economic power over the junior generation. It is part and parcel of the patriarchal system. This is perhaps why the inversion of the generational hierarchy in the Chinese family is often presented as a crisis of filial piety, with a strong sense of moral judgment. In a similar vein, the notion of intergenerational solidarity, one of the most commonly used concepts in American family sociology (Bengtson and Roberts 1991) adopts Western individualism and emphasizes the balanced flow of rights and obligations. In light of this perspective, family relations tend to be easily reduced to pragmatic functions. In contrast to both filial piety and intergenerational solidarity, intergenerationality does not take any ethical or ideological position nor does it place a priority on the perspective of any one generation.

The construction and exercise of privilege, prestige, and power across generational lines are still centrally important, but the dynamics should not be reduced to a story of generational winners and losers. Taking the downward intergenerational transfer of resources as an example, new studies show that urban parents regard their financial aid to their adult children as a moral obligation but they also genuinely feel the emotional rewards of continuing to show their love of their children and their strong sense of personal achievement (Zhong and He 2014). In contrast, adult children define their subjective happiness in terms of their emotional closeness with their parents or grandparents, even though they often must work far away from their hometowns and they often must receive financial aid from their parents (Hsu 2019). An intergenerationality perspective enables the researcher to go beyond the dichotomy of winners and losers in intergenerational contestation and conflict to uncover the underlying premises that tie together the members of the different generations in the endless process of family politics.

INTRODUCTION

Moreover, the notion of intergenerationality draws our attention to interactions instead of relations across generational lines. The difference lies in the dynamic nature of real life and the agency of individuals from different generations in any given interaction. Focusing on intergenerational relations, one may implicitly assume a more or less generational position and project it onto the subjects under study, often offering a static portrayal of the relational patterns.

Constrained by such a structural perspective of intergenerational relations, most existing studies tend to focus on the interlocking generations, such as parents and children, while overlooking the intersecting generations, such as grandparents and grandchildren, in a multi-generational household. One of the most important new features of family life, as indicated above, are the rapidly increasing interactions between grandparents and grandchildren. Intergenerational interactions may occur in the context of multiple generations, such as child-rearing that involves the child, the parents, and the child's maternal and paternal grandparents. This complexity tends to be obscured or overlooked when we emphasize only the dyadic interactions between two generations. The notion of intergenerationality, in contrast, emphasizes the agentic contribution of all *intersecting* and *interacting* generations in any given situation, and, by definition, it locates grandparenting at the core of contemporary intergenerational dynamics.

Furthermore, the notion of intergenerationality highlights individual agency and thus does not overlook the subjective aspects of intergenerational interactions, such as intimacy, affection, and moral reasoning, which may counterbalance the existing bias in favor of the economic and political aspects of intergenerational relations in the literature on family studies. This is particularly important for studying post-patriarchal intergenerational dynamics in the much more open and affluent Chinese society, in which individuals pay much more attention to and negotiate with more emotional and psychological issues, as evidenced by the concurrent rising importance of intimacy in family relations and the recent boom of family psychotherapy and counselling services (Hizi 2017). A newly added dimension to the subjective domain is the individual desire for self-development and, when it clashes with one's family duties, the associated conflicts, confusion, and compromises across generational lines. Such conflicts, confusions, and compromises may lead to an intergenerational trauma that in turn affects everyday life interactions across generational lines and reshapes the psychological and emotional lives of all the individuals in a given family (Shen 2013).

The increasing importance of self-development highlights another important aspect of the subjective domain in family life, that is, the focus on individual identity, or the social site of the construction of personhood. Chinese personhood is known to be relationally constructed and it is presented as a lifetime process of becoming, in the form of cultivating one's humanity (做人 in Chinese) instead of a structure being endorsed by a set of individual rights given at the moment one is born (see Yan 2017). The primary, and arguably the most important, relational thread in the process of making oneself a decent person is the vertical intergenerational relationship, which goes beyond the simple parent-child bond to include the grandparents, the grandchildren, and the other relatives across generational lines.

So much so that individuals of different generations constitute each other; for example, parents regard children as part of themselves and vice versa. I call this the intergenerational integration of personhoods or the integration/ wholeness of parents-children in terms of personhood and self-identity. It is the locus of the meaning of life that has to do with an extension of one's own life, a sense of eternity (more of the parents than of the children), and, in comparative terms, the marker of one's life achievements among one's peers. A striking example of the intergenerational integration of personhoods is found among those who lived their lives through the imagined eyes and experiences of their lost single children (see Chapter 8 by Shi). This aspect of intergenerational interactions was previously obscured by the patriarchal hierarchy but it has become increasingly visible and important as individuals gain more freedom and choice to deal with intergenerational relations.

In short, as a value-neutral, interaction-focused, and subjectivity-sensitive conceptual tool, intergenerationality allows us to reexamine both classical issues and emergent challenges from a new perspective. For instance, instead of lamenting the crisis of filial piety, one can delve deeper to analyze how two or three generations in a given family negotiate and redefine the moral responsibilities and practical work for elderly support, child-rearing, and individual self-development. More importantly, exploring post-patriarchal intergenerationality allows one to catch up with and make sense of the latest developments in Chinese family life, especially the inverted yet still significant generational axis of family relations that has given rise to a set of new topics waiting to be explored and analyzed.

3 Neo-Familism

The abiding theme running through the present volume is that intergenerational dependence and solidarity have regained so much saliency that the family institution has been reconfigured in innovative ways. The vertical parent-child relationship is outshining the horizontal conjugal tie and redefining the meaning of family life in a great number of families. Concurrently, the century-old pursuit of a small romantic family and individualism (Glosser 2003) has been sidetracked, the national project of a family revolution has long been aborted (Deng 1994; Stacey 1983; Zhao 2018), and the grand theory of the global modernization of the family (Goode 1962) has been found to be misleading (see Cherlin 2012 for the challenge to Goode's model in the global context). Yet, the new centrality of intergenerational relations does not indicate a simple return of parental power and authority; instead, it is part and parcel of the rise of neo-familism (Yan 2016, 2018), an important new social trend that is changing the identity of the individual, family life, and individual-state relationship in contemporary China.

The sociological concept of familism refers to the value system and social practices of the family in many traditional societies. It emphasizes the primacy of family interests over the interests of individual family members and of loyalty to the family over allegiance to any outside social organization. Ethically, familism is constructed through a discourse on obligations and self-sacrifice rather than through a discourse on personal rights and self-realization (Garzón 2000). In familism, the individual is defined as a means to a higher end, i.e., the continuation and prospering of the family group, and thus it antithetical to individualism. As a social practice, familism is manifested in the family as a cooperative organization dedicated to the survival and flourishing of the family as the basic building block in a given society that plays crucial economic, socio-cultural, and political functions. For both ideological and practical reasons, familism relies on a hierarchical arrangement of gender and generational relations, and it exists in opposition to equality and intimacy in family life. In traditional China, familism served as both the primary principle of association in social life and the foundational ideology of the imperial state (Fei 1992 [1948]).

The notion of Chinese neo-familism refers to the new discourses and new practices since the early 2000s that invoke familism as the primary strategy to pursue both individual happiness and family prosperity through the collective efforts of a multi-generational domestic group. As such, it demonstrates both similarities to and differences from traditional familism. The similarities focus on the foundational idea that the interests of the family take precedence over the interests of the individual family members, but the balancing of family interests and individual interests diverges across generational lines that is a nuanced difference. The differences between traditional familism and neo-familism become much more apparent in social practices because many people who claim to be followers of traditional values actually find themselves in today's competitive and risky social environment unable to practice what they believe, whereas many others employ familism merely as a resource to pursue their individual happiness. Most intriguingly, the party-state has been proactively evoking the political aspects of traditional familism, advocating integration of the family and the state, incorporating familism into patriotism, and drawing on the family as a means of governance (Chapter 11 by Yan). In this connection, the rise of neo-familism is also indicative of important social and political developments far beyond the boundaries of the domestic group.

Elsewhere, I sketched the contours of Chinese neo-familism and offer a detailed ethnographic account of certain practices of neo-familism in the everyday life of ordinary people (2015, 2016 and 2018). Here suffice it to list only the main features of neo-familism in social practices (cf. Harrell and Santos 2017: 31–32 for a number of similar findings in their framework of the new patriarchy):

(1) The focus of family life has shifted at both the spiritual and material levels from glorifying one's ancestors to enabling the youngest generations; consequently, the continuity of the descent line has lost its spiritual significance and the core value of filial piety no longer demands self-sacrifice by the junior generations.

(2) The patrilineal principles of Chinese kinship, which had already been undermined to a great degree in previous decades, and the newly surging centrality of children have led to bilateral arrangements in post-marital co-residence and child-naming practices, leading to diverse ways of forming one's own family.

(3) Intergenerational dependence and solidarity have gained a new saliency in both the pragmatic and emotional aspects of family life, so much so that a new intergenerational identity is in the making. The identity ties parents and adult children together as a unified whole, known as the "integrated oneness of parents and children" (亲子一体) in family discourse as well as practice (Liu 2016)

(4) An "intimate turn" has occurred in family life. An increasing number of people across generational and gender lines assert that familial emotions (亲情) are the most important value in one's life (Hsu 2019), and expressions of intimacy through communications, gifts, and shared leisure activities have gained popularity among both urban and rural families. With the redefinition of the traditional virtue of filial piety, the development of intergenerational intimacy is especially noteworthy (Evans 2008; Wang 2014; Zhu and Zhu 2013).

(5) The strong social pressure to achieve family prosperity constitutes the fifth feature of neo-familism practices; most people are compelled to show off

INTRODUCTION   17

their material wealth and, more importantly, the success of their children in education and career development, through circles of social media. As family prosperity is perceived as the visible and quantifiable measure of family happiness, this feature of neo-familism has hijacked hundreds of millions of Chinese to the run-away train of hyper-materialism.

(6) There are tensions between individual interests and family interests in the new patterns of family life because neo-familism recognizes the value of the individual while also emphasizing the priority of family interests, a paradoxical development that is replete with tensions but also new possibilities.

Under neo-familism, the conventional family script has disintegrated and a variety of new family scripts are in the making. Chinese individuals have to mobilize whatever resources available to them and to improvise their family life creatively, flexibly, and persistently on an ad hoc basis. Indeed, how people improvise neo-familism is the key to understanding the seemingly endless variations of household formation, the creative reinterpretation of structural principles, and a re-thinking of family values such as filial piety. This is precisely the major reason that I propose the notion of post-patriarchal intergenerationality as a conceptual tool for analyzing new intergenerational dynamics under neo-familism.

This conceptual tool would not be useful under traditional familism because the institutionalized inequality and hierarchy to a great extent exclude the possibility of generational interactions on an equal footing. Filial piety, for example, preemptively regulated the patterns of family relations and everyday life interactions; individual deviance from this prefixed model did occur but it was regarded as abnormal, unacceptable, ethically wrong, and socially punishable. Since the collapse of generational hierarchy, intergenerational interactions have become contingent on individual agencies rather than on established rules. This does not mean the achievement of equality among generations; on the contrary, in some cases this has led to a reversal of the previous generational hierarchy or the exploitation of one generation by another in a given family. Yet, it does open possibilities of all sorts, which often produce unexpected consequences.

A good example in this connection is the emerging practice of dual-local post-marital residence in both urban and rural areas among couples who are singletons. As both the singleton husband and singleton wife prefer to live close to his or her parents, they do not establish their own residence per se; instead, they have their own living quarters inside the home of their respective parents and they travel back and forth between the two homes (两头走). In the cities, the young couple stays with one side during the weekdays and then moves to the other side for the weekends (Shen 2013). In the rural areas, the young couple may alternate their primary residence to correspond with the busy and slack seasons in their work schedule or with the farming schedule of their respective parents. All else being equal, most young couples spend more time with the parents who can offer substantial help in their daily lives, such as child-rearing (Gao 2018; Wang and Di 2011). Yet, all such arrangements are derived from intergenerational negotiations on an individual basis. The dual-local residence provides strong support for Santos and Harrell's observation about the "hollowing out" of patriarchal kinship (2017:19). An associated change is the growing practice of combining the surnames of father and mother as the surname of their child, known as double-surname system (复姓制, for more details see Qi 2018; and Yan 2018:193–194).

In the context of post-patriarchal intergenerational dynamics, individuals define their own positionality and functional role in accordance with their own life situations and personal capacities. One telling example in this connection is the redefinition of motherhood in many multigenerational families, especially among the urban middle class. A number of recent studies have shown that the mother has assumed the role of manager in leading the entire family in the competitive enterprise of raising the perfect child. A good mother must be proactive and effective in obtaining the best education for her child, supervising her child in school work and all extra-curricular activities, and building a strong career path for her child from kindergarten through college. This managerial role is so demanding that the mother must shift most care-giving duties to her own parents or parents-in-law, effectively making the latter the de facto care-givers in family life. The father's role is affected as well because he must work harder to earn more money to support the family and, under the new idealism of child-rearing, he must also find time to play with his precious child (Yang 2018; and Chapter 7 by Xiao). In other words, because the new intergenerational dynamics occur in both intersecting and interacting generations, a change in the role of one person in family life alters the respective roles of all the other family members as well.

There is no secret recipe of doing neo-familism except for improvisation. Chinese people from all walks of life must find their own way to maximize their chance to reach to the ideal of happy family life by improvising what resources they have under specific circumstances, such as adopting the dual-local post-marital residence or redefining the motherhood. Indeed, improvisation seems to be the key to understand the seemingly endless variations of household formation, creative reinterpretation of structural principles, reinterpretation of family values such as filial piety, and pragmatic arrangement of power and hierarchy in intergenerational relations. Given its ubiquitous

INTRODUCTION

application across the boundaries of socio-economic standings, improvising family life is also a social phenomenon at the level of group behavior that is deeply embedded in the interactions between individual and society, family and social institutions, and social groups and the state (Yan 2018).

4   The Structure of This Book

Looking closely at the concurrent changes of the inverted generational hierarchy and the increased importance of intergenerational dependence, each of the chapters in this book deals with some nuanced issues that have yet to be fully understood or explored in the existing scholarship. The specific studies are anchored in a variety of scales, as far as the object of analysis and the date are concerned. Some of them deal with national trends and historical backgrounds, some make comparative analysis across cities or regions, and others delve deep in case studies of generational groups in rural or urban families or employ the method of person-centered ethnography to explore the lived experiences of key interviewees. By testing some uncharted waters and carrying out their investigation from oblique angles, all the authors of this volume actively engaged with the central theme of post-patriarchal intergenerationality and neo-familism. Except for chapters 10 and 11, they all privileged the everyday life experiences of ordinary people and their point of view on the ground. Collectively, the chapters offer vivid portrayals of people's efforts to come to terms with the new reality and improvising their responses to it. Most of these people do not have the benefit of hindsight that scholars have, as they are busy trying to make the best out of the rapidly changing, often confusing, life situations they live in; hence the intriguing and often unexpected developments of neo-familism in social practices.

In Chapter 2 Deborah Davis investigates the renewed parental commitment to and their large investments in the well-being of their adult children, primarily through financial investments in the latter's marriage formation and dissolution. This is a reversal of the urban practice in the 1970s–80s (Davis-Friedmann 1991; Whyte and Parish 1984) when, with the support of the work-unit and the influence of Maoist ideological socialization, urban youth in the 1970s–80s were mobilized to reject their parents' rather old, or at least non-revolutionary, mentalities and behavior. The intergenerational dynamics at that time were characterized by the young generation's reformist actions, such as collective weddings, the rejection of bridewealth and dowries, and the rejection of highly politicized standards of spouse selection. However, these have been replaced during the last four decades with some new developments, such as parent-driven divorces among urban youth. In searching for the causes for such a U-turn, Davis highlights the interplay between decisive state interventions and the emerging intergenerational dynamics among urban families.

The extent to which the return of parental commitments and contributions to their adult children's marriage and divorce will modify the inverted generational hierarchy or create a new dynamic remains an open-ended question. My early study shows that parental divorce arrangements among some urban youth indicate the strength of intergenerational dependence but not necessarily the return of parental authority (Yan 2015). Two chapters in this volume, by Vanessa Fong et al. and by Erin Thomason respectively, also implicitly show that receiving parental support does not change the inverted generational hierarchy.

The marriage of adult children remains an important life task for the parents, who place all kinds of pressures on the young to marry on time and in style in order to avoid the much stigmatized consequence of becoming older singles, known as left-over women or bare-stick men. In Chapter 3, Vanessa Fong, Greene Ko, Cong Zhang, and Sung won Kim present a radical departure from this well-established intergenerational responsibility or obligation as an increasingly large number of urban youth remain single by the age of 27 and they hope to continue this status quo. Among all social factors contributing to this new development, the comfort zone of living with one's own parents is particularly noteworthy. Given that the young generation is likely to have different values and life styles from their parents, how is the creation of such a comfort zone possible? Here the notion of intergenerationality is a convenient and useful tool because it requires the collective and combined efforts by both parents and their adult children to make co-residence so comfortable and attractive that no one wants to break it. Note that although parents are pressuring their children to marry, many seem to be reluctant to take radical actions of pushing their children out of the home. Instead, as this chapter shows, some parents simply veto the proposed candidates for their children, even though they themselves were the ones who initially introduced the marriage prospect. The mutual dependence and integration of identities among parents and adult children seem to play an equally important role here, and the two generations work together to de-stigmatize the threshold of an unmarried 27-year-old.

Erin Thomason in Chapter 4 explores how rural grandmothers take up the child-rearing duties from their daughters or daughters-in-law so that the latter are free to work in the cities as migrant workers. This is known as the "left-behind phenomenon," meaning the old and the very young are left in the village communities to form a de facto skipped generation household. These

INTRODUCTION   21

grandmothers attempt to make sense of their busy and often tiring daily chores in the context of intergenerational dependence and their individual duties to other members of the family group, hence eliciting inquiries about, and the pursuit of, the moral self. Particularly noteworthy is the fact that many of these middle-to-old-aged women belong to a sandwiched generation as they also must take care of their own parents or parents-in-law. Some cases may involve four generations whereby the young-old generation is located on the second tier and must exercise their agency to deal with the old-old, the adult-children, and the grandchildren in accordance with different norms and behavioral patterns. In these cases, intergenerationality not only occurs between any two generations but also cuts through and connects all four generations. The non-intersecting interactions between the grandparents on the one hand and the adult-married children on the other should also be noted.

Chapter 5 by Xiaoying Qi examines the challenges and coping strategies of those migrants who relocated with their grandparents and grandchildren, that is, the mirror image of the left-behind phenomenon. Focusing on the floating grandparents, Qi explores how these grandparents and their adult children reinterpret and renegotiate the intergenerational obligations and behavioral patterns to construct a multigenerational migrant household and to create happier lives in the cities. In so doing, the floating grandparents challenge the widely held individual-centered approach in migration studies because the intergenerational dependence and cooperation of the migrant household is more important than the individual migrant. Moreover, many floating grandparents proactively initiate, reinterpret, and renegotiate the meanings and practices of the multigenerational family, including pre-exchange obligations, emotional attachments, and symbolic values, in the precarious and nonstable migrant world. Together, Thomason's and Qi's chapters present a more comprehensive understanding of the latest changes in intergenerationality among migrant families, which account for about one-fifth of all families in China.

As indicated above, the notion of intergenerationality opens up new ways to understand the nuances in current intergenerational dynamics, such as the conflicts between individual happiness and family interests and/or generational duties. In Chapter 6, Claudia Huang highlights this issue by focusing on the conflicting demands between one's duties as a grandparent and one's newly gained freedom to live a life on one's own. The three cases Huang examines in her chapter represent quite different individual strategies to cope with the same challenge. The most intriguing development is that although none of these women, and many others in a similar position, can regain their lost authority and power or avoid their moral obligation to help their adult children in child-rearing, to a certain extent they all manage to find space of their own to seek self-development. It is also interesting to see how these grand-mothers interact with their own parents or parents-in-law on the one hand and their adult children on the other. However, the issue of the sandwiched generation is handled differently by urban retirees in contrast to how it is han-dled by their rural counterparts, as shown in Thomason's chapter; instead of "uniting to suffer" (to borrow Thomason's phrase), they choose to organize as group to pursue their own individual happiness. In this connection, these two chapters represent a direct dialogue among themselves.

How to raise a perfect child in the third generation constitutes the eye of the storm in family life where the parents and grandparents from both paternal and maternal lines contribute their love, attention, care and mate-rial resources. This is also the most important yet highly sensitive issue that intersects with existing categories of gender, age, generation as well as social-economic class in a given family, often highlighting tensions and intensifying conflicts. In Chapter 7, Suofei Xiao goes directly into the eye of the hurricane to explore the patterns of power relations and the mechanisms of exercis-ing power across generational lines in urban multigenerational families. She discovers a new power structure being made wherein the mother typically leads the enterprise of childrearing and education in an iron-fist and micro-management style, often assuming the role of tiger mom; while the father is on the sideline concentrating on money-making, grandparents become the care-givers in daily practices of childrearing, commonly receiving the moth-er's order without much negotiation power of their own. This new pattern of power relations, however, is manifested as the operation of intimate power which contains three dimensions: first, the formation of intimate relations provides the basis for the actual function of intimate power; second, an indi-vidual's exercise power is conditioned by the intergenerational intimacy; and third, overall it is the grandparents who relinquish power contestation for the purpose of maintaining intergenerational intimacy and support in the mission of raising the perfect child in the third generation.

The single most important issue in Chapter 8 by Lihong Shi is the inter-generational identification in the construction of personhood, or the integra-tion of individual selves across generational lines. This would be a latent issue under normal circumstances and often appears in the form of intensive mutu-ality in protection, care, love, and interference between the two generations. The sudden loss of one's single child completely radicalizes the person who is left, including the loss of his/her own moral self, which may be considered the deepest and most serious loss. The integration of individual identities also sets the Chinese case apart from its counterparts in the modern West where individual autonomy is the core of identity. As Shi's ethnography shows, many

INTRODUCTION   23

parents literally hold on to their children's ashes and refuse to accept that the child has passed on. What makes the situation particularly sad is the absence of religious beliefs among many of these *shidu* parents, who simply cannot find space to place the souls of their lost children with their own. One possible way out is to turn parental grief into a source of public action, for instance when the parents organize into self-help groups not only to provide counselling to one another but also to seek social justice; hence turning the lost intergenerational bonding into a common good to benefit others. Yet, when doing so some *shidu* parents have encountered cultural stigmatization due to government hostility to civic engagement (Kong 2018;).

Chapter 9 by William Jankowiak, offers a rather radical account of the new family configuration and intergenerational dynamics by tracing all major changes back to the 1980s when the Maoist work-unit culture still dominated in urban life. Jankowiak examines five areas representative of the gradual shift from the traditional family to the neo-family configuration: the good marriage, the parent-offspring relationship, the in-law relationship, individual expression and achievement, and residence preference. Based on his longitudinal field research in the northern city of Huhhot, Jankowiak argues that the new family configuration is being shaped by an independent, albeit coterminous, process: a heightened respect for the self as a cognitive and emotional entity. The expansion of an ethics of the self has reinforced support for valuing autonomy and self-expression, but it does not provide complete independence or self-sufficiency as is typically found in the United States. In this setting, emotional connections between spouses or with parents are no longer denied or rejected. In fact, to a large extent they are publicly affirmed. All of the changes that occurred in the 1980s, contends Jankowiak, set the stage for what would later become the neo-family.

Intriguingly, Jankowiak's historical ethnography also reveals that the early trend of the awakening individual autonomy and self-expression did not develop much further in the subsequent two decades. Many areas of family life in the 2000s appear to be similar to what already existed in the 1980s, and in some areas the early liberating change has been reversed in the 2000s, such as the increased parental power in their adult children's spouse selection, marriage, and childrearing. Such a trajectory of "two steps forward, one step backward" reflects the defining feature of neo-familism, that is, a rather complex combination of individualistic and familial features in both discourse and practice (Yan 2011, 2015, 2016, and 2018). It follows that the concoction of pursuing individual happiness and self-development by way of invoking familial support is the paradoxical point of entry for a better understanding of neo-familism practices, as evidenced in the ethnographic accounts of preceding chapters.

In the Chinese case of family change, the influence of the party-state can hardly be overstated. As Deborah Davis and Stevan Harrell noted nearly three decades ago: "Clearly, in the People's Republic of China (PRC) state power and policies have been the creators, not the creations, of a transformed society" (1993: 5). Policy making, however, has been a blind spot in English-language scholarship on family change in China. I devote Chapter 10 to fill this gap by examining how family policies have been made by the party-state as an instrument of governance to serve the national agenda from 1949 to the present. My central argument is that, in numerous ways and during different periods, the party-state took a statist approach in the making of family policies and in the reshaping of the Chinese family, and this statist model generated complex, inconsistent, and sometimes even conflicting policy results that affected the family wellbeing. This statist model of family policy making originated with the early attempts to reform the family for the purpose of nation-state building at the turn of the twentieth century, most particularly during the May Fourth New Culture Movement. Eventually, and to a great extent unexpectedly, the convergence of these historical and contemporary policy results contributed to the rise of neo-familism in the early twenty-first century.

Neo-familism also exists in social discourses on family values, behavior norms, the ideal family life, and the conceived relationship among individual, family, society, and state. This is why I conclude the present volume by taking a close look at three prevailing discourses of neo-familism in contemporary Chinese society in Chapter 11. The first is a popular discourse of neo-familism that emphasize the family as the only reliable resource for ordinary people to cope with the increasingly competitive, risky and precarious work place in particular and social life in general. It is highlighted in the motto of "family problems, family solution" and reflected in social surveys and individual testimonies in ethnographic research. The second is the official discourse by which the party-state redefines the family as a site of governance and incorporates familism into patriotism. The intellectual discourse of neo-familism is the third variation that invokes familism as a cultural capital to resist Western individualism and to construct a Chinese path to modernity. Both the official and intellectual versions regard the individual as the means to reach to a higher goal, be it the China Dream or rejuvenation of Chinese culture. Therefore, they merged into a united force through their shared preference of traditional familism and support each other with the common advocacy for some key Confucian notions such as the family-state (家国 *jiaguo*), the sentimental disposition of

INTRODUCTION

family-state (家国情怀*jiaguo qinghuai*), and the isomorphism of family and state (家国同构*jiaguo tonggou*).

Finally, it is noteworthy that nearly all of the new developments in family life and the emerging neo-familism are closely associated with the singleton generations (namely, those who were born in the 1980s and 1990s) who are taking the central stage in both private and public spheres in Chinese society. Their discourse and practice of neo-familism, therefore, will likely redefine many features and operating rules of the Chinese family and kinship, some of which have been explored in the present volume. Given that the singleton generations have grown up in the era of globalization and information revolution and indeed have stronger self-awareness and determination to pursue individual development and happiness, to what extent their heart and mind can be captured by the official and intellectual discourses of neo-familism remains an open question.

References

Baker, Hugh. 1979. *Chinese Family and Kinship*. New York: Columbia University Press.

Bengtson, Vern L. 2001. "Beyond the Nuclear Family: The Increasing Importance of Multigenerational Bonds." *Journal of Marriage and Family* 63 (1): 1–16.

Bengtson, Vern L. and Robert E. L. Roberts. 1991. "Intergenerational Solidarity in Aging Families: An Example of Formal Theory Construction." *Journal of Marriage and the Family* 53(4): 856–70.

Bregnbæk, Susanne. 2016. "From Filial Piety to Forgiveness: Managing Ambivalent Feelings in a Beijing House-Church." *Ethos* 44, 4: 411–26.

Brandtstädter, Susanne and Gonçalo D. Santos, eds. 2009. *Chinese Kinship: Contemporary Anthropological Perspectives*. London: Routledge.

Cherlin, Andrew J. 2004. "The Deinstitutionalization of American Marriage." *Journal of Marriage and Family* 66 (4): 848–861.

Cherlin, Andrew J. 2006 "On Single Mothers 'Doing' Family." *Journal of Marriage and Family* 68 (4): 800–803.

Cherlin, Andrew J. 2012. "Goode's 'World Revolution and Family Patterns': A Reconsideration at Fifty Years," *Population and Development Review,* 38(4): 577–607.

Cherlin, Andrew J. and Judith A. Seltzer. 2014. "Family Complexity, the Family Safety Net, and Public Policy." *The Annals of the American Academy* 654 (July): 231–239.

Chen Yingfang. 2015. "社会生活的正常化：历史转折中的 '家庭化'" (Normalization of Social Life: Analysis of "Familization" at the Historical Turn). 社会学研究(Sociological Studies), no. 5: 164–88, 245–46.

Choi, Susanne Y.P. and Luo Ming. 2016. "Performative Family: Homosexuality, Marriage and Intergenerational Dynamics in China." *The British Journal of Sociology* 67, 2: 260–80.

Croll, Elisabeth. 1987. "New Peasant Family Forms in Rural China." *Journal of Peasant Studies* 14, 4: 469–99.

Cross, Christina J. 2018. "Extended Family Households among Children in the United States: Differences by Race/Ethnicity and Socio-Economic Status." *Population Studies* 72 (2): 235–251.

Davis, Deborah S. and Sara L. Friedman. 2014a. "Deinstitutionalizing Marriage and Sexuality." In Davis, Deborah S. and Sara L. Friedman (eds.) *Wives, Husbands, and Lovers: Marriage and Sexuality in Hong Kong, Taiwan, and Urban China*, pp. 1–38. Stanford: Stanford University Press.

Davis, Deborah S. and Sara L. Friedman, eds. 2014b. *Wives, Husbands, and Lovers: Marriage and Sexuality in Hong Kong, Taiwan, and Urban China*. Stanford: Stanford University Press.

Davis, Deborah and Stevan Harrell, eds. 1993. *Chinese Families in the Post-Mao Era.* Berkeley: University of California Press.

Davis-Friedmann, Deborah. 1991. *Long Lives: Chinese Elderly and the Communist Revolution.* Stanford: Stanford University Press.

Deng Weizhi. 1994. 近代中国的家庭变革(Family change in modern China). Shanghai: Shanghai Renmin Chubanshe.

Di Gessa, Giogio, Karen Glaser, Debora Price, Eloi Ribe, and Anthea Tinker. 2016. "What Drives National Differences in Intensive Grandparental Childcare in Europe?" *Journal of Gerontology: Social Sciences* 71 (1): 141–153.

Ding, Renchuan and Wu Ruijun. 2009. "独生子女大规模进入婚育年龄对我国人口发展的影响" (The impact of the large cohort of singletons entering reproductive age on national demography), 西北人口 (*Northwestern Demography*) 30(2): 15–17.

Dykstra Pearl A. and Tineke Fokkema. 2010. "Relationships between Parents and Their Adult Children: A West European Typology of Late-life Families." *Ageing and Society*, 31(4): 545–569.

Evans, Harriet. 2008. *The Subject of Gender: Daughters and Mothers in Urban China.* Lanham, MD: Rowman & Littlefield.

Feng, Xiaotian. 2015. "四二一：概念内涵，问题实质，与社会影响" (4-2-1: The connotation of the concept, the essence of the problem, and its social impact). *Shehui Kexue (Social Sciences)*, No. 11, pp. 71–81.

Fei, Xiaotong. 1992 [1947]. *From the Soil, The Foundations of Chinese Society*, tr. Gary G. Hamilton and Wang Zheng. Berkeley: University of California Press.

Gao, Wanqin. 2018. "双系并重下农村代际关系的演变与重构：基于农村两头走婚居习俗的调查" (Changes and reconstruction of intergenerational relations under bilateral kinship—an investigation of dual-local postmarital residence in rural China). 中国青年研究(*Studies of Chinese Youth*), no. 2, pp. 11–17.

Garzón, Adela Pérez. 2000. "Cultural Change and Familism," *Psicothema*, 12(suppl.): 45–54.

Glosser, Susan L. 2003. *Chinese Versions of Family and State, 1915–1953*. Berkeley: University of California Press.

Goode, William. 1962. *World Revolution and Family Patterns*. New York: The Free Press.

Guo, Jiangang, Liu Jintang and Song Jian. 2002. "现行生育政策与未来家庭结构" (The current birth-planning policy and the future family structure), 中国人口科学(*Chinese Science of Demography*), no. 1, pp. 1–11.

Hanser, Amy and Jialin Camille Li. 2015. "Opting Out? Gated Consumption, Infant Formula and China's Affluent Urban Consumers." *The China Journal*, No. 74: 110–28.

Harrell, Stevan and Gonçalo Santos. 2017. "Introduction." In Santos, Gonçalo and Stevan Harrell, eds. 2017. *Transforming Patriarchy: Chinese Families in the Twenty-First Century*, pp. 3–36. Seattle: University of Washington Press.

Hizi, Gil. 2017. "'Developmental' Therapy for a 'Modernised' Society: The Sociopolitical Meanings of Psychology in Urban China." *China: An International Journal* 15, 2: 98–119.

Hopkins, Peter and Rachel Pain. 2007. "Geographies of Age: Thinking Relationally." *Area* 39, 3: 287–94.

Hopkins, Peter. 2008. "Is There More to Life? Relationalities in Here and Out There: A Reply to Horton and Kraftl." *Area* 40, 2: 289–92.

Horton, John and Peter Kraftl. 2008. "Reflections on Geographies of Age: A Response to Hopkins and Pain." *Area* 40, 2: 284–88.

Hsu, Becky Yang. 2019. "Having It All: Filial Piety, Moral Weighting, and Anxiety among Young Adults." In *The Chinese Pursuit of Happiness: Anxieties, Hopes, and Moral Tensions in Everyday Life*, ed. Becky Yang Hsu and Richard Madsen, 42–65. Berkeley: University of California Press.

Jankowiak, William R. and Robert L. Moore. 2017. *Family Life in China*. Cambridge, UK: Polity Press.

Kong, Xiangli. 2018. "风险社会视角下失独家庭的政策支持机制：实践困境及范式转制" (The Mechanism of Policy Support to the *Shidu* Families from the Perspective of a Risk Society: Practical Dilemmas and Paradigm Shifts). 北京行政学院学报 (Journal of Beijing Administration Institute), no. 5: 101–9.

Lesthaeghe, Ron. 2010. "The Unfolding Story of the Second Demographic Transition." *Population and Development Review* 36: 211–251.

Levine, Nancy E. 2008. "Alternative Kinship, Marriage, and Reproduction." *Annual Review of Anthropology* 37: 375–389.

Liu Wenrong. 2016. "转型期的家庭代际情感与团结" (Intergenerational affections and solidarity in families during social transition), 社会学研究 (Sociological Studies), no. 4, pp. 145–168.

Nelson, Margaret K. 2006. "Single Mothers 'Do' Family." *Journal of Marriage and Family* 68 (4): 781–795.

Ochs, Elinor and Tamar Kremer-Sadlik. Eds. 2013. *Fast-Forward Family: Home, Work, and Relationships in Middle-Class America*. Berkeley: University of California Press.

Parish, William L. and Martin King Whyte. 1978. *Village and Family in Contemporary China*. Chicago: University of Chicago Press.

Qi, Xiaoying. 2018. "Neo-traditional Child Surnaming in Contemporary China: Women's Rights as Veiled Patriarchy." *Sociology* 52 (5): 1001–1016.

Santos, Gonçalo and Stevan Harrell, eds. 2017. *Transforming Patriarchy: Chinese Families in the Twenty-First Century*. Seattle: University of Washington Press.

Shen Yifei. 2013. 个体家庭：中国城市现代化进程中的个体、家庭与国家 (iFamily: The Individual, Family, and the State in the Modernization Process of Urban China). Shanghai: Shanghai sanlian shudian.

Shi, Lihong. 2017. *Choosing Daughters: Family Change in Rural China*. Stanford: Stanford University Press.

Silverstein, Merril, Daphna Gans, Ariela Lowenstein, Roseann Giarrusso, and Vern L. Bengtson. 2010. "Older Parent-Child Relationships in Six Developed Nations: Comparisons at the Intersection of Affection and Conflict." *Journal of Marriage and Family*, 72(4): 1006–1021.

Stacey, Judith. 1983. *Patriarchy and Socialist Revolution in China*. Berkeley: University of California Press.

Steinbach, Anja. 2008. "Intergenerational Solidarity and Ambivalence: Types of Relationships in German Families." *Journal of Comparative Family Studies*, 39(1): 115–127.

Swartz, Teresa Toguchi. 2009. "Intergenerational Family Relations in Adulthood: Patterns, Variations, and Implications in the Contemporary United States." *Annual Review of Sociology* 35: 191–212.

Vanderbeck, Robert M. 2017. "Intergenerational Geographies in Theory and Practice." In *Establishing Geographies of Children and Young People*, ed. Tracey Skelton and Stuart C. Aitken, 1–23. Singapore: Springer Nature.

Wang, Feng. 2011. "The Future of a Demographic Overachiever: Long-Term Implications of the Demographic Transition in China." *Population and Development Review*, 37(supplement):173–190.

Wang, Hui and Di Jinghua. 2011. "两头走：双独子女婚后家庭居住的新模式" (Dual-local residence: A new pattern of post-marital residence among double-singleton couples), 中国青年研究 (*Studies of Chinese Youth*), no. 5, pp. 9–12.

Wang Yonghui. 2014. "城市化进程中农村代际关系的变迁" (Changes in Rural Intergenerational Relations during the Urbanization Process). 南方人口 (South China Population Studies), 28(1): 73–80.

Whyte, Martin. 2005. "Continuity and Change in Urban Chinese Family Life." *The China Journal*, no. 53: 9–33.

Whyte, Martin King and William L. Parish. 1984. *Urban Life in Contemporary China*. Chicago: University of Chicago Press.

Yan, Yunxiang. 1997. "The Triumph of Conjugality: Structural Transformation of Family Relations in a Chinese Village." *Ethnology* 36(3): 191–212.

Yan, Yunxiang. 2003. *Private Life under Socialism: Love, Intimacy, and Family Change in a Chinese Village, 1949–1999*. Stanford: Stanford University Press.

Yan, Yunxiang. 2010 "The Chinese Path to Individualization," *The British Journal of Sociology* 61 (3): 489–512.

Yan, Yunxiang. 2011. . "The Individualization of the Family in Rural China." *boundary 2* 38(1): 203–229.

Yan, Yunxiang. 2012. "Food Safety and Social Risk in Contemporary China." *Journal of Asian Studies* 70, 3: 705–29.

Yan, Yunxiang. 2015. "Parents-driven Divorce and Individualization among Urban Chinese Youth." *International Social Science Journal*, nos. 213/214: 317–30.

Yan, Yunxiang. 2016. "Intergenerational Intimacy and Descending Familism in Rural North China." *American Anthropologist* 118, 2: 244–57.

Yan, Yunxiang. 2017 "Doing Personhood in Chinese Culture: The Desiring Individual, Moralist Self, and Relational Person." *Cambridge Anthropology* 35, 2: 1–17.

Yan, Yunxiang. 2018. "Neo-Familism and the State in Contemporary China." *Urban Anthropology and Studies of Cultural Systems and World Economic Development* 47, 3/ 4: 181–224.

Yan, Yunxiang. 2021. "The Politics of Moral Crisis in Contemporary China." *The China Journal*, no. 85 (forthcoming).

Yang, Ke. 2018. "母职的经纪人化：教育市场化背景下的母职变迁" (Motherhood as an Educational Agent: Changes in Motherhood in the Context of Market-oriented Education). 妇女研究论丛(Journal of Chinese Women), no. 2: 79–90.

Zhang, Hong. 2017. "Recalibrating Filial Piety: Realigning the State, Family, and Market Interests in China." In Gonçalo Santos and Stevan Harrell, eds.. *Transforming Patriarchy: Chinese Family in the Twenty-First Century*, 234–50. Seattle: University of Washington Press.

Zhang, Ni. 2018. "2017 中国流动人口总量达2.44亿" (The floating population totalizes in 244 million in 2017), December 22, 中国新闻网 (China News Net) http://news.cctv.com/2018/12/22/ARTIquc9P3peRe218pIoIzoM181222.shtml (accessed May 20, 2019).

Zhao Yanjie. 2018. "为国破家：近代中国家庭革命论反思" (Destroying the family for the nation-state: Reflections on the family revolution in modern China), 近代史研究 (Journal of Modern History), no. 3: 74–86.

Zhong Xiaohui and He Shining. 2014. "协商式亲密关系：独生子女父母对家庭关系和孝道的期待" (Negotiated Intimacy: Expectations of Family Relationships and Filial Piety among Singleton Parents). 开放时代 (Open Times), no. 1: 155–75, 7–8.

Zhu Jinghui and Zhu Qiaoyan. 2013. "温和的理性：当代浙江农村家庭代际关系研" (Mild Rationality: A Study of Intergenerational Relationships among Rural Families in Zhejiang Province). 浙江社会科学 (Zhejiang Journal of Social Sciences), no. 10: 99–105, 129.

CHAPTER 2

"We Do"

Parental Involvement in the Marriages of Urban Sons and Daughters

Deborah S. Davis

1 Introduction

Historically parents in China played the central role in arranging a child's marriage, first by finding a spouse and then by negotiating the financial terms of the union. Because norms guiding the negotiations for marriages were more flexible than those for dividing an inheritance, a child's marriage offered a particularly important opportunity for parents to strategize long-term benefits for themselves and for their extended families, rather than for the happiness of the new couple (Watson and Ebrey 1991). Guiding the initial search was the principle of "matching doors" (门当户对). Wealthy parents sought daughters-in-law from equally wealthy families and middle-income parents sought in-laws of equal status. Many poor families adopted a young girl to be the future bride of a young, or even future, son so to reduce the costs and to hedge against conflicts with an adult daughter-in-law whose arrival might destabilize the existing household. Moreover, because traditionally wealthy men could have multiple consorts and infanticide of girls masculinized the population, sons in the poorest families were forced to delay or even forgo marriage. Nevertheless, parents of all economic strata could strategize how best to "marry off" a daughter to secure advantages for her natal family, if not necessarily for the young bride herself.

Over time as children were born and parents aged, the ties between husband and wife as well as between adult children and their parents evolved. The power and authority of the elder generation declined and that of the middle generation increased. Yet the principle of filial piety as well as the practicalities of co-residence and the rituals of ancestor veneration reinforced the primacy of vertical loyalty between married men and their parents. Thus, as Margery Wolf discovered in Taiwan during the 1960s, village women concentrated their efforts on strengthening the vertical loyalties with their sons rather than focusing on the horizontal conjugal ties with their spouse (Wolf 1993).

Yet, even as marriage emotionally and economically binds together family members, marriage is simultaneously a public institution through which

© DEBORAH S. DAVIS, 2021 | DOI:10.1163/9789004450233_003

governments control their citizens and subordinate idiosyncratic family ambitions to national goals (Glosser 2003). In the decades before 1949, both Nationalist and Communist leaders prioritized marriage reform and each passed regulations to reduce parental control and promote monogamous free-choice marriages (Glosser 2003). In practice, however, because neither political party exercised effective control over the country and because most young adults lacked economic autonomy, throughout the first half of the twentieth century parents continued to determine the timing and conditions of their children's marriages.

However, the first item of official legislation after 1950 was a new Marriage Law. Prohibiting concubinage and child brides (童养媳), requiring registration of marriages, and mandating a minimum marriage age of 18 for women and 20 for men, the legislation directly limited parental interference in the marital lives of their children (Marriage Law 1950). The subsequent collectivization of land and private businesses further reduced parental power and authority. In cities where education was free for both girls and boys through early adolescence and where loyalty to the party determined promotion in the workplace, parents were generally disempowered. Directly arranged matches became rare and parents became less entangled in the marriages of their children (Whyte 1990), or, as Yunxiang Yan (2003) has so succinctly noted: "conjugality triumphed."

However, recent observations indicate a decided move toward more intense and sustained parental involvement in the lives of adult children, a trend that Yan (2017/2018) characterizes as "descending familism," whereby a downward flow of family assets from the older to the younger generations both heightens financial and emotional interdependence and disrupts the traditional patriarchal hierarchy. In this volume, Yan elaborates on how, due to the increasing economic and social insecurities, parent-child relations have become inverted and post-patriarchal. Drawing on both documentary sources and fieldwork in Shanghai, this chapter focuses on parental involvement in mate choice and wedding celebrations to ground the conceptual heuristic of "post-patriarchal intergenerationality" in one specific moment in the family life course.[1]

---

1 Between 2014 and 2016 I interviewed seventy men and women about their weddings that took place between 1978 and 2016. I also observed twenty-five wedding videos with my respondents, interviewed four wedding planners, and directly observed eight weddings at several wedding halls. I met these men and women through many channels: some were old friends, others were friends of colleagues or former students, and some were contacts of my research assistant, a recently retired office worker. In addition, I drew on focus groups that I ran with colleagues Hanlong Lu, Peidong Sun, and Jun Zhang in 2004, 2006, 2008, and 2015

2 Matchmaking in Shanghai's People's Park

On every weekend since 2005, thousands of parents in their fifties and sixties have gathered in one corner of People's Park in Shanghai to find a partner for their unmarried son or daughter. When the corner first became a matchmaking venue, parents carried a shopping bag, and later on an umbrella, to which they had attached a summary of their child's demographic profile: birth date, educational credentials, height, current job, and usually their *hukou* status (Zhang and Sun 2014). Ten years later, when I was a frequent visitor at the corner, parents had added their child's yearly salary, and whether or not the child owned a car and/or an apartment.[2] Most surprising to me was that in such a public space, parents provided a cell number for anyone who wanted to pursue an introduction, and on one occasion, an anxious mother pushed her daughter's ID card and bus pass into my hand.

When my colleague Peidong Sun (2012) analyzed her visits to the corner in 2007–8, she found that most parents displayed the background details of their child so that anyone passing by could collect the information. But in the fall of 2015 and early spring of 2016, I observed two distinct patterns of outreach. About one-half of those in the park sat on a folding stool or a garden wall, with an umbrella opened to publicize the child's situation. Some were parents, others were acting for an agency or for a friend. Another approach was to circulate along the nearby pathways. Many among those on the pathways circulated as a couple. Also, they were often better dressed than those sitting with the umbrellas. Rarely did they openly display the demographic profile of their child. Instead, they moved slowly, appraising others who passed by, and when they perceived a possible match, they would ask in very low voice, "Is your child a son or daughter?" If they were looking for a daughter and the other parent(s) had a son, they would stop to chat. Although I have no systematic evidence, I sensed that those circulating saw themselves as superior to those who were huddled under the umbrellas.

If the initial exchange of pleasantries went well, parents would share photos on their phones and inquire more about the lives of their children. If after twenty minutes of conversation, they felt that the other parents were sincere and a match seemed promising, they might exchange phone numbers, which

---

to probe attitudes toward the division of conjugal property, grounds for divorce, and parental matchmaking.

2 Between July 25, 2015 and April 17, 2016, I visited the corner fifteen times. On each visit, I spent at least one hour walking along all the pathways where the parents were sitting and I spoke to three or four parents about their respective child.

they would later pass on to their child. It was then up to the young man or woman to set up a meeting.

In September 2015 when interviewing a cadre who supervises commercial enterprises on the periphery of the park, I asked why Shanghai parents did not use the mobile matchmaking apps in the safety of their homes. Why did they venture out into public, where they might be recognized and/or cheated? He responded with surprise:

> Because by meeting face to face, seeing their clothes, their posture, and their language they have already conducted a first screening. Just like today, from your posture, your make-up, and your way of speaking I can make a judgment. Parents are just like that. People make their first assessment (判断) via the person (人) not via the written word (字) People make their first judgments via their hearts (心).

On a short visit in September 2019, I met two men who were watching the crowds drift past in the park. When they saw me read a notice in Chinese, they called out and engaged me in conversation. They assumed that I was a curious tourist who would benefit from their local knowledge and, given that travel guides now list the corner as one of the top ten tourist attractions in Shanghai, their assumption was not far-fetched (https://www.travelchinaguide.com/attraction/shanghai/marriage-market.htm, accessed January 15, 2020). After we briefly exchanged travel experiences, theirs in the United States and mine in China, the younger man volunteered his assessment of the small dramas unfolding before us in the park: "These are parents looking for a family like their own; they are not searching for an ideal daughter or son-in-law." The older man agreed.

In addition to the men and women crouched under their umbrellas or slowly circulating along the pathways, there were clusters of semi-professional match-makers displaying large laminated booklets or charts with fifty or more potential mates. Periodically suppressed by city officials, these semi-professionals were present during about one-half of my visits in 2015 and 2016, but they were largely absent when I returned in 2019. These matchmakers often charged for an introduction, but most only received their fee if an introduction resulted in a date.

I have never found official estimates of the success rate, but whether they exchanged phone numbers while sitting under an umbrella or met while circulating through the crowds, all whom I interviewed reported that successful matches were extremely rare. Nevertheless, one colleague reported that his son had recently married a woman whose father he had met at the corner.

Stories such as his encouraged others to return to the corner week after week in the hope that they and their child would be another such lucky exception.

When Peidong Sun and Jun Zhang analyzed Sun's 2007–8 fieldwork at the marriage corner, they characterized the parents as individuals on a "historical mission" (Zhang and Sun 2014: 133) who were driven by their sense of duty and responsibility to help their children find a suitable spouse. In terms of their emotional affect, they also exemplified Yan's new form of filial piety where the emotional core of enduring family obligations centers on the parents' "undying devotion" to their children's happiness rather than on their children fulfilling obligations to their parents (Zhang and Sun 2014:137).

During my conversations in 2015 and 2016, most mothers and fathers stressed that marriage was necessary and remaining single was not normal (不正常). In some cases, the parents emphasized the necessity of a grandchild and that without a grandchild their own lives would be incomplete. But equally often parents prefaced their remarks about the necessity of marriage in terms of the universal need for someone to provide care in old age. If their child did not marry, they asked who would provide care in times of sickness or in times of need after they themselves had passed away. Furthermore, because in China childbearing outside of marriage is stigmatized and legally problematic, arguing for the necessity of children is equivalent to arguing for the necessity of marriage.

Although Hangzhou, Shenzhen, Tianjin, Shenyang, Suzhou, Luoyang, and Ji'nan have had similar matchmaking corners, most people I met in Shanghai consider matchmaking in a public park to be aberrant as well as embarrassing. We certainly cannot presume that the parents whom Sun and I interviewed were statistically representative; they were more desperate as well as more fearless than most. But in terms of age, education, and occupations, these parents were not exceptional. Moreover, the current popularity of the television show, "Chinese-Style Matchmaking" (中国式相亲), launched in December 2016, suggests that parental participation in matchmaking, although a source of entertainment, remains an accepted practice.

In "Chinese-Style Matchmaking," five young people accompanied by two family members interview a possible spouse. The young man or woman first lists the qualities they most prize in a mate, followed by their accompanying parents also presenting a list. After the five young adults depart to a nearby room from where they can see possible choices and they can confer by phone with other family members, the potential candidate appears on a small stage. Each of the families then pose questions, and the audience watches the reaction of the five young adults who are sitting off-stage. I do not know how contestants are selected or coached, but in the opening minutes of the February

16, 2019 show, the master of ceremonies announced that thirty-seven participants had married since the showed first premiered (https://www.youtube.com/watch?v=UaTt7KL8sUk, accessed January 15, 2020).

The contrast between "Chinese-Style Matchmaking" and the equally popular but longer running "If You Are Not Sincere Don't Bother Me" (非诚勿扰) on Jiangsu television is revealing. In "If You Are Not Sincere Don't Bother Me," which was launched in 2010, one man interacts with twelve young women who stride down a runway in revealing ensembles before standing behind a podium. In addition, two commentators, referred to as "teacher" (老师) provide commentary on the performance of the young man and his ranking of the young women. During its first six years, the show was quite raucous, but after one female participant rejected a poor but sincere young man by saying she would rather be unhappy riding in a BMW than sitting on the back of a bike, the show was rebooted to stress more wholesome values. Most importantly, "If You Are Not Sincere Don't Bother Me" in contrast to "Chinese-Style Matchmaking" features only unattached young men and women. No parents or grandparents appear on stage.

Reality lies somewhere between the hype of both shows. Thus, for example, in a 2013 survey of married men and women born between 1980 and 1989 who were living and working in Shanghai, Felica Tian and I found that 55.8 percent of the women and 53.5 percent of the men had met their spouses on their own and 24.2 percent of the women and 26 percent of the men had met their spouses through introductions by friends or a dating organization (Tian and Davis 2019). However, 19.9 percent of the men and 20.5 percent of the women had met their spouse through an introduction through their parents or other close kin. The key predictor of independence from one's parents was graduation from a four-year college. By contrast, a local Shanghai *hukou*, which aligns with geographic proximity to one's parents, reduced the self-reliance among women but not for men. Whereas for men, but not women, having a father who was a CCP member, an indicator of parental prestige and local social capital, inclined a child to turn to his/her parents to find a spouse. Because the median age of our married respondents was 28 and most people assume that finding a mate after the age of 30 becomes increasingly difficult, particularly for women, Tian and I hypothesize that the percentage who ultimately rely on their parents will rise above 20 percent, and that this increase will be particularly marked for women in families where both parents and daughter have a Shanghai *hukou* and for men without college degrees whose fathers are CCP members.

Yet, at the same time as our survey documented that only a minority had met their mate through a parental introduction, these percentages, surprisingly exceed those Martin Whyte reports for Chengdu women who married between 1958 and 1987 (1990: 184). Moreover, recent qualitative research confirms the current centrality of what Sandra To (2015) identifies as "marital filial strategies," whereby parents establish criteria for an acceptable mate and rarely will adult children marry someone whom the parents do not explicitly endorse. As a result, few men or women are willing to marry someone of whom their parents strongly disapprove. Thus, even if individuals report that they found their spouse on their own, it is unlikely that the parents were totally excluded from their mate search. Arranged marriages are extremely rare, but many parents will guide a search and some will exercise veto power.

In summarizing recent trends in Chinese family relations, and specifically in his exchange with Uncle Lu, Yunxiang Yan foregrounds the emotional dimension of "inverted" family relations. During my initial visits to People's Park in fall 2015, I too was impressed by the strong emotions that surfaced during even short conversations; they were not primarily expressing love, affection, and devotion, but rather anxiety, fear, and in some cases anger. I also was impressed by the gender distinctions. When mothers were looking for a match for a daughter, they more often expressed guilt than did fathers. Yet both expressed regret (后悔)that when their daughter was younger, they had pushed her to focus on her schoolwork and had discouraged, or even prohibited, her from dating. In addition, mothers, more often than fathers, more directly expressed shame when a daughter whose superior performance in school had been a source of constant pride had subsequently fallen behind her peers in terms of reaching the next life milestone. When the unmarried child was a son, the mother's emotions were more muted than when the child was a daughter; strikingly, many fathers but no mothers overtly expressed anger, and several times the fathers, but not the mothers, made direct comparisons between the son's failure and their own success.

To explore these initial impressions of emotional variation by gender, Peidong Sun recruited twenty-five university students to interview parents at the park following a script of fifteen questions that probed expectations of marriage and experiences in searching for a mate for their son or daughter at the corner.[3] During a period of six weeks in November and December 2015, the students spoke with thirty-three mothers searching for a mate for a daughter,

---

3   The fifteen questions on the interview schedule include: 1. When did you first visit the corner? and how long did you stay? 2. What kind of partner (什么样 的对象) for your child are you looking for? 3. What information (择偶信息) do you want from other parents or agents? 4. What is most important （最看重什么） when selecting a spouse for your child? What is most unacceptable? 5. If your child were the opposite sex, would you be using the same criteria? 6. Have you used channels other than the park to find a spouse for your child? 7. What does your child and your spouse think of your going to the corner? 8. What is your impression

nineteen mothers searching for a mate for a son, twenty-three fathers searching for a mate for a daughter, and twenty fathers searching for a mate for a son. In addition to transcribing the answers to the specific questions, the students were asked to describe the interviewees' varied emotions.

Overall, the students confirmed my initial impressions, but they also offered important corrections. First, anger was not restricted only to the fathers. Second, both the mothers and the fathers connected their anxieties over their child's marriage prospects to broader fears that both they and their child would be cheated in the turbulent urban society that no longer observed the more predictable norms of earlier decades. Such fears resonated with the results from focus groups that I coordinated in 2004, 2006, and 2008 in Shanghai, Guangzhou, and Beijing (Davis 2010), where in response to questions about the use of prenuptials, men and women with and without college degrees who were born in the 1950s or after 1980, consistently emphasized that the primary attribute of a good spouse is one whom they can trust in this era of instability. Parents seeking a match at the corner did not as overtly articulate the need for trust as did the participants in my focus groups, but their repeated concern about avoiding a man or woman who would cheat their child reflected the same priority.

In addition to probing parental anxieties and hopes for their child, the students asked the parents to compare their own search for a mate with that of their child. Because 90 percent of the parents had married between 1980 and 1985, these interviewees provide a window into norms for mate selection among the first generation to marry after promulgation of the new Marriage Law of 1980 and implementation of the one-child policy. In reviewing over 100 interviews, I was impressed how simple the criteria were for a successful match and I was surprised at how few had found their spouse on their own. For example, when asked to list attributes that they sought in finding a mate, most responded they would be satisfied if the person was not bad looking (顺眼) and were an adequate companion. The key persons to make the introduction, however, were not their parents but supervisors at their place of work or older neighbors with whom they had grown up. The explanation for relying on supervisors and neighbors was that these elders had wider social networks

---

of the other parents whom you have met at the corner? 9. Have you had any success? 10. Have your attitudes about the corner changed at all? Why? 11. Do you think every person should marry? Why? 12. Is marriage more important for women than it is for men? 13. If after two years your child has still not yet married, about what would you most worry (担心)? 14. Is it more difficult to find a mate today than it was when you married? 15. Is destiny (缘分) important? What does 缘分 mean?

than parents and were more aware of a person's strengths and weaknesses. In reflecting on their own mate search, many interviewees lamented the loss of neighborhoods where everyone knew everyone else's business and the collapse of the large state units where trade union and youth league cadres considered matchmaking to be part of their jobs. These fathers and mothers emphasized that people today live in high-rise apartments where everyone is a newcomer and people prize their privacy. Most young adults no longer work in large enterprises and their work hours are extremely long. As a result, once out of school it becomes increasingly difficult for young people to find a spouse on their own and the role of their parents becomes more important. With regard to this shift to greater reliance on one's parents, I summarize below an exchange on November 14, 2015 with a 60-year-old Shanghai-born father who had been going to the park nearly every weekend for the past year on behalf of his daughter who was born in 1984. He explicitly said that he was looking for a son-in-law whose family background matched his own (门当户对) and he believed that going to the park was an ideal way to identify families whose conditions are about the same (家里条件和自己差不多的). He explicitly rejected using professional matchmakers on the grounds that such people simply cheat people. Of note are his reasons why he also felt he could no longer turn to relatives for introductions.

> Q6. Have you also used avenues other than the park to help your child find a spouse? For example, relatives? friends? or the web?
>
> A. Previously our relatives and friends did make introductions, but they were all rather casual. Then once my daughter became so old, our relatives did not dare to make more introductions because they feared that if the man were not good, there would be problems after they married. Thus, now that my daughter is so old, it is too embarrassing to ask relatives for help.

Although tied closely to his wider circle of kin, this father deliberately no longer sought help from those who best knew him and his daughter. Rather, like the other parents I met at the park, he felt an intensified sense of individual responsibility to resolve his child's marital status on his own.

3   Nuptial Celebrations

In 2014 the average cost of celebrating an urban wedding in China was 200,000 yuan (about $33,000), a sum almost ten times the per capita disposable income

FIGURE 2.1   Number of Shanghai marriages and divorces, 1980–2017
SOURCES: *SHANGHAI STATISTICAL YEARBOOKS 2010–18*

(Davis 2019). Moreover, 200,000 yuan is the national average; in Shanghai, recently married college graduates estimated they spent closer to 300,000 yuan (about $50,000). Some have hypothesized, and one of my respondents confirmed, that the celebrations have become increasingly elaborate and costly because the turbo-charged industry of wedding planners play on the parents' need to match or exceed the displays at the weddings of children of relatives or colleagues. Several also admitted that they believed that the larger their investment in the public celebration of the wedding, the more likely the couple would be to escape the trend toward ever higher rates of divorce. (see Figure 2.1). However, in this chapter I do not highlight increased financial investments by parents, but rather I focus on the emotional and performative dimensions that distinguish contemporary wedding practices from those when today's parents were married during the 1980s.

In Shanghai, a couple is officially married when they register at a district office. The process is an entirely bureaucratic transaction that requires that the two parties appear in person and submit copies of their identity cards, household registrations, a health certificate, and two color photos of standard size.[4] If the office is not busy, the procedure takes no longer than twenty minutes.

---

4   Before 2003, the registries also required a letter from the employer of both the bride and groom granting approval for the marriage. Today, there is no role for employers. (Davis 2014a).

When I observed more than 100 couples registering their marriage during the spring of 2016, the lines moved rather quickly. Most surprising to me was that I rarely saw a couple kiss or even embrace during or after the registration. In fact, one couple seemed most preoccupied that their illegally parked BMW would be towed, with the groom stepping out in the middle of the registration procedure to confirm that the car had not been ticketed. Most arrived without parents or friends. And when I asked my respondents if anyone had accompanied them when they had gone to register their marriage, most were surprised by my question. However, the behavior of couples in the registry did not indicate that parents did not play any role in the nuptial celebrations. Rather, registration recognized marriage in the eyes of the state; the real celebration and the socially significant confirmation of this major life transition occurred when the parents hosted an elaborate and highly choreographed banquet before as many as two hundred guests. Typically the ceremonies begin when the father of the bride enters the banquet hall leading his daughter, dressed in a white gown and with a veil, to meet the groom waiting on a raised stage. A master of ceremonies, supplied by the hotel or wedding planner, then leads the couple through an exchange of rings and at many weddings the master of ceremonies helps the couple cut a multi-tiered wedding cake that is placed on the edge of the stage. After completing these rituals, the couple will exit, while the guests might eat a first course and the master of ceremonies will engage them in various guessing games. Shortly thereafter, the bride reappears in a full-length evening gown. However, for this second segment of the ceremony, the parents as well as the new husband will join the master of ceremonies on the stage. The respective fathers then speak about the bride and groom, after which the children often present gifts to their parents and thank them for their life-long love and care. After completing these exchanges, the couple exits, and when the bride returns, she will be wearing a third outfit, often a red brocade *qipao*, and will circulate through the banquet room with her husband and both sets of parents to toast the guests. After the couple toast each table, the guests depart (Davis 2019).

Prior to this highly choreographed evening banquet, most couples and their parents had celebrated the nuptials with tea ceremonies at the home of each set of parents. During this ceremony, preceded by elaborate teasing of the groom at the entrance to the home of the bride' s parents, the couple would kneel before the parents and the parents would present the couple with substantial cash gifts. As in the case of the banquet rituals, the wedding planners directed the participants through the sequence; they also directed a professional videographer to record the event (Davis 2019). Most of my respondents who married after 2005 said that they would have preferred a destination wedding or a small celebration for a few close friends and relatives. But because a large and elaborate wedding banquet is essential for their parents to demonstrate to their relatives and colleagues that they are successful parents, none of my respondents hosted a banquet with fewer than eighty guests. For the couple to have spurned a banquet would have hurt or humiliated their parents. As one 2014 working-class bride (Mrs. W. below) commented: "I guess I would have preferred a simple ceremony with friends, but the wedding was so important to my parents and I had to think about them because their feelings, not mine, were most important" Similarly, when I asked an office worker, who married at the age of 30 in May 2015, about the significance of weddings and marriage, she replied: "A wedding represents your love and your relationship with your parents. Marriage is evidence that you have grown up and now have adult responsibilities."

When the parents of today' s brides and grooms married in the 1980s, the celebrations were far less elaborate. At that time, there were no wedding planners and no multiple changes of clothing. Nor were there professional masters of ceremonies. However, it is not the case that Shanghai weddings in the 1980s were small gatherings at the workplace where the couple distributed wedding candy. On the contrary, among my ten respondents who married in the 1980s all had invited at least forty guests to dinner at a restaurant where each table cost approximately one month' s wage. Moreover, unless the parents were deceased, the parents usually paid for the banquet. However, in other ways the parents were far less the focus of attention. For example, at the dinner the couple would ask a favorite teacher or supervisor to say a few words of welcome; the fathers, not to mention the mothers, would rarely speak. The couples did not offer gifts to their parents, and the parents did not present any large gifts of cash at a tea ceremony.

To illustrate the new centrality of parental roles in marriage, below I present my interviews with either a parent or a newly married child in four cases drawn from among twenty-four weddings celebrated between 2013 and 2016. In two cases (Mrs. D. and Mr. S.) I also watched professionally edited videos that followed the couple through the entire wedding day. Without a representative survey, such as that Felicia Tian and I used to analyze mate selection, I cannot identify any specific characteristics of either the parent or the child that increased the degree of parental investment. But demography is clearly consequential. Whether from the perspective of an only child or from the perspective of a parent with only one child, a child' s wedding is a once-in a lifetime event for both generations. Also, when one contrasts the socio-economic status of the parents, it appears that the downward flow of resources and control from the parents to the children is more pronounced when two wealthy families "match doors" than when the parents are from poor working-class families or are migrants from rural Anhui or Fujian.

Mrs. T.

I interviewed Mrs. T. (R# 20154a) in March 2016 in the small apartment she rented with her husband and her eight-week-old son. Dominating the crowded rooms were two large wedding photos. In the photo displayed over the folding table in the outer room Mrs. T. is seated in a bright red formal gown and is wearing a tiara. In the second photo, in the bedroom, Mrs. T is wearing a white wedding gown and the couple is posing on a bridge. Mrs. T. tells me that she is imagining they are visiting Paris, the original destination for the honeymoon, which was delayed because of her pregnancy.

Mrs. T. was born in rural Anhui in 1993 and raised by her paternal grand-mother after her parents migrated to Shanghai to run a breakfast cart. She joined her parents and two younger siblings when she entered junior high school; she later completed a vocational high school with a major in account-ing, and for several years she kept the books for several small companies before joining the family restaurant. Her husband was born in 1991 in Fujian province. His father emigrated to Shanghai and worked as a middle-man in Baoshan. Mr. T. and his two older brothers joined their father when they were in their late teens, and he met Mrs. T. when they were junior high-school students. They began to date in 2012 after both already had full-time jobs. Mrs. T. said that they became romantically involved after he asked her to take care of his dog. When she became pregnant, they decided to marry.

Unlike his wife, Mr. T. had completed senior high school and had an associ-ate post-secondary degree. He had initially worked for a company in Baoshan, but he later started a delivery business with one of his brothers. At the time of the interview, he was working in Mrs. T's parents' restaurant. Mrs. T, is already planning to start a mail-order business that she can run from their home.

Once they announced their plans to marry, her husband accompanied her father to her natal village to present engagement gifts to her paternal grand-mother. Later that day, her entire family, including her great-grandmother, drove to Kunshan where her fiancé's father had already purchased apartments for each of his three sons. Two weeks later, his father drove the couple to his natal village to register the marriage. They had originally planned to register on May 20, but because her husband's paternal grandmother had said that date was unlucky, they moved it up one day. In June they took the photos (described above) and used two of the shots to send slightly humorous invitation cards for the wedding celebration to their friends; in contrast, the parents sent tradi-tional invitations. As Mrs. T. commented when I expressed surprise: "Our tastes (品味)are not the same."

They held a fourteen-table wedding banquet on the National Day holiday at a Shanghai hotel; each table cost 5,000 yuan, and for an additional 10,000 yuan the hotel supplied make-up, decorations, and a video service. By 2014 standards, 5,000 yuan represented a budget choice. Nevertheless, she chose Tiffany blue as the thematic color for the decorations and the candy boxes. The hotel objected, but she insisted, and then paid an extra fee. There were also several other ways in which Mrs. T. maximized her options but minimized the costs. She decided that there would be cigarettes only at the tables occupied by his family and she bought the bridesmaids' dresses on Taobao (an on-line discount service.) Each family paid for the tables where their family or friends sat. Mr. T.'s family only had three tables, Mrs. T. said, because his village was farther from Shanghai. It is also the case that his mother had remarried and his father had several girlfriends.

On the morning before the banquet, the couple held two tea ceremonies, first at her parents' home and then at the home of his father. At each home, the couple paid their respects to the elder generation, and the parents presented red packets of monetary gifts. During the banquet, however, the parents did not appear on the stage at the front of the banquet hall. Nor did the couple ask either parent to come forward to speak. However, Mrs. T.'s father did lead her into the banquet hall and later he offered a few words of welcome.

Mrs. W.

I interviewed Mrs. W. (R#20147a) two years after her June 2014 wedding. Born in Shanghai in 1986, Mrs. W. is the only child of a father who has worked as a security guard since the state shoe factory where he had worked went bankrupt. Her mother recently retired from her job as a cashier at a state food market. Mr. W., also a Shanghai native and an only child, was born in 1983. The couple first met in 2005, when she was 19 and he was 22, during a picnic organized by his cousin. When they met, he had just broken up with his university girlfriend and for the next two years the new couple remained simply good friends. After Mr. W. moved to a job closer to her workplace, they began a relationship, and for nine years they dated on and off. Several times they considered breaking up. He had taken money from his parents to start a company that had failed and he felt they should break up because he had no future. When describing her decision to stay with him and marry, she said: "My mother pushed me to stay with him saying: "You are getting old and you won't have many more chances to have a healthy baby. I really wanted a baby and I didn't care about money issues. Also, my Dad was already 65 years old and both he and my husband's parents really wanted a grandchild. So, at the end of 2013, we decided to marry. We registered in February 2014, but we had to wait until June to hold the banquet because all the good dates had already been taken. We had twenty-five tables, fifteen for my side and ten for his side. The tables cost 5,000 yuan each and his parents paid the entire cost."

Mrs. W. searched for the hotel online and her primary concern was that the LED screen be large enough for everyone to see the videos. She also stressed that she wanted a location that would not require her relatives to travel a long distance. Once she had chosen the hotel, she took her boyfriend and then his parents to assess her choice, and the six ate lunch there to try the food. His parents also paid for the wedding rings, but they allowed the couple select the rings on their own.

After she reviewed all the other choices she had made about the wedding, I asked if there had been any tensions with her in-laws or her parents about the banquet arrangements. She said: "I would go first and review the possibilities, and if my husband agreed, we went ahead. My in-laws had no say. However, when it came to the renovation of the second-hand apartment his parents had purchased, his parents made all the decisions and they also purchased the furniture. The young couple only shared the labor. Mrs. W. finds the two room apartment of 56 square meters completely adequate for a family of three; it also is very close to where her mother lives.

Currently Mrs. W. lives with her husband and six-month-old son. Monday through Thursday, her mother cares for the baby and at night the young couple goes to her mother's home for dinner and then to bring their infant son back to their apartment. Her mother has six siblings and each day one them goes to care for their blind mother who is 94 years old. On the day her mother goes to care for her mother, Mrs. W.'s mother-in-law cares for the baby.

Mrs. D.

I met Mrs. D. (R# 20141), the mother of a recent bride, at a Shanghai Starbucks in early September 2015. One month later I spent over an hour watching the video of her daughter's wedding, guided by my 60-year-old research assistant who was a distant acquaintance of Mrs. D.

Mrs. D. was born in 1960 and she married in 1986. When we first met, I presumed she was my respondent; her nails were perfect, she wore a large new diamond wedding band, and her jewelry and tailored suit were understated but exquisite. Mr. D. is a high-level executive in a multinational firm, whereas Mrs. D. no longer works. Their only daughter, born in 1988, studied law in France and then received further legal training in Switzerland. She became romantically involved with her future husband when they both were in Europe. Although the couple had shared a desk at an elite Shanghai junior high school, the mother reported that they only met by chance via an online dating service when working in Europe.

While in Europe, the daughter spoke with her parents every day. When her parents learned that she had met someone who was pursuing her, her parents insisted that she return to Shanghai. Mrs. D. emphasized that this is her only child and that she and her husband wanted her close by. After the daughter returned, she first worked first for a state firm and then transferred to a U.S. firm. The boyfriend also returned to Shanghai and joined a German firm. The couple then dated for one year before announcing their engagement.

Immediately, Mrs. D. said she and her husband started to plan for the wedding. Her husband wanted fifty or sixty tables, but she wanted something smaller and more elegant (精致). In the end, they settled for twenty tables, ten for each side. The parents also chose a date that would not be too close to the holidays in September and October when, Mrs. D. noted, many of their guests would be traveling. They chose November 8 which is also a lucky day. However, she noted that they did not check an almanac or consult the couple or the groom's parents. However, once they had selected a date and venue, they did need his parents to approve the final plans because his parents were paying for the wedding. Mr. and Mrs. D. had previously bought their daughter an apartment in a building adjacent to theirs where the young couple now lives.

When Mrs. D. described the wedding ceremony, she said that the exchange of rings was held in a chapel-like room that could only accommodate sixty of the two hundred guests. After this ceremony, the wedding party moved to the banquet hall and the other guests filed in, but only after they had been photographed and received a souvenir identity card overlaid on the wedding invitation. Later, there would be a lucky draw and the photo of the winners would be flashed up on the LED screen at the front of the banquet hall.

When I interviewed Mrs. D., she was vague about the exact role of the parents during different parts of the ceremony, but when I watched the edited video of the wedding day, it was clear that both sets of parents were central participants. For example, after the couple exchanged the rings in the chapel, they turned to the audience and openly thanked their parents. The parents, including both mothers, then came to the front of the chapel and, as featured on the video, they shook hands. At the banquet, all four parents were called to serve as witnesses (证婚人). Although the master of ceremonies orchestrated the movements on the stage, Mrs. D. told me that her husband had written the script for the master of ceremonies. Finally, before the young couple left the stage to toast all their guests, the master of ceremonies asked the parents to join the couple. Mrs. D. wore a red *qipao* and the groom's mother wore an elegant red and black cocktail dress. In the background, balloons floated upward on the LED screen and the parents again shook hands. The father of the groom spoke first to the guests and then Mr. D. spoke before both set of parents left the stage via a translucent glass runway. From the perspective of the video, the focus was clearly on the parents.

For the third, and final, segment of the ceremony, the hall had been decorated as a night club. The bride and groom in formal evening dress expressed their gratitude to their parents. The bride then read from a letter Mr. D. had sent to her when she was 10 or 12 years old. Overcome by emotions, she started to cry, and then Mr. D. also started to weep uncontrollably. The groom put his arms around his new father-in-law and then both bride and groom embraced her parents. The master of ceremonies then asked Mr. D. to speak about the new couple. Having regained his composure, Mr. D. shared his observation that after two years of watching the couple, he never saw them quarrel, therefore he indicated that he could stop worrying (放心). The video then records Mrs. D. saying: "My work is over; my daughter has grown up." Nevertheless, until 2016, the couple continued to live in the apartment adjacent to that of the bride's parents and they ate most of their meals with Mrs. D. and her husband.

Mr. S.

I interviewed Mr. S. (R#20162a) in March 2016 as we viewed the video of his wedding that had taken place the previous month. An only son born in Shanghai in 1988, he was currently working part-time on an MBA degree after receiving a BS degree in electrical engineering from one of Shanghai's top universities. His wife, also a Shanghai singleton, was born in 1994 and was still a college student. Their parents had previously worked in the same state enterprise and the couple had known each other since childhood. He casually noted that in the past the parents had joked that one day their children would marry. But the couple only began to date during the previous year, and when she realized she was pregnant in December, they quickly went ahead with plans for an elaborate wedding. After the baby is born, they plan to leave the child with his parents, and he will accompany her when she goes to the UK for a master's degree in industrial design.

With money from his parents, they spent over 10,000 yuan on the wedding photos, which were so exceptional that the company asked to use them during their next promotion at the wedding expo. In exchange, the couple received two free copies of the largest portraits. Two weeks later, together with both sets of parents, they registered their marriage in the district where his parents live. Several weeks earlier, the four parents had consulted an almanac to identify a lucky day and after they had chosen several possibilities, they asked the couple to make the final selection. Mr. S. then showed me a picture of the couple (without their parents) holding the certificate at the registry.

One month later, immediately after Chinese New Year's, they held a wedding celebration at one of Shanghai's most expensive hotels. Through his parent's personal connections, they were able to book nineteen tables: nine for his family and ten for hers. This hotel usually does not do weddings, but business was down so it agreed to host the banquet. Not coincidentally, the groom's parents had married at the same hotel in 1987. They did not use a packaged wedding planner for the banquet, in part because this hotel charges by the guest and not by the table.

The groom, who is also an amateur musician, selected a master of ceremonies whom he knew through his own performances. He also chose the videographer, also someone with whom he had previously collaborated. However, his parents, who hired a wedding planner to direct the two tea ceremonies, covered all the expenses.

During the banquet, the parents were present and frequently played key roles. At the lucky time of 6:28 the bride's father. led her into the banquet hall and handed her over to the groom. The couple then exchanged rings, after which a witness stepped forward to address the couple, the two sets of parents, and the guests. The witness was a leader in his father's previous state factory; he also had served as a reference for Mr. S. on his application for the MBA program. After changing into an evening gown, the bride returned, and while a ppt telling "their story" was projected behind them, all four parents joined them on the stage and both fathers spoke in praise of their child and new in-law. As we watched the video, Mr. S. was overwhelmed to hear the two fathers speak. In the final segment of the banquet, the young couple, accompanied by their parents, circulated to all nineteen tables.

4 Conclusion: The Inverted Family and Party-State Initatives

In a 2015 essay Yunxiang Yan identifies several state policies that have made parent-child loyalties "the central axis" of Chinese family life. Most decisive for urban residents are the one-child policy, the reduction of enterprise welfare benefits, and the privatization of housing. In this volume, Yan also emphasizes how specific policies interact with the broad economic and political trends to invert the flow of resources along this core vertical axis. Yan even goes so far as to conclude that an increasingly "competitive, precarious, and risky society" threatens the survival of the nuclear family.

The first and most obvious party policy that has inverted urban families is the 1979 one-child policy that has effectively universalized 4-2-1 families among non-migrant Shanghai residents, regardless of a mother's education or occupation. Furthermore, even if they choose to have a second child, the ratio of adults to children favored, even dictated, a downward flow of resources from old to young.

The second recent state initiative that has inverted urban families is the post-1993 decision to commodify, commercialize, and financialize healthcare, education services, and housing. Most consequential for family life is the decision in 1998 to privatize urban real estate and eliminate further construction of low-cost rental units (福利房) (Davis 2000b 2001, 2003, 2010). Subsequently, sky-rocketing housing prices have made young couples more financially dependent on their parents and in some cases financial dependence has increased co-residence after marriage (Nauck and Ren 2018)

A third state intervention that has increased parental involvement in their children's marriages arises from several Supreme People Court (SPC) interpretations of the 2001 amended Marriage Law and a 2003 State Council decision simplifying registration for marriage and divorce. For example, Provision 22 of the 2003 SPC interpretation specifies that absent other arrangements, parental investments before a marriage should be regarded as a gift (赠与) to their child alone (SPC 2003). Eight years later, Provision 7 in a third SPC interpretation of the Marriage Law states that when parents give their child money to purchase "immovable property" (不动产) after a child's marriage and the property is registered in their child's name then according to Article 18 of the Marriage Law, the property is considered a gift to their child alone and the individual property of one spouse (夫妻一方的个人财产). The interpretation further notes that in cases where the parents of both the husband and the wife have invested in the purchase of the home, absent other arrangements, ownership will be apportioned on the basis of the parental investment. Were the lower courts to strictly follow this logic, in the event of divorce they could grant to the parents who had paid the largest share of the down-payment or mortgage a larger share of the marital home than to the co-resident spouse. (Davis 2014a, 2014b)

In addition to these SPC interpretations, a State Council regulation (*minfa* 2003) that eliminates the need for written permission from an employer for individuals to initiate a divorce has indirectly served to increase parental involvement in a child's marriage. From the view of the state, the core objective of the new regulation is to reduce non-essential burdens on industrial enterprises and to minimize the number of divorce cases in court dockets. Henceforth, when two persons decide to divorce, they need only to swear before a registry clerk that they both desire to end their marriage because of loss of affection, and then they must submit a short document (协议) in which they specify how they will divide their property and provide for any minor children. With no further investigation or any intervention by court officers, the

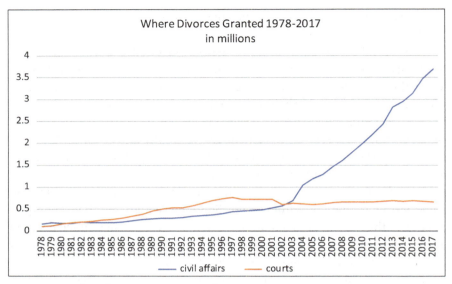

FIGURE 2.2   Where divorce cases are granted, 1978–2017
SOURCE: 1978–2013 *ZHONGGUO TONGJI NIANJIAN 2014*, AT HTTP://WWW.INFOBANK.CN/IRISBIN/TEXT.DLL?DB=TJ&NO=626026&CS=14782858&STR=%C0%EB%BB%E9, ACCESSED APRIL 5, 2015
Note: Of the 669,000 divorce cases handled by a court, only 207,000 divorces were granted and 328,000 were rejected. *Zhongguo minzheng tongji nianjian 2018*.

registry clerk may finalize the divorce. Today, 80 percent of divorces are finalized outside of a court (see Figure 2.2).

Ostensibly, the removal of employers from the divorce procedures should have had no impact on parental entanglements in their adult children's marriages. Yet, the simplification of government regulations has not meant that decisions to dissolve a marriage involve only the two principles. On the contrary, given the simplified routines to finalize a divorce, the new rules have created conditions for others, aside from the husband and the wife, to dictate the terms of the division of property and compensation. Furthermore, because the parents have become so deeply involved in financing the new marital homes and in providing childcare, the new regulations have inadvertently increased the opportunities for vertical parent-child loyalties to override those of horizontal conjugal relations (Yan 2015).

Parentally arranged marriages largely disappeared in urban China after 1950, and during the first decades of the economic reforms, horizontal conjugal relations were dominant, or at least co-equal with the vertical ties between the parents and their adult children Yet, more recently as marketization and privatization have heightened economic insecurities, urban kinship has been re-verticalized around the parent-child axis. Whether one considers the search for a mate, the elaborate marriage celebrations, or the handling of the divorce proceedings and the division of conjugal assets, urban parents during the first two decades of the twenty-first century have become ever-more deeply involved in the lives of their adult children. The unprecedented one-child policy established the demographic foundation for this re-verticalization of urban kinship, but the ongoing economic restructuring, legal reforms, and cultural shifts continue to create and reproduce a social matrix that routinely privileges parent-child ties over those between the spouses.

Selected Bibliography

Alford, William P. and Yuanyuan Shen. 2004. "Have You Eaten? Have You Divorced? Debating the Meaning of Freedom in Marriage in China." In *Realms of Freedom in Modern China*, ed. William C. Kirby, 234–63. Stanford: Stanford University Press.

Cai, Yong and Wang Feng. 2014. "(Re)emergence of Late Marriage in Shanghai." In *Wives, Husbands, and Lovers: Marriage and Sexuality in Hong Kong, Taiwan, and Urban China,* ed. Deborah S. Davis and Sara L. Friedman, 97–117. Stanford: Stanford University Press.

Chan, Anita, Richard Madsen, and Jonathan Unger. 1984. *Chen Village: The Recent History of a Peasant Community in Mao's China*. Berkeley: University of California Press.

Davis, Deborah, ed. 2000a. *The Consumer Revolution in Urban China*. Berkeley: University of California Press). Translated as中国城市的消费革命,with a new introduction by Lu Hanlong. Shanghai: Shanghai shehui kexue chubanshe, 2003.

Davis, Deborah. 2000b. "Reconfiguring Shanghai Households." In *Re-drawing Boundaries: Work, Households, and Gender in China*, ed. Barbara Entwisle and Gail E. Henderson, 245–60. Berkeley: University of California Press.

Davis, Deborah. 2001. "When a House Becomes His Home." In *Popular China: Unofficial Culture in a Globalizing Society,* ed. Perry Link, Richard P. Madsen, and Paul G. Pickowicz, 231–50. Lanham, MD: Rowman & Littlefield.

Davis, Deborah. 2003. "From Welfare Benefit to Capitalized Asset: The Re-commodification of Residential Space in Urban China." In *Housing and Social Change: East-West Perspectives*, ed. Ray Forrest and James Lee, 183–98. London: Routledge.

Davis, Deborah. 2010. "Who Gets the House? Renegotiating Property Rights in Post-Socialist Urban China." *Modern China* 36, 5: 463–92.

Davis, Deborah. 2014a. "Privatization of Marriage in Post-Socialist China." *Modern China* 40, 6: 551–77.

Davis, Deborah. 2014b. "On the Limits of Personal Autonomy." In *Wives, Husbands, and Lovers: Marriage and Sexuality in Hong Kong, Taiwan, and Urban China*, ed. Deborah Davis and Sara Friedman, 41–61. Stanford: Stanford University Press.

Davis, Deborah. 2019. "Performing Happiness for Self and Others: Weddings in Shanghai." In *The Chinese Pursuit of Happiness: Anxieties, Hopes, and Moral Tensions in Everyday Life*, ed. Becky Yang Hsu and Richard Madsen, 66–83. Berkeley: University of California Press.

Davis, Deborah S. and Sara K. Friedman, eds. 2014. *Wives, Husbands and Lovers: Marriage and Sexuality in Hong Kong, Taiwan, and Urban China*. Stanford: Stanford University Press.

Davis, Deborah and Stevan Harrell, eds. 1993. *Chinese Families in the Post-Mao Era*. Berkeley: University of California Press.

Diamant, Neil J. 2000. *Revolutionizing the Family: Politics, Love, and Divorce in Urban and Rural China, 1949–1968*. Berkeley: University of California Press.

Farrer, James C. 2002. *Opening Up: Youth, Sex, Culture and Market Reform in Shanghai*. Chicago: University of Chicago Press.

Glosser, Susan L. 2003. *Chinese Visions of Family and State, 1915–1953*. Berkeley: University of California Press.

Greenhalgh, Susan. 2008. *Just One Child: Science and Policy in Deng's China*. Berkeley: University of California Press.

Huang, Phillip C. C. 2005. "Divorce Law Practices and the Origins, Myths, and Realities of Judicial 'Mediation' in China." *Modern China* 31, 2: 151–203.

Kong, Travis S. K., 2011. *Chinese Male Homosexualities: Memba, Tongzhi and Gold Boy*. London: Routledge.

Marriage Law of the PRC. 1950 （Chinese original http://www.npc.gov.cn/wxzl/wxzl/2001-05/30/content_136774. Accessed Jan 22,2020.

Marriage Law of the PRC. 1980. Chinese original http://npc.people.com.cn/n/2014/0929/c14576-25761144.html English translation at https://www.cecc.gov/resources/legal-provisions/marriage-law-of-the-peoples-republic-of-china-amended, accessed at January 5, 2020.

Marriage Law of the PRC. 2001. Chinese original at www.hun-yin.com; English translation at http://www.lawinfochina.com/display.aspx?id=1793&lib=law, accessed January 5, 2020.

Minfa (Civil Law). 2003. 婚姻登记工作暂行规范 (Temporary Regulations on Work for Registering Marriages), September 24. *Minzheng falü fagui* (November): 421–43, at http://www.gov.cn/banshi/2005–08/21/content_25046.htm, accessed January 5, 2020.

Nauck, Bernhard and Qiang Ren. 2018. "Coresidence in the Transition to Adulthood: The Case of the United States, Germany, and Mainland China." *Chinese Sociological Review* 50, 4: 443–73.

Ocko, Jonathan K. 1991. "Women, Property, and Law in the People's Republic of China." In *Marriage and Inequality in Chinese Society*, ed. Rubie S. Watson and Patricia Buckley Ebrey, 313–46. Berkeley: University of California Press.

Palmer, Michael. 1995. "The Re-emergence of Family Law in Post-Mao China." *China Quarterly*, no. 141: 110–34.

Sharygin, Ethan J. 2011. "Marriage in Uncertain Times: Modeling Human Capital, Demographic Change, and Marriage Outcomes in China." Unpublished paper.

Sun Peidong. 2012. 谁来娶我的女儿: 上海相亲角与"白发相亲" (Who Will Marry My Daughter? Shanghai Blind Date and "White Haired Blind Date"). Beijing: Zhongguo shehui kexue chubanshe.

Supreme People's Court (SPC). 2001. 最高人民法院关于适用《中华人民共和国婚法》若干问题的解释（一） (First SPC Interpretation of Several Questions in Regard to the "Marriage Law of the PRC"), at www.law-lib.com/law/law_view.asp?id=16795, accessed January 5, 2020.

Supreme People's Court (SPC). 2003. 最高人民法院关于适用《中华人民共和国婚姻法》若干问题的解释（二） (Second SPC Interpretation of Several Questions in Regard to the "Marriage Law of the PRC"), http://www.court.gov.cn/fabu-xiangqing-36972.html . accessed Jan 22, 2020.

Supreme People's Court (SPC). 2011. 最高法关于适用婚姻法若干问题解释 (三) (全文) (Third SPC Interpretation of Several Questions in Regard to the Marriage Law of the PRC) (Complete Text), at http://pkulaw.cn/fulltext_form.aspx?db=chl&gid=156539 accessed January 22, 2020.

Tian, Felicia F. and Deborah S. Davis. 2019. "Reinstating the Family: Intergenerational Influence on Assortative Mating in China." *Chinese Sociological Review* 51, 4: 337–64.

To, Sandy. 2015. "My Mother Wants Me to Jiaru Haomen" (Marry Into a Rich and Powerful Family! Exploring the Pathways to 'Altruistic Individualism' in China's Professional Women's Filial Strategies of Marital Choice." *Sage Open* 5, 2: 1–11.

Watson, Rubie and Patricia Ebrey. 1991. *Marriage and Inequality in Chinese Society*. Berkeley: University of California Press.

Whyte, Martin King. 1990. "Changes in Mate Choice in Chengdu." In *Chinese Society on the Eve of Tiananmen: The Impact of Reform*, ed. Deborah Davis and Ezra F. Vogel, 181–213. Cambridge: Council on East Asian Studies, Harvard University.

Whyte, Martin King and William L. Parish. 1984. *Urban Life in Contemporary China*. Chicago: University of Chicago Press.

Wolf, Margery. 1993. "Uterine Families and the Woman's Community." In *Talking About People: Readings in Contemporary Cultural Anthropology*, ed. William A. Haviland and Robert J. Gordon, 166–69. Mountain View, CA: Mayfield Publishing.

Woo, Margaret Y.K.. 2003. "Shaping Citizenship: Chinese Family Law and Women." *Yale Journal of Law and Feminism* 15: 99–134.

Xu, Anqi and Yan Xia. 2014. "The Changes in Mainland Chinese Families During the Social Transition: A Critical Analysis." *Journal of Comparative Family Studies* 45, 1: 31–53, 5, 9–10, 13.

Xu, Qi, Jianxin Li, and Xuejun Yu. 2014. "Continuity and Change in Chinese Marriages and the Family: Evidence from the CFPS." *Chinese Sociological Review* 47, 1.

Yan, Yunxiang. 2003. *Private Life under Socialism: Love, Intimacy, and Family Change in a Chinese Village, 1949–1999*. Stanford: Stanford University Press.

Yan, Yunxiang. 2009. "Conclusion." In *The Individualization of Chinese Society*, 273–94. Oxford: Berg.

Yan, Yunxiang. 2011a. "The Changing Moral Landscape in Contemporary China." In *Deep China: The Moral Life of the Person, What Anthropology and Psychiatry Tell Us About China Today*, ed. Arthur Kleinman et al., 1–35. Berkeley: University of California Press.

Yan, Yunxiang. 2011b. "The Individualization of the Family in Rural China*." boundary* 2 38, 1: 203–29.

Yan, Yunxiang. 2015. "Parent-Driven Divorce and Individualization Among Urban Chinese Youth." *International Social Science Journal* 64, 213–14: 317–30.

Yan, Yunxiang. 2016. "Intergenerational Intimacy and Descending Familism in Rural China." *American Anthropologist* 118, 2: 244–57.

Yan, Yunxiang. 2018. "Neo-Familism and the State in Contemporary China." *Urban Anthropology and Studies of Cultural Systems and World Economic Development* 37, 3/4: 4–42.

Yan, Yunxiang and Li Tian. 2019. "Self-Cultivation of the Socialist New Person in Maoist China," *The China Journal*, no, 82: 88–110.

Zhang, Jun and Peidong Sun. 2014. "When Are You Going to Get Married? Parental Matchmaking and Middle-class Women in Contemporary Urban China." In *Wives, Husband, and Lovers: Marriage and Sexuality in Hong Kong, Taiwan, and Urban China*, ed. Deborah S. Davis and Sara L. Friedman, 118–44. Stanford: Stanford University Press.

CHAPTER 3

The "Leftover" Majority

Why Urban Men and Women Born under China's One-Child Policy Remain Unmarried through Age 27

Vanessa L. Fong, Greene Ko, Cong Zhang, and Sung won Kim

Drawing on surveys, interviews, and participant observation conducted as part of a longitudinal study of Chinese singletons carried out between 1998 and 2019, this chapter examines how and why most of a cohort of 406 Chinese young adults (who attended the same middle school in Dalian City, Liaoning province, in 1999) ended up unmarried through the age of 27. In recent years, Chinese state, media, and popular discourse have described unmarried Chinese women over the age of 27 as *shengnü,* or "leftover women" (Hahn and Elshult 2016; To 2015; Ji 2015; Fincher 2016) who would be highly stigmatized, have great difficulty getting married in the future, and be forced to select a future marriage partner from among a tiny pool of men who remained unmarried past 27. A related discourse about the social dangers and personal suffering of men who remain unmarried, as *guanggun* ("bare branches") throughout their lives, has also been widespread. However, this discourse assumes that such men wanted to marry but were too poor or uneducated to find any women willing to marry them, rather than that they were as picky as the "leftover" women were assumed to be (Jiang and Sánchez-Barricarte 2012; Ebenstein and Jennings 2009). Though many unmarried male and female research participants are aware of such discourse and are nervous about becoming "leftover" or "bare branches," most of them find that such concerns are outweighed by the factors that prevent them from marrying by the age of 27, such as their desire to continue to focus their time and money on their pursuit of more education and better jobs instead of on marriage, childbearing, and childrearing, their desire to retain the independence, freedom, and high quality of life they enjoy as single singletons living with their parents for as long as possible, and/or their desire to not settle for a spouse who did not meet all of their own as well as their parents' expectations. Concern about becoming "leftover" or "bare branches" has been ameliorated somewhat, however, by the fact that the majority of their male as well as female former middle school classmates in this study remained unmarried after the age of 27, and most men as well as women of their cohort were either divorced or had never married by the age

© VANESSA L. FONG, GREENE KO, CONG ZHANG, SUNG WON KIM, 2021 | DOI:10.1163/9789004450233_004

of 28, thus ensuring that those who wanted to delay marriage or get divorced would still have many potential partners to choose from through their early thirties, and that remaining unmarried would not be as much of a minority status, and thus not as stigmatized, as it had been for their parents' generation, or as the "leftover women" and "bare branches" discourses warned would be the case for their generation.

1   Research Methods

This chapter is based on a longitudinal mixed methods project, drawing on surveys of 406 respondents in 1999, 2012–13, and 2014–15, on interviews and surveys conducted with a representative sample of 48 of the respondents between 2012 and 2019, and on participant observation that Fong conducted with the respondents and others in their neighborhoods in Dalian, between 1997 and 2019 (for more details about our survey and interview research methods and sample, see Kim, Brown, and Fong 2017, 2018; Kim, Brown, Kim, and Fong 2018). Our survey respondents (n = 406) were on average 30 years old in 2014, and 96 percent of them had no siblings.

From 1998 to 2000, Fong carried out participant observation among the survey respondents in this study (who were then in either eighth or ninth grade), among students at a nearby vocational high school and a nearby college-prep high school, and among the friends, families, and neighbors of these students and survey respondents. Fong also visited some of them in China almost every summer between 2002 and 2019 and visited some of them outside of China between 2003 and 2019 (Fong 2011). In addition, each summer between 2008 and 2014, Fong organized homeroom reunions in Dalian for all survey respondents who were willing to attend, and encouraged them to bring their girlfriends, boyfriends, spouses, and children. The reunions were organized not only for the survey respondents this chapter focuses on, but also for alumni of the vocational high school and the college-prep high school who had also been part of Fong's longitudinal study since 1998. Fong lived with research participants' families and participated in many of their social activitiesm including weddings, parties, meals, and even a few first dates to which some of the couple's friends, including Fong, were invited so as to reduce the awkwardness of the date. Our surveys and interviews are drawn only from the middle school alumni because they had the highest response rates and because they had the demographic and socioeconomic characteristics most similar to those of the overall same-age population of Dalian. However, the study also draws on Fong's participant observation among the much larger community.

THE "LEFTOVER" MAJORITY   57

The first wave of surveys was collected in 1999 when Fong taught English and conducted participant observation between 1998 and 2000 at our respondents' middle school as well as at a vocational high school and a college-prep high school in the same city, and in the homes and at social gatherings of some of the survey respondents and their families, friends, neighbors, and classmates from 1998 to 2000, during the summers of 1997, 2002, 2014, and 2018, and every summer between 2004 and 2012 (Fong 2004, 2011; Kim, Brown, and Fong 2017, 2018). The middle school from which our respondents were originally recruited was purposively selected because it included proportions of various groups defined by socioeconomic status, demographics, and levels of academic achievement that were similar to those of the middle-school population of Dalian City at that time. This chapter draws on the surveys of the 406 who responded to the 1999 survey when they were in eighth or ninth grade, and to the 2012–13 survey as well as to the 2014–15 survey and were living in Dalian and had not spent more than one month outside of China when they responded to the 2012–13 survey. Our survey data analyses exclude those who at the time they completed the 2012–13 survey were living elsewhere in China instead of Dalian or were living in other countries, had spent more than a month abroad, and/or had not responded to questions about where they were living or how much time they had spent abroad, because the diversity of experiences and expectations they may have had in other Chinese cities or in other countries (Fong 2011) could skew the findings about the 406 of the former classmates who at the time they completed the 2012–13 survey were living in Dalian and had not left China for more than one month. Although Fong designed and conducted the 1999 survey on her own, Fong, Zhang, and Kim worked together on the research design beginning in 2012 and Fong, Ko, Kim, and Zhang collaborated on the data analysis, writing, and revision process for this chapter.

2   Remaining Unmarried through the Age of 27

Among respondents to our 2014–15 survey, 56 percent of men (n=202) and 52 percent of women (n=204) were divorced, married when they were 28 years old or older, or had never married (see Figures 3.1 and 3.2), and the mean age at which those who were married reported the year in which they first legally married was 27 for both men and women. The actual percentage of those who had remained unmarried through the age of 27 is probably even higher, as 5 percent of married women and 14 percent of married men did not indicate what year their current marriage had started. Even though we know that they were married by age 28–33 (their age range when completing the survey), we do not know how old they were when they first entered into their marriages. The mean age at the first marriage will probably be even later for our entire survey sample by the end of their lifetime, given that, at age 28–33, 26 percent of women and 28 percent of men had never married, and some of them are likely to eventually marry. Our respondents remained unmarried much later than the average for the representative sample of the Chinese population that Ji and Yeung (2014) found, based on the 2005 Population Survey Data, in which the singulate mean age at marriage was 25.7 for men and 23.5 for women. This is probably because, unlike most respondents in representative national surveys of China, our respondents live in a coastal city, were born between 1982 and 1986, and were surveyed in 2014–15, 9–10 years after the last national-level survey on marriage rates was conducted; urban residence and eastern coastal residence are associated with later marriages, even in previous studies, and the rise of individualism and neo-familism among the generation born after China's one-child policy began in 1979 has made this generation even more likely to marry later than previous generations.

For married male respondents (n = 102) to our survey, the mean year of birth is 1984, and the mean year of birth for their spouses is 1985; male respondents thus married women who were on average only one year younger. While the average year of birth for women (n = 136) is 1984, their husbands' average year of birth is 1982, which means that female respondents on average married men two years their senior. Mu and Xie, whose study is drawn from the China 2005 1% Population Inter-census Survey that includes data about marriages that occurred between 1960 to 2005, observed the return of the trend toward greater age hypergamy and a decrease in age homogamy among the post-1990 reform era generation in China (Mu and Xie 2014). The age hypergamy that Mu and Xie found among the youngest generation in their study was not as apparent among our respondents, however, most likely because all our respondents were urban residents, while the nationally representative survey Mu and Xie used included both rural and urban residents and because our survey only captured our respondents' marriages by age 28 to 33, when age hypergamy is not as necessary as it may be when the respondents grow older and have fewer potential marriage partners.

3 Adolescent and Young Adult Fears of Marriage and Childbearing

When the respondents were in eighth or ninth grade, 22 percent of our female respondents (n=190) and 14 percent of our male respondents (n=180) indicated

THE "LEFTOVER" MAJORITY 59

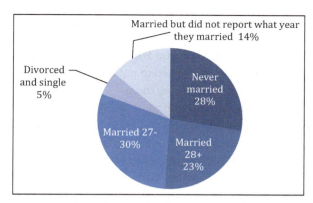

FIGURE 3.1   Marital status of male survey respondents (n=202) in 2014–15

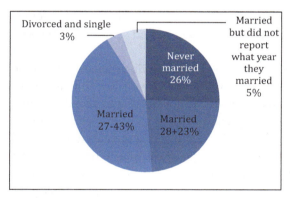

FIGURE 3.2   Marital status of female survey respondents (n=204) in 2014–15

in our 1999 survey that they wanted to remain unmarried their entire lives. Even as teenagers, some were skeptical of the value of marriage, given the marital unhappiness and divorce rate that many of them observed among some of their parents, grandparents, aunts, uncles, and family friends. Even more were skeptical of the value of childbearing: 39 percent of the female respondents (n=186) and 15 percent of the male respondents (n = 176) indicated that they wanted to remain childless their entire lives. Female respondents were especially likely to be averse to marriage and childbearing because they saw that their parents had to make tremendous personal sacrifices in terms of time, effort, money, and deferral of one's personal dreams and aspirations in order to provide the intensive parenting considered necessary to insure that their singleton children develop the outstanding skills, academic credentials, and physical and psychological health that will propel them toward upward mobility (Fong 2004). Female students in particular saw that this burden fell disproportionately on the shoulders of mothers (Fong 2004; Kim and Fong 2013; Kim and Fong 2014). As teenagers, some research participants told Fong that they hoped to not have to sacrifice as much as their parents had to in the process of raising them.

Throughout their twenties, many male and even more female research participants frequently expressed skepticism and fears about the prospects of marrying and having children. They worried about experiencing divorces or unhappy marriages if they were to settle for a spouse with whom they were not completely satisfied, both in terms of personal rapport and in terms of attributes such as health, family wealth, earning potential, educational attainment, and physical appearance. Some worried that, even though they loved their partners, their parents disapproved of them for not having enough education, wealth, good health, earning potential, attractiveness, acceptable moral character, and/or polite and filial attitudes; many also wondered whether they should "settle" for their current partners or wait to find someone better with regard to all of the above criteria.

Some men, and more women, worried about marrying spouses who would cheat on them and break their hearts. Many who already had romantic partners were worried that their partners would not be able to remain faithful to them throughout their lives, especially if their partners were currently attracted to others, just generally flirtatious, or working in fields that required working closely with many members of the opposite gender. Worries about the faithfulness of a current partner was a particularly significant concern among those who knew that their partners had previously had sex with multiple partners or had histories of divorce or of breaking up with previous partners, all of which are situations that are common among their generation. Many were also worried because they sometimes had fights with their partners, felt annoyed by their partners, felt their partners were annoyed with them, or felt that their partners did not love them enough or that they did not love their partners enough; they worried that these problems would grow worse after marriage, after the excitement of a new romance wears off and they have to deal with the stresses of shared finances, parenting, and chores, and with each other's diminishing physical attractiveness as they age and encounter health problems. As one such single, childless Dalian woman, age 31, told Fong, "Many of my friends were too anxious to marry. They married too quickly and later they had problems in their marriages. So, I want to wait until I can find someone who is really suitable."

Meanwhile, premarital sex was increasingly considered acceptable by the research participants' generation, and grudgingly was even considered acceptable by some of their parents' generation as long as it was in the context of a long-term relationship likely to lead to marriage. Our research participants therefore could remain single and still have the sex, romance, and companionship that among previous generations had been mainly reserved for married couples, and thus had served as an incentive for young people to marry. Remaining single while dating, and in some cases having premarital sex, allowed them to have many of the advantages of marriage, without the long-term legal and social commitments and the pressures to bear and raise children that frightened many of them.

The challenges of buying neolocal housing, given the high price of housing, also caused many research participants to postpone marriage, and in many cases to postpone looking for a spouse. As in many other Chinese cities (Sito and Liu 2019), housing in Dalian became increasingly unaffordable after the marketization of housing in the 1990s. Men and their families were expected to pay for most or all of the costs of neolocal housing before women would be willing to marry them, though in practice this condition could be waived or modified by women who really wanted to marry them; in those cases, the bride and her family might pay for some, most, or all of the neolocal housing; the bride and groom would each pay about half of the down payment and then each pay about half of the monthly mortgage from their incomes; the young couple would rent an apartment drawing on both their incomes (the cost of rent was far less than the cost of a mortgage); the young couple would live with the bride's parents or the groom's parents while saving up for neolocal housing; or the bride would live with her parents while the groom would live with his parents most of the time, with conjugal visits to each other's homes on weekends and holidays. Still, the lack of an ability to buy neolocal housing appliances, furnishings, and a car to start the newlywed couple off in terms of wealth and comfort meant that a man would be disadvantaged in the marriage market, and the lack of an ability to at least help with the purchase of these things meant that a woman could also be disadvantaged in the marriage market. Because the ability to pay for neolocal housing would potentially enable men to attract higher-quality wives, many male research participants postponed looking for wives until they had at least enough money to pay the down payment on a mortgage for neolocal housing. Even in some cases where a woman was willing to marry a man who did not have the ability to buy neolocal housing, her parents would still insisted that they wait. Waiting to marry would also give women more time to save money to contribute, if necessary, to neolocal housing, furnishings, appliances, and cars, and to avoid having to live with her in-laws or having their husbands live with his in-laws or having the wife live with her parents and the husband live with his parents and having only occasionally conjugal visits, all of which were considered undesirable conditions for the newlyweds. Because parents were expected to draw on their own savings to help buy neolocal housing, appliances, home furnishings, and cars for their newlywed children's new household, especially in the case of sons, many parents were also reluctant to encourage their children to commit to a marriage with someone less than ideal, and they had significant incentives to allow or even to encourage their adult children to postpone marriage until the adult children and their potential spouses earned more and saved more so they could contribute to the purchase of their own neolocal housing, appliances, home furnishings, and cars. As a single, childless 28-year-old Dalian man told Fong, "I have to work hard for a while longer before I can buy housing, and only then can I consider marrying. My parents are anxious for me to marry, of course, but they cannot afford to buy housing for me, so there's nothing they can do."

Childbearing and childrearing caused even more fear than marriage among our research participants, especially the women. Most men and women shared the widespread Chinese cultural assumption that childbearing and childrearing are the main reasons for marriage, and therefore childbearing and childrearing should very likely take place very soon after the wedding. This made them fear marriage even more because they knew, based on what they observed of their parents' lives, that raising a child would require them to devote most of their time, money, and emotional energy to their child.

Women were also worried about what pregnancy and childbearing would do to their bodies, both aesthetically, in terms of causing stretch marks, caesarian section scars, and weight gain, and in terms of health problems that could result from difficult pregnancies and births. The research participants also worried about the high medical costs that could ensue from pregnancies and childbearing, especially if they had complications or children born prematurely or with birth defects or disabilities. Even in the best-case scenario of an easy, low-cost pregnancy and birth, the high costs of having a child begins as soon as the infant is born and the parents and grandparents must be taught how to care for the infant during the traditionally required maternal postpartum confinement period of 30–40 days, which most research participants believed were necessary to protect the mothers from serious long-term illnesses and disabilities. Most of our research participants could not afford to hire full-time nannies, but many had to hire people part-time to help with the tutoring, babysitting, or household chores. Competitive social pressures also encouraged parents to pay for educational and enrichment classes for infants, and toddlers, and to pay for their caregivers. Almost all of our respondents who had children sent their children to preschool starting at age 3; some sent their children to nurseries even earlier due to lack of child-care resources at home. While there were some affordable private schools, they were often of such low quality that they were considered dangerous to the physical, psychological, and intellectual well-being of the child. Higher-quality private schools often cost a large proportion of the parents' salaries, and in some cases cost even more than the parents' salaries. While public preschools had affordable tuitions, the waitlist to get into them was so long that parents often had to pay bribes for admission, making them cost the same as the high-quality private preschools. While public school education was free and universally available for children between first grade and ninth grade, different school districts varied greatly in terms of the quality of the teachers, facilities, and peer groups, and it was extremely expensive to buy or even rent an apartment that would qualify one's child to attend a top-quality public school. While top students could test into public college-prep high schools and could attend them for free, the majority of students could not, and their parents would have to pay bribes or extra fees to get them into public college-prep high schools, or, failing that, they would have to pay high tuitions for private schools, study abroad, or even technical or vocational high schools (which almost all students could get into, even though they were charged tuition). Most college programs charged tuition, and many research participants also wanted to send their children abroad, which would cost even more.

Research participants of both genders worried about how much time they would have to spend caring for and educating their children. Though most men expected not to have to quit their jobs or take lower-paying jobs to care for their children, they worried about the loss of free time for leisure and social activities, as they would have to spend much of their time after work helping with childcare and household chores. Men also worried about being unable to earn enough for their families, especially given that their wives might have to stop working or be underemployed in order to take care of a child. Women were particularly worried about how much pregnancy, childbearing, and childrearing would harm their careers and earnings. The demanding parenting their generation believed would be necessary to ensure that their children grew to be healthy, happy, and successful required so much time and effort that both parents, as well as both sets of grandparents, would have to devote most of their time outside of work with the child, either tutoring the child or doing chores for the child for at least 18 years. Mothers were expected to do so much of this that many of them had to spend some number of years not working or they would have to transfer to less time-consuming, lower-paying jobs in order to free up more time and flexibility to care for their child. Though employers were legally required to give women paid maternity leave and let them return to their old jobs after the end of their leave, some employers skirted these laws by keeping employees on short-term contracts that they could refuse to renew once a woman became pregnant; this was allowed because employers had no obligation to renew any contracts. Some women felt compelled to voluntarily quit their jobs after their maternity leaves ended because they had to spend more time caring for and breastfeeding their children. Research participants of both genders also worried about the burdens that childcare would place on their aging, increasingly ill, or disabled parents, as child-care responsibilities often fell primarily to the child's grandparents, given the high earning ability and career ambitions common among both men and women of the generation born after China's one-child policy. As a single, childless 28-year-old Dalian woman told Fong, "I feel that right now having a child would be a big burden."

4 Single, Childless Young Adults Living with Their Parents: The Golden Years of Neo Familism

In contrast to all the burdens that would descend upon them as soon as they married and had a child, the lives of our single young adult research participants were relatively fun, comfortable, and full of potential. Most of those who found jobs in Dalian lived with their parents, in the same room they had grown up in. Of the 101 never-married respondents who answered our 2014–15 survey questions about who they were living with, 85 percent lived with one or both parents. Moving out and renting their own apartment when living with one's parents was still an option would have been considered an embarrassing sign to all who knew them since it would indicate that there was something wrong with their relationship with their parents. Singles whose relationships with their parents were so bad that they wanted to live separately did not perceive of marriage as the only or the best way to escape their parents; on the contrary, they feared that marriage and childrearing would most likely make it even more difficult for them to escape from their parents, given that they would need their parents' help with childcare and often with the costs of purchasing neolocal housing and paying for the children's education, and, in a worst-case scenario, they might even need to live with their parents after marriage, either because they could not afford neolocal housing or because they needed their parents' help with childcare. Moving to another city or abroad for education or work, while remaining single and childless, was a much more effective way to escape their parents, and it was used by a number of our research participants who had particularly strained relationships with their parents.

Those who wanted to stay in Dalian but did not want to live with parents also had the option of moving to a separate apartment and accepting the higher financial costs, emotional strains, and social stigma (social stigma which in any case would fall more heavily on the parents than on the children, as bad parent-child relationships are more likely to be blamed on the parents rather than on the children). Fong observed several such cases; however they were relatively rare.

Though most of our research participants had incomes much higher than those of their parents, most parents did not require them to pay rent. Most single young adults who were working while living with their parents chose to help buy groceries for the household, and some who had much higher incomes than their parents ended up paying for most or all of the household's expenses. Some whose relationships with their parents were especially strong turned their entire paychecks over to their parents, but most of those parents tried to spend as little as possible of their adult children's money on household expenses and tried to save as much as possible of their children's earnings for their children's likely future expenses, such as a car, neolocal housing, and education for their child; in most of these cases, children could ask for money from some or all of their parents' savings at any time, with only minor complaining from the parents if the children wanted to spend the money on something the parents considered frivolous, such as a vacation in another city or abroad.

Most of our research participants believed that their upward-mobility trajectory had the potential to continue throughout their twenties and early thirties, as they earned higher academic degrees, received promotions or better jobs, and/or studied abroad. This belief was validated by the outcomes of our survey, as many who were not accepted into college immediately after high school earned associate degrees and bachelor's degrees in their late twenties and even late thirties, some studied abroad, and the vast majority found better jobs, received promotions, and/or higher salaries over the course of their twenties and early thirties. If they waited to marry, instead of "settling" for a marriage to someone in their current social circle who was willing to marry them, it was likely that they would be able to meet and marry people with a higher socioeconomic status as their own upward mobility trajectories enabled them to move in higher socioeconomic social circles and to be considered acceptable spouses by other singles in those circles. Marriage, childbearing, and childrearing could end the young adults' upwardly mobile trajectories by preventing them and their parents from investing time and money in their own pursuits of higher education, study abroad, and/or better jobs, and by redirecting the entire family's time and resources toward concern about their child's health, happiness, and educational success. Waiting to marry was thus often considered a wise and rational strategy, not only by young adults who believed their upwardly mobile trajectories would take them even higher within a few years but also by their parents, relatives, and friends. As a single, childless 30-year-old Dalian man told Fong, "After a few years, I will be very likely to be promoted and have better conditions, and even better choices, so I'm not anxious to look for a match right now. My parents support me in this decision."

In most families, single research participants in their twenties and thirties were not responsible for household chores, just as they had not been responsible for such chores while growing up. Their parents did most of the cooking, cleaning, and washing for them, both because the parents believed they were better at it and because the adult children were too busy with work (that brought in much more income than what the parents earned from their pensions or their blue-collar jobs positions) or because the children sometimes continued to pursue their educations. Of the 94 never-married survey respondents who were living with one or both parents and answered our 2014–15 survey question about who did the most housework, only 4 percent indicated that they, rather than one of their parents, did most of the housework. Most single young adults as well as their parents felt that the young adults had "earned" the right to more leisure time after the pressure-cooker years of their childhood and adolescence and they also felt they needed a lot of time to pursue friendships, widen social networks that could help them with work opportunities as well as with finding a suitable partner, and meeting and dating people who might be their future spouses. Many of them pursued higher educations, which they considered essential both for social status and for future earning potential, given that the vast majority of their generation had college degrees. Some pursued graduate education and/or studied abroad (Fong 2011); many more saved their money to visit foreign countries as tourists. Though they were anxious about their marriage and childbearing decisions that increasingly loomed on the horizon as their marriage market and their biological clocks ran out and about whether they would achieve the upward mobility in education and work that they and their parents desired, many research participants considered their lives as single young adults living with their parents to be more rewarding than the more constrained, academically stressful years that preceded this period and also more rewarding than the more burdensome years of marriage, childbearing, and childrearing that lay ahead. They were therefore in no hurry to put an end to this relatively fun, carefree, and potential-filled life stage. As a 29-year-old single, childless woman living with her parents told Fong, "I want to continue to enjoy this beautiful time of my life. I'm not anxious to marry and have a child."

5 Ambivalence about Parental and Social Pressures, and Personal Desires in Favor of Marriage and Childbearing

Despite their misgivings about marriage and childbearing and their desire to remain in the fun-filled life stage of the single, childless young adult, the vast majority of our research participants did not view this life stage as permanent. Even though many of them had wanted to remain single and childless their entire lives when they were in eighth or ninth grade, almost all had changed their minds by their late twenties or early thirties; only 4 percent of 391 respondents to our 2014–15 survey indicated that they planned never to have children. (They were not asked about whether they wanted to marry, since it could be assumed that those who want children also want to marry; due to strong Chinese legal as well as cultural sanctions against having children outside of marriage, it was extremely rare, and undesirable, for Chinese young adults to give birth out of wedlock.)

Though they feared ending up like the unhappily married or divorced couples they knew, they admired, and hoped to emulate, the happily married couples whom they knew, and they sometimes told Fong how envious they were of those couples who derived happiness from marriage and childbearing. A 33-year-old single, childless Dalian woman told Fong that even passing by a seemingly happy couple with a seemingly happy child in a park was enough make her feel "envious to death."

Compared to their parents' generation, our research participants had higher incomes and savings and better old-age insurance policies, as well as stronger desires to encourage their own future children to pursue their personal interests and happiness and not to be burdened by filial obligations to provide nursing care and financial support to aging parents (Kim, Brown, and Fong 2018; Yan 2016, 2009). Nevertheless, they still hoped that a spouse and an adult child would provide socioemotional support and companionship in their old age and they feared growing old alone. They also recognized that it was possible that their plans for relying on retirement income and paid nursing care would be inadequate in their old age. While this recognition was only theoretical for most in their early twenties, it was increasingly based on empirical experience due to the inadequacy of insurance and paid help for caring for their own parents as the research participants and their parents grew older. When discussing their desire for a child, many referred to the Chinese aphorism *yang er fang lao* (a phrase that historically meant to "raise a son for old age," but it was re-interpreted by our research participants as to "raise a child for old age" (Kim and Fong 2014b).

Like their parents, many of our research participants were atheists or agnostics, though many were practicing Buddhism to varying degrees, and a few practicing Christianity to varying degrees. Even many of their parents' generation were skeptical of traditional beliefs about the dead needing elaborate funerary rituals or offerings of food and burnt paper money and commodities to ensure a pleasant afterlife, especially given that such beliefs had been reviled during their own youth during the Cultural Revolution, and were still discouraged by the state. Having grown up with such skeptical parents, aunts, uncles, and teachers, our research participants were even more likely to dismiss such beliefs as "superstitions," or respect and practice them as traditions without believing that they actually had an effect on an afterlife, or even that an afterlife exists. Nevertheless, some of our research participants were saddened and somewhat fearful at the thought of having no spouse or children to organize their funerary rituals or to offer them food or burnt offerings after they died. They were also fearful of loneliness in the present, as more of their friends married and had children and could spend less time with them, and even more of loneliness in their old age. Some told Fong that, even though they enjoyed the fun they had with friends and the achievements they had at work, they would feel like something is missing if they do not have a spouse and child. Some who disliked their work, social circles, and/or parents eagerly looked forward to having a spouse and child who would make their lives more worth living. As a 31-year-old single, childless Dalian man told Fong, "Life is too boring without a family."

In addition to their personal desires for an ideal neo-familistic family that would give their lives meaning, the research participants also recognized that they would be stigmatized if they remained single and childless throughout their lives. They feared that others would believe that they were physically, personally, and/or socioeconomically unattractive to find a spouse or that they were gay or lesbian. As in most of China, LGBTQ identities were heavily stigmatized in Dalian (Zheng 2015). Of the thousands of research participants Fong met in Dalian, none admitted to her that they were lesbian, bisexual, transgender, or gender queer, and only one had ever told her that he was gay, and even he asked her to keep this a secret from all of their mutual friends and acquaintances.

When asked in 1999 how old they hoped to be when they married, female respondents (n = 166) stated a mean age of 27, and male respondents (n = 158) stated a mean age of 26. When asked in 1999 how old they hoped to be when they had a child, female respondents (n = 135) and male respondents (n = 142) both stated a mean age of 29. By 2014–15, the mean age of a first marriage was 27 for both men and women, and the mean age for when their first child was born was 28. Thus, if all of our respondents who had not married or had a child by 2014–15 stayed unmarried and childless throughout their lives, our

THE "LEFTOVER" MAJORITY 69

respondents would have proven able to time their marriage and childbearing to match the timing they envisaged even when they were in eighth or ninth grade. It is likely that, eventually, at least some of the 29 percent of the respondents (n = 406) who were unmarried in 2014–15 will marry, and that at least some of the 63 percent of the respondents (n = 406) who were childless in 2014–15 will have children, given that almost all of them want children, thus driving up the mean age at which respondents first marry and have a child. Still, it is clear that the high rate of being single past age 27, which previous generations had defined as the final deadline for women's marriageability (and close to the final deadline for men's marriageability, given the high rate of age homogamy among the respondents), for both male and female research participants is very much in keeping with their long-held life goals and understandings of cultural norms. Based on what they told Fong about their continuing desire to marry, their single status was not due to a determination to remain single throughout their lives.

The anxieties that caused and were promoted by the popular discourses about "leftover women" and "bare branch" men were nevertheless reflected in the nagging that both male and female research participants frequently heard from their parents, relatives, friends, and co-workers with regard to the urgency of finding, dating, and then marrying someone by the age of 27. They were discouraged by parents, teachers, and school administrators from having sex, marrying, or even in some cases from dating while they were still full-time students in high school or college due to fears that a romantic relationships would distract them from their studies and fears about the difficulty of maintaining a relationship after graduation sent them on different socioeconomic and/or geographic trajectories. But social pressures to find a partner to marry began as soon as they were no longer full-time students (part-time adult education college student status did not count as an excuse for not marrying). Such pressures intensified with each passing year between the singles' late twenties and early thirties. Most of their friends, parents, relatives, and co-workers considered matchmaking a helpful, kind, and generous gesture on behalf of a single person. Anyone who was single was likely to be encouraged to go out on dates with suitable singles in the social circles of those who cared about them (even those who themselves were postponing marriage). Singles who claimed that they wanted to postpone marriage until their thirties, or who claimed that they hoped never to marry or have children, were frequently subjected to matchmaking efforts, on the (often valid) assumption that they secretly were eager to find a spouse but they were claiming that they were not eager simply because they feared the stigma of being perceived as someone who was unable to attract a suitable spouse.

In many cases, even singles determined to postpone marriage for many years were grateful for such matchmaking, as they eventually wanted to marry and felt that they had to go on many dates with other singles who were potential future spouses before they would find an ideal spouse. Many considered dating a fun activity in itself and a valuable opportunity to learn about what kind of partner one might prefer, what kinds of partners might be available and interested, and how one might cultivate social skills that would make one better at attracting a desirable partner. Dating also widened one's social circles, which was valuable for social networking that might be useful for one's career or other aspects of one's future. Chatting on social media, either with friends of friends in one's social media circles, or with strangers online, was also considered a way to look for a spouse; those who were particularly comfortable with the Internet or eager to find a spouse also frequented matchmaking websites.

While many of their friends of a similar age responded sympathetically to their desire to postpone marriage, childbearing, and childrearing, agreeing with them about the risks and burdens of marriage and childbearing and the fun and opportunities available to those who remained single and childless, our research participants' parents, older relatives, and older co-workers commonly responded by nagging them about the importance of marrying and having children. Parents and older relatives and co-workers warned our research participants about the social stigma if they were to remain unmarried and childless into their thirties, about the loneliness they would feel without a family, especially after their parents are deceased, and about how no one will provide nursing care or emotional or financial support for them when they are old if they are still single and childless. Fong not only observed such nagging and efforts at matchmaking among her research participants' friends, parents, relatives, and co-workers but also experienced it herself from those same research participants (including some who were themselves trying to delay or resist marriage) as well as from their friends, parents, relatives, and co-workers. From the time she first started doing research with them at the age of 24, through her twenties, thirties, and early forties, Fong had continuously told them that she intended to remain single and childless throughout her life, both because she shared her research participants' concerns about the long-term stability of marriages and because the academic career she wanted would most likely require too much time and travel and would allow too little choice about the geographic location of her job to enable her to be the kind of wife and mother she would have wanted to be. Nevertheless, many of Fong's research participants and their parents, relatives, and friends still assumed that her protests were not a definite decision but merely a rhetorical face-saving strategy, similar to that of her single research participants and they tried to match her with single men whom they knew. Such matchmaking efforts and nagging about the value of marriage and childbearing were especially intense when Fong was between the ages of 24 and 29 but it continued to some extent even when she was in her thirties and forties.

Despite the frequent and widespread nagging and matchmaking attempts the research participants experienced, most single research participants did not find such nagging and matchmaking as painful or compelling as some media portray it to be because they (and most of the naggers and matchmakers) understand that the costs and risks of remaining single are no longer as high as they were for their parents' generation (Jankowiak and Moore 2016). There was ambivalence even in their parents' nagging and matchmaking. Many parents nagged their young adult children about the importance of marrying and having children in the abstract but they also expressed disapproval of just about every potential partner their children introduced them to, believing that their children deserved a spouse who was "better," not only socioeconomically but also in terms of appearance, likeability, and character. As a 31-year-old single, childless Dalian woman told Fong, "My Ma keeps pressuring me to look for a match, but in the past, she always disapproved of my boyfriends. I don't know what she's thinking."

The research participants as well as their parents knew that conflicts between parents-in-law and sons/daughters-in-law were common and likely; even though all hoped that a match could be made that would avoid such conflicts, they recognized that such an ideal was extremely rare (Yan 2015; Wolf 1985). The emotional intensity of the bonds between parents and their singleton children were so strong (Shi 2017; Fong 2004; Kuan 2015; Yan 2018) that in practice many parents were actually happy to postpone the "losing" of their child to a spouse. Abstract, general comments about the importance of finding a spouse that were expressed by such parents thus did not pack much of a punch, given how much they seemed to encourage their children to postpone marriage while waiting to find a better match in practice. Many research participants' parents had experienced divorces or unhappy marriages, and even those who had not were quite aware of how common divorces and unhappy marriages were and they were thus reluctant to push their children into a marriage with a potentially unsuitable partner. Some research participants' parents even told their children that it would be fine for them to stay single their entire lives if they could not find a suitable partner who would make them happy, and whom they were unlikely to divorce. Many research participants' parents were also happy that their children wanted to focus on pursuing further education, study abroad, or better jobs—goals that these parents also strongly desired—, often as much as, or more than, they wanted to see their children marry and have children. The research participants' parents also shared some of their children's ambivalence about how much time and money everyone in the family (including the research participants' parents, who were likely to have to contribute a lot to the purchase of neolocal housing, appliances, furnishings, and a car for the newlyweds, as well as take on the brunt of child-care responsibilities at least during early childhood) would have to sacrifice for their children to marry and have children. As a 30-year-old single, childless Dalian man told Fong, "My parents sometimes say I should find a match, but they know marriage is expensive, and we may not be able to afford it now, so they are not too anxious."

6 Conclusion: Redefining the Value and Proper Age of Marriage for a Neo-Familistic Generation

Our research participants and their parents were highly aware that the divorce rate, as well as the mean age of a first marriage, were rising, based both on their own observations and on reports in the media. This awareness increased their wariness of rushing into a marriage that could end in divorce and it also alleviated some of their fear about being "leftover" after all the more suitable potential spouses had been taken. The new norm of late marriage has actually become so commonly accepted for the research participants' generation that some women and men who were considering marrying in their early twenties actually faced criticism from their parents as well as friends, relatives, and co-workers for wanting to rush into marriage, and they were encouraged to receive more education, find better jobs, and/or save more money in order to buy or at least to be able to put a down payment on a mortgage for neolocal housing before marriage.

Though most of the parents wanted their adult children to eventually marry, many of our research participants' parents were ambivalent about the practical implications of pushing their children to marry and have children in the near future. The neo-familistic bonds between parents and children were so strong that many parents and their adult children were reluctant to hasten to bring a disruption to those bonds, which was likely to occur with a marriage. Because the dominant practices of neo-familism required parents to contribute most of their time, energy, and savings to help their adult children for the purchase of neolocal housing and to provide the costs or work of caring for and educating their young children, parents were concerned about the greater burdens that marriage and childbearing would bring to themselves as well as to their adult children. Moreover, the intense emotional and financial investments that parents

THE "LEFTOVER" MAJORITY 73

had made and believed they would have to continue to make meant that parents had much to lose if their children married someone who did not get along with the parents or whom the parents and/or the child considered less than ideal. It was therefore common for parents to be so picky about who their children dated or considered marrying that their objections reduced the likelihood of their children marrying by the age of 27 in practice, even though these same parents believed in theory that they wanted their children to marry by age 27.

At the same time, many of our single research participants greatly enjoyed the comfortable lives they had as single young adults living with their parents and therefore they were in no rush to exchange what they considered to be the best time of their lives for the burdens of marriage and childbearing. As single young working adults, they could enjoy the same love, care, and freedom from household chores that their parents had always provided them but without the intense pressure to succeed academically that their parents had inflicted on them while they were students. Many of them had strong, loving relationships with their parents, and the removal of the academic pressures even improved these relationships. Our research participants also greatly enjoyed being able to use the money they earned while living with their parents (which was often much more than the money their parents received from their pensions) to spend on things they enjoyed, to fulfill their filial duties by improving their parents' lives, and to increase their savings instead of using their salaries to deal with the stress-inducing expenses of starting their own households. They enjoyed the conditions of their lives as single, working young adults living with their parents and they did not feel strongly motivated to trade their lives for the much more difficult lives they anticipated they would lead as young new-lywed working parents.

It is clear, however, that, at least for now, most research participants still want to marry and eventually have children. Unlike in many other countries where single childless people, married childless people, divorced people, single parents, adoptive parents, stepparents, blended families, and LGBTQ relationships are becoming increasingly accepted, the heterosexual married couple with a child remains the hegemonic vision of the ideal family in China, even among the youngest generation of adults. It remains to be seen how much the hegemony of this vision will erode, however, as many of the neo-familistic generation of those who want to postpone marriage become so comfortable during their single and childless life stage that they will not want to leave it, as they end up waiting so long to marry that they can no longer find a suitable partner, as the media discourse warns, or as biological constraints on childbearing cause them to rethink the value and purpose of marriage once childbearing becomes more difficult or impossible.

References

Ebenstein, Avraham Y. and Ethan Jennings. 2009. "Bare Branches, Prostitution, and HIV in China: A Demographic Analysis." In *Gender Policy and HIV in China: Catalyzing Policy Change*, ed. Joseph D. Tucker and Dudley L. Poston, 71–94. Dordrecht: Springer Netherlands.

Fincher, Leta Hong. 2016. *Leftover Women: The Resurgence of Gender Inequality in China*. London: Zed Books Ltd.

Fong, Vanessa L. 2004. *Only Hope: Coming of Age Under China's One-Child Policy*. Stanford: Stanford University Press.

Fong, Vanessa L. 2011. *Paradise Redefined: Transnational Chinese Students and the Quest for Flexible Citizenship in the Developed World*. Stanford: Stanford University Press.

Hahn, Christina and Katarina Elshult. 2016. "The Puzzle of China's Leftover Women." http://lup.lub.lu.se/student-papers/record/8882495, retrieved October 28, 2019.

Jankowiak, William R. and Robert L. Moore. 2016. *Family Life in China*. Oxford: Polity Press.

Ji, Yingchun. 2015. "Between Tradition and Modernity: 'Leftover' Women in Shanghai." *Journal of Marriage and Family* 77, 5: 1057–73.

Ji, Yinchun and Wei-Jun Jean Yeung. 2014. "Heterogeneity in Contemporary Chinese Marriage." *Journal of Family Issues* 35,12: 1662–82.

Jiang, Quanbao and Jesús J. Sánchez-Barricarte. 2012. "Bride Price in China: The Obstacle to 'Bare Branches' Seeking Marriage." *The History of the Family* 17, 1: 2–15.

Kim, Sung Won and Vanessa L. Fong. 2013. "How Parents Help Children with Homework in China: Narratives across the Life Span." *Asia Pacific Education Review* 14, 4: 581–92.

Kim, Sung Won and Vanessa L. Fong. 2014a. "Homework Help, Achievement in Middle School, and Later College Attainment in China." *Asia Pacific Education Review* 15, 4: 617–31.

Kim, Sung Won and Vanessa L. Fong. 2014b. "A Longitudinal Study of Son and Daughter Preference among Chinese Only-Children from Adolescence to Adulthood." *The China Journal*, no. 71: 1–24.

Kim, Sung Won, Kari-Elle Brown, and Vanessa L. Fong. 2017. "Chinese Individualisms: Childrearing Aspirations for the Next Generation of Middle-Class Chinese Citizens." *Ethos* 45, 3: 342–66.

Kim, Sung Won, Kari-Elle Brown, and Vanessa L. Fong. 2018. "How Flexible Gender Identities Give Young Women Advantages in China's New Economy." *Gender and Education* 30, 8: 982–1000.

Kim, Sung Won, Kari-Elle Brown, Edward J. Kim, and Vanessa L. Fong. 2018. "'Poorer Children Study Better': How Urban Chinese Youth Perceive Relationships Between Wealth and Academic Achievement." *Comparative Education Review* 52, 1: 84–102.

Kuan, Teresa. 2015. *Love's Uncertainty: The Politics and Ethics of Child Rearing in Contemporary China*. Berkeley: University of California Press.

Mu, Zheng and Yu Xie. 2014. "Marital Age Homogamy in China: A Reversal of Trend in the Reform Era?" *Social Science Research* 44 (March): 141–57.

Shi, Lihong. 2017. *Choosing Daughters: Family Change in Rural China*. Stanford: Stanford University Press.

Sito, Peggy and Pearl Liu. 2019. "China Property: How the World's Biggest Housing Market Emerged." *South China Morning Post*, November 26, 2018. https://www.scmp.com/business/article/2174886/american-dream-home-ownership-quickly-swept-through-china-was-it-too-much, retrieved October 27, 2019.

To, Sandy. 2015. *China's Leftover Women: Late Marriage among Professional Women and Its Consequences*. London: Routledge.

Wolf, Margery. 1985. *Revolution Postponed: Women in Contemporary China*. Stanford: Stanford University Press.

Yan, Yunxiang. 2009. *The Individualization of Chinese Society*. Oxford: Berg.

Yan, Yunxiang. 2015. "Parent-Driven Divorce and Individualisation among Urban Chinese Youth." *International Social Science Journal* 64 (213–214): 317–30.

Yan, Yunxiang. 2016. "Intergenerational Intimacy and Descending Familism in Rural North China." *American Anthropologist* 118, 2: 244–57.

Yan, Yunxiang. 2018. "Neo-Familism and the State in China." *Urban Anthropology and Studies of Cultural Systems and World Economic Development* 47, 3/4: 181–224.

Zheng, Tiantian. 2015. *Tongzhi Living: Men Attracted to Men in Postsocialist China*. Minneapolis: University of Minnesota Press.

CHAPTER 4

United in Suffering

Rural Grandparents and the Intergenerational Contributions of Care

Erin Thomason

解放前，大部分群众都作难
Before the revolution, almost everything was difficult for the masses.

光作难还不算，部分群众去要饭
Not only did people face difficulties, some of them begged for food.

光要饭还不算，部分群众饿死完[1]
Not only did people beg for food, some of them starved to death.

开放改革三十年, 现在群众变化完
It has been thirty years since the reform and opening, right now everything has changed for the masses.

以前就是男管女，现在就是女管男
Before it was "the man commands the woman," now it is "the woman commands the man."

女管男还不算，现在的儿媳妇都是出去打工完
The woman commands the man comes up short, right now all the daughters-in-law go to work.

打工完还不算，孙子都交给奶奶看
Going out for work comes up short, the grandsons all are given to their grandmothers for care.

奶奶看不好了，还得把奶奶埋怨
Care by the grandmother is not good, and the grandmother is blamed for every single thing.

---

1 The careful linguist might note that here 完 is used to mean the end of something, in this case the end of a life from starvation. In Henan dialect to say 完 indicates the end, such as "完结，完蛋". Here, Auntie Tang is using 完 to add poetic symmetry to her lines.

© ERIN THOMASON, 2021 | DOI:10.1163/9789004450233_005

現在改革开放三十年，现在的什么社会都改变
It has been thirty years since the reform and opening, everything in society has changed.

∴

Tang Chunrong wrote this poem while she was tending to her four grandchildren. She recited it to me as she was breaking up sticks and twigs to add to her stove, preparing the evening meal for her family. As she recited the poem, her pacing became rapid and the lyrics took on a rhythm of their own. "Everything has changed," the poem's refrain laments, as her pacing takes on a feeling of speed. It is as if no one—not even the poem's author— can keep up with the vast number of changes in rural China. The poem is partially a platform for complaints, illuminating the contours of the economic and institutional transformations that affect Tang's everyday life. The physical suffering that characterizes life after the revolution continues in a dizzying array of social suffering. Although gender roles have flipped, giving Auntie Tang more authority within the household, "everything is now the responsibility of the grandmother," including raising, feeding, and clothing grandchildren, while the parents—her sons and daughters-in-law—migrate in search of employment. This significant change in household responsibilities shifts not only the power dynamics within the family but also the very expectations of family ideology, causing ripples in how the family is imagined, invoked, and implemented in daily life.

Auntie Tang's family situation is illustrative of new living arrangements and family obligations in rural China. Her two sons and their wives have both migrated to different urban areas to work in factories. Her own husband has part-time employment in the township, and Auntie Tang cares for the four grandchildren almost single-handedly. The oldest two grandsons live at a boarding school for most of the school year; every two weeks, they return home for four days. The youngest two grandchildren, a girl, aged 3 years and a toddler boy, aged 18 months, live full time with the grandparents. This kind of separate living arrangement affects approximately 68 million children in rural China (Chan and Ren 2018). In addition, like approximately 60 percent of the grandmothers in my sample, Auntie Tang also cares for an elderly relative, in this case, her husband's bachelor uncle who lives in the family courtyard and is dependent on Auntie Tang for his meals in exchange for some agricultural work.

While grandparenting is not a new or unique phenomenon in rural China, the specific arrangements of intensive grandparental care in the absence of the migrant parents create new roles and responsibilities for grandparents such as Aunt Tang. Accompanying these radical changes in family composition there are corresponding shifts in the social and economic structure that affect the ways in which the cohort of grandparents, in particular, participates in the contemporary economy. Grandparenting, as I argue throughout this chapter, is one way that older adults continue to participate in the family economy, despite their exclusion from other forms of labor. In this sense, grandparenting also provides a source of ethical meaning, a way for older adults to understand their roles and obligations in a changing social context.

In this chapter I explore how everyday care-giving arrangements affect the grandparents' sense of self, well-being, and the moral fields upon which they draw to understand their new roles as the primary caretakers of their grandchildren, while still shouldering their traditional burdens as filial adult children. A key notion in the concept of intergenerationality is how the various generations both conflict and collaborate to form a unified family—a family that in terms of structural composition differs significantly from the traditional forms of the extended filial family, such as those described in the 1930s by Fei Xiaotong and others (Fei 1992; Baker 1979; Wolf 1972).

Grandparenting, argues Arber, Virpi, Herlofson and Hagestad (2012), must be understood in three dimensions: cultural, structural and demographic. This chapter offers insight into the cultural and structural changes that inform grandparental experience in rural China. I explore two key terms developed from my research findings: suffering and family harmony. Whereas at the outset these concepts may seem to be at odds with each other, I show how they reinforce each other to create an everyday morality, defining the expectations of daily life while re-inscribing the self in a sphere of belonging that shapes the ways in which grandparents understand themselves within the kinship networks of obligation, companionship, and community.

I argue that grandparents do not share the same kind of emotional and material mobility enjoyed by the younger generation of migrant workers who have been raised to value happiness and reflexive freedom (c.f. Coe 2008). While no one wants to return to the traditional authoritarian family hierarchy, older family members must also find a way to reconcile heavy care-taking responsibilities with new values of happiness and self-suficency. Suffering becomes a way for the older generations to understand that their contributions are valuable, and meaningful, if not entirely always enjoyable. The grandparents in my study draw on revolutionary-era values, such as bearing burdens, carrying out one's duties, and suffering. These values are re-inscribed as a generational and national morality. By following their family obligations to provide caretaking, grandparents use their suffering to paint themselves as the moral champions of the family. Instead of being abused or left-behind, these grandparents challenge the narrative of abandonment by pointing to their moral victory, heralding their roles as moral stalwarts of the family.

1 Site and Methdology

This chapter is based on thirteen months of ethnographic fieldwork undertaken in an agricultural village, which I call Jiatian village, located in northwest Henan province. About one mile outside of a busy township, the county surrounding Jiatian village has been the target of government poverty alleviation investment and an urbanization scheme since 2012, bringing in local employment, businesses, and improvements in the township infrastructure. I first visited Jiatian village in 2013 before I then returned for eleven months from 2014 to 2015 for my dissertation research. As a postdoctoral scholar in Shenzhen, I also returned to Jiatian in 2018–19 for two follow-up visits of 1–2 weeks. My research methodology utilized person-centered interviewing methods and focused on the narrative reflections of nine women between the ages of 40 and 75. In this chapter, I focus on the lower age limit of this cohort, those between 40 and 60 years old. I followed these key families throughout my four years of research, tracing their shifts in migration and changes care-taking, observing their family life, and recording their everyday struggles. I also conducted more traditional village-based ethnography, tracking the village demographic information and conducting a small-scale survey about family change.

2 Suffering and the Chinese Family

"See for yourself, are we or are we not facing hardship? (*xinku bu xinku*)," Aunt Xu poured steaming water into the large iron wok holding the dirty dishes from breakfast, pausing to wipe sweat from her brow that had formed despite the bitter cold in the room. "With three kids, how can life not be hard?"

"What can I do?" she continued. "If I don't care for the kids, then how can their mother go to work? And if their mother doesn't go to work, who will pay for the household expenses? The recent marriage of my grandson cost over 160,000 RMB—and this was only for the gift to our granddaughter-in-law. The wedding, the house, they all cost more."

Aunt Xu, as in 40 percent of the households I met in Jiatian village, cared for her three grandchildren while her son and daughter-in-law were working some ten hours away. In the parents' absence, the bulk of the household chores and the demanding childcare when the children were small all fell on Aunt Xu's shoulders. Aunt Xu's hardships were actually quite normal among the grandparents whom I met. Her everyday tasks included the daily laundry, sweeping the courtyard, feeding and clothing the children, and making three meals per day using the large stove that utilized agricultural refuse as fuel.

Aunt Xu justified the hard work of grandparents as part and parcel of the experience of having kin in contemporary rural China. Being a grandparent involves suffering, Aunt Xu seems to imply. This idea of a suffering grandparent was shared among many of my diverse rural informants; regardless of their actual care-taking burdens, almost all agreed that caring for the children in the absence of their parents and also caring for their aging parents and relatives were tiring and difficult jobs, but it was also normal, representing an inherent part of being a grandparent in the countryside. Likewise, it was universally agreed that suffering was part of the generational experience of those between ages 55 and 70 who had experienced the bitter years of collectivization and famine in the days before the reform and opening. In the words of one grandmother, "hardship is just part of our generation."

Suffering, and complaints about suffering, which are constantly repeated by grandparents to describe their everyday experiences and contributions to the family, are subject to cultural and historical configurations of moral attitudes that shape the ways that people imagine and talk about hardships and dysphoric experiences (Wilce 2003). Suffering is a virtuous part of identity, especially for older people who imagine their contribution not only to the family but also to the nation in terms of their ability and experiential sacrifice of bodily comforts during the early years of the People's Republic. Suffering becomes a meaningful cultural category which organizes the experience of being a grandparent and instills a sense of generational and collective identity in this rural community.

Suffering for the family, I argue, not only is a material condition or a description of poverty or bodily fatigue but it is also an affective state, a feeling of being ill at ease or facing hardships and troubles. Suffering is a kind of emotional posturing toward the family, which is expressed by my informants in the following Chinese terms, *xinku* (辛苦, to experience great hardships), *ai* (挨, to endure), and *shou kunnan* (受困难, to bear difficulties). Based on these linguistic terms, suffering is not simply passively experienced but rather it is borne and endured. Suffering can either enable family harmony or it can lead to isolation, depending on how the experience of suffering is (or is imagined

UNITED IN SUFFERING   81

to be) shared and distributed among the different generations of adults within the family. Thus suffering, and especially acts of shared suffering, can be one important way of instilling family harmony, unity, and a moral spirit of working together with a shared purpose.

In the face of the rapid social change, China has experienced a profoundly radical restructuring of the economic conditions that shape individual and family lives in a short amount of time (Yan 2010; Alpermann 2011; Chang 2010), leading to strong and divergent impacts of these conditions on the various age cohorts. The possibilities afforded by the employment, education, and labor markets all have resounding effects on the individuals' understanding of their obligations to the family. The kind of contribution that each generation is able to offer to the family is configured not only by its individual experiences but also by larger economic forces, such as state retirement and benefit policies and the generational distribution of social resources. To understand how the contemporary intergenerational family operates as a unit of economic cooperation and a source of moral personhood, it is necessary to explore the history of the labor market in rural China.

3   A Short History of the Laboring Rural Family

In prerevolutionary China, family divisions of labor were based on age and gender, with hierarchies linked to one's age and status. The logic can be summarized by the saying *nanzhuwai, nüzhunei*, or "men manage the outside, while women manage the inside." Outside tasks included culturally recognized forms of leadership, management, income-earning, and commercial activities, whereas women's inside work included all domestic household tasks, such as sericulture, spinning, weaving, and sewing (Mann 2000). Although not necessarily recognized as major economic players, women's inside work contributed significantly to the household economy and the women's internal divisions of labor were quite important (Brown 2016). Older women were the recipients of the younger women's labor as part of the filial code of honoring one's parents. Thus younger women, namely the newly married daughters-in-law, shouldered the greatest burdens of the household labor and childcare (Wolf 1972).

During revolutionary China, age began to configure new ways of understanding worth within the family. In the rural context, for example, older women were awarded less work points than younger women (Li 2005). Along with the campaigns calling for an end to age-based patriarchy, the new economic policies, legal reforms, and the thriving youth culture began to shift the family system in favor of the younger members of the family (Blake 1979; Yan 1997;

Davis and Harrell 1993). In my interviews with older women and men in Jiatian village, I discovered that during the collective era, even though elders were not remembered as important to the economic work-point system or the collective labor system, they were particularly vital to the family household labor, which were largely ignored by the revolutionary calls for gendered equality (Brownell and Wasserstrom 2002). For women with young children, having a mother-in-law became a potential source of labor cooperation which would ultimately enable the family to occupy a better economic position.

Because of the work-point system, all able-bodied men and women had to work. Many families could not sacrifice work-points for childcare or household work, such as weaving, sewing, or cooking. In particular, women with young children were left to make hodge-podge rearrangements for childcare. The strategies I recorded included tying infants to mattresses, bringing toddlers to the fields, and, importantly, engaging both the maternal and paternal grandparents to take care of the children. Poverty, hunger, and desperation meant reconsidering the previous practice of mother-led care and led my informants to comment, "whoever is able to care for the child should do so." Under this ideology of pragmatism, and with the increasing importance of participation by younger women in wage and agricultural labor to national productivity, the ideal family structure slowly shifted along age-based lines. Divisions of inside and outside labor that previously were tied to gender increasingly came to be tied to age divisions (Lou 2011). This shift was further solidified by the tidal wave of rural-to-urban migration that began in the mid-1990s and continues to this day.

Following both market and political logic, many rural families divided their labor participation based on the pragmatism of the new migrant labor market in the urban areas. Low-skilled industries were largely based on labor capacity (or perceived labor capacity), such that gender and age determined individual access to secure, stable, and well-paid work. Older women ranked at the bottom of such evaluations, since they were assumed to lack the education, technical knowledge, or beauty of younger women or bodily strength of men in similar age-cohorts. Therefore, the migrant labor market tended to value younger more flexible workers and to undervalue older workers.

Accompanying this new economic dynamic, the household registration system (*hukou*) limited social welfare, health care, and school registration in urban communities so that children's access to schooling and elder's access to state-sponsored healthcare were linked to one's place of origin (for a comprehensive review, see Young 2013). Low-skilled workers, who likely could not earn a merit-based residency transfer or could not have access to work-unit–sponsored schools or benefits, made economic and practical calculations, effectively dividing the family by age and ability to work. Elders and children thus remained in the countryside, maintaining the agricultural landholdings and preserving the access to rural benefits.

Jiatian village, like many other agricultural areas (C. C. Fan 2008), has been profoundly shaped by rural-urban migration, with more than 50 percent of all young adults relocating to city centers for work in factories, at construction sites, or in small businesses. In 2015, 23 percent of all children lived in split-generation households headed by the paternal grandparents, while their parents worked in the cities; 42 percent lived with their mothers and paternal grandparents; and another 11 percent lived in divorced-households without their mothers. In 2019 when I returned to the village, the number of children living without their parents had increased by 10 percent, in part because a large cohort of young children in the village had entered kindergarten, freeing up maternal time to migrate to the cities for paid employment.

The grandparents' efforts to provide care are not always valued or recognized, even by the members of their own family. Most daughters-in-law with whom I spoke were dissatisfied with various aspects of the ways in which their mothers-in-law cared for their children and they complained about the grandparents' lax discipline, lack of supervision over their child's education, and their inability to control their child's access to technology and their use of the Internet. In turn, grandparents complained that they were ill-prepared to supervise schooling, and they often made self-critical statements indicating that because of their own illiteracy, their grandchildren were falling behind in school. They did not understand how to use cell phones or the Internet and therefore, as reported, they had no idea how to limit usage.

Portraying grandparental care as lacking, inadequate, or incomplete was also echoed in the numerous campaigns that urged the migrant parents to return to the countryside. These well-intentioned attempts to reunite migrant parents and rural children portray the nuclear family as essential for psychological well-being. The unintended target of these campaigns was the care by the grandparents, which was deemed to be both overbearing and inadequate. School teachers in the township described children cared by their grandparents as "dirty," "pitiful," and "sad." Scholarly reports based on numerous survey-based studies on left-behind children echo similar sentiments (see, for example, Fan et al. 2010; Ye and Murray 2010; Ye and Lu 2011).

Simultaneously, most of these rather young grandparents, in their early fifties or sixties, also bear traditional filial responsibilities toward their own aging parents and relatives. A report by the Economist Intelligence Unit estimates that 37 percent of Chinese adults between the ages of 20 and 70 are caught in "the sandwich generation," meaning they have family care responsibilities spanning more than one generation: 83 percent of working-age adults in China support their parents financially; 45 percent of individuals dually caring for both older and younger family members report that they are "struggling to cope" with the financial and time commitments needed for them to care for both their children and their aging relatives. In rural China, the pressures may be even more keenly felt by not only the grandparents' generation, whose perspective I describe in this chapter, but also by the middle generation of migrant parents who are providing financially for three different dependent generations—their children, their own parents, and their parent's parents. In tangible terms, those between the ages of 40 and 65 bear the bulk of everyday caring tasks, such as cleaning, cooking, dressing, bathing, and managing medications and hospital visits. As I discuss below, these care-giving tasks may be felt differently depending on the perception of the moral obligations borne by each generation and the experience of unexpected or unanticipated difficulties along one's life course. I propose that the key to understanding of their caring efforts is found in the concept of suffering, which allows grandparents to construct their experience as morally virtuous and socially productive.

In the cases I present below, I feature three grandparent-headed households in order to examine the ways in which the elder generation understands their affective and economic contributions to the multi-generational family. I show how their emotional contributions of suffering contribute to the undervalued care economy (Folbre 2006; England and Folbre 1999) in an increasingly trans-local China. Exploring both economic and emotional labor, I review how ideas of suffering are employed to reinforce family unity. My argument highlights the importance of emotional labor in intergenerational exchanges and illuminates the role of suffering in creating feelings of caretaking ambivalence.

Among all of these families, care responsibilities span four generations. The Jia family and Honglin's family each care for a paternal matriarch, whereas Yuejie's family bears responsibility for an elderly unmarried uncle. Their care situations are largely representative of many of the cases I encountered during my fieldwork. Even though each individual family has worked out its own care arrangements, their narratives reveal three major ways of dealing with the concept of suffering as a value that allows them to conceptualize and construct their experience within a moral and ethical framework.

4 "We Are United as a Family"

When I returned to Jiatian village in 2018 and 2019, I discovered that my neighbor's two sons and daughters-in-law had migrated for work, leaving their three

UNITED IN SUFFERING

young children in the care of the elderly grandparents. The younger couples had returned during Spring Festival and when I saw them I was shocked because all four of the young people had become much thinner, losing close to 15 pounds each.[2] I immediately remarked how thin they were and how I barely recognized them. Aunt Lu agreed with me, "Working as migrants, they have suffered (*xinkule*). They work twelve hours per day and they don't have time to eat." She shook her head and amended her statement, "Actually, we all have suffered."

Uncle Jia piped in, "Their thinness is good! (*shou shi hao*); in fact, before we were all too idle (*lan*). With nothing to do at home, everyone got fat. Now everyone is thin, but we are all productive and thin."

In the three years during which I had known them, the family had improved their life circumstances considerably, building a stand-alone house for the elderly couple. The oldest grandchildren, now ages 4 and 6, had entered a private kindergarten and in the last year the family had been able to afford a costly medical expense—the removal of a uterine tumor. They also had been able to sign up for the government poverty benefit system and they receive a small monthly subsidy from the local government, easing the household budget and allowing the family to focus on saving for the children's future education and marriage expenses. Additionally, the family was shouldering part of the burden of caring for the elderly matriarch, who at the time of this writing close to 95 years of age. She rotates between living with her three local sons for one month at a time (c.f. Jing 2004).

Later, I recorded an interview with the family about the recent shifts in their care-taking arrangements.

> UNCLE JIA: Here is the way it is, I'll tell it to you very simply. Right now, why do we care for the children? All the young people have each found their own jobs; they all have their own things to do (*shi ganqu*). But for us older people, finding a job is usually really difficult. In addition, the kids need someone to look after them (*zhaogu*), so we enable (*rang*) [the young couples'] labor; we stay at home to take care of the kids, in that way we divide the labor.
>
> ERIN: Okay, so it's a division of labor

---

2   Admittedly, the average weight at my field site is quite high, due in part to the radical reduction in physical activity and the widespread availability of snack foods and high-caloric staples like meat, oil, and refined flour. My neighbors previously had been heavy set, but now they appeared to be more healthy and fit.

UNCLE JIA: It is not like it was before! Right now, we've developed technology, we've saved a lot of labor power (*renli*). ... In one day, we can finish our [agricultural] work [for the season]; in the past, we would have to work for two months in order to finish what we can now accomplish in one day. Labor power is saved and we can earn money; the children can find jobs. ... So we use our time to care for the kids. In the past, we didn't have any extra time, so how could we take care of kids? Right?

VASILIKKI (THE RESEARCH ASSISTANT): Is there anyone who is *not* willing to care for their grandchildren?

AUNT LU: I'm sure there are such people, but I don't know any of them.

ERIN: Right, there is no one in our village who doesn't care for their grandchildren, right?

UNCLE JIA: Right now, it's actually voluntary. We do this because we care about our own children. According to common logic, we will often say, if you give birth [to a child], then you should care [for them]. If she gives birth, then she should care for the child. I give birth to a kid, and I take care of it completely by myself. If I have to look after your kid ... I will suffer too much and I will not have any good times in my life. ... But now, we enable our kids to earn money and get experience—that is, to go out and earn a salary. I myself can't earn any money. But you can earn money, so I'll stay at home and take care of the kid, and you can relax and focus on your labor. You earn the money, and we'll stay at home. We are united together as a family (*jia jieheqilai*). ... Because we cannot work, we have to depend on what they earn. If they didn't give us any money, then we would have a legitimate reason to say that we can't take care of their child. Basically, if we didn't care for these kids, the two of us elderly people would starve to death. We want (*yao*) to spend our energy [taking care of the kids] so that we can meet the demands of this situation.

In the above discussion, a central organizing tension in the logic of care is the division between productivity and idleness. Productivity exists simultaneously with suffering and hardship. Idleness, on the other hand, consists of remaining in the countryside without access to productivity. Uncle Jia specifically links the development of labor-saving technology, such as mechanized harvesters and tractors, to the increase in leisure time, and thus idleness in the countryside. The untying of human labor from agriculture is what ultimately frees up the time of the grandparents to care for the children, which in turn enables the middle generation to engage in migrant labor. According to Uncle Jia's thinking, this rearrangement of caregiving is a positive sign of progress mutually enabling the elder and parental generations to avoid the trap of idleness. Now,

UNITED IN SUFFERING

Uncle Jia states, they are thin, but being productive and thin is better, both morally and economically, than being idle and fat.

This is reminiscent of the traditional value in Chinese culture of industriousness, or what Stevan Harrell (1985) has called the "entrepreneurial effort." The Chinese term for the concept is *qinlao*, a quality of laboring diligently. Harrell argues the family has long been a motivating factor for Chinese individuals since the kin group can determine one's social and economic standing. During the revolutionary era, this value was channeled for the benefit of the national collective, yet it seems that the entrepreneurial ethos remained a central core in the way the family is joined together both ethically and morally.

With the convergence of new technologies that have transformed human labor in the countryside and with improved health and nutrition from education and healthcare campaigns, elders in rural areas are living longer and more comfortable lives. Yet psychologically and morally, some elders feel ungrounded without labor. In many families that I followed, men and women both worked in sideline industries, such as piecework beading and sewing or informal food carts, even though did not actually need the very low wages they earned from such endeavors. The common way to describe this sideline work was that there was "no money, but I have nothing else to do anyway." In doing these small tasks, elders could stave off the boredom that comes from leisure as well as fight the trap of becoming useless, giving moral grounding to their everyday lives.

A second theme revealed from the above conversation is that the family is understood as a sort of bounded organism and it must solve its problems on its own. The key to this conception of the family is Uncle Jia's framing of the ideal family as united (*jiehe qilai*) by an economic and practical dependency. Dependency, according to the logic presented here, strengthens the intergenerational family because the family has little choice but to work together. Uncle Jia even goes so far as to say that he would starve to death without the remittances from his adult children. In fact, this assertion is exaggerated because the elderly couple does receive a poverty-benefit ration and their yield from farming should enable hearty consumption of wheat and vegetables. But the other elders who live in the village without migrant remittances do face real economic hardships and they have no room in their budgets for any spending on consumption.

In a conversation several months earlier, Aunt Lu told me that if the young children were not in her care, then she would feel as if the house were empty. "They add excitement and liveliness (*renao*)," she asserted. While we spoke, the children were pushing small toy cars around the room and shouting gleefully. Aunt Lu and Uncle Jia both relished their care-taking responsibilities, often purchasing small treats for the children, teasing them, and doting upon them. Aunt Lu recounted with laughter that the youngest child loved to wash his feet before bed and the eldest child always chased the chickens. Despite Uncle Jia's assertion of a simple financial exchange or an intergenerational division of labor, the daily acts of caregiving as part of grandparental care were much more emotional, involving a moral and ethical sense about what is right, good, and important in kinship relations. This is also clarified in Uncle Jia's statement that their care is voluntary, motivated not by a sense of duty or financial desperation but because "we care about our own children."

In Uncle Jia and Aunt Lu's conversation, there is a real sense that if the family cannot pull itself together and collaborate economically, then the emotional ties that bind the family will be lost. Suffering, then, is a kind of affective tool that measures the family collaboration. In its ideal form, suffering is shared and distributed across the generations such that the entire family suffers together for the sake of economic progress. The Jia family narrative of suffering is a narrative of positive collaboration, in which the suffering is a visible sign of one's hard work. Suffering, in this sense, is the way in which the traditional value of economic cooperation meets the more modern emotional sentiments that tie the family together in modern times.

Although some families might measure their unity based on happiness (see for example Yan 2003), the Jia family uses suffering as a key moral and ethical indicator. Suffering represents an important contribution by everyone to the family, but for Uncle Jia and Auntie Lu, in particular, suffering is an especially important contribution due to their lack of wage-remunerated labor. In this way, suffering becomes an affective contribution to the intergenerational family, binding together the family's sentimental and economic standing and including both the sentiments and practical arrangements of everyday life.

5   "All These Troubles I Bear Myself"

At 9:00 AM, when most of the neighbors had long since eaten breakfast, it seemed to Yujie that her family was the only one that was behind schedule. At 7:30 AM the 7-year-old twin girls had knocked on the door of their older brother's house. I was staying with the family during the Spring Festival and I answered the door. Guests had come, we needed to quickly dress and brush our teeth and head to the larger family home just 25 meters down the road. I dressed in a rush, throwing on a layer of long johns before climbing into the thick pair of cotton-padded pants that had been loaned to me for the week. My haste, however, was in vain as the 21-year-old sister-in-law, Meihua, remained in bed scrolling her phone while her 3-year-old daughter played at her feet. Despite the repeated insistence by the younger sister-in-law that she get up quickly, we waited for over an hour, playing with the 3-year-old, while Meihua continued to lay in bed, her eyes glued to her smart phone's screen and oblivious to the growing anxiety of her younger sister-in-law and me. When we finally arrived at the family complex, Meihua immediately closed herself in the small bathroom since she had not spent anytime brushing her hair or washing her face when we were waiting for her. The young girls reported to Yujie, their mother, about how they had spent the last hour, how Meihua had spent the entire time looking at her phone and was still not ready to meet the family guests. Yujie was visibly upset, her eyes facing downward in a contemptuous grimace and her fingers drumming repeatedly against her legs to hide her anger. I quickly said hello to the visiting aunt and uncle who had traveled over 10 km in a small three-wheeled electric cart to make the visit before I retired to the kitchen to help prepare breakfast.

Yujie was still pacing, and I laughed saying that I had never seen anyone stay in bed so long. I was trying to bring some levity to the situation. Yujie spit back, "She is the laziest person I've ever met. Lazy, lazy, lazy!" Then, changing the subject, we began to prepare the dishes for the morning meal.

Later, when Yujie was no longer angered by the family drama, I asked what she thought about her daughter-in-law. When I had first met Yujie three years earlier, she had just arranged for her 18-year-old son to marry Meihua and, although overcome with anxiety about financing the wedding, Yujie was hopeful that the marriage would anchor her eldest son in the family, bringing a pause to his propensity to play and waste money. In the three years since, the young couple had given birth to a pretty daughter and had found work in a pork factory outside of Guangzhou. Meihua's personality was continually jovial, she laughed heartily, teased her husband, and played with her daughter. But she seemed bent on asserting her power as a daughter-in-law, such as refusing to greet guests early in the morning. During the marriage negotiations, she had demanded bridewealth that matched that of her peers, an amount totaling almost 150,000 RMB. Yujie stated that in the past a daughter-in-law was expected to be docile and respectful, but in the current state of affairs she could do little to control, influence, or change her daughter-in-law's behavior. Since her children spanned the ages of 22 and 7, she imagined herself in the position of being both an ideal mother-in-law and an ideal daughter-in-law at the same time.

"I like a peaceful family (*heping jiating*)," she insisted. "So even if there is trouble, I'm not going to say anything. In fact, I have so many difficulties—with earning money, with daily chores. All these troubles, I bear them all myself.

I don't share them with others. In that way, the others are happy. This year I couldn't afford to buy the kids new clothes [for New Year's]. I told them; we can eat bitterness ourselves (*chiku*). But I was afraid that she [her mother-in-law] would get angry. So, I spent 300 RMB —money I didn't have— to buy her a new coat. I want others to be happy, then we can have harmony."

This strategy of bearing trouble and avoiding confrontation actually seemed to work very well for the family. Yujie's daughter-in-law regularly praised Yujie's morality and personality, highlighting the ways in which she was tolerant and loving. Despite her reluctance to support Yujie in material and practical ways, she seemed to offer emotional support in the form of praise, affection, and general goodwill. Even though this offering of emotional affection seemed inadequate to Yujie, my discussions with other daughters-in-law of Meihua's generation reveal that they calculate their duties toward their mothers-in-law quite differently. One recent bride summarized her attitude toward her in-laws as "If they won't respect me, I won't respect them." This reciprocal calculation of emotional exchange means that during the first several years of marriage, daughters-in-law are basically testing out their relationships with their mothers-in-law in order to see how tolerant, loving, and mother-like the new family will be. The attitudes of the mothers-in-law form the basis for the later filial negotiations. This is the foundation for what Clara To calls "the gendered intergenerational contract" (To 2014), the role of each generation of women to contribute to the family caretaking responsibilities.

While Yujie and other mothers-in-law complain about the rising power of their daughters-in-law, they also seem reluctant to return to a more traditional mother and daughter-in-law relationship that largely characterized their experiences with their own mothers-in-law. For Yujie, this meant scraping together money for a gift to demonstrate her filiality and gratitude toward her mother-in-law. Yujie, on the other hand, did not expect or receive a gift from her own daughter-in-law.

In the family drama that unfolds above, Yujie's thoughts on *heping jiating* point to the central value of suffering, or eating bitterness, in the sentiments that determine the family. Family, John Borneman writes, is not only a matrix of a relationship but also of sentiment (Borneman 2001). The moral ways of being in a family, and particularly a family that is united in peace, require particular kinds of affective, emotional, and material labor. Among the three generations of women, there is a significant difference in the ways that each woman contributes to family peace. The eldest family member, still able-bodied and in her late sixties, offers labor, cooking, and childcare, while Yujie and her husband work. Her practical labor expresses little in the way of emotional or sentimental platitudes and I never heard her praise or encourage her daughter-in-law.

The youngest woman, Meihua, entering the family just three years earlier has the advantage of a long-term temporal plane in which to repay her mother-in-law for her current kindness and the large bridewealth she received at her wedding. She offers emotional support in the form of praise, but still seems unsure if and when she will offer more deferential or practical support, such as a ritualistic New Year's gift. Yujie, however, is caught in between two kinds of demands—to be both a good daughter-in-law and a good mother-in-law requires no small amount of emotional and practical gymnastics.

Yujie's statement—"All of these troubles, I bear them all myself"—demonstrates the ways in which she feels caught in between two kinds of obligations as well as the ways in which she imagines herself to be morally victorious despite being exasperated by the moral pivoting. Like many other women in their early forties in Jiatian village, Yujie had missed out on schooling and she could not read or write even her own name. Because of her illiteracy, she was limited to doing base-line factory, restaurant, or cleaning work, so her financial worries were already predetermined by her past. Her efforts therefore had to be directed morally, and her work involved bearing these troubles.

Yujie completes this emotional labor through emotional regulation—a silencing of perceived negative emotions in service to a moral attitude (Wikan 1990; Abstract 1989; Hochschild 2003). In effect, her attitude is very self-sacrificing. She understands her moral personhood to be stemming directly from this ability to create a peaceful and harmonious family. In her narrative, Yujie emerges as a moral victor in the family because she suffers not only to make others happy but also because the family enjoys peaceful harmony due to her suffering. In bearing the family's troubles, she emerges as a moral victor.

As much as Yujie's discussion of bearing trouble is a lament or a complaint, it is also a cultural and local assertion of her own moral personhood. Unlike Kleinman (1988b; 1988a), who argues that suffering is an expression of disorder, the suffering expressed by Yujie and other grandmothers are statements of order—they are proof that they are conforming to the correct sets of ethical and cultural demands of a moral personhood. In a different context, Jason Throop (2008) examines the role of suffering in the South Pacific community of Yap. Drawing from Lévinas (1998) and Scarry's (1985) reflections on pain, Throop argues that narratives help shape pain from a meaningless experience into a virtuous moral engagement. Throop (2008:176) outlines the many ways that Yapese culture constructs enduring pain as a positive moral attitude, including laboring without food, enduring medical treatment, and surviving war injuries, and he points out that suffering has value within the Yapese community through the connection to others. This positive valence of "suffering-for" allows individuals experiencing pain to transform an otherwise useless and meaningless tragedy into a purposeful event. Likewise, in Yujie's narrative, bearing trouble becomes a moral gloss to enable the happiness of the family. Even if the suffering is solitary, it is transformed into a collective act of suffering on behalf of the family.

6   "That's The Difficulty For Us Women in Our Forties"

From her friend and neighbor, I had heard that Honglin's situation had worsened. Honglin had always worked long hours, and when I had first met her, she was spending most of her days mixing cement at a local construction site. She was saving money to pay for her second son's new house, she told me, since the one that they had previously constructed was rejected by his future bride. Now, three years later, Honglin was no longer working in construction but instead she had become a full-time caretaker for her 2-year-old grandson. However, instead of enjoying her new role, she found herself even more anxious because a series of unfortunate events had led to a huge financial and care-taking burden.

Her eldest son, who had been happily married and living in a different city, had returned home, despondent and heartbroken when his marriage had ended in divorce. Honglin immediately began planning to arrange a second marriage to a local girl, trying to mend his broken heart. She soon discovered that since he was divorced, not only would the matchmaker demand more than twice the normal fee, she could expect that the new daughter-in-law would demand an extra-large bride price. In the meantime, there were other financial obligations, hospital bills from her husband's recent car accident, a fine for her grandson who had not filed on time for his household residence permit, and the everyday cost of living.

Her sons and husband worked, but she complained that her second son did not, in fact, provide sufficient financial support. "My second son doesn't buy [us] anything. ... He pays for the formula, and that's pretty much it. Every two months, he gives us about 500 RMB, but everything else, we must take care of it by ourselves. Nevertheless, whether or not he gives us any money, I still have to care for his son." She continued to describe her financial situation in terms of a competition between care and finances, "I cannot earn any money because I also have to look after my mother-in-law. In Zhengzhou, my husband is only paid once a year; the rest of the year we live on loans."

Her daughter-in-law was neither helpful or supportive; "For a whole year she [the daughter-in-law] did nothing. I mean not a single thing. She didn't get out of bed, she didn't cook food, she didn't even wash a dish. She just would

UNITED IN SUFFERING 93

leave the bowl by her pillow. So incredibly lazy. In fact, all young people of her generation are like that. Doesn't get out of bed, demands good food, and after she has eaten she just leaves. If you behaved like this in the past, you could not have survived; you would enrage the elder generation. Even my own mother-in-law, if I don't give her good things, if I don't care for her well, she will be very angry. If there is anything that I don't do well, she will give me an unhappy look (*gei lianse kan*). That's the difficulty for us women in our forties. When I got married and left home, my brothers didn't care one bit. But my daughter-in-law will dare to demand things for herself."

Honglin, just like Yujie and Aunt Lu, can be classified as what is known in the United States as a member of the "sandwich generation" (Roots 2014; Zal 2001). Faced with the triple burden of caring for her adult children, grandchildren, and elderly parents-in-law, Honglin not only faces extreme financial burdens to support her eldest son's remarriage but also the emotional and practical troubles of dramatically different expectations about roles and attitudes within the family. These radically different generational expectations contribute to her daily financial struggles, since her son fails to remit adequate funds for the young child and for her practical daily life. And now she has now added one additional member to the family [her daughter-in-law] who also requires care instead of contributing to the household labor.

Complaints about daughters-in-law, as noted in the latter two cases, are incredibly common. While a good number of mothers and daughters-in-law cooperate well and divide household responsibilities fairly, common disagreements between the two generations of women often stem from different expectations about their chores. Even when the younger woman moves to a separate residence, it is common for the older generation to continue to provide a large portion of the cooking and cleaning tasks. Given these complaints about the general character of daughters in law, many mothers-in-law with whom I spoke were happy when their daughters-in-law migrated for work, even if it meant that they were left with a larger child care-taking burden. Mothers-in-law actively encouraged their daughters-in-law to find wage labor, complaining that at home the daughters-in-law were too prone to laziness and if they were to earn an income, they could at least contribute to the family economy.

A series of demographic studies record the rise of grandparenting in both urban and rural China (Cong and Silverstein 2008; Silverstein and Cong 2013; Xu, Silverstein, and Chi 2014; Ko and Hank 2013; Nyland et al. 2009; Zeng and Xie 2014). For example Chen, Liu, and Mair (2011) note that beyond the first year of life, paternal grandmothers spend as much time with the children as the mothers do. This is true in both urban and rural China, despite the differential access to quality daycare. Feinian Chen (2014) analyzes data from a large-scale social survey and finds that the daughter-in-law's professional standing is often determined by the availability of the mother-in-law's labor. In this volume, Qi explores the phenomenon of "floating grandparents" who accompany their extended family in urban centers and Huang's chapter highlights the role of urban grandparents. All of these data point to the idea that grandparenting has become an enduring family strategy to deal with the challenges of contemporary economics and the demands for dual-wage families.

In European and East Asian contexts, researchers have pointed out the connection between the paucity of state welfare systems and the increase in grandparental involvement (Bordone, Arpino, and Aassve 2017; Arber et al. 2012; Glaser et al. 2013). Coupled with a demographic transition and increasing numbers of younger women in formal or migrant employment, grandparents fill the practical gaps in childcare (Emick and Hayslip 1996; Shore and Hayslip 1994; Chen, Liu, and Mair 2011). The conversations with Honglin and Yujie also point out that custodial grandparenting and migration may be a strategy to ease relations among the generations. Most families I met agreed that while the mother was the best person to care for their own children, grandmothers enabled mothers to work outside the home allowing for extra income as well as clear expectations for each family members. With more firm divisions of household roles, intergenerational relationships may be smoothed avoiding the daily conflict and negotiations of chores and responsibilities.

Still, many grandparents have a profound ambivalence toward their caretaking responsibilities, describing the obligation as a moral and ethical task to be undertaken regardless of the amount of remittances provided by their adult children. Ambivalences in intergenerational relationships exist because of structural and ideological contradictions (Luescher and Pillemer 1998). On the one hand, grandparenting is fraught with exhausting and tiresome routines of caretaking, while on the other hand, grandparents can derive satisfaction from an active role in the intergenerational family (Backhouse and Graham 2012; Doley et al. 2015; Hoang, Haslam, and Sanders n.d.; Park 2018)

Honglin's ambivalence about her care-taking responsibilities is most keenly felt in the conflict between her responsibility toward her eldest son and her commitment to her grandchild. She wants to work to earn income, but her time is taken up with caring for her grandson. She cannot earn the cost of a new bridewealth for her heartbroken son and spend her days chasing a toddler at the same time. Traditionally, Chinese kinship studies describe the horizontal conjugal and vertical intergenerational relationships as being in direct conflict with each other (Fei 1992). Rubie Watson (1985) famously analyzed relationships among brothers as a source of tensions in the distribution of kinship resources. Honglin's situation brings a new twist to these traditional conflicts,

UNITED IN SUFFERING

adding not only competition among brothers but also competition among brothers and the brothers' children. Honglin's situation reveals a new kind of intergenerationality, one that cannot be explored simply by comprehending the vertical and horizontal relational pulls; those that are directed diagonally both upwards and downwards at the same time must also be examined. As the family becomes increasingly expanded, so too are commitments increasingly in conflict. Honglin finds herself unable to meet all of these obligations.

Honglin's complaints express a desire for recognition for her unfair burdens. Meeting kinship duties through suffering is not always a sign of moral fortitude or virtuosity. Rather, Honglin's complaints highlight a profound disconnect between family expectations and contemporary ideals of the rights and responsibilities of family membership. While the grandparents with whom I spoke never anticipated the state to care for them in their old age (in contrast, see the chapter by Huang in this volume), they certainly did not expect there to be such radical shifts in terms of their positionality. "The difficulty for women in their forties," Honglin reminds us, is that not only have social changes radically restructured their economic value but also they themselves have suffered as daughters-in-law in service to the patriarchal family, and then are only to be disappointed by the partial dismantling of the family structure. They find themselves once again at the bottom of the family hierarchy with no hope of climbing to the top.

Honglin's story does have some unique points—she has an unusually large number of sons, for instance, and her son's remarriage makes her family's economic situation especially precarious. However, she shares in common with the grandparents I feature above the struggle to manage the new expectations for intergenerational cooperation and the divisions of labor. She, like many grandparents, is worried about the financial contributions of her adult children but she seems embarrassed to directly ask for more.

Discussions about suffering and hardship are a vehicle to draw attention to the mismatch between one's expectations and reality. Grandparents all utilize narratives about suffering to draw attention to this uncomfortable fit between the ideal and the reality. In some cases, these realities are shared across an entire generation, requiring a shift not only in how one thinks about one's individual life but also about how one engages with society.

7   Conclusion

I began this chapter with Auntie Tang's poem "Everything changes" to point out the ways in which a radically shifting social structure has reorganized the family as a basic unit of moral personhood and as a unit of economic survival, necessitating even more intensive intergenerational cooperation. Many authors researching intergenerational families highlight the ways in which reciprocity (Cong and Silverstein 2008; Zhang, Gu, and Luo 2014; To 2014; Coall et al. 2018) and emotional ambivalence (Hoang, Haslam, and Sanders n.d.; May, Mason, and Clarke 2012; Sadruddin et al. 2019) shape grandparenting obligations. My discussion explores suffering as a key concept in both of these theoretical frames. The struggles of three different grandparent-headed households demonstrate that suffering can be included as collaborative emotional work in reciprocal intergenerational exchanges. At the same time, suffering can lead to emotional ambivalences and complicated attitudes that characterize intensive caretaking responsibilities.

Suffering has become a key way that older people understand their labor in the intergenerational family. Without access to high-wage income, suffering becomes one benchmark affective contributions. Given that household care and labor are often invisible and devalued, the grandparents must find ways to measure their investments of time, effort, and energy. Discussions about suffering and hardship thus become a central way to frame their daily lives in an ethical and moral framework that historically has been valued as a central part of Chinese citizenship.

In referencing suffering, the above grandparents are drawing from a cultural imaginary propagated in part by the Chinese party-state. During the collective era, to suffer for the revolution was considered the highest ethical good. Attitudes of altruism, endurance, and selfless acts of nationalism were honored and encouraged by the party. A typical example of encouragement of these attributes is found in the memorializing of Lei Feng, a young martyr in the People's Liberation Army. His diary was published in 1963 and became the basis for a number of propaganda campaigns that encouraged individuals to sacrifice their lives and physical comfort for the sake of national progress (Farquhar 2002).

Vera Schwarcz argues that personal suffering is also utilized by the Chinese government to "enforce amnesia about unspeakable portions of one's own history" (1997:126). In ritualized "speak bitterness" sessions, older members of the community tell tales of woe and sorrow to indirectly praise the contemporary situation. By drawing attention to the bitterness of the past, the community frames their current sufferings in a meta-narrative of progress, which ultimately places responsibility for the progress on the actions of the party-state. In her analysis, Schwarcz (1997:121) notes the make-up of the Chinese word "*ku.*" Alternately bitterness or sadness, *ku* 苦 is made of the radical grass (⁺⁺) and the radical ancient (古), and it conveys a "notion of an old hurt grown terribly sour over time ... this appreciation for bitterness at the heart of suffering is key to all Chinese expressions of grief." In the contemporary context, suffering is found in both past and present and a progressive narrative is not always easily found in the vicissitudes of state policies.

These bitterness campaigns served to solidify class formation and unite over the hatred of the old society. A similar function can be seen when grandparents share complaints about novel kinship expectations. It is important to note that *ku* also has a healthy, positive valence as well, even without the coopting of suffering for political means. For example, eating bitter melon is thought to be beneficial to health, hence children and the elderly are often required to eat bitter melon to nourish the body. Additionally, *neng chi ku* (the ability to eat bitterness and endure suffering) is a quality that is highly regarded by my neighbors and interlocutors. While suffering has been utilized by the Chinese Communist Party to support a grand narrative of progress, suffering is a central part of the local moral code in the village. The ability to endure suffering, to work hard, and to perform heavy labor are all important ways in which villagers understand themselves and their community. In contrast to urbanites, intellectuals, and individuals who do not contribute to the family economy, rural grandparents feel that their ability to withstand hardships and to work is an important marker of identity. Suffering centers prominently in such narratives not only because everyone truly did suffer or is suffering but also because suffering is a quality that is socially desirable. Suffering is politically beneficial to the national narrative, but it is locally beneficial as well.

In effect, the values instilled by revolutionary China—a fear of idleness, a compulsion to work hard, and the nationalistic desire to contribute to a progressive narrative—have all been reinvigorated by the economic changes that have brought the family together. The dismantling of the collective system and the establishment of a totally new kind of migrant labor market effectively disenfranchised the rural elders. Simultaneously, the national household registration system radically limited the movement of children who were tied to their places of origin because of restrictive access to education. Thus two distinct generations are thrown together and are dependent upon the wage labor of the middle generation. This dependency creates new opportunities for both intimacy and conflict.

Yet suffering can only create family unity when it is shared among all parties. Whereas Uncle Jia's family demonstrates the profound emotional and practical productivity of suffering together, this kind of harmony is not shared among all the families in my study. When one party does not suffer, or seem to suffer, this places greater demands for sacrifice on one or more of the other family members. Yujie's and Honglin's cases are both effectively illustrative as they both struggle with the unequal contributions of their daughters-in-law to the household economy and labor.

A discussion about suffering, however, does not always contain a moral meaning, and the sufferer does not always end up as the moral victor. Rather, sufferers may point to suffering because of a lack of control. In other words, suffering is sometimes meaningless, random, and without a cure. The suffering of grandparents caught in changing kinship expectations is not easily alleviated. The struggle of those who suffer at the random hand of generational fate is to bear, to endure, and to find an ethically meaningful life.

References

Abstract, Nicky James. 1989. "Emotional Labour: Skill and Work in the Social Regulation of Feelings." *The Sociological Review* 37 (1): 15–42.

Alpermann, Björn. 2011. "Class, Citizenship and Individualization in China's Modernization." *ProtoSociology* 28 (April): 7–24.

Arber, Sara, Timonen Virpi, Katharina Herlofson, and Gunhild O. Hagestad. 2012. "Transformations in the Role of Grandparents across Welfare States." In *Contemporary Grandparenting: Changing Family Relationships in Global Contexts*, 27–50. Bristol: Policy Press.

Backhouse, Jan, and Anne Graham. 2012. "Grandparents Raising Grandchildren: Negotiating the Complexities of Role-Identity Conflict." *Child & Family Social Work* 17 (3): 306–15.

Baker, Hugh. 1979. *Chinese Family and Kinship*. New York: Columbia University Press.

Blake, C. Fred. 1979. "Love Songs and the Great Leap: The Role of a Youth Culture in the Revolutionary Phase of China's Economic Development." *American Ethnologist* 6 (1): 41–54.

Bordone, Valeria, Bruno Arpino, and Arnstein Aassve. 2017. "Patterns of Grandparental Child Care across Europe: The Role of the Policy Context and Working Mothers' Need." *Ageing & Society* 37 (4): 845–73.

Borneman, John. 2001. "Caring and Being Cared For: Displacing Marriage, Kinship, Gender, and Sexuality." In *The Ethics of Kinship: Ethnographic Inquiries*, edited by James D. Faubion, 29–46. Lanham, MD: Rowman & Littlefield.

Brown, Melissa J. 2016. "Dutiful Help: Masking Rural Women's Economic Contributions." In *Transforming Patriarchy: Chinese Families in the Twenty-First Century*, edited by Gonçalo D. Santos and Stevan Harrell, 91–112. Seattle: University of Washington Press.

Brownell, Susan, and Jeffrey N. Wasserstrom. 2002. *Chinese Femininities, Chinese Masculinities: A Reader*. Berkeley, Los Angeles: University of California Press.

Chan, Kam Wing, and Yuan Ren. 2018. "Children of Migrants in China in the Twenty-First Century: Trends, Living Arrangements, Age-Gender Structure, and Geography." *Eurasian Geography and Economics* 59 (2): 133–163.

Chang, Kyung-Sup. 2010. "East Asia's Condensed Transition to Second Modernity." *Soziale Welt* 61 (3/4): 319–28.

Chen, Feinian. 2014. "Patterns of Grandparents Caring for Grandchildren in China." In *The Family and Social Change in Chinese Societies*, edited by Dudley L. Poston, Jr, Wen Shan Yang, and Demetrea Nicole Farris, 165. The Springer Series on Demographic Methods and Population Analysis 35. Heidelberg, New York, London: Springer Science & Business Media Dordrecht.

Chen, Feinian, Guangya Liu, and Christine A. Mair. 2011. "Intergenerational Ties in Context: Grandparents Caring for Grandchildren in China." *Social Forces* 90 (2): 571–94.

Coall, David A., Sonja Hilbrand, Rebecca Sear, and Ralph Hertwig. 2018. "Interdisciplinary Perspectives on Grandparental Investment: A Journey towards Causality." *Contemporary Social Science* 13 (2): 159–74.

Coe, Cati. 2008. "The Structuring of Feeling in Ghanaian Transnational Families." *City & Society* 20 (2): 222–50.

Cong, Zhen, and Merril Silverstein. 2008. "Intergenerational Time-for-Money Exchanges in Rural China: Does Reciprocity Reduce Depressive Symptoms of Older Grandparents?" *Research in Human Development* 5 (1): 6–25.

Davis, Deborah, and Stevan Harrell. 1993. *Chinese Families in the Post-Mao Era*. Berkeley, Los Angeles: University of California Press.

Doley, Rebekah, Ryan Bell, Bruce Watt, and Hannah Simpson. 2015. "Grandparents Raising Grandchildren: Investigating Factors Associated with Distress among Custodial Grandparent." *Journal of Family Studies* 21 (2): 101–19.

Emick, Michelle A., and Bert Hayslip. 1996. "Custodial Grandparenting: New Roles for Middle-Aged and Older Adults." *The International Journal of Aging and Human Development* 43 (2): 135–54..

England, Paula, and Nancy Folbre. 1999. "The Cost of Caring." *The ANNALS of the American Academy of Political and Social Science* 561 (1): 39–51.

Fan, C. Cindy. 2008. *China on the Move: Migration, the State, and the Household*. London: Routledge.

Fan, Fang, Linyan Su, Mary Kay Gill, and Boris Birmaher. 2010. "Emotional and Behavioral Problems of Chinese Left-behind Children: A Preliminary Study." *Social Psychiatry and Psychiatric Epidemiology* 45 (6): 655–64.

Farquhar, Judith. 2002. *Appetites: Food and Sex in Post-Socialist China*. Durham, NC: Duke University Press.

Fei, Xiaotong. 1992. *From the Soil, the Foundations of Chinese Society: A Translation of Fei Xiaotong's Xiangtu Zhongguo, with an Introduction and Epilogue*. Berkeley; Los Angeles: University of California Press.

Folbre, Nancy. 2006. "Measuring Care: Gender, Empowerment, and the Care Economy." *Journal of Human Development* 7 (2): 183–99.

Glaser, Karen, Debora Price, Giorgio Di Gessa, Eloi Ribe, Rachel Stuchbury, and Anthea Tinker. 2013. *Grandparenting in Europe: Family Policy and Grandparents' Role in Providing Childcare*. London: Grandparents Plus.

Hoang, Nam-Phuong T., Divna Haslam, and Matthew Sanders. 2019 "Coparenting Conflict and Cooperation between Parents and Grandparents in Vietnamese Families: The Role of Grandparent Psychological Control and Parent–Grandparent Communication." *Family Process*.

Hochschild, Arlie Russell. 2003. *The Managed Heart: Commercialization of Human Feeling, Twentieth Anniversary Edition, With a New Afterword*. Berkeley; Los Angeles: University of California Press.

Jing, Jun. 2004. "Meal Rotation and Filial Piety." In *Filial Piety: Practice and Discourse in Contemporary East Asia*, edited by Charlotte Ikels, 53–62. Stanford University Press.

Kleinman, Arthur. 1988a. *The Illness Narratives: Suffering, Healing, and the Human Condition*. New York: Basic Books.

Kleinman, Arthur. 1988b. *Social Origins of Distress and Disease: Depression, Neurasthenia, and Pain in Modern China*. New Haven: Yale University Press.

Ko, Pei-Chun, and Karsten Hank. 2013. "Grandparents Caring for Grandchildren in China and Korea: Findings From CHARLS and KLoSA." *The Journals of Gerontology Series B: Psychological Sciences and Social Sciences*, December.

Levinas, Emmanuel. 1998. *Entre Nous: On Thinking-of-the-Other*. Translated by Michael B. Smith and Barbara Harshav. New York: Columbia University Press.

Li, Huaiyin. 2005. "Life Cycle, Labour Remuneration, and Gender Inequality in a Chinese Agrarian Collective." *The Journal of Peasant Studies* 32 (2): 277–303.

Lou, Vivian W. Q. 2011. "Life Satisfaction of Chinese Grandmothers: The Impact of Grandparenting Role Changes." *Journal of Ethnic & Cultural Diversity in Social Work* 20 (3): 185–202.

Luescher, Kurt, and Karl Pillemer. 1998. "Intergenerational Ambivalence: A New Approach to the Study of Parent-Child Relations in Later Life." *Journal of Marriage and Family* 60 (2): 413–25.

Mann, Susan. 2000. "Work and Household in Chinese Culture: Historical Perspectives." In *Re-Drawing Boundaries: Work, Households, and Gender in China*, edited by Barbara Entwisle and Gail Henderson, 97–110. Berkeley; Los Angeles: University of California Press.

Mattingly, Cheryl, and Linda C. Garro. 2000. *Narrative and the Cultural Construction of Illness and Healing*. Berkeley; Los Angeles: University of California Press.

May, Vanessa, Jennifer Mason, and Linda Clarke. 2012. "Being There, yet Not Interfering: The Paradoxes of Grandparenting." In *Contemporary Grandparenting: Changing Family Relationships in Global Contexts*, edited by Sara Arber and Timonen Virpi. Bristol: Policy Press.

Nyland, Berenice, Xiaodong Zeng, Chris Nyland, and Ly Tran. 2009. "Grandparents as Educators and Carers in China." *Journal of Early Childhood Research* 7 (1): 46–57.

Park, Eon-Ha. 2018. "For Grandparents' Sake: The Relationship between Grandparenting Involvement and Psychological Well-Being." *Ageing International* 43 (3): 297–320.

Roots, Charles R. 2014. *The Sandwich Generation: Adult Children Caring for Aging Parents*. London: Routledge.

Sadruddin, Aalyia F. A., Liliana A. Ponguta, Anna L. Zonderman, Kyle S. Wiley, Alyssa Grimshaw, and Catherine Panter-Brick. 2019. "How Do Grandparents Influence Child Health and Development? A Systematic Review." *Social Science & Medicine* 239 (October): 112476.

Scarry, Elaine. 1985. *The Body in Pain: The Making and Unmaking of the World*. Oxford, UK: Oxford University Press.

Schwarcz, Vera. 1997. "The Pane of Sorrow: Public Uses of Personal Grief in Modern China." In *Social Suffering*, edited by Arthur Kleinman, Veena Das, and Margaret M. Lock, 119–48. Berkeley; Los Angeles: University of California Press.

Shore, R. Jerald, and Bert Hayslip. 1994. "Custodial Grandparenting." In *Redefining Families: Implications for Children's Development*, edited by Adele Eskeles Gottfried and Allen W. Gottfried, 171–218. Boston, MA: Springer US.

Silverstein, Merril, and Zhen Cong. 2013. "Grandparenting in Rural China." *Generations-Journal of the American Society of Aging* 37 (1): 46–52.

Throop, C. Jason. 2008. "From Pain to Virtue: Dysphoric Sensations and Moral Sensibilities in Yap (Waqab), Federated States of Micronesia." *Transcultural Psychiatry* 45 (2): 253–86.

To, Clara Wai-chun. 2014. "Domestic Labor, Gendered Intergenerational Contract, and Shared Elderly Care in Rural South China." In *Social Issues in China*, 67–84. International Perspectives on Social Policy, Administration, and Practice. Springer, New York, NY.

Watson, Rubie S. 1985. *Inequality among Brothers: Class and Kinship in South China*. Cambridge [Cambridgeshire]; New York: Cambridge University Press.

Wikan, Unni. 1990. *Managing Turbulent Hearts: A Balinese Formula for Living*. Chicago: University of Chicago Press.

Wilce, James M. 2003. *Eloquence in Trouble: The Poetics and Politics of Complaint in Rural Bangladesh*. Oxford, UK: Oxford University Press.

Wolf, Margery. 1972. *Women and the Family in Rural Taiwan*. Stanford, CA: Stanford University Press.

Xu, Ling, Merril Silverstein, and Iris Chi. 2014. "Emotional Closeness between Grandparents and Grandchildren in Rural China: The Mediating Role of the Middle Generation." *Journal of Intergenerational Relationships* 12 (3): 226–40.

Yan, Yunxiang. 1997. "The Triumph of Conjugality: Structural Transformation of Family Relations in a Chinese Village." *Ethnology* 36 (3): 191.

Yan, Yunxiang. 2003. *Private Life Under Socialism: Love, Intimacy, and Family Change in a Chinese Village, 1949-1999*. Stanford, CA: Stanford University Press.

Yan, Yunxiang. 2010. "The Chinese Path to Individualization." *The British Journal of Sociology* 61 (3): 489–512.

Ye, Jingzhong, and James Murray. 2010. *Left-Behind Children in Rural China*. Reading, UK: Paths International Ltd.

Ye, Jingzhong, and Lu Pan. 2011. "Differentiated Childhoods: Impacts of Rural Labor Migration on Left-behind Children in China." *The Journal of Peasant Studies* 38 (2): 355–77.

Young, Jason. 2013. *China's Hukou System: Markets, Migrants and Institutional Change*. Berlin: Springer.

Zal, H. Michael. 2001. *The Sandwich Generation: Caught Between Growing Children And Aging Parents*. Cambridge: Da Capo Press.

Zeng, Zhen, and Yu Xie. 2014. "The Effects of Grandparents on Children's Schooling: Evidence From Rural China." *Demography* 51 (2): 599–617.

Zhang, Zhenmei, Danan Gu, and Ye Luo. 2014. "Coresidence With Elderly Parents in Contemporary China: The Role of Filial Piety, Reciprocity, Socioeconomic Resources, and Parental Needs." *Journal of Cross-Cultural Gerontology* 29 (3): 259–76.

CHAPTER 5

Floating Grandparents

Rethinking Family Obligation and Intergenerational Support

Xiaoying Qi

1 Introduction

In discussion of China's internal labour migration attention is given to the 'left-behind' elderly. The aged parents of mobile adult children who themselves relocate and are therefore not "left behind" tend to be overlooked. China's internal migration involves approximately 10 million people annually, 85% of whom are from rural areas and many of these married (Lu and Piggott 2015). During the past decade, the age of migrant workers has risen, and more of them are married with children. Previously migrant workers' children typically stayed behind with grandparents in the countryside. But migrant parents increasingly have their children with them in their destination city where opportunities for young people are greater than in their village or hometown.

When both spouses of a migrant couple work fulltime, as they typically do, a grandparent or grandparents may join them to provide childcare. Through my fieldwork a population of elderly men and women, described here as 'floating grandparents', was identified that is absent from the literature. For reasons indicated below the aged portion of the floating population is likely to continue to grow. Interviews with floating grandparents revealed that they relocated to care for their grandchildren, and indicated an intention to return to their hometown after their grandchildren reach school age. Factors relating to these decisions are explored below.

People create their lives by responding to and thus affecting social structural and institutional factors that lie beyond their immediate apprehension but with which they are intimately integrated. It will be shown that economic pressures, family law, and policies regarding pensions contribute to the need for and the pattern of intergenerational support, forces which also affect a family's capacity to provide such support. Exploration of floating grandparents adds a new dimension to understanding not only the provision of care within families in present-day China but also the relationship between mobility, family support and social reproduction. China's Sixth National Population Census reveals that in 2010 persons aged 65 years or more constituted 3.77 % of the

© XIAOYING QI, 2021 | DOI:10.1163/9789004450233_006

floating population, over 8.3 million individuals. An examination of floating grandparents sheds light not only on changes in intergenerational relations but also on changing perceptions and practices of filial obligation. This chapter is a first attempt to examine an emergent social category in China, namely 'floating grandparents' who are not 'left behind'.

2 A Neglected Population, Individualization and Family Obligation

Theorization complimentary with the literature on the 'left-behind', the women, children and elderly who remain in villages and small towns, holds that marketization in China leads to individualization, including disintegration of the family bond and of the obligation of adult children to their elderly parents (Hansen and Svarverud 2010; Yan 2011). Contrasting studies, though, show that the conditions of the left-behind elderly are likely to be materially improved by having a migrant son or daughter. Though elderly parents may receive less hands-on support from their migrant children they enjoy increased monetary support. Remittances constitute a dimension of family ties that generate interaction between migrants and families at home (Murphy 2002, 2008). Emotional ties and social relations between elderly parents and their migrant children are not necessarily abrogated by geographical distance (Cong and Silverstein 2008; and Chapter 4 by Thomason). Family obligation continues to play an important role in China, even though economic, social and cultural changes modify the expectations, attitudes and emotions through which it operates (Qi 2015, 2016).

An influential approach to intergenerational family obligation draws on social exchange theory, holding that the provision of 'rewarding services' obligates the recipient to provide 'benefits' in return (Blau 1964, 89). From this perspective childcare contributed by grandparents is reciprocated by an adult child's provision of aged care (Fingerman et al. 2009; Lei 2013). Yan (2011, 227) similarly argues that in China 'the new game of intergenerational reciprocity [is] based on market logic rather than the logic of filial piety'.

Such accounts of intergenerational exchange are arguably qualified by evidence that parents provide more help to poorer children in an effort to equalize the status and circumstances of their offspring (Grundy 2005; McGarry and Schoeni 1997). Indeed, mothers provide extensive unreciprocated support to young children, typically providing more support to children than they receive while reporting very high levels of satisfaction in their relationships with adult children across the life course (Fingerman et al. 2012; Suitor et al. 2011; Sechrist et al. 2014). Discussion below provides additional support for a nuanced understanding of intergenerational exchange that relates to need rather than equity purposively achieved.

Traditionally Chinese sons receive more from their parents than daughters, including inheritance of family property. Sons are thus traditionally responsible for supporting their aged parents. After their marriage daughters traditionally are obliged to support their in-laws, not their parents. In China today daughters increasingly provide support to their own aged parents and married daughters may provide not only more emotional but also more financial support to parents than sons (Cong and Silverstein 2008).

The present study indicates more varied and complex factors in intergenerational support than merely social exchange obligations. It does so by identifying significant emotional and symbolic aspects of intergenerational ties. Changes in the role of both adult son and daughter in providing support to aged parents are also discussed, pointing to not only the complexity of what is provided in intergenerational exchange but also by whom.

3   Method

The present chapter arose out of a larger study concerning changes in the social bases and forms of family relations in mainland China. After becoming aware of the phenomenon of floating grandparents the author sought additional interviewees, recruited through snowballing and informal contacts. Qualitative methods are particularly useful in identifying the complexities of emergent phenomena, including floating grandparents, and the dynamic contexts in which they are located. Such approaches refine existing theoretical perspectives and prepare the ground for an empirically-based and theoretically-informed examination of 'floating grandparents' in mainland China.

The present study draws on eighty-eight semi-structured in-depth interviews conducted in Beijing, Changshu, Dongguan, Guangzhou, Hefei and Shenzhen during 2015 and 2016. These cities have received a continuing influx of migrants. A company in Dongguan where interviews were conducted has a total of 151 employees, including 112 migrants. Eighteen or 16% of the latter have aged parents who relocated to help with childcare. Seven out of this 18 are blue-collar employees and 11 are white-collar. In Shenzhen, Dongguan and other cities where migrant populations are significantly larger than the local population, the numbers of floating grandparents who provide childcare precipitate civic needs that highlight aspects of general social conditions in China today and government policy designed to deal with them.

Interviews were conducted with two distinct age-groups from villages and small towns. They include 25 adult migrant workers (11 female and 14 male) and also 63 elderly respondents (40 female and 23 male). Elderly respondents' ages range from 50 to 80 years. Information provided by these distinct age-groups encourages conceptualization of concerns that are interactively negotiated by the parties involved, each with their own agency. Migrant workers interviewed include individuals in blue-collar employment (14) and white-collar employment (11). This distinction of employment type corresponds to access to different forms and amounts of resources as well as manifesting distinct orientations and adoption of different social strategies. Gender-related issues are informed by representation of men and women in the interview sample. Interviews lasted approximately one and a half hours although some were longer, the longest being three and a half hours.

Data was sorted and coded according to thematic constructions. Coding was in terms of name, age, sex, employment, income, village/town origin, reasons for relocation, relocation strategy, childcare strategy, domestic helper, health, health insurance, elderly care plan and strategy, negotiating practices, conflict patterns, conflict resolving strategies, obligation and other thematic influences. The final stage of coding focused on hypothesizing for theory development. Transcripts were read and coded for indicators of themes. Themes were labeled and organized in terms of the connections between them. Clusters of themes were then organized to create higher-order concepts. Respondent's names reported below are pseudonyms and the titles 'Mrs' and 'Mr' are indicated here for gender identification only as they are not used in China.

4 Reshaped Obligation: Relocation at an Old Age

Given high living costs, including rent or mortgage payments, employed respondents reported that it was not feasible for one spouse to remain at home while the other worked. Respondents also indicated that hiring a domestic helper was not practicable. Even middle-income white-collar workers reported that a hired domestic helper would require a considerable portion of their income, and simply beyond the means of migrant manual workers. It was reported that a domestic helper would cost approximately CNY 3,000 per month and that a 'high quality' helper, responsible, patient and skilled in communication, would cost a minimum of CNY 4,000 per month. A majority of young blue-collar male respondents earn between CNY 3,000 to CNY 4,000 per month and young blue-collar females CNY 2,000 to CNY 3,000 per month. Respondents also reported that domestic helpers could not be trusted and expressed concern that a

FLOATING GRANDPARENTS

domestic helper might physically abuse their child. From the perspective of young parents, grandparents provide the best option for childcare; they are cost effective and can be trusted to look after their grandchildren lovingly with proper care. Grandparents from small towns with a pension are perceived to have time at their disposal.

All of the aged respondents indicated that as parents they wished to reduce their own children's burden. Assistance to their adult children is seen by aged respondents as a contribution to family well-being. They indicated that it was through their assistance with childcare that their adult children are able to work and earn an income in order to support the family and pay their rent or mortgage.

Obligations of filial piety traditionally favour seniority, requiring adult children to practice '*fumu zai, bu yuanyou*' (when parents are alive, children should not travel too far afield). The elderly parents in the study's sample have themselves *yuanyou* (traveled far) to satisfy their adult children's needs. Aged respondents actively redefined their roles to satisfy the needs of their adult children, expressing strong sympathy for them; they acknowledged the demands of their children's jobs and rent or mortgage commitments, and indicated *their* obligation to support them. Rather than individualization and the erosion of family ties these patterns suggest that family connection and obligation remain strong, supported by family practices marked by innovation and variation exemplified in 'floating grandparents'.

5   Innovative "Strategies Of Action": Agency of the Elderly

Respondents indicated different relocation and childcare strategies. The arrangements entered into by floating grandparents may be complex, possibly involving more than one childcare responsibility which in turn may have a number of variant forms. One common practice involves a grandparent or grandparents relocating to provide childcare for the family of an adult child for a certain period of time in one city and then moving to another city (or another part of the same city) to provide childcare for the family of another adult child. Another common practice involves a grandparent or grandparents relocating to an adult child's city to provide childcare and another adult child's children are brought into this household so that childcare can be provided for them also. These arrangements are typically entered into when grandchildren are born in the destination city of their migrant parents. Another type of arrangement involves leaving a child with grandparents in the village or hometown of its migrant parents and after a period of time a grandparent or grandparents relocate with the child to their adult children's city to provide childcare there.

Relocation of grandparents may involve one (usually the grandmother) or both. Grandparents from small towns with pensions typically relocate together, supporting their adult children with childcare and homecare. Another possibility, typical of grandparents from the countryside with blue-collar migrant adult children, is relocation of both, with the grandmother taking responsibility for household chores and childcare and the grandfather finding employment. Sometimes the grandfather may not relocate when the grandmother moves to provide childcare but continues farming or working. This strategy also has many variant forms, including the grandfather working for part of the year and joining his wife for another part, or the grandmother moving back and forth, taking the child with her, or alternately providing support in the countryside and caring for her grandchild in the city. Windowed grandmothers most readily move to join their adult children to provide childcare.

Against a still dominant idea, that rural grandmothers are backward, passive, dependent and ignorant, the blue-collar grandmothers in the study sample demonstrate flexibility and a capacity to take initiative. Fifty-year old Ji from Guizhou joined her eldest daughter's family in 2009 when their first child, a daughter, was three and half years old. Prior to this the child was left with her paternal grandmother in a village in Shanxi but was returned to her parents when the grandmother relocated to join her younger son's family in Hubei to look after his newly born child. At this time Ji relocated to provide childcare. When her granddaughter enrolled in a childcare centre Ji remained with her daughter and son-in-law and took paid employment as a cleaner, thus contributing to the family income. When her daughter had a son in 2012 she left paid employment to resume childcare. When the grandson recently started attending a childcare centre Ji returned to work as a cleaner. While Ji alternates between providing childcare for her daughter and paid employment, another grandmother in the sample, Yue (54-year old), performs these two roles at the same time.

Yue capitalizes on the task of looking after her own grandchild by concurrently providing paid childcare for another young couple. She earns CNY 1,000 a month, which covers a number of expenses, including buying milk powder and clothes for her 83-year old mother, *hongbao* (money in red-envelopes) and presents for relatives when she returns to her village during Chinese New Year. The conventional view of aged countryside grandmothers, as helpless and passive, does not correspond with the proactive, independent and innovative senior women effectively creating new cultural forms. These grandmothers not only employ culture as a 'tool kit' for constructing 'strategies of action' (Swidler 1986), but are able to produce new 'tools'. These emergent forms arise out of the interaction between family members in dealing with new contingencies in response to their practical needs and those of their family members, in turn shaped by the wider social context in which they live.

6 Continuation and Transformation of Gender Roles

Studies show that paternal grandparents from the countryside, rather than maternal grandparents, predominantly provide childcare to their adult son's families (Chen et al. 2011, 581). This may be taken as evidence of the persistence of patriarchal tradition in rural China. Fieldwork reveals, however, that grandparents' involvement in childcare is more complex and diverse than this conclusion suggests. Grandparents from villages did report that providing childcare to sons is a taken-for-granted responsibility. Typical of the floating rural grandparents I interviewed Mr Lu (aged 63) and Mrs Luo (aged 61) from Henan lived with their elder son for more than two years in order to look after his son; they then moved to live with their younger son to look after his child. Every year they alternate between Shenzhen and their hometown, staying for half a year in each place, taking their grandsons with them when they return to their hometown. Mrs Hou arrived in Guangzhou three years prior to my interview with her from the countryside, followed by her husband Mr He, two years later, to look after their son's daughter. Together with their son, daughter-in-law and grandchild, they live in an apartment of 30 square meters, which has two small bedrooms, one occupied by the aged couple and the other by the young couple and their child. The priority of adult sons' needs suggests continuation of a rural patriarchal tradition as sons carry the family linage and responsibility for supporting aging parents. And yet paternal grandparents may provide childcare regardless of the gender of their grandchild.

Against the tradition that grandmothers provide support for their adult sons' household fieldwork findings indicate that grandmothers from the countryside increasingly provide childcare to their daughters, especially if the daughter is unable to obtain support from her mother-in-law. If an adult daughter has a child before her brother's wife, then it is highly likely that her mother shall provide childcare for her. Grandmother respondents indicated that support for their daughters did not interfere with their support for their sons. Interviewee Qiu was proud of her capable household management. She looked after her eldest daughter's first child until she was able to attend a childcare centre. By the time this daughter's second child will attend the childcare centre she anticipates that she will be able to help her second daughter with childcare. When this daughter's child is 4 or 5 years old she anticipates that her son's wife will have a child.

Fieldwork findings show that both paternal and maternal grandparents from towns are likely to provide childcare for their adult children. This parallels the urban situation reported by Jankowiak (2009) in which paternal and maternal grandparents equally care for their grandchild. With more stringent enforcement of the now lapsed one-child policy in cities and towns than in the countryside there are significant numbers of daughter-only families. In these cases grandparents readily provide childcare to their daughters. Fieldwork reveals that grandparents and grandparents-in-law may compete to provide childcare, thus generating situations in which a mother of a young child must choose between them. One possible outcome is that paternal and maternal grandparents alternate in providing childcare. Typical of the floating grandparents from small towns I interviewed, Mr Fang (aged 72) and Mrs Fu (aged 68) moved from their hometown in Hunan to Shanghai more than six years earlier to help look after their daughter's child, which they did for four years, periodically alternating childcare with their daughter's mother-in-law. The enhanced status of women and weakening preference for boys in towns and cities is one of the unintended consequences of the previous one-child policy (Fong 2002).

Daughters are reported to play an increasingly important role in providing support for elderly parents (Cong and Silverstein 2008; Hu 2017). Fieldwork findings reveal that some adult daughters from the countryside, through various strategies, are able to decide which set of grandparents provide childcare. Mrs Chu complained that her son's first child was brought up by her son's mother-in-law as her daughter-in-law preferred her own mother, using her mother's younger age as justification. Mrs Chu was called upon to join her son's family to look after their second child after her son's mother-in-law died.

Through provision of childcare gender relations between floating grandparents also change. In providing childcare grandfathers take a role traditionally reserved for women. Unlike the Muslim grandfathers who relocate from Bulgaria to Spain, reported to experience shame in this role reversal (Deneva 2012), respondents in the present study expressed a sense of achievement in their ability to care for a grandchild and thus contribute to the well-being of their adult children. Their doing so may reflect continuing adherence to an element of traditional gender difference, however, in which men operate outside the household and women within it. Grandfathers' childcare includes taking the child to kindergarten in the morning, picking the child up in the afternoon,

FLOATING GRANDPARENTS

and minding the child in the playground. Grandmothers typically engage in meal-preparation, washing and cleaning, tidying the house and baby-care.

Indeed, grandmothers' role in childcare is much more extensive than grandfathers' (Buchanan and Rotkirch 2016). During interviews and through observation I became aware that grandmothers typically play a more dominant role than their husbands in effectively expressing and enforcing views regarding domestic concerns. The greater involvement of grandmothers in household chores and grand-parenting provides them with continuing status in their multi-generational family and an affirming role, thus enhancing their own sense of importance. The place of tradition, as persistent or eroded, is a constant theme in discussion of family relations subject to social change. Examination of floating grandparents shows that cultural forms are both a resource for action and at the same time an outcome of practices which are necessarily contextualized, politically and socially (Jackson et al. 2013; Porpora 1993). Cultural change occurs not through an internal dynamic but evolves through interaction with the larger institutional framework in which it is situated (Qi 2018).

7 Intergenerational Ambivalence and the Elderly's Strategies

Floating grandparents' sense of duty and also joy in providing childcare for their adult children, and affection for their grandchild, should not be taken to imply that there is no ambivalence or conflict in these intergenerational relations. Generationally different childrearing values and practices is a frequently reported area of disagreement. Interviewees reported managing their child's academic development while leaving other aspects of upbringing to grandparents. When asked how differences between themselves and their daughters-in-law are resolved concerning childrearing, a majority of the rural grandmothers reported that they respected their daughters-in-law's views, particularly those relating to the child's academic needs. This suggests a desire to maintain a boundary of non-interference, reported for grandparents among local urban families in Beijing (Chapter 7 by Xiao) and families in Singapore and Japan (Thang et al. 2011).

Strong differences of opinion exist, nevertheless. Mrs Fu and Mr Fang did not approve of their son and daughter-in-law's buying Barbie dolls for their granddaughter: 'Barbies have long legs and naked bodies. Don't you think this will poison a child's mind?' Their son and daughter-in-law held another view: 'Wanting Barbie dolls is a small request. We only have this child. Our daughter should have what other children have'. Another child-raising difference separates the generations in this family. Mrs Fu habitually criticizes her granddaughter's shortcomings, in order for her to improve. The constant criticism makes the grand-daughter unhappy. Mrs Fu's daughter-in-law expressed the view that a child should be encouraged rather than criticized. I observed that Mrs Fu acts in her own way but at the same time avoids open confrontation with her daughter-in-law, retreating when she is present but resuming her own approach when she is not. There is a tendency to interpret intergenerational relationships in a way which either emphasizes solidarity or conflict. Ambivalence seems to be a general feature of intergenerational relations (Mehta and Thang 2012); understanding how they are managed and negotiated is important (Goh 2011; Luescher and Pillemer 1998), as indicated here.

Interview findings support recent research showing that young women reinterpret filial piety and, among other things, feel that their mothers-in-law are not entitled to unconditional deference (Shi and Pyke 2010). Mothers-in-law and not only daughters-in-law take initiative in reinterpreting and renegotiating traditional meanings of filial obligation and hierarchical intergenerational relations. Rather than make a scene regarding her daughter-in-law's open challenge to her approach in child-rearing Mrs Fu practices 'tolerance' and avoids confrontation. A number of grandparents I interviewed reported similar strategies: 'I would criticize my son straightforwardly but I would be more polite to my daughter-in-law. My son wouldn't harbor bad feelings but with a daughter-in-law *geceng dupi*' (literal: a barrier of tummy; didn't give birth to her). Grandparents' flexibility and strategies in resolving disagreements and conflicts reflect their reshaped expectations. These developments are not exclusively associated with the movement of grandparents who provide childcare to their migratory adult children. But the reconfiguration of family and household associated with the phenomenon of floating grandparents encapsulates these trends, including the active role which grandparents play in resolving family problems.

8 Refashioning Family Obligation: the Elderly's Initiatives

Traditionally family obligation operates upward, from the younger to the older and from female to male. In providing childcare to their adult children a number of grandmothers in the sample left their home and husband in order to join their adult children. This element of renegotiated family obligation is in a downward direction, aptly described as 'descending familism' (Yan 2016) or, as more recently termed, families 'upside down' (Chapter 1 by Yan). It was reported that if a husband or parent-in-law requires care because of ill health then a grandmother providing childcare away from home is likely to return, but typically through negotiation. Aged parents consistently reported directing their resources to their adult children and grandchildren, a significant break with tradition. Cooperation between family members engaged in migration invariably involves deployment of human resources and cultural repertoires in making and remaking households and therefore families which depart from traditional forms and expectations. Traditionally adult children subordinate their conjugal family to a consanguine interest. This study shows that today grandparents manage their resources to ensure the economic security of their adult children's conjugal family.

When asked about their future plans most aged respondents indicated that when their grandchildren reach school age, and their childcare is no longer needed, they intend to return to their village or town. A number of floating grandparents from small towns also indicated a preference to live close to their adult children. The reality for the majority of floating grandparents, however, is a pension that is inadequate for them to continue to live close to their adult children in the cities of their employment. A considerably improved but still under-developed state system of pensions and aged-care means that many aged parents continue to depend, wholly or partially, on their adult children for financial support and physical care. It is reported that 'just under a quarter of the mainland's elderly residents survive on pensions, while more than 40 per cent seemingly rely on family members' (Yan 2012; see also Zhou 2015).

A major concern for floating grandparents is health insurance. Some respondents have required expensive medical and dental treatment. Though a majority of them have health insurance, all except one is unable to claim expenses in their city of residence as their insurance is valid only for the area in which they have *hukou* or household registration. If a large expense is anticipated, aged respondents indicated that they would return to their local area to access health insurance. Under these circumstances travel costs constitute a further burden in addition to disruption of childcare and other household activities. Outstanding medical costs of the rural aged in the sample are generally paid by their adult children. I was told that if this is beyond their means, then other family members are likely to contribute. Aged respondents from small towns, on the other hand, typically manage to pay for their own medical expenses.

Aged respondents from small towns with pensions are typically financially independent provided they avoid serious illness and unaffordable medical expenses. Many respondents indicate that through diet and exercise they try to maintain good health and physical mobility. A shared expression among aged respondents: 'we don't want to become our children's burden'. Expectations of aged parents concerning the discharge of their adult children's filial obligations are also shaped by a realistic appreciation of practical circumstances. As Mrs Bao (aged 62), from a small town in Hubei and mother of a white-collar migrant indicated:

> I see very clearly, look at my child, can you rely on her? ... She isn't able to look after her own child. Is she able to look after us? If I'm sick, she can accompany me to the hospital. But can she stay at the hospital and look after me every day? Surely impossible! We now try our best to help her. When the day comes that we can no longer move around, we won't be able to rely on her.

Aged respondents from the countryside indicated that they want to support themselves while physically able and plan to work when they return to the village after completion of childcare. Many indicated the importance of not falling ill, to reduce their adult children's burden. Mo went back to her village for the Chinese New Year, became ill and saw a local doctor. Through allergic reaction to medication she suddenly stopped breathing. Her children, two daughters and a son, as well as sons-in-law and daughter-in-law, took leave from their work in the city and rushed to her side. She reported: 'I realize that my physical condition is not only my own concern but closely connected with the well-being of the whole family. I have to look after myself to make sure that I'm healthy and won't affect my children's work'. Aged respondents claim it is their duty to remain healthy so as to reduce the burden on their adult children. Respondents expressed relief that their aged parents have not had a major health problem with remarks such as: 'the elderly's health is our treasure'.

A number of aged parents from towns indicated their willingness to go to an elderly-care home when they could no longer look after themselves. Several grandmothers from towns indicated that they discussed their future prospects with friends, agreeing that when they can no longer look after themselves they will go to the same elderly-care home to support each other. Two grandmothers from villages expressed their willingness to go to an elderly-care home. One had indicated this wish to her three children who, as white-collar employees, she believes would be able to share the cost. Another respondent, with blue-collar children, requested that I, as a researcher, advise the central government that people like her be given sufficient pension to afford elderly-care residence. Floating grandparents place a high value on their independence and have a sense of their own agency in shaping their lives.

As noted, aged respondents express the view that they wish not to burden their adult children. Instead of emphasizing traditional filial expectations they appreciate the constraints on their adult child's time and financial capability.

FLOATING GRANDPARENTS

Discussion in the literature concerning Chinese individuals' reinterpretation and renegotiation of the meanings and practice of filial obligation focuses on young people, their preferences and behavior (Yan 2011). The initiatives which aged parents take, however, in reconstructing the established meanings of filial obligation tend to be given insufficient attention.

9 Intergenerational Support, Family Obligation, and Emotion

Through the prism of exchange theory a grandparent's provision of childcare is taken as the basis of an adult child's provision of aged care (e.g. Croll 2006). Fieldwork findings reported here, however, reveal that grandparents may sacrifice their own interests for the welfare of the whole family without expectation of a return provision. While the aged parents in the sample willingly relocated to care for grandchildren they reported that the decision to do so was not necessarily easy as they gave up a familiar lifestyle and had to adapt to a new environment. A number of grandmothers confided that they missed their hometown friends and grandparents from the countryside reported a sense of loss in giving up a big house in the village, fresh air, food of their own taste, and enjoyable activities such as planting trees, taking their food-bowl away to chat with neighbors, playing *majiang* with friends and so on.

Some grandparents reported that their decision to relocate to join their adult children to provide childcare led to a serious inner struggle because relocation entailed sacrifice, including financial loss. Two out of 26 respondents from small towns had to give up their after-retirement employment in order to join their children. With one exception, grandparents from the countryside were previously engaged in agriculture or an agricultural sideline, or worked in a local enterprise or a small shop. Respondents with employment prior to joining their adult children reported financial loss as a result of relocating. Three grandmothers from the countryside were previously migrant workers themselves and gave up employment with earnings between CNY 1,500 and CNY 2,500 per month. Interestingly, it was upon the request of their daughters-in-law that two grandmothers gave up employment and relocated to their son's city to provide childcare so that their daughters-in-law could work.

In addition to financial loss, joining adult children may entail additional deprivation for floating grandparents. Before joining her daughter's family in Guangzhou Mrs Kang, who lived in a remote village in Sichuan, enjoyed working in a relative's shop. She proudly reported that over ten people volunteered to learn fitness dance from her in the evening. She not only had many friends in the village but also a sense of satisfaction and achievement. After painstaking inner-struggles she decided to leave her home to provide childcare so that her daughter could work.

The strongly intergenerational form of Chinese families means that grandparents' sense of obligation toward their adult children and affection for a grandchild are inter-related. Obligation and affection are combined in motivation to support others (Sanghera et al. 2011). Time with grandchildren is reported in interviews as enjoyable even while its strenuous aspects are acknowledged. Grandfather Heng remarked: 'Playing with the child is joyful, nothing to worry about. An old man, being with a child, has a childlike heart, like an "old" child'. Some grandmothers remarked proudly that their grandchildren are very close to them, even closer than to their own mothers. Hu, the mother of a young child, commented on such *qinqing* (family attachment) when reflecting on her parents' and in-laws' relations with her child:

> The joy of being with their grandchild comes from their hearts, which we cannot directly give. They like being with the child, touching her head, pulling her ear, giving a kiss, giving a hug ... They are willing to spend a long time feeding my daughter ... seeing her eat gives enormous joy to them. When my daughter says things such as 'I like *nainai* (grandmother from father's side) the most', 'I like *laolao* (grandmother from mother's side) the most', *nainai* and *laolao* feel that no matter how tired they are, all the efforts are worthwhile.

Spending time with a grandchild is an engagement that provides a sense of meaning and, as a form of agency, removes anxieties. Grandfather Teng remarked, 'If we stay at *laojia* (hometown), [we'll be] idle for the whole day, nothing to do ...' Grandmothers frequently indicated that their worries went when their grandchild danced and said sweet things to them.

Role obligations and emotional aspects of intergenerational ties reported by respondents are quite unlike the instrument of exchange assumed in standard exchange theory. In social exchange theory, obligation is taken to arise from and within the exchange relation (Blau 1964, 92, 133–136; Cox and Rank 1992) but family obligation in China is prior to exchange. Feeling obligated and providing support to family members involves complex emotions and beliefs (Finch and Mason 1993; Unger 1993; Chapter 2 by Davis and Chapter 6 by Huang). Grandparents not only reported emotional satisfaction from interaction with their grandchild but also achievement of self-realization and

FLOATING GRANDPARENTS

self-pride in making a contribution to their adult children's career through provision of childcare. A number of grandparents remarked that they experience hopefulness and gain energy through the growth of their grandchildren. Through contact with their grandchildren some feel that they also 'grow'.

In addition to relief of their adult children's burden is a concern for floating grandparents' own future wellbeing. One consideration expressed by a number of respondents is that if elderly parents go to an elderly-care home, then their adult children will lose face; in the words of one young respondent: *'women nali doushi fumu gen erzi de. Buguan fumu, bieren yao ma nide'* (At our hometown elderly parents depend on sons. If sons don't provide support they will be scolded). Mr Deng from a small town, father of white-collar sons said:

> Our sons and daughters don't want us to go to an elderly-care home ... My children are concerned that they might be laughed at ... I said to my children, don't listen to other people. Many high-ranking officials, who have a lot of money and who have everything, go to elderly-care homes ... *Yanglaoyuan* are different from *jinglaoyuan* which are for those who don't have sons and daughters. Those who have money go to an elderly-care home. The service and conditions at elderly-care home are very good ... We've visited elderly-care homes in our *xian* (county), very good ...

Adult children from the countryside reported that it is still a norm in their villages that adult children have a duty to support their elderly parents. When asked about the prospect that their parents can no longer look after themselves, blue-collar migrants reported a number of possible arrangements. First, it is assumed that the dependence of their aged parent will coincide with the independence of their own children, so that they will be able to return to their village to discharge their duty to care for their aged parents. Another scenario is that their daughter-in-law may return to the village to look after her elderly in-laws, her husband remaining in employment in the city. Indeed, this is a common pattern adopted by people from the countryside. Another possibility is that adult children will take turns to care for their aged parents.

Different strategies are indicated by white-collar migrants in the sample. A hometown apartment purchased by adult child(ren) for their aged parents is a leading choice. Another approach of white collar migrants is to provide financial support to hire a domestic helper if they are themselves unable to provide physical support to aged parents. Finally, interviewees indicated a willingness to pay for residence in an elderly-care home, provided their aged parents agree. A number of adult children admitted that in comparison with their parents' generation, in which priority was given to *their* parents, the primary concern and emotional involvement of the present generation is with their children rather than their parents. They attributed this to the pressures of paid employment. A number of professional respondents regretted their inability to perform household chores, resulting from parental encouragement to focus on only academic achievement.

In spite of changing priorities, adult children indicated that they are duty-bound to support their aged parents. Qin's remarks are typical: 'I should set a good example for my children; if I'm unfilial, my children will also be unfilial'. Respondents recognized that their conduct toward their parents set an example to their child(ren) regarding their own future treatment. Given the continuing underdeveloped state-provision for aged care in China, adult children expect that their own old-age care will be provided by their children. It is thus in their interest to set a good example in their treatment of aged parents. Within internal family relationships, then, it is not contradictory that self-interest leads adult children to promote the moral virtues of filiality, which is best demonstrated by their support of their aged parents. Self-interest here does not relate to intergenerational exchange directly but to the socialization of children for their future filial responsibility. In this way the interactive effect of state regulation on the one hand and individual interests on the other articulate in advancement of values that draw upon the language of filiality, even though its form and practice depart from traditional codes.

Intergenerational support does not simply reflect the Confucian principle of filial obligation, but is cemented in current law. The Marriage Law of 1950 and all subsequent related legislation explicitly stress the reciprocal obligations of family members for support. Similarly, the 2012 Law on the Protection of the Rights and Interests of Seniors, which replaced the 1996 law, strengthens family obligation requirements. Article 13 states that 'aged care is primarily home-based; family members should respect, care about and look after the elderly'; the statements concerning 'primarily home-based' care and 'respect' are new elements in the law (LPRIS2012, Article 13). The new Article 18 goes so far as to require that 'family members should care about the elderly's spiritual needs ... [and those] family members who do not reside with the elderly should frequently visit or pay respect to the elderly' (LPRIS 2012, Article 18). The emphasis on family obligation in the law reflects China's undeveloped welfare infrastructure. Chinese elderly people have never benefitted from social rights of citizenship in which state support is assumed. The basis in Europe of state-subsidized aged care comes from a long history of not only a liberal economy, social democracy and the welfare state, but also two world wars in which universal military service led to post-war welfare entitlements, none of which occurred in China's history.

10 Conclusion

It has been shown that a problem of childcare arises for families in China's floating population of rural-to-urban migration when both spouses are in paid employment. A self-generated solution is migration of grandparents to sites of their adult children's residence. A conventional image persists of vulnerable children and elderly 'left behind' in the villages and towns from which mobile young adults depart. The research reported here, though, identifies a distinct development in which aged parents join the floating population rather than remain behind; they provide childcare in the cities where their adult children are employed. This chapter contributes to a more complete representation of the so-called 'floating population' and therefore to a more comprehensive understanding of internal migration and family processes in mainland China.

Migration studies 'continue to be dominated by the treatment of people as labor moving across borders or, at best, as movement of individuals in a family, but not as a process related to the continuity of the household in social reproduction' (Douglass 2006, 421). The present study shows how grandparents may move between localities and social settings to provide childcare facilitating their adult children's participation in paid urban employment. It empirically demonstrates the importance of treating the household rather than the individual as a unit of analysis in migration studies. The literature shows that migration decisions are taken by families rather than individuals. The present study empirically confirms the research benefits of treating grandparents' childcare as a form of reproductive labor enabling the continuation of their adult children's labor force participation, thus contributing to social reproduction (Misra et al. 2006). It also shows that the migratory movement of elderly parents exacerbates issues concerning their welfare. Indeed, the chapter contributes to the growing broader interest in grandparenting (Buchanan and Rotkirch 2016; Mehta and Thang 2012; Thang et al. 2011).

The chapter contributes to the literature on family relationships, including family obligation. Cultural and social changes promote new norms and modify established norms, including conventions associated with filial obligation. Political reform and marketization in China have impacted on family life, including family responsibilities and the capacities through which they are discharged. In general terms, intergenerational family responsibility continues to have high salience in China even though geographic mobility changes the context in which it operates. While changes in family obligation initiated by young people has received much research attention, this chapter shows that grandparents, rather than maintaining traditional meanings of filial obligation, may initiate, reinterpret and negotiate current meanings and practices.

The chapter also contributes to the development of our understanding of intergenerational support. Research which theorizes intergenerational support in terms of exchanges of resources and resulting obligations tends to overlook the important role of pre-exchange obligation, emotional attachment and symbolic values in intergenerational interactions. The discussion here presents an empirically-based approach to intergenerational support through examination of an emergent social group, floating grandparents.

References

Blau, Peter. 1964. *Exchange and Power in Social Life*. New York: Wiley.

Buchanan, Ann and Anna Rotkirch, eds. 2016. *Grandfathers: Global Perspectives*. London: Palgrave/Macmillan.

Chen, Feinian, Guangya Liu and Christine Mair. 2011. "Intergenerational Ties in Context: Grandparents Caring for Grandchildren in China." *Social Forces* 90(2): 571–594.

Cong, Zhen and Merril Silverstein. 2008. "Intergenerational Support and Depression among Elders in Rural China." *Journal of Marriage and Family* 70(3): 599–612.

Cox, Donald and Donald Rank. 1992. "Inter-vivos Transfers and Intergenerational Exchange." *Review of Economics and Statistics* 72(2): 305–314.

Croll, Elizabeth. 2006. "The Intergenerational Contract in the Changing Asian Family." *Oxford Development Studies* 34(4): 473–491.

Deneva, Nede. 2012. "Transnational Aging Carers." *Social Politics* 19(1): 105–128.

Douglass, Mike. 2006. "Global Householding in Pacific Asia." *International Development Planning Review* 28(4): 421–445.

Finch, Janet and Jennifer Mason. 1993. *Negotiating Family Responsibilities*. London: Routledge.

Fingerman, Karen, Laura Miller, Kira Birditt and Steven, Zarit. 2009. "Giving to the Good and the Needy: Parental Support for Grown Children." *Journal of Marriage and Family* 71(5): 1220–1233.

Fingerman, Karen, Jori Sechrist and Kira Birditt. 2012. "Intergenerational Ties in a Changing World." *Gerontology* 59(1): 64–70.

Fong, Vanessa. 2002. "China's One-Child Policy and the Empowerment of Urban Daughters." *American Anthropologist* 104: 1098–1109.

Goh, Esther. 2011. *China's One-Child Policy and Multiple Caregiving*. London: Routledge.

Grundy, Emily. 2005. "Reciprocity in Relationships." *British Journal of Sociology* 56(2): 233–255.

Hansen, Mette and Rune Svarverud, eds. 2010. *iChina: The Rise of the Individual in Modern Chinese Society*. Copenhagen: NIAS Press.

Hu, Anning. 2017. "Providing more but Receiving less: Daughters in Intergenerational Exchange in Mainland China. *Journal of Marriage and Family* 79(3): 739–757.

Jackson, Stevi, Petula Ho and Jin Nye Na. 2013. "Reshaping Tradition? Women Negotiating the Boundaries of Tradition and Modernity in Hong Kong and British Families." *Sociological Review* 61(4): 667–687.

Jankowiak, William. 2009. "Practicing Connectiveness as Kinship in Urban China." In *Chinese Kinship*, edited by Susanne Brandtstadter and Goncala Santos, 67–91. London: Routledge.

Lei, Lei. 2013. "Sons, Daughters, and Intergenerational Support in China." *Chinese Sociological Review* 45(3): 26–52.

LPRIS. 1996. Zhonghua Renmin Gongheguo Laonianren Quanyi Baozhangfa. (*Law on the Protection of the Rights and Interests of Seniors*).

LPRIS. 2012. Zhonghua Renmin Gongheguo Laonianren Quanyi Baozhangfa (*Law on the Protection of the Rights and Interests of Seniors*).

Lu, Bei and John Piggott. 2015. "Meeting the Migrant Pension Challenge in China." *CESifo Economic Studies* 61(2): 438–464.

Luescher, Kurt and Karl Pillemer. 1998. "Intergenerational Ambivalence: A New Approach to the Study of Parent-child relations in Later Life." *Journal of Marriage and the Family* 60(2): 413–425.

McGarry, Kathleen and Robert Schoeni. 1997. "Transfer Behavior within the Family." *Journal of Gerontology, Social Sciences* 52B (Special Issue): 82–92.

Mehta, Kalyani and Leng Leng Thang, eds. 2012. *Experiencing Grandparenthood: An Asian Perspective*. London: Springer.

Misra, Joya, Jonathan Woodring and Sabine Merz. 2006. "The Globalization of Care Work: Neoliberal Economic Reconstructing and Migration Policy." *Globalizations* 3(3): 317–332.

Murphy, Rachel. 2002. *How Migrant Labor is Changing Rural China*. Cambridge: Cambridge University Press.

Murphy, Rachel. 2008. "Migrant Remittances in China." In *Labor Migration and Social Development in Contemporary China*, edited by Rachel Murphy, 47–72. London: Routledge.

Porpora, Douglas. 1993. "Cultural Rules and Material Relations." *Sociological Theory* 11(2): 212–229.

Qi, Xiaoying. 2015. "Filial Obligation in Contemporary China: Evolution of the Culture-system." *Journal for the Theory of Social Behaviour* 45(1): 141–161.

Qi, Xiaoying. 2016. "Family Bond and Family Obligation: Continuity and Transformation." *Journal of Sociology* 52(1): 39–52.

Qi, Xiaoying. 2018. "Neo-traditional Child Surnaming in Contemporary China: Women's Rights as Veiled Patriarchy." *Sociology* 52(5): 1001–1016.

Sanghera, Balihar, Mehrigiul Ablezova and Aisalkyn Botoeva. 2011. "Everyday Morality in Families and a Critique of Social Capital." *Theory and Society* 40(2): 167–190.

Sechrist, Jori, Jill Suitor, Abigail R. Howard and Karl Pillemer. 2014. "Perceptions of Equity, Balance of Support Exchange, and Mother-adult Child Relations." *Journal of Marriage and Family* 76(2): 285–299.

Shi, Lihong. 2017. *Choosing Daughters: Family Change in Rural China*. Standford: Stanford University Press.

Shih, Kristy and Karen Pyke. 2010. "Power, Resistance, and Emotional Economies in Women's Relationships with Mothers-in-Law in Chinese Immigrant Families." *Journal of Family Issues* 31(3): 333–357.

Suitor, Jill, Jori Sechrist, Megan Gilligan and Karl Pillemer. 2011. "Intergenerational Relations in Later-Life Families." In *Handbook of Sociology of Aging*, edited by Richard Settersten and Jacqueline L. Angel, 161–178. New York: Springer.

Swidler, Ann. 1986. "Culture in Action: Symbols and Strategies." *American Sociological Review* 51(2): 273–286.

Thang, Leng Leng, Mehta, Kalyani, Tsuneo Usui and Mari Tsuruwaka. 2011. "Being a Good Grandparent: Roles and Expectations in Intergenerational Relationships in Japan and Singapore." *Marriage and Family Review* 47(8): 548–570.

Unger, Jonathan. 1993. "Urban families in the Eighties." In *Chinese Families in the Post-Mao Era*, edited by Deborah Devis, and Sevan Harrell. Berkeley: University of California Press, pp. 25–49.

Yan, Alice. 2012. "Most elderly rely on family, not pensions." *South China Morning Post* (October 24).

Yan, Yunxiang. 2011. "The Individualization of the Family in Rural China." *Boundary 2* 38(1): 203–229.

Yan, Yunxiang. 2016. "Intergenerational Intimacy and Descending Familism in Rural North China." *American Anthropologist* 118(2): 244–257.

Ye, Jingzhong and Congzhi He. 2008. *Jingmo Xiyang: Zongguo Nongcun Liushou Laoren* (Lonely sunset: The Left-behind Elderly in China's Countryside). Beijing: Shehui Kexue Wenxian Chubanshe.

Zhou, Laura. "Home for Aged who Lose Only Child." *South China Morning Post*, June 23, 2015.

CHAPTER 6

Families Under (Peer) Pressure

Self-Advocacy and Ambivalence among Women in Collective Dance Groups

Claudia Huang

1 Together on Their Own

Retired women living in urban China must contend with a fundamental tension in their lives: on the one hand, they are freer than ever before to live their lives on their own terms; on the other hand, expectations that older women devote themselves to their families remain salient in Chinese society and can become especially intense as these women become grandmothers. For women who participate in common-interest social groups, such as congregational dance groups, known colloquially as *da ma* in Chinese or "dancing grannies" in English, an additional layer of complications may arise as they struggle to balance these two diametrically opposed forces. Dance groups are made up of people who come together of their own volition in order to pursue their personal interests. With the exception of some groups that are formed by community officials, urban dance groups are almost entirely self-organized. The groups are, in essence, held together by the participants' desires to engage in self-cultivation and to spend time on relationships and hobbies of their own choosing. This means that when any one person chooses to honor her family obligations over her own interests, including dancing, others in the dance group are also affected.

This chapter examines the uneasy balance that retired women try to strike when confronted with the tensions between self-interest and morally laden family obligations in post-reform urban China as well as how friendships figure into this fraught calculus. Most of urban China's *da ma* belong to the so-called sandwich generation (see Zhang and Goza 2006; Tu 2016) and perform the lion's share of care-giving duties in their families. In addition to often being expected to care for their grandchildren, many also have elderly parents and parents-in-law who require attention and resources. The result, as scholars have noted, is widespread exhaustion and stress associated with care-giving among women in this age cohort (Chen, Liu, and Mair 2011; Goh 2011). Further complicating matters is the fact that the relative social status of middle-aged and elderly women has declined in recent years. While elders—and grandmothers would

© CLAUDIA HUANG, 2021 | DOI:10.1163/9789004450233_007

have certainly been counted as elders—commanded a great deal of respect in traditional Chinese kinship hierarchies, the gravitational center of Chinese families has recently begun to shift away from elders and toward young children (Fong 2002; Kipnis 2009; Yan 2016).

All this is to say that the tide has shifted against Chinese elders and people in the sandwich generation have plenty to complain about. Their current predicament can be traced to the numerous changes in the traditional family structure that have occurred since the middle of the past century, including Chinese Communist Party policies that destabilized patriarchal authority as well as pressures from the market economy that rendered traditional family structures untenable (Davis and Harrell 1993; Yan 2003; Santos and Harrell 2017). None of these changes have made the bonds of kinship insignificant. They have, however, introduced new challenges to family cohesion as well as emerging opportunities for individual family members to negotiate their relationships with one another.

The nature, content, and stakes of these negotiations are the focus of this chapter. Elsewhere in this volume, Erin Thomason argues that long-suffering grandparents in rural areas invoke their misery as their contribution to their families; without the ability to offer their children financial support and without the means to support themselves in later life if they do not receive care from these same children, they have no choice but to frame the indignity of their present situations as necessary sacrifices made on the altar of family solidarity. Though retired urban women echo many of the same complaints about inverted family dynamics, their relative financial independence from their children (due to high rates of home ownership and monthly pension payments from their former public-sector employers) allow them more options to navigate the trend of descending familism that is experienced by all Chinese elders.

Given their relatively privileged circumstances, many urban retirees have the option to prioritize personal interests over family obligations, particularly if they believe their family dynamics are too heavily skewed to their disadvantage. I have argued elsewhere (Huang 2016) that women who participate in congregational dance groups use these groups as vehicles for self-expression and as places where they can carve out meaningful lives on their own terms. But because this self-cultivation takes place within a collective enterprise, the demands of personal interest and friendship are closely interlinked. In a society where putting one's family before one's own personal interests is still widely considered the morally righteous course of action, choosing to honor one's own concerns over those of one's family requires the support, validation,

FAMILIES UNDER (PEER) PRESSURE

and in some cases forceful persuasion from one's friends. In other words, in order for these women to live lives of their own, they must stick together.

While the study of kinship has a long tradition in anthropology, the literature on friendship is considerably thinner. According to scholars such as Pitt-Rivers (1973) and Carrier (1999), this relative oversight can be attributed to an often-held assumption that kinship ties are permanent, universal, and compulsory, whereas and friendships are ephemeral, idiosyncratic, and voluntary. There have been a few notable studies that challenge these assumptions by highlighting the ways in which solidarity among friends can be important not only for mitigating risks and creating social cohesion, but in some cases they are even crucial for survival (see Abrahams 1999; Gratz 2004; Santos-Granero 2007). The retired women who participate in congregational dance groups are not grappling for survival. They are, however, engaged in a struggle to maintain their senses of self while inhabiting the bottom tier of the family hierarchy. Even though the friendships I examine in this chapter vary in terms of closeness and intensity, they are all, as Jane Dyson (2010) would say, settings for social production because, for those people who participate in them, they function as avenues for self-preservation or self-improvement.

1.1   *Setting and Methods*

The chapter is based on my dissertation research on China's uniquely popular congregational dancing phenomenon. I conducted this research over a period of eighteen months between 2014 and 2018 in Chengdu, Sichuan province. I was born in Chengdu and spent eight years of my childhood there; returning to Chengdu to conduct research was a logical choice for me, both because my fluency in the local Sichuanese dialect allowed for easy conversations with retirees (many people in Sichuan over the age of 55 do not speak Mandarin well) and because it offered me a chance to revisit a place where I have many memories. In 2014 and 2015, I began by surveying more than two dozen groups throughout the city to get a sense of the overall composition, structure, and governance of the groups. After two summers of preliminary research getting to know as many groups as possible, I spent eleven months doing participant observation with the members of two dance groups: the "Dancing Beauties Group," consisting of twenty members who meet to dance together once a week in a studio space, and the "Sunset Dance Group," consisting of about thirty members who dance on a daily basis in a small square near a market. (These group names are what they use to refer to themselves on the popular social media app WeChat.) Of the total of forty-eight women who participated in either the Sunset Dance Group or the Dancing Beauties Group at the end of 2017 when I left the field, no fewer than thirty-nine were new grandparents, meaning that they had a grandchild or grandchildren under the age of 6. Five women were not (yet) grandmothers, and four women had grandchildren who were already in primary school or older.

In addition to dancing with them on a regular basis, I also joined the groups for meals, shopping trips, and occasional social outings. Though the congregational dancing phenomenon was the focus and organizing principle of my research, the scope of my study expanded over the course of my time in Chengdu as I learned more about the women and their changing outlooks about their families, their personal goals, and the future.

In what follows, I present three cases that showcase just how tensions between family duties and individual interests can collide for retired urban women who are grandmothers, and I focus on how their friendships are interwoven into these already complex situations. The first case demonstrates the ways in which congregational dancers use social pressure to bully a group member who, according to the group's estimation, spends too much time and energy tending to her family duties. The second case further illuminates how much dance groups rely on the participants' continued commitment to the group and how the group dynamics may be threatened when participants have other priorities. In the third case, I zero in on two friends whose very different styles of managing the aforementioned tensions between self-interest and family duty threaten to come between them. I conclude with some conjectures about where these rumblings of discontent might lead and the implications of the greater emphasis on personal happiness in the family lives of Chinese urban retirees.

2   Three Case Studies

2.1   *Case One: Bullying Qiu*

The Dancing Beauties Group held its annual end-of-year party at an upscale karaoke bar in one of Chengdu's ritziest neighborhoods. Karaoke in China is perhaps best known as an evening activity for groups of young professionals and businessmen; deals are negotiated between rounds of singing and young female hostesses lubricate the conversation with ample amounts of liquor. But at two o'clock in the afternoon, when private rooms are available at an early-bird discount, karaoke bars are havens for retirees who wish to belt out songs from revolutionary-era films and pop singles from the 1980s and 1990s. Afternoon karaoke was a favorite pastime of the Dancing Beauties, and on this occasion, the group's de-facto leader Teacher Yuan booked a private room with

FAMILIES UNDER (PEER) PRESSURE 127

money left over from the group's membership dues. On the appointed day and time, the group met in the lobby and made its way to the second floor, where private rooms lined both sides of a long, brightly lit corridor.

Everyone was settling in with the usual greetings, snacks, and song selections when a woman whom I had never seen before walked into the room. She was short statured, had auburn-hair, and looked to be in her late fifties. She glanced around a little nervously before someone spotted her and ran toward the door where she stood, shouting greetings along the way. She was soon mobbed by nearly everyone in the room. Someone asked her if she had lost weight. Someone else complimented her on her purple sweater. Everyone wanted to know how the baby was. I was left sitting alone in the far corner, utterly confused by the fact that this seeming stranger was being treated like an old friend. By that time, I had already been a member of the Dancing Beauties Group for four months. Though some people attended the dance practices only sporadically, it did not seem possible that I could have completely overlooked someone. The mystery was short-lived. I soon learned that the newcomer was actually a four-year veteran of the group named Qiu. Her son and daughter-in-law had welcomed their first child less than two weeks prior to my arrival in Chengdu, and Qiu had been away because she had taken on full-time caregiving duties for her infant grandchild.

I was not the only one who found Qiu's seemingly abrupt re-appearance to the dance group's social scene noteworthy. As the afternoon wore on and people took turns singing their karaoke selections, Qiu fielded a number of questions—some of them quite pointed—about why she had failed to keep in touch during her absence and why she had been away for so long. She demurred on most of the questions, claiming that she was simply too busy to keep up with the online group chats and she was too tired to come to the dance classes. Her friends did not let her off the hook so easily. As the karaoke session concluded and the group made its way to a nearby restaurant for dinner, group members continued to harangue her about how she was handling her transition into grandmotherhood.

It was apparent from the start that Qiu prioritized maintaining good relations with her son and daughter-in-law. It became clear that most of the other women interpreted Qiu's devotion to her son's new nuclear family as a weakness or even a sense of capitulation. "When is your daughter-in-law going to let you have your next night off?" a group member named Jiaming asked as we sat down to eat. Her thinly veiled suggestion that Qiu was at the mercy of her daughter-in-law—a direct reversal of the customary hierarchy in traditional Chinese families—caused quite a stir around the table. Several of the women chuckled and even clapped, and everyone directed glances at Qiu to see how she would respond. Qiu laughed along but did not answer. The teasing reached a peak when, at the end of the meal, Qiu ordered extra portions of food to bring home for the young couple. "Oh, you are such an obedient mother-in-law!" exclaimed a normally soft-spoken group member named Yun. Again, everyone at the table burst into laughter. Perhaps because it had come from the gentle-tempered Yun, or perhaps because the comment was particularly barbed, Qiu's shoulders dropped and her cheeks became engulfed in a deep blush. The word Yun had used for "obedient" was *ting hua,* literally translated as "listen to words" [of authority]. It is a term that is often used when praising young children for good behavior (see Xu 2017), but it is never used to refer to an adult without some sense of irony or deprecation as the subtext.

For the first time that day, Qiu attempted to defend herself: she explained that her son and daughter-in-law loved the type of food served at the restaurant but had not had a chance to enjoy it since the baby's arrival. Unfortunately, this explanation only added fuel to the fire. Several people laughed, and someone pointedly jeered, "look at you being so filial!" Again, by "praising" Qiu in a manner usually reserved for children (after all, filial piety is defined as respect for one's elders), the women in the group aimed to draw attention to Qiu's (from their perspective) transgressive behavior and to shame her for it.

It is crucial to note that although the women in the Dancing Beauties Group invoked the language and norms of the traditional family hierarchy and used them as rhetorical weapons, they actually were not trying to enforce these norms. On the contrary, by taunting and insulting Qiu for her devotion to her family, they were building solidarity in an effort to establish new norms— norms that do not take a grandmother's financial and emotional resources for granted. This was a feat that they could not accomplish as individuals. The group's overt cruelty toward Qiu can be explained by the fact that Qiu was crossing the picket line, so to speak, by continuing to make sacrifices on behalf of her adult children. As the women's reactions to Qiu's relatively compliant disposition toward her son and daughter-in-law demonstrate, there was significant social pressure to show one's willingness to "fight back" against the inverted family dynamics.

But it turned out that Qiu had given more thought to the inherent tensions in her situation than her friends had given her credit for. At the end of the evening, Teacher Yuan suggested that Qiu and I catch the bus together since we happened to live in the same part of town. Under the increased scrutiny of her friends and group-mates, Qiu had been good-natured but cagey, rarely adding more than a few words to any exchange for fear that the conversation might turn on her. It was only after we sat down on the bus that Qiu started speaking with me candidly. At my gentle urging, she revealed that she longed to return to the group and that although she adored her grandson, she resented that he kept her from participating in her own social life. She even admitted that she was glad that the end was in sight: her daughter-in-law's six months of maternity leave would soon be over, after which the baby would be sent to live with the daughter-in-law's parents in another city, thus releasing Qiu from her care-giving duties.

Qiu is hardly alone in her ambivalence: confusion and doubt seem to be the primary emotions among many women with whom I spoke about the choice between taking care of their grandchildren and enjoying their retirement on their own terms. They are all-too-aware of the inverted power dynamics in the family and they must weigh their own wishes against the risks of displeasing their adult children. Whereas Qiu made major social sacrifices in order to take care of her grandson, in her mind there would have been even greater repercussions had she refused: her daughter-in-law who would have had to go to live with her own parents for the duration of her maternity leave unless Qiu had agreed to help care for the infant in Chengdu. By all accounts, Qiu got along quite well with her son and daughter-in-law and it is unlikely that they were intentionally taking advantage of her. Nevertheless, they put her in the situation of having to choose between giving up her social life for six months or giving up the chance to bond with her infant grandson. Throughout our thirty-minute conversation, Qiu alternated between saying that she was looking forward to resuming her regular activities and that she was dreading the day when she would be separated from her grandchild.

Despite the relentless onslaught of not entirely good-humored taunting, the women in the Dancing Beauties Group stopped short of asking Qiu to abdicate her grandmotherly responsibilities in favor of spending more time with the group. Though at some point every woman asked her when she would be able to come dance again, no one actually pressed her to take time off from her childcare duties or offered her any practical suggestions on how she could get away from the family. Nevertheless, the group's bullying was clearly meant to send the message that Qiu's behavior was unacceptable. Moreover, by casting Qiu in a child-like position in their pointed jokes about filial piety and obedience, the group members were also seeking to undermine Qiu's sense of personal autonomy and to impress upon her that she would not receive the group's support until she demonstrated that she could assert her independence from her son, his wife, and her grandchild. The result was that at the end of the evening, Qiu was more conflicted than ever about how to balance her duties to her family, to her dance group, and to herself.

2.2   *Case Two: Committing to Teacher Yuan*
A few weeks after the end-of-year karaoke party, Teacher Yuan told the Dancing Beauties Group that her son was expecting a child with his fiancée, due in late

spring. The announcement immediately threw everyone into a panic. People assumed that Teacher Yuan would cancel dance classes for an indefinite amount of time after the baby's arrival. Teacher Yuan took great joy in correcting this assumption. "Not only will I keep teaching classes," she proclaimed," I have also signed up for both the singing class *and* the African drum class at Old Age University during the summer term!" When incredulous group members asked how she planned to balance these activities with her care-giving duties, Teacher Yuan replied that the two sets of grandparents (meaning herself and her future daughter-in-law's parents) would take turns caring for the baby. "It's unreasonable to expect me to drop everything," she explained. "I have my own life to live, you know!" At this, the group enthusiastically praised Teacher Yuan for her independent attitude and a few women who did not yet have a grandchild vowed to emulate her when their time came.

Teacher Yuan is intensely dedicated to the Dancing Beauties Group and leads it with the precision and iron will of a military commander. Not only does she teach the group's weekly dance classes but she also single-handedly manages the group's finances, sets its agendas, and makes announcements via WeChat. I will admit I was skeptical that Teacher Yuan would be able to follow through on her intentions after the baby arrived, but she proved me wrong. Her granddaughter was born in early May and the dance classes resumed after a brief two-week hiatus. Teacher Yuan attended the courses at Old Age University as planned and in early July she even organized a group day trip to the countryside to pick peaches.

As it turned out, the group was threatened not by Teacher Yuan's family commitments but rather by her disappointment in the other members' inability to match her dedication to the group. In late September, a few hours before the afternoon dance class was scheduled to begin, the Dancing Beauties' WeChat group was flooded with messages from people excusing themselves from attendance due to various scheduling conflicts and illnesses. A few people usually excuse themselves each week, but this week had an unusual number of absences. It soon became clear that a majority of the class would not be in attendance. Teacher Yuan remained silent while people were sending their regrets and excuses, but just a few minutes prior to the start of the class she finally replied: "It looks like everyone is quite busy. After this semester is over, we will no longer hold this dance class."

When I arrived a few minutes late to the dance studio where the classes were held, I saw that there were only five people present—a very low turnout. Teacher Yuan made no mention of the absences and carried on as usual. No one spoke of the ominous WeChat announcement until the class had ended. As we filed out of the studio building and into the parking lot, Jiaming gently

FAMILIES UNDER (PEER) PRESSURE

approached Teacher Yuan, who had headed straight for her electric scooter and was busy stuffing her belongings into the front basket. "Please give us another chance," Jiaming began. "I'll go home and tell the others that they have to stop taking breaks for no good reason." The rest of us gathered around. "I'll tell them to respect your time more," Jiaming continued as Teacher Yuan fussed with her scooter, pretending not to hear. "You take such pains with us! It's not right that they don't come." At this, Teacher Yuan finally looked up and began airing some of her long-held grievances. "It's not that I don't want to teach the class anymore," she complained. "It's that people really don't seem to have the time. I don't know why they don't have the time! I had to bathe my granddaughter before I came! And I still made it here on time!"

All of us gathered around her scooter agreed that it should not be so difficult to make a commitment for just a few hours per week, but Teacher Yuan was not satisfied. "I have never taken a break, you know! I have never a missed class, never! In all these years!" Jiaming agreed: "Yes, Sister Yuan," she said, switching to an affectionate term of address. "*Ni zhen xinku le*" [You really have worked so hard/suffered so much.] And in the future if you need to take a break, just let us know!" Teacher Yuan, however, was entirely immune to their entreaties. She declared that we could all still be friends, and that she would organize get-togethers once in a while so that everyone could stay in touch.

Later in the evening, Jiaming wrote a long message to the WeChat group thanking Teacher Yuan for her generous guidance, pledging that everyone will work harder in the future and begging Teacher Yuan to continue leading the classes. Others, including those who had been absent, soon chimed in. Most people offered similar assurances that things would be different going forward, but a few went even further. Someone posted an appointment confirmation for an optometry visit. Someone else posted a photo of a thermometer showing a feverish temperature. Yun wrote a lengthy explanation that she had been recruited for a *qipao* (a type of traditional Chinese dress) modeling competition and that against her wishes the organizers had scheduled rehearsals that day. She shared the rehearsal schedule, emphatically adding that she hated missing class. It was only when Ying, one of the group's most dedicated participants, wrote to say that her husband was in the hospital with appendicitis and expressed her regrets for her absence that Teacher Yuan finally broke her silence: "I know about your husband, Ying! You should take care of yourself too!"

After several more days of intermittent pleading, Teacher Yuan finally relented. The Dancing Beauties Group continued to hold weekly classes at the dance studio. But the short-lived episode not only provided further proof that dance groups demand loyalty and commitment from their members, it also revealed the internal logic of how the members' loyalties are assessed and enforced. It is noteworthy that Teacher Yuan made a big deal about not allowing her new granddaughter to take precedence over the dance group, and she broke her silence only upon hearing of Ying's husband's illness. Over the course of the year that I spent with them, I slowly learned that there was a hierarchy of excuses for missing class among the women: taking care of grandchildren was seen as the least legitimate reason, choosing to honor another personal commitment (such as Yun's *qipao* competition) was somewhere in the middle, and skipping class for a spouse or parent's illness was universally accepted and supported. For example, though the group bullied Qiu for dropping out of the group for several months to attend to her newborn grandson, people were quite supportive when another group member had to take a similar-length leave to help her father recover from a stroke.

The Dancing Beauties are not the only group to have these sorts of unspoken rules. In the weeks leading up to a major dance competition, Auntie Wang, the de-facto leader of the Sunset Dance Group, sent the group a very serious WeChat message explicitly stating that the only acceptable reasons for missing practice were medical issues for one self or for one's parents. Though children and grandchildren were not mentioned in the directive, the implication was understood by all: the demands of the younger generations cannot supersede those of the group. This point was further confirmed when Auntie Wang's pregnant daughter went into labor a month earlier than expected, which prompted Auntie Wang (who missed several days of rehearsals to tend to her daughter and new granddaughter) to send continuous apologetic messages from the hospital maternity ward asking her dance group friends for their understanding.

By the end of my fieldwork, the at-times murky attitudes toward different types of kin relations that shaped the dance groups' strategies to ensure dedication among the members began to coalesce into a clearer picture: participants were duty-bound to tend to their parents and to their spouses in times of need, but extending this same care to one's children and grandchildren was often regarded as a personal choice somewhat different from, or outside of, one's family obligations. Although the traditional moral frameworks of filial piety and family duty apply when dealing with the older generations, these women know very well that their children may never be able to reciprocate these acts of care, and thus they approach the latter relationships with a shrewder, more calculating attitude that provides more space for placing a priority on their own self-interest. But because these internal rules run contrary to the official discourse on family matters, and because they are often left unspoken and unratified by the groups themselves, they require constant—and at times painful— negotiations. The next case is an example of how such negotiations

FAMILIES UNDER (PEER) PRESSURE

can bring emotionally fraught tensions to the surface, which in turn can test the bonds of both kinship and friendship.

2.3 Case Three: Putting a Price on Care

My final example focuses on a dispute between two Sunset Dance Group women, named Wenxie and Liwei. Though they share a close friendship and generally get along well, their different approaches to grandmotherhood is a source of continuous tension. They had apparently been fighting about this for years, but I first learned of their conflicts in the winter of 2016, when one day Wenxie, Liwei, and I decided to go shopping together after a dance practice. There was a seasonal mall on the outskirts of the city that specialized in food and decorations for the upcoming Spring Festival, and our plan was for each of us to go to our respective homes after practice, change clothes, eat lunch, and then meet at a nearby bus station. The holiday was just a few weeks away and we all wanted to buy snacks and gifts for our families. Liwei and I met at the appointed time and sat down at the bus stop to wait for Wenxie. Five minutes passed. Liwei sent a text message to Wenxie. No response. After another five minutes, Liwei called Wenxie demanding to know her whereabouts. From overhearing Liwei's half of the conversation, I gathered that Wenxie was delayed at home because her three-year-old grandson was eating his lunch very slowly and Wenxie could not leave until the boy had been properly fed. She would be at least another fifteen minutes late. This infuriated Liwei. When she hung up the phone, she immediately turned to me to complain. "The boy has parents!" she began. "Why does she have to feed him when she knows there are people waiting for her?" Liwei has two grandchildren of her own and she takes pride in the fact that she does not let them interfere with her own social life. For the next ten minutes, Liwei continued to send angry messages to Wenxie telling her to hurry up.

Despite having very little in common on the surface, Liwei and Wenxie are indeed good friends. Whereas Liwei grew up in Chengdu and has educated relatives who are government officials and university professors, Wenxie is from the countryside and she moved to Chengdu about ten years ago to accompany her daughter, a self-made entrepreneur who now makes about one million RMB per year.[1] They speak with different accents: Liwei in her standard Chengdu dialect and Wenxie with a melodic provincial drawl. Liwei prefers long dresses in floral patterns and she towers above Wenxie, who is less than

---

1 In 2016, one million RMB was equal to approximately 150,000 USD. A person with such an income in Chengdu would be considered very wealthy and would have access to all the luxuries the city had to offer.

five feet tall and likes to wear athletic gear. Their different backgrounds are so readily apparent and their friendship so unlikely that they sometimes draw curious looks from strangers. Had they not joined the same dance group, it is unlikely that they would have ever met at all. However, most of the time Liwei and Wenxie did not let their differences get in the way of their friendship, but as this scene at the bus stop clearly demonstrated, certain situations could reveal raw disagreements beneath the surface.

When Wenxie finally arrived some thirty minutes after our agreed-upon time, Liwei greeted her by venting her frustrations about having to wait. Wenxie tried to defend herself by explaining that her grandson wanted second helpings and the food had to be re-heated. Liwei, however, became even angrier upon hearing this. "Well then his parents could have taken care of him! You could have just gotten up and left and let somebody else feed him more food! Why do you have to be the one to give him seconds? We were waiting for you!" Wenxie offered a placating smile, but did not answer. Liwei tried again, this time even more forcefully: "There were other people to take care of your grandson, but we were waiting for you!" Wenxie laughed and shrugged but again she did not answer. She seemed to know that there was nothing she could say to smooth over the differences in outlook she and Liwei had on the subject; while Liwei believed that honoring appointments with friends should take precedence over a toddler's whims, Wenxie placed a priority on her grandchild's needs even if it meant making her friends wait outside in the cold. I stayed out of it. This was clearly an old disagreement and neither woman was likely to be moved by the thoughts of a young interloper.

We boarded the bus after a few moments of rather awkward silence. Thankfully, normal conversation resumed well before we reached our destination and Liwei did not raise the issue again for the rest of the afternoon. We all headed home at the end of the night in good spirits with full shopping bags. I left with the impression that Wenxie simply had more traditional ideas about family obligations than Liwei did. What I did not learn until later was that Wenxie had already taken actions regarding her child-care duties that could not be considered "traditional" by any stretch of the imagination.

Wenxie lives with her son, her son's second wife, and her young grandson. Her son moved to Chengdu soon after his wedding to his first wife in hopes of replicating his sister's phenomenal success. Instead, he found a middling sales job that required frequent travel. Tired of being left to care for their daughter alone, his wife took the child—Wenxie's only grandchild at the time—back to her natal city of Mianyang, located about two hours north of Chengdu. She soon remarried and limited her ties to her ex-husband and to Wenxie, her former mother-in-law. Wenxie's son's second wife is a woman from a rural village in eastern Sichuan, not far from where Wenxie herself was raised. Wenxie disapproved of this relationship from the outset, mostly because she believed her son should not settle for a rural woman now that he had a stable job in the city. However, the woman became pregnant and a wedding was quickly arranged. Wenxie, still stung by the loss of her first grandchild, seemed to have a total change of heart when she learned that she would again have a chance to dote on a baby. She invited her son and her new daughter-in-law to move into her own apartment, which her wealthy daughter had bought for her. After the child— a boy named Wei Wei— was born, Wenxie fed and clothed him from her own modest income of 3000 RMB (about 450 USD) per month, 2000 RMB of which was given to her by her daughter as an allowance.

The whole family lived together for a year and a half until Wenxie's daughter-in-law convinced her husband to move their nuclear family into their own apartment. Wenxie was devastated. By both her own and Liwei's accounts, Wenxie was inconsolable that yet another daughter-in-law had denied her the chance to be a doting grandmother. Liwei told me that she used every tactic she could think of to convince Wenxie to stop dwelling on the matter: "I told her, 'if they won't let you take care of the baby, then there's nothing you can do about it. Crying about it certainly won't help.'" Liwei invited Wenxie out for evening walks on a daily basis and told her to try to forget about her family troubles by focusing instead on her own personal life.

After several months of cajoling from Liwei and other members of the Sunset Dance Group, Wenxie finally took this advice to heart and began devoting more of her energy to her own social life. Whereas before she would frequently skip dance practices when her presence was needed at home, she began attending morning practices on a daily basis. Her dancing improved, and she took on additional responsibilities for the group by making WeChat group announcements, collecting dues, and re-scheduling rehearsals when the weather prompted cancellations. She began spending more time socializing with Liwei and a few other friends, and she even went on a few overnight sightseeing trips with other dance group members.

Just as Wenxie was beginning to become accustomed to her new life, her son and daughter-in-law suddenly asked to move back in with her. Like many young couples, they were finding it too difficult to work and raise a child at the same time and they could not afford to pay for childcare; they wanted the round-the-clock childcare that only Wenxie could provide. Against Liwei's and other group members' urgings, Wenxie agreed to let them move back in. ("I told her to never complain to me about them again!" Liwei grumbled as she recounted this story.) Wenxie did, however, surprise her friends by placing new conditions on the living arrangement, requiring her son and daughter-in-law to compensate her for her efforts. She had previously performed all duties related to her grandson's care, including shopping and preparing his meals, but she now demanded monthly payments in exchange for this work.

Wenxie asks for—and receives—300 RMB (about 45 USD) from her son each month, an amount so minimal when compared to the general costs of urban living that it hardly even covers her grandson's room and board, not to mention the fact that live-in nannies who provide the same service cost at least ten times that amount. Moreover, Wenxie confided to me that she does not actually need the money; she doesn't have to save because she knows her daughter will provide for her. Instead, she charges this fee in order to regain a sense of control and dignity over a situation that previously had left her feeling humiliated. "What did they think?" she wondered out loud as we chatted about it after dance practice one day. "That they could just drop me and then pick me back up when it was convenient for them? I won't be taken for granted again."

It is quite unusual for a Chinese grandmother to charge her own son for childcare. There have been some reports of elders suing young couples for a so-called "grandchild care fee" (*dai sun fei*) in recent years, but such cases are still rare and controversial.[2] Even though exchanging cash, favors, and other valuables among extended family members is a common and indeed foundational feature of Chinese social life (Yang 1994; Yan 1996), putting a price on the everyday acts of caregiving that occur within a domestic unit—much less for one's own grandson— is such an affront to the established norms that Wenxie has only told a few of her closest friends about the arrangement for fear of judgment. For Wenxie, the money served as a simple proxy for a complicated array of impulses. She wanted to convey her pain at having been cast aside, to mete out punishment to her son for mistreating her, and, above all, to make sure that it never happened again. Rather than communicating these fraught emotions directly—an endeavor that offered no guarantee of a satisfactory outcome— Wenxie instead chose to take a symbolic stand that was both easier to ask for and could also serve as a monthly reminder that the terms of the family arrangement were now under her control.

Despite the unorthodox nature of Wenxie's conflict-resolution strategies, scholars have noted elsewhere that blurring the boundaries between care and

---

2   Some high-profile cases of elders successfully suing their children for a *dai sun fei* (grandchild-rearing fee) have appeared on various Chinese news sites since 2014. Most cases seem to involve acrimonious divorces in which one spouse leaves the other and takes the child. The parent of the jilted spouse then sues to recoup the costs of the childcare for the child who has been taken away. See example http://inews.ifeng.com/yidian/46075914/news.shtml?ch=ref_zbs_ydzx_news, retrieved October 28, 2019.

FAMILIES UNDER (PEER) PRESSURE

resources has become commonplace for matters of kinship in the post-reform era. For example, Hong Zhang (2017) has argued that filial piety has been "recalibrated" in order to adhere to post-reform realities, and paying for a nurse for one's ill parent now "counts" as a filial act, even if one is not actually doing the nursing. In Wenxie's case, she was not up to the task of directly asking her son to be more attentive to her feelings. She was, however, able to extract something that counts as more or less the same thing.

Wenxie managed to negotiate an adequate solution by using her ability to provide childcare for her grandson as leverage against her son and daughter-in-law, but it came at the cost of much heartache to all concerned. Her demand for monthly compensation surprised her son and it especially unsettled her daughter-in-law. In the struggling rural areas where all three of them had grown up, a grandmother would be hard-pressed to attempt such a risky maneuver. This sort of affront to intergenerational solidarity is ill-advised when families must operate as a cohesive unit in order to survive (Chen, Liu, and Mair 2011; Luo and Zhan 2012; Yan 2016), and rural elders may also lack the social support to act in such an outspoken manner. Wenxie, backed by the financial security offered by her daughter and the social alliances offered by her dance group, successfully came out on top in this intergenerational dispute. Having regained her sense of dignity while also having secured the ability to spend time with her grandson, Wenxie is now eager to avoid further disturbances to her family harmony; she has gone as far as she is willing to go.

Of course, Liwei believes that Wenxie should be willing to go even further in confronting her son and daughter-in-law by refusing to perform certain child-care tasks when these tasks interfere with her personal interests and plans. Liwei's own approach to intergenerational conflict is to maintain the upper hand at all costs, even if it means permanent damage to family ties. Like Wenxie, Liwei's son has two children— a boy and a girl. Also like Wenxie, for a time Liwei's family attempted to live together as three generations, but this arrangement was cut short when her son and daughter-in-law announced that they wanted to get their children away from Liwei's "old-fashioned" child-rearing practices. Liwei was both hurt and furious. Rather than biding her time to find an acceptable outcome like Wenxie did, Liwei instead chose the scorched-earth method: she told her son and daughter-in-law that once they left, they would never again be welcomed back. To this day, Liwei told me, she remains on shaky terms with her son and oneven worse terms with her daughter-in-law, but she stubbornly maintains that she does not care. "I have lots of other things to occupy my time!" she insisted. She is certainly correct in this regard: Liwei is extremely active in the Sunset Dance Group and is seemingly always flitting between one social outing to the next. And as is obvious in how she reacted to Wenxie's plight, Liwei now is also a staunch evangelist for living life on one's own terms.

Confronted with similar challenges, the friends reacted according to their temperaments and priorities. But in both cases, the Sunset Dance Group—or the friendships among the women in the group, to be more precise—played a key role in how the women made their decisions and how they carried out their strategies. For Wenxie, the group provided social support and a diversion when she was feeling abandoned by her son and his wife. It also provided constant pressure to stand up to her son and daughter-in-law and to advocate for her own needs in the form of her friend Liwei, whom she likely would have never met had they not both been members of the same dance group. For Liwei, the group offers constant social connections, many opportunities for recreation, and, ultimately, because the others treat her as something of a leader, it gives her a sense of self-importance.

Wenxie and Liwei have different personalities and different approaches. The same can be said of Teacher Yuan, Qiu, Auntie Yu, and every other retired woman who participates in congregational dance groups. What they have in common is that they are all in the unfamiliar territory of trying to juggle grand-motherhood, friendship, and self-interest at the same time. There is no play-book for maintaining this delicate balance. However, the common-interest social groups in which they take part certainly provide fertile ground for new strategies and norms to grow, develop, and circulate.

3   Conclusion

Grandmothers with young children are a ubiquitous sight throughout urban China. In Chengdu, I often saw clusters of middle-aged and elderly women chatting on park benches while toddlers played underfoot and infants napped in strollers. Grandparents lined the sidewalks outside preschools and primary schools in the afternoons, and when hundreds of pairs of little feet finally came streaming out of the gates, the elders craned their necks anxiously until the children found their way to each of their waiting caregivers. Book bags would soon be transferred onto the elders' backs, and small hands would be gripped firmly by the large ones before they began the journey home together.

Sweet moments like these are commonplace, but being a grandparent in urban China today can still be a thankless task. As members of the post-eighties and post-nineties generations struggle to balance their high-pressure careers with the demands of childcare, their own parents are often called upon to help ease the domestic burdens on the young couple. Grandparents—and

FAMILIES UNDER (PEER) PRESSURE

grandmothers in particular— feed, bathe, soothe, and entertain their grand-children until the little ones are old enough to attend preschool, at which time dropping off and picking up the children may be added to the grandmother's care-giving duties. This intense period of childcare may also be exacerbated and lengthened due to the revision of the one-child policy in 2015 and the sub-sequent addition of second children to many urban families (Zhong and Peng 2020). Many young couples are grateful for their parents' efforts, of course, but there are also cases where the grandparents' labor is taken for granted or even—as in Liwei's case—scrutinized and criticized. Chinese media reports and my own observations are filled with stories of elders feeling taken advan-tage of or being humiliated by this dynamic. As one dance group interlocutor complained, "sometimes I feel [my daughter and son-in-law] see me as noth-ing more than a *baomu* [nanny or housekeeper]."

Like their rural counterparts, urban grandmothers have few resources at their disposal to wage a counter-insurgency against the seismic shift in family dynamics. Many—like Qiu and to a certain extent even Wenxie—are afraid that upsetting the younger generation will backfire and so they do what they can to maintain family harmony. They are all too aware that their children hold most of the cards in any negotiations. This does not mean, however, that urban grandmothers belonging to the sandwich generation must accept China's new inverted family structure at face value. The women I write about in this chapter are all finding new ways of relating to their families that also allow them more space to prioritize their own feelings, needs, and desires. More significantly, they are accomplishing this through conversations with their friends. In each of my examples, I examined how retired women take the initiative to cultivate and maintain friendships out-side of their family circles and in turn they lean on these friendships to achieve their personal goals. This is not to say that social groups can neces-sarily function as respites from interpersonal difficulties. My examples also revealed the potential pitfalls of such groups of friends: because they are venues where people can test out emotional intimacies, they are also places where values can clash and conflicts can arise.

Despite these limitations, the social power of groups of friends among retired women should not be underestimated. Regular interactions with peo-ple in similar circumstances can expose struggling grandmothers to new cop-ing strategies or alternative negotiating tactics when they otherwise would have to suffer in silence. Internal discussions among groups of grandmothers on the subject of family dynamics and grandparenting—while seldom arriving at a full consensus— can bring forth new value systems to which the group members feel beholden and accountable.

Of course, although the grandmothers in my examples may have won a few battles, it is far from clear whether they, or any other urban grandparentswill be able to reverse or even stem the trend of the inverted family dynamics that has been taking place for the better part of a century. Such a feat would require social organization and solidarity on a far larger scale than groups of twenty to thirty people can foster. The idea that thousands or even millions of elders will band together to advocate for their collective interests may sound like a grandiose fantasy, but I think it is too soon to completely discount the possibility. I discovered early on in my fieldwork that my dance group interlocutors spent a great deal of time on the social media platform WeChat. The vast majority of their communications with one another consisted of logistics, personal photos, and funny videos, but the conversation did occasionally veer onto more serious topics. Someone may share an Internet meme that speaks to the retirees' concerns about being squeezed for resources, or, as I observed just recently, a witty poem like the following may appear in the chat transcripts:

In the past, there were three ways that a person could fail to be filial
Now a new type of lacking filial piety has appeared:
Young people only give birth to children but they do not care for them;
They put all of the burden of childcare on the backs of the elderly.

The dance group member who shared the poem did not write it. Instead, she found it on "*Laonian hai* [old kids]," a popular website that focuses exclusively on issues of interest to elders. Webpages, blogs, and social media accounts geared toward retirees have proliferated across the Chinese Internet in recent years, and sentiments like those conveyed in the above poem are easy to find. A brief search for "grandparenting" yields innumerable results, including blog posts with titles like "I am the child's grandmother, not the nanny!" (https:// kknews.cc/zh-cn/story/zpljoyg.html 2019), and think-pieces pondering whether child-rearing is the "fate" of all Chinese elders (https://known.ifeng. com/a/20180905/45152277_0.shtml 2018). Retired netizens often fill these webpages' comments sections with additional remonstrations about care-giving– related exhaustion or the ungrateful manner in which they are treated by their adult children.

While no amount of grousing on the Internet is equal to a real-life social movement (especially when a majority of the complaints are logged anonymously or under pseudonyms), the existence of space devoted to the airing of such complaints allow Internet-savvy elders to learn from one another and to offer each other support. Chinese grandparents are far from alone in their desire to enjoy their "golden years" and their ambivalence about providing

FAMILIES UNDER (PEER) PRESSURE 141

childcare; the experiences of elders from nations that have already undergone similar demographic and social transformations may prove useful in the Chinese context. We must wait to see whether the collective and cumulative effects of peer-to-peer information-sharing can exert sufficient pressures on the child-centric family structure to amount to tangible changes. What is already clear at this moment, however, is that some urban Chinese elders have begun to realize that they can fight back, even if they must fight back with the short end of the stick.

References

Abrahams, Ray. 1999. "Friends and Networks as Survival Strategies in North-East Europe." In *The Anthropology of Friendship*, ed. Sandra Bell and Simon Coleman, 155–68. Oxford: Berg.

Carrier, James G. 1999. "People Who can be Friends: Selves and Social Relationships." In *The Anthropology of Friendship*, ed. Sandra Bell and Simon Coleman, 21–38. Oxford: Berg.

Chen, Feinian, Guangya Liu, and Christine A. Mair. 2011. "Intergenerational Ties in Context: Grandparents Caring for Grandchildren in China." *Social Forces* 90, 2: 571–94.

Davis, Deborah and Stevan Harrell, eds. 1993. *Chinese Families in the Post-Mao Era*. Berkeley: University of California Press.

Dyson, Jane. 2010. "Friendship in Practice: Girls' Work in the Indian Himalayas." *American Ethnologist* 37, 3: 482–98.

Fong, Vanessa. 2002. *Only Hope: Coming of Age Under China's One-Child Policy*. Stanford: Stanford University Press.

Goh, Esther. 2011. *China's One-Child Policy and Multiple Caregiving*. London: Routledge.

Gratz, Tilo. 2004. "Friendship among Young Artisanal Gold Miners in Northern Benin (West Africa)." *Afrika Spectrum* 3, 1: 95–117.

Huang, Claudia. 2016. "'Dancing Grannies' in the Modern City: Consumption and Group Formation in Urban China." *Asian Anthropology* 15, 3: 225–41.

Kipnis, Andrew. 2009. "Education and the Governing of Child-centered Relatedness." In *Chinese Kinship: Contemporary Anthropological Perspectives,* ed. Susanne Brandstädter and Gonçalo D. Santos, 204–22. London: Routledge.

Luo, Baozhen, and Heying Zhan. 2012. "Filial Piety and Functional Support: Understanding Intergenerational Solidarity Among Families with Migrated Children in Rural China." *Ageing International* 37, 1: 69–92.

Pitt-Rivers, Julian. 1973. "The Kith and the Kin." In *The Character of Kinship*, ed. Jack R. Goody, 89–105. Cambridge: Cambridge University Press.

Santos, Gonçalo D. and Stevan Harrell. 2017. *Transforming Patriarchy: Chinese Families in the Twenty-First Century*. Seattle: University of Washington Press.

Santos-Granero, Fernando. 2007. "Of Fear and Friendship: Amazonian Sociality beyond Kin-ship and Affinity." *Journal of the Royal Anthropological Institute* 13, 1: 1–18.

Tu, Mingwei. 2016. "Chinese One-child Families in the Age of Migration: Middle-class Transnational Mobility, Ageing Parents, and the Changing Role of Filial Piety." *Journal of Chinese Sociology* 3, 1: 1–17.

Xu, Jing. 2017. *The Good Child: Moral Development in a Chinese Preschool*. Stanford: Stanford University Press.

Yan, Yunxiang. 1996. *The Flow of Gifts: Reciprocity and Social Networks in a Chinese Village*. Stanford: Stanford University Press.

Yan, Yunxiang. 2003. *Private Life under Socialism: Love, Intimacy, and Family Change in a Chinese Village, 1949–1999*. Stanford: Stanford University Press.

Yan, Yunxiang. 2016. "Intergenerational Intimacy and Descending Familism in Rural North China." *American Anthropologist* 118, 2: 244–57.

Yan, Yunxiang. 2018. "Neo-Familism and the State in Contemporary China." *Urban Anthropology and Studies of Cultural Systems and World Economic Development* 47, 3/4: 181–224.

Yang, Mayfair. 1994. *Gifts, Favors, and Banquets: The Art of Social Relationships in China*. Ithaca: Cornell University Press.

Zhang, Hong. 2017. "Recalibrating Filial Piety: Realigning the Family, State, and Market Interests in China?" In *Transforming Patriarchy: Chinese Families in the Twenty-First Century*, ed. Gonçalo D. Santos and Stevan Harrell, 234–50. Seattle: University of Washington Press.

Zhang, Yuanting and Franklin W. Goza. 2006. "Who Will Care for the Elderly in China? A Review of the Problems Caused by China's One-child Policy and their Potential Solutions." *Journal of Aging Studies* 20, 2: 151–64.

Zhong, Xiaohui and Minggang Peng. 2020. "The Grandmothers' Farewell to Childcare Provision Under China's Two-Child Policy: Evidence from Guangzhou Middle-Class Families." *Social Inclusion* 8, 2: 36–46.

"我是孙子的奶奶，不是保姆！" https://kknews.cc/zh-cn/story/zpljoyg.html, retrieved September 24, 2019.

"带孙费"到底该不该要 老人与儿女都有话说" http://inews.ifeng.com/yidian/46075914/news.shtml?ch=ref_zbs_ydzx_news, retrieved October 28, 2019.

"带孙子，是中国老年人全部的宿命吗？" https://known.ifeng.com/a/20180905/45152277_0.shtml retrieved September 23, 2019.

CHAPTER 7

Intimate Power

Intergenerational Cooperation and Conflicts in Childrearing among Urban Families

Suowei Xiao

1 Introduction

In Western societies, particularly the United States, the majority of grandparents follow a norm of noninterference in intergenerational relationships and do not assume a central role in caring for or rearing of their grandchildren (Cherlin and Furstenburg 1986). However, their involvement with grandchildren may increase when their adult children face difficulties, such as unemployment, bankruptcy, divorce, incarceration, or drug abuse (Gibson 2005). By contrast, in contemporary China it is a prevalent for grandparents to participate in the care of their grandchildren. According to a pooled 1991–2004 sample drawn from nine provinces as part of the China Health and Nutrition Survey, 45 percent of grandparents lived in the same household with their grandchild from birth to age 6. In families where three generations lived together, grandparents, especially grandmothers, played an extremely important caregiving role, spending as much time as the mothers in caring for preschool-aged children. Nonresidential grandparents also served as important alternative childcare providers. In 27 percent of the surveyed families, children were cared for in the paternal grandparents' households and nearly 13 percent were cared for in the maternal grandparents' households (Chen et al. 2011). Other large sample surveys in urban China indicate that more than one-half of the respondents received help with childrearing from their parents or in-laws (Goh and Kuczynski 2010; Ma et al. 2011).

China has a long history of grandparent involvement in the taking care of grandchildren. Historians note that in traditional Chinese society most young couples lived with the husband's family when their children were born, and grandparents, as well as other female relatives, played an important role in the raising of the young children (Hsiung 2005). However, departing from the traditional image that old people simply enjoyed playing with the grandchildren, the contemporary intergenerational childrearing is more complicated. On the one hand, the grandparents' participation in the raising of their grandchildren

© SUOWEI XIAO, 2021 | DOI:10.1163/9789004450233_008

constitutes an important source of support for their adult children, helps to cultivate a close grandparent/grandchild relationship, and enhances the grandparents' satisfaction in life (Goh and Kuczynski 2010). On the other hand, contradictions and conflicts regarding childrearing issues frequently occur between the grandparents and the parents. Due to differences in parenting styles and beliefs, the nurturing and educating of the grandchildren are likely to result in conflicts in the intergenerational parenting coalition (Goh and Kuczynski 2010, 2012; Luan 2009). Furthermore, grandparents and adult children often engage in delicate competition to establish intimate bonds with the children (Shen 2013). Several scholars have noted the tendency for grandparents to become "nannies" in the intergenerational parenting coalition, i.e., they assume the lion's share of the housework and the childcare, while, at the same time, ceding their voice in family decision making (Goh and Kudznski 2010; Shen 2013).

These findings indicate that contemporary intergenerational parenting coalitions remain a traditional form of intergenerational cooperation, but the findings also reveal a new feature regarding intergenerational relations in general and the changing power relations among the generations in particular. By studying the intergenerational parenting coalition, this study seeks to address the following questions: In the contemporary intergenerational collaboration of childcare in urban China, what is the division of labor and the power relations among the family members? Is there an emerging pattern of intergenerational power relations and how is it challenged and maintained among family members? Based on an in-depth investigation into the intergeneration cooperation and conflicts in childrearing, this article seeks to deepen our understanding of power relations in intergenerational cooperation and assistance and to illuminate the intertwining of power and intimacy in the family.

This chapter draws on in-depth interviews and observations of parents and grandparents who collaborated in the raising of children. The analysis focuses on thirteen families residing in Beijing between 2010 and 2013. All of the parents in this study had a junior college degree or higher. The majority of the fathers held professional or managerial positions or ran their own business. Most mothers worked, or had worked in research, managerial, or administrative jobs, such as secretary or accounting.[1] Their annual household income was no less than 150,000 yuan (about US $22,869). In only one family were the

---

1 Among the mothers, four were not employed at the time of the interviews, but only one did not plan to find a job in the near future. The remaining three were all considering freelance jobs in education, training or consulting, which would allow them to work at the same time that they were taking care of their children.

parents both born in Beijing; all the others had migrated to work in the city and had purchased private homes in Beijing. Twelve out of the thirteen children in the participating families had Beijing *hukou* (household registrations). Ten out of the thirteen children in the participating families were between the ages 3 and 6 years old, and the other three were school-aged (7 to 10 years old). Except for one family in which the grandparents lived separately and were not involved in childcare, all the other families had three generations living under the same roof for more than one year, with the grandparents providing childcare in varying forms on a daily basis.

I conducted multiple interviews that lasted between a total of three to six hours with all thirteen mothers, and one two-hour interview with two fathers respectively. I asked the parents to elaborate on their childrearing experiences since the birth of their child. Complementing the parent sample, eight grandparents who engaged in caring for their grandchildren were also interviewed. All of these grandparents lived in Beijing, were between the ages of 60 and 80, and had stable incomes at the time of the interview. In addition, I also visited the homes of seven of the participating families and joined three families on weekend trips, thus enabling me to observe the interactions among the various family members and to better understand the family dynamics. For reasons of confidentiality, all names used in this article are pseudonyms.

2 Intergenerational Cooperation in the Family in Reform-Era China

Intergenerational cooperation and reciprocity are important traditions in Chinese families. Culturally, familism is a value system that maintains and enhances the stability of Chinese society, of which the family is the basic unit. Family members and kin linked by blood ties have a natural and unique closeness, and they undertake unconditional and unlimited responsibilities and obligations of mutual care and support (Liu 2013). Since the market reforms, along with the nuclearization of the family and the prevalence of the independence of an adult son's conjugal family from his natal family in terms of residence, property, and finance, parents and their adult children have shifted from intra-family to inter-family relations, and intergenerational relations have become the connection between the two nuclear families (Wang 2010). The tradition of mutual support and aid across generations has persisted; the parental family is closely connected with the adult children, constituting a new pattern of "[nuclear] families in [kin] networks" (Wang 2010; Ma et al. 2011). The existing literature on intergenerational cooperation and reciprocity focuses primarily on two dimensions, i.e., resource flows and cultural ethics.

First, in regard to resource flows, extensive attention has been paid to fairness and equity in intergenerational exchanges of economic, physical, and emotional means. Some researchers argue that the pattern of intergenerational cooperation and reciprocity is "reciprocal" or "feeding back" (*fanbu*), i.e., adult children maintain close reciprocal exchanges with their parents but tend to provide more economic resources and caregiving to their parents than the other way around (Xiong 1998; Xu 2011; Bian et al. 1998). Others point out that adult children, singletons in particular, receive extensive parental financial, emotional, and physical support, which may exceed the amount of support they provide to their parents. This is referred to metaphorically as "downstream grace" (*en wangxia liu*) or "tears dripping down" (*yanlei wangxia liu*) (He 2009; Ma et al. 2011; Liu 2005; Liu 2012; Shen 2013). In recent years, the increasing phenomenon of *ken lao* (i.e., adult children being dependent on their elderly parents for financial, physical, and other forms of support) and the tragic cases of children failing to properly provide for their rural elderly parents have aroused much debate on whether the equilibrium and fairness in the traditional "feeding back" model of intergenerational exchange has been altered (Guo 2001; He 2009; Liu 2012).

Second, regarding cultural ethics, the central issue concerns changes in the ethical foundations of intergenerational cooperation. Some scholars point out that traditional family ethics that emphasizes responsibility and obligations among family members has faded, and, under the veil of individualism, ideas are emerging that stress the subjectivity of the younger generation (Liu 2011; Kang 2012; Shen 2013; Yan 2003). Nevertheless, there is a difference in the two generations' views of family ethics. Some studies find that members of the elder generation still have a firm sense of "responsibility-oriented ethics," i.e., they fulfill their responsibilities and obligations toward their descendants, generously offering support and assistance to their children (and grandchildren) through various means and they attempt to lessen their children's burdens in terms of providing elderly care and by being forgiving when their children do not "feed back" in a proper manner (Yang and He 2004). However, other scholars argue that despite the fact that the elder generations selflessly support their children, they no longer adhere to the notion of unlimited responsibilities and obligations (Liu 2013). There have also been debates concerning the younger generations' notion of family ethics. Informed by individuation theories, one group of scholars argues that the family has become the pool of resources and means by which individuals achieve their personal goals, with the basis of intergenerational ties shifting from mutual obligations to individual desires, choices, and needs (Shen 2013; Yan 2003, 2012). Other studies challenge the above-mentioned view of the "individuation of the family," arguing that emotional ties still predominate in nuclear families, while economic benefits outweigh family ethics in intergenerational relations (Tan 2010). The term "new familism" (*xin jiating zhuyi*) has been coined, referring to family notions held by the younger generation that seeks to accommodate both personal and family interests. It has been argued that adult children, despite a growing strong sense of individualism, value the family as a whole, and they are willing to maintain a mutually supportive relationship with their parents (Kang 2012).

To better understand the mechanism and process of intergenerational cooperation, another dimension of the power relations among generations is essential yet understudied in the existing literature. One exception is Shen's study of urban families in Shanghai. This work finds that in families where three generations live under the same roof, young mothers are relieved from most of the housework and have more power in making decisions and arranging family affairs, while the grandparents relinquish their authority. Shen (2013) claims this is a reversal in the power relations of the parent-child axis. But Shen's study examines power in intergenerational relations from a relatively static view, highlighting the shift in the relative position and status of the grandparents and parents in the family that result in changes in the resources, rights, responsibilities, and obligations of the two generations. However, as scholars of family studies have pointed out, family politics is a dynamic process, constantly negotiating interests and demands. Individuals seek a greater voice and respect in family affairs and tend to achieve their goals by accumulating moral capital and strategizing in terms of family politics (Wu 2009; Zheng and Yang 2003).

Viewing power as dynamic and flowing is illuminating for an understanding of power relations in the contemporary intergenerational parenting coalition. In the modern transition of Chinese families, the traditional patriarchal family power structure, relying on hierarchies of gender, generation, and age, has been challenged. On the one hand, the cultural and moral authority granted to parents through their status in the family has been weakened, the power of the younger generation is on the rise, and the women's, especially the young women's, status in the family has been enhanced (Ma et al. 2011; Shen et al. 2009; Wang 2009; Xiao 2002; Yang 2011). On the other hand, the institutionalized and well-defined hierarchy among family members has been loosened. The weakening of the institutionalized power structure allows room to negotiations among family members and produces more flexible and diversified power relations in the family (Wu 2009; Shen 2013; Yan 2012). In other words, in the traditional family where rules of seniority and hierarchy were strictly enforced, individual power was closely linked with one's role and status in the family and little room was left for individual maneuvering. In contrast, in the modern family, with its relatively loose hierarchical structure, individuals have more space to maneuver to have a voice in family affairs. For instance, a recent study finds that many parents subsidize their children's purchase of housing, either by taking initiatives or positively responding to their children's requests, in order to establish a "negotiative intimacy" (*xieshangshi qinmi guanxi*) with their children (Zhong and Ho 2014). By willingly providing financial resources, parents capture the chance to take part in their children's family affairs and to cultivate a relationship characterized by emotional exchange, respect, and close ties. This finding challenges the stereotypical image of parents being "the victim" and "the disadvantaged" as they sponsor their children's real-estate and other financial pursuits.

Based on a close examination of the intergenerational parenting coalition, this article seeks to illuminate the characteristics of intergenerational power relations in contemporary China, highlighting both the general power structure and the dynamic process of exercising power. I argue that a new pattern whereby young mothers act as powerful "managers " of the childrearing project, and grandparents serve primarily as caretakers who are marginalized in family power relations, has emerged with respect to both the division of labor and the power structure among generations in the intergenerational parenting coalition. However, patterns of intergenerational power relations are fluid rather than institutionalized, susceptible to negotiations and interactions among family members, and largely confined by the construction and maintenance of specific intimate relations between the parents and the grandparents.

I use the term "intimate power" to describe the particular features of the exercise of power in the intergenerational parenting coalition, highlighting the connection between intimate relations and power in the family. This concept includes the following three features. First, in the intergenerational collaboration, the establishment of an intimate relationship among family members is the premise for the exercise of power. Second, the individual exercise and negotiation of power is mediated by intimate relations among family members. Finally, as in the specific case of the intergenerational parenting coalition, grandparents forgo their negotiating authority and power so as to maintain mutual assistance and cooperation as well as to sustain emotional intimacy with their offspring.

Two main features of "intimate power" will be covered in the remainder of this chapter, the division of labor and power relations in the intergenerational parenting coalition, and intimate relations and the exercise of power in childrearing. Before we address these main themes, a brief discussion of the transition in childrearing in modern China is presented to help readers understand the background under which the contemporary intergenerational parenting coalition has been formed.

INTIMATE POWER 149

3 The Transition of Childrearing in Modern China

Chinese traditional childrearing was highly functionally oriented. The child's main task was to learn to behave as a person, that is, to grow up into a socially recognized adult so as to honor his/her family and ancestors and to perpetuate the family line. Early child training was characterized by respecting one's seniors and by being pragmatic, moral, and disciplined (Hsiung 2005). A common pattern in childcare was that mothers would nurture and fathers would educate. To be more specific, mothers were responsible for physiological care, i.e., bringing up the young in terms of daily feeding, dressing, and tenderness. They empathized with the bodily and emotional needs of their children and formed intimate bonds with their children. Fathers, in contrast, were responsible for sociocultural reproduction, assuming responsibility for the children's moral and behavioral training as well as their intellectual skills. The affection between the father and the child was thus inhibited. Paternal grandparents and female relatives were also involved in the daily care of the children since most young couples were still living with the husband's family when they had their first child (Fei 1998; Hsiung 2005).

The transition of Chinese society has brought enormous changes in childcare practices. During the pre-reform socialist era, children were regarded as the future of the nation rather than as the private property of the family. Attempts were made to collectively reorganize childcare. In the cities, public preschools and childcare facilities were established to alleviate the family's childcare burdens. Although many women entered the labor force, the gender division of labor in the family still persisted. In general, urban women suffered the double burden of work and housework and they relied on kin networks for support in caregiving (Zuo and Jiang 2010).

With the market reforms we have witnessed a trend of marketization and privatization in childcare. With the decrease in public childcare facilities, families again assumed the primary, if not the sole, responsibility for the raising of their children. There has also been a proliferation of discussions on parenting. A parenting magazine, *A Must Read for Parents* (*fumu bidu*), which first appeared at the beginning of the 1980s, introduced a new concept of "parenting," referring to those who adopt scientific methods to foster the healthy development of their children (Dong 2014). Furthermore, in recent years many popular readers on family education have proliferated. Informed by Western child-development psychology, such readers advocate good parenting that is characterized by being child-centered rather than adult-centered and by cultivating comprehensive qualities rather than being exam-oriented. These new views stress the importance of providing early education, engaging in emotional communications, and cultivating the child's interests (Chen and Wang 2005). Such popular views of childrearing in the name of scientific parenting (*kexue yuer*) have been well received by young urban parents, especially the newly emerging middle-class families. Furthermore, due to the one-child policy and the intensified market competition since the reforms, many parents have high expectations of upward mobility for their only child, and thus they seriously invest in their child's education (Lin 2009; Fong 2004). Along with the burgeoning markets for children's education and consumption, childrearing has become a complicated project that involves extended roles for parents, schools, experts, and markets. First, the roles of the parents have been extended. Good parents are not only caretakers but also learners of parenting skills and consumers in the educational market. They actively acquire new knowledge and skills to perceive and respond to their children's needs. They also attentively seek information about nutrition and education; choose desirable educational institutions, toys, books, and consumer products; and they arrange appropriate activities for their children.

Second, childrearing has become consumer-oriented and extremely expensive. Parents not only seek to facilitate their children's development by purchasing professional educational services but also to cultivate class-coded lifestyles and tastes in their children through the adoption of consumption patterns. For example, among the families in my study, only one mother was able to send her son to a good public preschool, affiliated with the university where she taught, at an affordable price. All the other families chose to send their children to private preschools which cost an average of 2,500 yuan (about US $381) per month (varying from 1,800 yuan to 4,200 yuan), while the monthly wage for the working population in Beijing averaged at 4,672 yuan (about US $ 712) in 2011. Other educational expenses, such as early child-development programs, extracurricular activities, and private tutoring, totaled on average of over 1,500 yuan (about US $229) per month. Parents also paid attention to what their children ate and wore. Rather than simply feeding their children and keeping them warm, the parents chose clothing of good quality and expensive taste for their little ones. Some parents purchased organic food and fashionable outfits for their children on a regular basis. Social and leisure activities for children, such as birthday parties, vacation trips, and summer camps, have also become important household expenses.[2]

---

2 Large-scale surveys have validated the pattern of increasing expenses/consumption of childrearing. A large-scale ten-city survey finds that families with children between the ages of 3 and 6 spend an average of 1,454.92 yuan (about $222) per month on preschool education. In high-income families (with monthly incomes of 10,000 yuan or more), the expenses for

As childrearing becomes more complicated and expensive, families require more labor and money to provide "proper" care for their children. This care can be divided into different sets of tasks: mental work, such as learning, decision making, teaching, and playing; manual work, such as taking physical care of the children; and auxiliary work, such as cooking, washing clothes, and house cleaning.

4 Grandparents Take Care, Mothers Take Charge: The Division of Labor and Power Relations in Childrearing

Among the middle-class families I studied, a new pattern that I call "grandparents take care, mothers take charge" has emerged regarding the division of labor in the intergenerational parenting coalition. In this pattern, the mothers become the manager of the childrearing project, taking full charge and assuming the responsibilities for sociocultural rearing, whereas the grandparents become helpers and engage in the physical care but lack authority in terms of the childrearing practices. Fathers concentrate on earning money to facilitate their children's development, but they are largely absent from everyday childcare practices. However, they do participate in decision making via their connections with the mothers. This pattern points to the power relations among family members in the parenting coalition. However, young mothers do not have the institutionalized symbolic and moral resources to ensure their supervisory role and authority in childcare practices. There is much room for negotiation among family members, who strategize to change or to maintain the particular power relations in the family. In this sense, power relations in the intergenerational parenting coalition are flexible and diversified. The story of the Wang family provides an excellent example.

4.1 A Story of the Wang Family
Meimei Wang was a 4-year-old girl. Since her birth her grandparents on both sides rotated to help take care of her. Meimei's maternal grandmother came to help until she was 8 months and then her paternal grandparents

---

preschool education total 2583.7 yuan (about $394) per month, or about 18.17 percent of the family income (Liu and Song 2013). Xu (2004) finds that families in Shanghai spend more on their children than on their parents. In families with children between the ages of birth to 16 years old, the annual cost of raising a child is between 13,000 yuan (about $1983) and 19,000 yuan (about $2896), accounting for 39–51 percent of total household expenses. The higher the family income, the more they spend on their child.

took over. After Meimei went to preschool at the age of 2.5, her maternal grandparents returned since the paternal grandparents were no longer able to provide childcare due to deteriorating health conditions. But because they had another daughter who also needed childcare help, the old couple had to separate, with each one staying with one daughter's family and then rotating on a regular basis. They made it clear to their daughters that if they were needed, they would be happy to help but they would not insist on providing help.

At the time of the research, Meimei's grandfather, Grandpa Lin, was living with his daughter's family. Every morning he was the first one to get up, prepare breakfast for the family, and then send Meimei to preschool at 8:00 a.m. He then did the grocery shopping, cleaned the apartment, and washed the clothes. At noon, Grandpa Lin fixed himself a quick lunch, took a nap, and then started preparing dinner and snacks for Meimei. At about 5:00 p.m. he picked up Meimei from preschool. When he cooked dinner for the family, he kept an eye on Meimei as she would play in the living room. Usually Grandpa Lin would wait until everyone had returned home to eat dinner. But if the young couple was unable to return home until very late, he and Meimei would eat alone. After dinner, if his daughter was home, he would go out for a walk; if his daughter had not yet returned home, he would skip his daily exercise.

With the help of the grandparents, Meimei's mother, Yang, earned her PhD and completed a two-year postdoc appointment. She then took a teaching position at a small private college even though she had other job offers. The young couple made this decision collectively after deliberate discussion. Working in a small college did not earn much, but due to its flexible schedule, two one-month breaks, and lower demands for research and publications, compared to that of large research universities, Yang would be able to devote more time to take care of her family.

Yang read extensively on topics related to childrearing, such as the *Parenting Encyclopedia*, *A Good Mother Is More Important than a Good Teacher*, *Capturing Children's Sensitive Periods*, and *Effective Parent Training*. She also followed childrearing information and discussions on online forums and attended lectures by education professionals. She stated that she was not very concerned about practical things, such as her daughter's future career; her top priority was to "teach her daughter how to be a good person; other things, such as learning knowledge, would come later."

When Meimei was a preschooler, Yang focused on nurturing Meimei's emotional stability and cultivating her communication skills. For instance, when Meimei was fussy and began to cry, Yang would not cajole or scold her; instead, she would hold her gently and then try to reason with her until she calmed

INTIMATE POWER

down. Sometimes Meimei was fussy for quite a while and Yang had to make a great effort to remain patient. When Yang was disciplining Meimei, the grandparents normally would keep silent and leave them alone. However, Yang's mother was short-tempered and would try to "help" discipline the child in ways with which Yang did not agree, such as using mandatory language or intimidating the child. Yang could not help but complain about this to her mother and she would often ask her mother to leave the room.

On most days Yang returned home before 6:00 p.m. and ate dinner with the family. After dinner, she spent time with her daughter, playing games, singing songs, drawing pictures, reading books, or together visiting the neighbors. At 9:00 p.m. Yang helped Meimei get ready for bed by brushing her teeth, washing her face, and reading her bedtime stories. When Meimei was 1 year old, Yang began to arrange outdoor activities for the family on weekends. The parents would take Meimei to parks, museums, swimming pools, organic farms, and so on. The grandparent(s) sometimes joined them on the weekend activities. Yang had to make considerable effort in advance to arrange these outings, checking the venue, getting directions, checking the weather and other details, and informing her husband about the arrangements.

Ever since her birth, Yang was concerned about finding a good preschool for Meimei. Over the course of several years she sought out information from Web sites and online forums as well as from neighbors and friends. When Meimei was 1 year old, Yang was already well-informed about all the preschools within a five-mile radius of their residence. When Meimei was about 2 years old, Yang began contacting several preschools in which she was interested. She attended more than ten orientation meetings organized by various organizations and she personally visited six preschools. Her top choice was a private preschool because the principal's vision of education resonated with her own. She took her husband, Mr. Wang, on the campus visit, and both were quite satisfied with the facilities and the teachers. However, the high expense of 3,600 yuan (about US $549) per month made her hesitate.[3] Mr. Wang helped her make up her mind by saying, "You won't be able to get a good education by choosing a cheap school."

After Meimei turned 2 years old, Yang signed her up for art, dance, and English classes. Meimei liked to paint, so Yang sent her to an art class recommended by the neighbors. Meimei attended dance classes because Yang liked to dance and she found that Meimei had a good sense of rhythm. Yang also

---

3 The cost increases annually. At the time of the interview, it had reached 4,200 yuan (≈$640) per month.

sent Meimei to English classes because the children of most of her neighbors and friends who had children of Meimei's age were also learning English. Mr. Wang was enthusiastic about his daughter learning English at an early age, but it was Yang who called the English-training centers for information and audited three different classes with Meimei. Yang did not expect her daughter to be an artist or a professional dancer in the future; rather, these classes made good use of her daughter's time by learning useful skills and cultivating good taste. The total cost of the art, dance, and language classes as well as preschool totaled over 6,000 yuan (about US $915) per month, far exceeding Yang's salary.

Fortunately, Mr. Wang made a good salary. After working for consulting companies for over ten years, he was earning more than 200,000 yuan (about US $30,492) annually, which he attributed to his hard work, including his regularly working overtime and taking business trips. During Meimei's first year of life, he was working on a project in another city and only returned home every two weeks. Yang commented, "At that time, I could not count on him [to take care of the baby]. He had changed her diaper only once or twice and he recorded it because he thought it was interesting. But if I asked him to do it [change the diaper] every day, no way!" Mr. Wang later began to resent the fact that his job kept him away from his family and so he found a new job that allowed him to work in Beijing most of the time, taking only one or two short business trips each month. Although he was able to return home every day, Mr. Wang still had little time to spend with Meimei. On the few days that he finished work early, he arrived home at about 8:00 p.m. He would play with Meimei after dinner, doing somersaults or carrying her on his neck. "They are just like friends," Yang commented. Father and daughter would have fun for about half an hour until it was time for Meimei to go to bed. However, on most nights Meimei was already asleep when her father returned home.

Although Yang had some complaints, she was generally satisfied with her husband for being the primary breadwinner for the family and making an effort to be a good father. Mr. Wang did not have much face-to-face interaction with Meimei, but his wife kept him informed, and he regularly talked to Meimei over the phone when he was away on business trips. When it came to important decisions, such as choosing a preschool or leisure activities, Mr. Wang would be involved, sharing thoughts, providing suggestions, and even making the final decision when his wife had hesitations. During the past year, due to the influence of Grandpa Lin, Mr. Wang's available time had improved: he tried not to work on weekends, joining the family for outdoor activities or taking Meimei to different classes. He even spent several weekends preparing for a school play with other parents, which would be performed for all the children in Meimei's preschool on International Children's Day.

INTIMATE POWER   155

4.2   *The Division of Labor in Childrearing*

In terms of the intergenerational division of labor in childrearing, the case of the Wang family is typical among the families I studied. As the manager of the childrearing project, the young mother usually engages in three main responsibilities.

First, the primary responsibility of the mother involves making plans and decisions for her child's development, from selecting educational institutions to arranging daily activities, including choosing a preschool, early childhood education programs, and leisure activities; making arrangements for weekends and holidays; and shopping for food, clothes, and toys that are age-appropriate for her child. To be able to make good decisions, the mother has to invest enormous time and effort in collecting and analyzing relevant information, surfing the Internet, reading books, talking with other mothers, and consulting experts as well as taking field trips.

The second responsibility of the mother is to educate and train the child in terms of intellectual development and the building of a good character. To stimulate the child's intellectual development, mothers engage in various activities such as reading to the child, assessing and cultivating the child's talents, and developing and maintaining relationships with preschools and training centers. Furthermore, mothers are also concerned about building good character and habits in their children. Modern ideals of child development emphasize self-discipline, emotional management, communication skills, and adaptive habits. Training to instill these characteristics is integrated into the process of daily caretaking. To achieve these goals, mothers not only discipline the child, setting rules and regulating the child's behavior, but they also monitor others, usually the grandparents, who are taking part in the family childcare.

The third responsibility involves take partial care of the child's daily life. The extent to which mothers personally care for the physical needs of the child varies, affected by the demands of the mother's paid work, the health condition of the other caregivers (the grandparents in particular), and, most importantly, the mother's perceptions of whether certain activities are important to her child's development. Like Yang, most mothers I interviewed bathed their child and put them to bed on their own because they believed that taking part in these activities helped to build intimate bonds between mother and child.

Grandparents are responsible for taking bodily care of the child and for performing household chores, such as doing the grocery shopping, cooking, cleaning the house, washing the clothes, and taking the grandchildren to school and bringing them back home. In some families, grandparents have additional tasks, such as preparing special meals for the children and feeding them, bathing them, and putting them to sleep. For instance, Niuniu was a three-year girl. For the first three years of her life, she had been primarily tended to by her grandma since her mother took business trips on a regular basis. Her mother had reduced the number such trips in order to spend more time with her daughter. Each night, Niuniu was allowed to choose whether she would sleep with her grandparents or with her parents; with whomever Niuniu chose to sleep was responsible for the "getting-reading-for-sleep" routine (such as brushing her teeth, giving her a bath, and reading her a bedtime story) as well as helping her to get dressed the next morning.

Grandparents also serve as a childrearing safety net for the parents. The division of labor between the mother and the grandparents is defined, but it is not strictly enforced. Most of the time, to accommodate the mother's work schedule, the grandparents willingly undertake more tasks than are originally "assigned" to them to ensure that the grandchild is well cared for. For instance, in the Wang family it was usually Yang who played with Meimei after dinner; however, if Yang did not return home from work on time, the grandparents would automatically "work" overtime to play with Meimei.

Departing from the traditional image of an authoritative figure in the family, fathers in this study have shifted from being their children's disciplinarians to being their children's playmates, spending quality time and having fun together. Serving as a playmate is an important characteristic of the "new father," a paternal ideal that has emerged in recent years. Unlike the authoritative father figure, the "new father" is more involved in childrearing and engages in face-to-face interactions and emotional communications with his child (Wang 2014; Lamb 2000). However, among the interviewed families, fathers had limited time to spend with their children. Only two of the thirteen fathers spent more than an hour with their children on weekdays; quality time between father and child primarily occurred on weekends or holidays. Not all fathers were like Mr. Wang who reserved his weekends for his family; quite a few of the fathers placed a priority on their work and would only join the other family members on weekend activities when they did not have to work overtime.

In addition to serving as playmates, fathers also act as backup or supplementary helpers in times of emergency. For example, the fathers would attend parent-teacher meetings when the mothers were unavailable, take a sick child to the hospital, or discipline the children for difficult issues (usually upon the mother's insistence). These situations occur only occasionally, in contrast to the daily routine of providing childcare and imposing discipline that are performed by the mothers and grandparents. When it comes to important decisions regarding the children's education, such as choosing a kindergarten or selecting a program to cultivate talent, many fathers become involved by offering their thoughts. That said, the mothers discuss the situation with the fathers and solicit their opinions. If the couple cannot reach agreement, however, it is usually the mother who has the final say.[4]

Largely absent from providing daily care for their children, the fathers' main responsibility is to provide financial resources for the expensive child-development plans that the mothers make. Most of my respondents were working parents and both made significant financial contributions to the family. However, many families tended to follow the traditional conceptions of the gender division of labor in the family whereby the man serves as the primary breadwinner. Driven by the high cost of modern childrearing, the role of the father is highlighted by his financial provisions for his child's development, which to some extent rationalizes his absence from the child's daily life.[5]

4.3   *Intergenerational Power Relations*

The story of the Wang family also illuminates a particular power relationship between the parents and grandparents in the intergenerational parenting coalition, i.e., young mothers taking charge and grandparents being marginalized in decision making regarding childcare. As the manager of the childrearing project, young mothers are in charge of decision making, from those decisions related to their child's formal education to arrangements for the child's daily activities. In addition, mothers enjoy more discursive power. On matters such as providing proper care and training as well as cultivating the child's talents, the mother's opinion shapes how things should be perceived and handled. This is often rationalized by their better knowledge of scientific parenting. As a result, the mother assumes the role of supervising the other family members and she intervenes when the latter handle the child in an "inappropriate" way. As illustrated in the case of the Wang family, when Yang's mother attempted to discipline the child, Yang asked her to stay away. In other families, it was not unusual for mothers to monitor the behavior of other family members. For instance, one mother made a no-smoking rule at

---

4   However, a small number of fathers were more involved in decision making. For instance, Xinxin's father read extensively about childrearing in books or online, and he shared that information with his wife. This couple also regularly discussed issues related to Xinxin's upbringing, although normally it was the mother who handled such issues. Xinxin's father explained, "We have much in common regarding our ideas about childrearing. I am more logical, and she is more emotional. Normally, I tell her what to do and she will do it."

5   In a number of the interviews mothers mentioned that they had complicated feelings about the fact that their husbands "did not mind spending money on the child." On the one hand, they complained that their husbands simply spent money but did not know how to provide good guidance for the child. On the other hand, only when the fathers did not mind spending money were the mothers able to effectively implement their child-development plans.

home for the sake of her child's health; her husband had to go outside if he wanted to smoke. Another mother of a 2-year-old boy felt it was a bad habit to hold her son and rock him to sleep and she believed that his grandmother should no longer do this. The 2-year-old screamed and cried for hours when the mother attempted to put him to sleep.. Out of empathy, the grandmother interceded; the mother criticized her, "Letting him be [without proper training] is to spoil the child."

Fathers partially participate in decisions about childrearing, especially when the decisions focus on important matters in their child's development. However, unlike the traditional authoritative figure in the family, fathers are more of a participant and a counselor in the decision-making process rather than being the primary decision maker. Fathers have the right to be informed and share their opinions. However, their opinions matter only if their wives buy into them. For instance, although Mr. Wang had suggested that Meimei participate in a weekend English class, it worked out only because Yang had agreed with the idea that it was important for their daughter to learn English at an early age. The few fathers who actively learn scientific methods of childrearing, however, are usually more influential in terms of how the child should be raised.

In contrast to young mothers, grandparents generally lack power in the decision-making process and they are muted in discussions about childrearing issues. In most families, the grandparents do not participate in decisions related to their grandchildren's formal education. In the Wang family, for instance, Yang never consulted the grandparents when she was selecting a preschool or any programs to cultivate Meimei's talents. In her view, the grandparents were neither interested in nor knowledgeable about these issues. In other families, however, the grandparents may express their opinions but their opinions are rarely considered. For instance, one grandmother objected to her daughter's idea of sending the child to talent-cultivating classes because she believed they were not worth the money. Her daughter offered several reasons why the classes were important, and the grandmother, although not convinced, no longer argued about it.

Grandparents normally take charge of the household chores that they perform, such as choosing what to cook for the family for dinner. In order to ensure that everyone eats well, many grandparents will solicit opinions from other family members. One grandmother told me that she would ask her daughter and son-in-law every night what they would like to eat the following day and she found it easier to make a decision if they gave her a definite answer.

However, providing proper care for the grandchildren is likely to lead to disagreements between the parents and the grandparents. The "old" experiences

INTIMATE POWER 159

of the grandparents are different from "new" methods the young mothers have learned. Taking clothing as an example, the grandparents were often concerned that the child would become cold if he/she did not wear enough, whereas the mothers believed that wearing too much would cause them to feel cold. Young mothers are more likely to win such arguments since they are supported by scientific evidence. Some grandparents learned to ask for the opinions of the parents when they took care of their grandchildren. For example, Grandma Luo, a woman in her late 50s, helped to take care of her 2-year-old granddaughter. As the weather was becoming warmer, she considered putting a thinner coat on her granddaughter. She then checked with her daughter, "Should I change to another coat for the child? If you think it is okay, I will do that; if you believe it is still too cold, I will wait."

In the rare cases when the grandparents are able to prove that their "old" experiences are more effective than the new methods, they tend to obtain some authority and autonomy in taking care of the grandchildren. For instance, the paternal grandmother of 5-year-old Xuanxuan had some previous training in traditional Chinese medicine. When Xuanxuan had a fever, she used indigenous methods, i.e., mixing white spirits, spring onions, and Chinese medicines, and then wiping Xuanxuan's arms and legs with the mixture to help reduce the fever. Xuanxuan's mother was initially suspicious; however, the grandmother's method worked and was more time- and money-saving than taking Xuanxuan to the hospital. Xuanxuan's grandmother was later given authority to take care of Xuanxuan whenever he had a fever.

4.4 A Sociocultural Explanation of Intergenerational Power Relations in Childrearing

Several sociocultural factors contribute to the emergence of the pattern of "grandparents-take-care-and-mothers-take-charge" in the division of labor and power relations in the intergenerational parenting coalition. These factors include the changing discourses on parenting, intergenerational social mobility, and transformation of the family structure. The emergence of modern scientific methods of parenting, the development of the education industry, and the increasing costs of childrearing all led to a revolution in the ways families raise their children. The old experiences of the grandparents may not fit well with the new conditions of child development in contemporary society and thus are useless at the operational level. In addition, popular discourses on scientific parenting, often drawing on various and sometimes divergent theories of child development and parenting skills, foreground their superiority over the traditional ways of childcare, thus further devaluing the grandparents' experiences in childrearing at a symbolic level. Among the interviewed families, young parents often perceived the grandparents' understanding of raising a child as outdated, defective, or even misleading, as illustrated by a quote by one mother:

> When we were little kids, our parents did not know much about parenting. After the family ate together, adults would go about their own business and we children would simply play on our own. There was no such concept as "family education. "My family was living in the countryside then and my parents had not had much education. ... Nowadays, things are very different, and the grandparents' old experiences from a long time ago are no longer useful.

Some grandparents admitted that they were "out of date." Grandma Wang, for example, lived with her son's family and helped to take care of her grandson. She dressed and prepared food for the child every day, but it was her daughter-in-law who decided what the child should wear and eat. Grandma Wang explained, "This [arrangement] is good because it won't cause any conflicts [between me and my daughter-in-law]. Everything is better and more modernized now. We are outdated and cannot keep up with the new things. We need to take it easy, otherwise it does no good."

The fact that older people are losing their authority in terms of how to raise their grandchildren illuminates the features of what Margaret Mead calls the "prefigurative culture" era (Mead 1970). Furthermore, intergenerational social and spatial mobility have inverted the positions of the grandparents and their adult children in the family. Among the interviewed middle-class families, most of the young parents had achieved upward social mobility through education. They were better-educated, had more income, and a higher social status, and were thus regarded as more knowledgeable and capable than their parents. They also had more financial, social, and cultural resources that enabled them to make better arrangements for their children. All these factors gave them more authority and power in the family. Among all the families that I studied, there was only one exception in terms of intergenerational upward mobility. In that case, the grandfather was a retired high-ranking military officer who was receiving a high pension, and his son and daughter-in-law were university professors. However, after the former military division commander moved to Beijing in order to take care of his grandson, the rich social and cultural resources he used to enjoy in his hometown were largely compromised because of the move.

In terms of family structure, most grandparents leave their own homes and move into their children's homes in order to take better care of their grandchildren.[6] The newly formed intergenerational family is an extension of the nuclear family of the young parents. The distinction between the parents as "masters" and the grandparents as guests/helpers is clear. The fact that young mothers are positioned at the center of power in the intergenerational parenting coalition is attributed to two factors associated with the family dynamics. The young mother serves as the mistress of the family and assumes responsibility for all domestic affairs. In addition, handling the important affairs related to the child's development renders the young mother the *de facto* power and authority in terms of making decisions and arrangements for the children.[7]

5　Intimate Power: Intergenerational Intimacy and the Exercise of Power in the Family

In the previous section, I illustrate that in the intergenerational parenting coalition young mothers have more power in decision making and in the discourse on childrearing affairs. Nevertheless, young mothers do not have institutionalized symbolic and moral resources to ensure their authority, and it is not guaranteed that all other family members, especially the grandparents, will comply with the decisions and arrangements that these mothers make for their children. This is a form of uninstitutionalized intergenerational power that leaves room for competition and negotiation within the family, i.e., family members may strategize either to change or to maintain their status in the family. Within this flexible power structure, the maintenance of power relations in the intergenerational parenting coalition is intertwined with the specific pattern of intimacy established between the parents and the grandparents. The young mothers' exercise of power in terms of parenting largely depends on whether the grandparents put up with their marginal status and are willing to make compromises for the sake of maintaining desirable intergenerational intimate relations.

6　It is common among migrant families for the grandparents to leave their hometowns to live with their children in the city (Beijing). Even among Beijing families, some grandparents relocate to live together with their children in order to provide convenient childcare.

7　In traditional families women held *de facto* power to make important family decisions because they were responsible for performing housework and taking care of the family members, but their husbands, who symbolized the head of the family, would give formal approval for their decisions (Li 2010). Departing from the fact that women exercise power implicitly in traditional families, the mothers interviewed for this study had explicit power in decision making, and in most cases, they only involved their husbands in discussions or simply informed them about their decisions.

5.1 Grandparents: Tolerance and Expectations of Intergenerational Intimacy

The main reason why young parents live with the grandparents is that they need help in childcare; their main concern is the development of the children. The grandparents, however, regard helping to raise the grandchildren as a part of intergenerational cooperation. Through such intergenerational cooperation, they hope to maintain continuing mutual assistance in family affairs and emotional bonds with their offspring. When addressing the reasons why they were willing to help with the childcare, most grandparents emphasized the joy of "raising a child." For instance, Grandma Zhang, an old lady in her early 60s who was helping her son with childcare, stated: "We old people enjoy staying with the little ones. This gives us something to occupy [our minds]. My neighbors [an elderly couple] just live alone by themselves. Their son and other children all live apart. Life is rather boring for them."

It is also important for the grandparents to sustain mutual support with their children. They perceive looking after the grandchildren as a way of helping their children, and they expect to receive assistance from their children when they are too old or too sick to take care of themselves, as mentioned in the following by Grandma Zhang:

> Jobs nowadays are highly demanding and competitive for our children. ... We are still healthy; we do not have serious health problems and we are able to take care of ourselves. We should support our children. We do more for them now and then in the future when we are ill, we can count on them [for support].

Grandparents do not seek equality in intergenerational exchanges. Rather, they hope to sustain ongoing reciprocity with their children. They are well aware of the fact that the payback from their children will be delayed and will depend on ongoing positive interactions with their offspring. As Grandma Wang, a local Beijing native who had moved with her husband into their son's apartment to take care of their grandchild, said: "If we have a good relationship with our children, they will stay around [to take care of us] in the future." She and her husband had reached an agreement:

> The two of us realized a long time ago that we would stay out of our children's business since there is definitely a generation gap between us. If we express our opinions about their business, they won't listen to us. It will do nothing but upset us. It is better for us to keep our mouths shut. Whatever they say, we will just listen and not argue. Even if [we believe]

INTIMATE POWER   163

what they are doing is wrong when they discipline him [the grandson], we will remain silent. Too much quarreling does not make for a good life.

Grandma Wang also regarded not arguing with the younger generation as a way of showing tolerance and understanding: "She [her daughter-in-law] is still young and immature. She easily becomes anxious and makes a fuss. On occasion, when we make some comments, she realizes that she made a mistake and then she is more careful in the future. But other times, she simply ignores our suggestions." This quote indicates that the reason why grandparents choose to concede when disagreements come up with their children is not because they accept the authority of their children but because they want to maintain a peaceful relationship that will be beneficial to the entire family.

The grandparents also want to be respected by their children. They desire an intergenerational relationship that includes feelings of intimacy among family members who care about one another and a sense of dignity and status within the family. For instance, Grandma Liu, another grandparent/childcare helper whom I interviewed, took seriously any greetings and expressions of care from her son and daughter-in-law. She said: "We old people do not want money from them. We want kind words. For instance, when they return home, they will say, 'Oh mom, you are still up. What did you eat today?'[8] It is as simple as that." Like many grandparents who in the interviews recalled the moments when their children expressed concern for them, Grandma Liu happily shared one such moment. One day her son-in-law noticed that the old couple planned to fix a simple lunch of noodles. He went out and bought some porridge, Chinese pancakes, and two dishes for them. "I felt very content," Grandma Liu commented.

Respect and understanding from the younger generation are important to the grandparents. For Grandma Wang, filial piety meant forming an equal relationship with her children and not picking on one another. She said:

What is filial piety? It means [the younger generation] does not talk back when I say something, whether I am right or wrong. I am old, a bit slow, and I have a bad memory, so please keep silent even if I am wrong and do not talk back. If there is some disagreement between us, pretend to agree with me. I serve you food, drink, and take care of your daily life, so do not be fussy and create conflicts. I do not pick on you, so do not pick on me.

---

8   This is a common greeting among Chinese people, which is similar to "How was your day?"

However, as discussed in the previous section, in many families young mothers often interfered with the grandparents when they took care of their grandchildren. This not only constituted a direct challenge to the face/dignity of the grandparents but also negatively affected the intergenerational relationship of mutual understanding and tolerance that the grandparents expected. As a result, rather than being cooperative, the grandparents often turned to the grandchildren to build an emotional alliance in an attempt to challenge the maternal power.

Many young mothers whom I interviewed mentioned that the grandparents often undermined their efforts to discipline their child. Many grandparents would intervene to protect a child who was being punished by the mother for not obeying. For instance, Jingjing's mom, who had an MA in art studies from a British university, did not allow her son to eat sweets on a regular basis because she believed they were bad for his health. Five-year-old Jingjing was well-behaved when his mom was present, but his mom later discovered his little secret:

> This child is so clever; he discovered early on when he should go to his grandparents and when he should go to his parents. He goes to his grandpa for candies and roasted sunflower seeds because his grandpa will give him whatever he wants. He very much likes candies and chocolates. I later found out that he was able to sneak a few treats every day. But he did not know to throw away the candy wrapper and he instead left them in a drawer. One day I happened to open the drawer and was astonished to find a full drawer of candy wrappers. I asked my mom (who was taking care of him) about it, and then she admitted to me that she would give the child one piece each day.

Apart from indulging the grandchildren by acquiescing to their demands, some grandparents also try to defend their grandchildren against the parents. The following is an example offered by a young mother who was "defeated" by a "grandparent-grandson-alliance." Because her 4-year-old son would throw his toys everywhere, the young mother asked him to put them back in the toy box. Her son refused to do so and started to cry. Seeing him being unreasonable and acting out, the mother decided to discipline him. The paternal grandfather jumped in, cuddled his grandson, and said, "It's OK! Grandpa will help you clean up!" In a similar manner, other mothers reported, many children have learned to seek protection from their grandparents, crying out for their help when they are being disciplined or punished by their parents.

INTIMATE POWER

In the contemporary intergenerational parenting coalition, mothers who are responsible for the sociocultural rearing of the child tend to train their children according to social demands or according to ideas from modern parenting theories. In contrast, grandparents, who are in charge of satisfying the physiological needs of the children, are prone to take the children's standpoint and empathize with them, offering emotional support when they [the children] are being disciplined (Fei 1998). However, children are little agents who are good at catching the discrepancies between their various caretakers and finding space for negotiation and manipulation (Goh and Kuczynski 2009). By acquiescing and providing defense and protection, grandparents form alliances with their grandchildren, thus undermining the power of the young mothers. The grandparents highly value their relationships with their grandchildren. In my interviews many grandparents offered examples of their close relations with their grandchildren or expressed regret that "the child is still closer to his/her mom."

5.2   *Managing Intergenerational Intimacy and the Maintenance of Maternal Power*

The alliance between grandparents and grandchildren may hinder the mothers' child-development plans and impair the mothers' "managerial" position in childrearing. Aware of the problem, some mothers work on their relationships with the grandparents. Specifically, they attempt to maintain their leadership in parenting by meeting the grandparents' expectations for intimate family relations. In the following, Qing provides a good example.

Qing was a mother of Yuanyuan, a 3-year-old girl. Qing worked in a travel service company as an assistant director and her husband was a vice president of a communications company. When Yuanyuan was eight months old, Qing's in-laws, who had been living in a northern town, moved in with them to help take care of Yuanyuan. The grandmother attended to Yuanyuan's daily needs, and the grandfather took care of the household chores, preparing food for the family and cleaning the apartment. With the help of her in-laws, Qing was able on occasion to watch a movie online or to enjoy tea with friends. For the sake of Yuanyuan's development, Qing believed it was necessary to "educate" her in-laws how to modernize their perceptions and behavior. Given the numerous disparities between her and her in-laws regarding how to raise a child, she prioritized her demands, stressing those that were the most important to her. For instance, she turned a blind eye when the grandparents insisted on feeding Yuanyuan rather than having Yuanyuan feed herself, as Qing preferred. When it came to issues associated with the child's psychological development, however, Qing was rather strict and persistent. For instance, when Yuanyuan fell down, the grandparents were not allowed to comfort her by blaming the floor (such as saying "It was the fault of the floor that our baby got hurt") since Qing felt that this represented an act of misattribution. Most importantly, she did not want the grandparents to intervene when she was disciplining her daughter. She said, "I will continue to reason with them and not give up. But I won't say 'It is absolutely wrong for you to do this' or 'You can never do that.' Quarrelling with them or confronting them is not helpful to family relations. After all, we are all living under the same roof."

Qing paid close attention to the needs of her in-laws. Her mother-in-law had rather large feet and had difficulty finding comfortable shoes at affordable prices. When Qing went to London on a business trip, she bought five pairs of Clark shoes for her mother in-law. Qing also joined the grandparents in conversations about their relatives, although she personally found such conversations to be boring. She generously offered help when her husband's relatives needed it; for example, she helped arrange the wedding when one of his cousins got married and she housed another cousin when he came to Beijing for a visa interview. She commented with humor: "We are the 'reception office in Beijing' [for his relatives]."

Taking advantage of her job, Qing arranged several vacation trips for the entire family. She put her mother-in-law in business class to reduce her air sickness, and she made detailed schedules to ensure that everyone enjoyed themselves without becoming exhausted. She was quite content with her arrangements, and said, "Last time when we were in Singapore, my father-in-law [a CCP member] said that he had never enjoyed such good things when following the party, but now he is able to enjoy himself by following his son. ... My mother-in-law corrected him that it was not his son but rather his daughter-in-law who had made the arrangements."

When Qing was disciplining her child, her mother-in-law gradually agreed to stay out of the way in her own room. However, her father-in-law, who was used to his role as the head of the household, continued to intervene, which sometimes ended in an open conflict. Qing said:

> I said to the grandparents: 'If you disagree with me, we can discuss it after Yuanyuan falls asleep. We should not argue about it in front of her. We can have a family meeting to talk about our disagreements.' But this was really difficult for them [the grandparents]. Sometimes he [the grandfather] acted out on the spot, and I became annoyed and argued with him directly. [I have to admit that] conflicts did exist, but there was no way to avoid them.

INTIMATE POWER 167

However, after these conflicts Qing usually approached her father-in-law and apologized. She gradually managed tó persuade him to leave their apartment when she was disciplining her child. She explained:

> I am living with this family, so sometimes I have to be resigned to this situation. I am not idealistic. I am not a princess. There are certain things I have to accept. Why should I initiate reconciliation with my father-in-law? It makes no sense to argue about who is wrong. Just say what you have to say. After all, he is an old man. I should respect him simply because of his seniority. Even if he is acting ignorant or stubborn, he cleans the apartment and prepares meals for us each night, right?

Qing is strategic when dealing with her relationship with her in-laws. She made it clear that she did not want to be a housewife and that she wanted time and space of her own. Therefore, she required help from her in-laws. Although she might not spontaneously feel close to her in-laws, Qing treated them as family. In her words, "If I do not regard them [the grandparents] as family, how uncomfortable I will feel at home!" Thus "I do and say whatever I should."

Qing's management of the intimate relations with her in-laws includes the following: First, by buying clothing for her in-laws, taking them on family trips, and taking care of her husband's relatives, Qing is properly expressing her care and mindfulness toward her in-laws, and she is making them feel proud in front of other relatives, which in turn wins her a good reputation as being filial. Second, she partially yielded to her in-laws, giving them some autonomy when they took care of her child. Third, in dealing with conflicts with her in-laws she adopted certain strategies, such as making ritualized apologies and holding family meetings. In so doing, she is showing her in-laws respect and giving them the right to express their opinions on certain family affairs. Finally, by making arrangements for the entire family that not only satisfied but actually exceeded her in-law's expectations, she delicately is able to present herself as capable and sophisticated in managing family affairs. Because of these efforts, Qing earned recognition and appreciation from her in-laws and enhanced her status within the family. Positive interactions were thereby established and maintained across the generations, the grandparents received respect and care, and, in turn, they were more willing to trust and to be tolerant of their daughter-in-law.

5.3   *Weak Intergenerational Bonds and the Intergenerational Struggle for Power*

An intimate relationship based on mutual understanding and consideration, which is crucial to the intergenerational parenting coalition, is difficult to establish, especially in families where the coalition is formed between young mothers and in-laws who did not have strong emotional connections before living together. During the initial stage, conflicts often occur between the young mother and her in-laws due to differences in lifestyle, habits, and even in their respective ways of speaking. To avoid conflicts, some families adopt a distancing approach. With a lack of intimate bonds across the generations, young mothers may encounter more challenges in managing the childcare, as revealed in the case of Xuanxuan's family.

When Xuanxuan was one month old, his paternal grandparents moved from their home in southern China to help take care of the baby. At the time of the interview, the grandparents had already been caring for Xuanxuan for more than five years. Xuanxuan's mother, Rong, described her relationship with her in-laws as being "polite but distant." When she was staying at home during her maternity leave, there were some arguments with her mother-in-law on minor issues, which gave her the impression that "it does not work for the two of us to spend every moment together." She thus decided to minimize the number of interactions with her in-laws in order to avoid open conflicts. Therefore, she went to her office every day and stayed as long as possible, despite the fact that her job offered her the opportunity of working from home. In contrast, the grandparents were busy in her home, cooking, washing, cleaning, and so on. Rong was fully in charge of arranging talent-cultivating classes and extra-curricular activities for Xuanxuan, and the grandparents seldom asked about these activities. When it came to Xuanxuan's birthday parties, weekend activities, and vacation trips that the parents organized, the elderly couple rarely participated.

Although Rong was free from performing any household chores, she often felt suppressed at home. She did not have many dinner-table conversations with her in-laws and she had little say about those affairs that her mother-in-law handled. For instance, Rong thought that a big dinner with a lot of meat and fish was delicious but unhealthy. She suggested that her in-laws cook less, but her in-laws ignored her requests. When at home, she also felt that she was under the surveillance of her mother-in-law, which made her feel rather uncomfortable. One time, after she took some fruit out of the refrigerator for her son, her mother in-law called out, "The door is not tightly closed!" These encounters sometimes ended up in confrontations between the two women, which further contributed Rong's strategy of minimizing her interactions with her in-laws.

With the help of the grandparents, Xuanxuan grew up to be healthy, tall, and strong. Rong appreciated her in-laws for their childcare skills, but she found it difficult to discipline Xuanxuan at the home. If Xuanxuan was unwilling to follow her directions, he would simply "turn a deaf ear and refuse to listen." Rong did not consider herself to be strict; rather, she believed in the power of encouragement. However, once in a while when she attempted to discipline Xuanxuan after he misbehaved, he would quickly find shelter with his grandparents. For example, on one occasion when at bedtime Xuanxuan said he was hungry, Rong believed that this was simply a ploy for his not having to go to bed, so she ignored him. However, the grandmother immediately went to the kitchen and provided him with some treats. As another example, Xuanxuan always asked for new toys, which Rong believed was a bad habit. She made an agreement with him that they would not buy any new toys for him for a period of one month since they had already bought him several toys. However, when, on the following day, Xuanxuan went out with his grandpa, he returned home with several new toys.

Rong tried to communicate with her in-laws, typically by announcing at the dinner table her agreement with Xuanxuan over some issue. For instance, "I bought quite a few things for Xuanxuan today, and we agreed that he should not get any new toys for the next month. Grandma and grandpa, please do not buy any new toys for him. But this strategy did not work well at all. So Rong resorted to keeping Xuanxuan out of the house for as long as possible, since she had found it impossible to discipline him in the home. She sometimes felt helpless because her home gradually became "just a place to sleep in."

In Xuanxuan's family, his mother and grandparents maintained a relationship in which they were functionally cooperative but emotionally distant. This helped buffer any open conflicts between them.[9] However, it prevented the possibility of establishing any intimate relations whereby his mother and grandparents would be able to empathize and communicate with one another. In this "polite but distant" intergenerational relationship, the grandparents found it difficult to feel that they were receiving any care or empathy from their daughter in-law, and there was a lack of any emotional bonding between them. Since the buffering effect of intergenerational intimacy was missing, the grandparents tended to apply the principle of unity of responsibility and power. They did not intervene in family affairs in which they were not involved, but by constantly contributing to the family, they accumulated

---

9 Undoubtedly, managing a relationship that is "friendly but distance" is an active attempt to maintain some intergenerational intimacy, a way of avoiding an unsatisfactory intergenerational relationship.

some moral capital,[10] which they converted into total control over their housework. In addition, the grandparents turned to their grandson to build an emotional alliance. By fulfilling their grandson's demands, they consolidated the grandparent-grandson ties that served to maintain their status in the family.

6 Conclusion

Drawing on in-depth interviews and ethnographic data from urban middle-class families, I argue that the building of an intergenerational parenting coalition is a family strategy adopted by urban families in order to cope with the privatization and marketization of childcare in contemporary China. With the family division of labor by gender and generation, a pattern of "grandparents-take-care-and-mothers-take-charge" has emerged in the organization of childcare. Young mothers act as managers of the childrearing project. Equipped with scientific parenting methods, they tend to take the lead in decision making and in the discourses on childcare, making plans for child development and engaging in social rearing, such as the intellectual cultivation and character building of the child. In contrast, the grandparents join the family to provide childcare. They perform a large amount of housework and remain in charge of the physiological rearing of the child, but they are marginalized in terms of family decision making. The rise of this particular pattern of power relations is associated with modern parenting ideologies, intergenerational social mobility, and the shift in family structure.

I further argue that this is a set of fluid, uninstitutionalized power relations modified by affection and interactions among family members. In the intergenerational parenting coalition, young mothers are more concerned about the outcome of their child's development, whereas the grandparents tend to value the maintenance of intimate intergenerational ties, which consist of not only duty-based exchange and assistance but also positive affection and interactions between the generations. In order to maintain desirable intimate intergenerational relations, the grandparents learn to be tolerant, to make concessions, and to yield their authority, thus facilitating the exercise of power by the young mothers. However, when intimate intergenerational relations cannot be established or sustained, the grandparents tend to make fewer concessions and

---

10   "Moral capital" is a term coined by anthropologist Fei Wu to explain family politics. It refers to the behavior and status of an individual that is considered beneficial to the entire family. Wu argues that in family politics or power games, moral capital is an important factor that determines the winner (Wu 2009, 48).

to dilute the power of the young mothers by building an emotional alliance with their grandchildren. I thus use the term "intimate power" to characterize the exercise of power in the intergenerational parenting coalition. I argue that intimate intergenerational relations constitute the premise behind maternal power in the intergenerational parenting coalition, mediating the individual negotiation of power in the family. The term "intimate power" highlights the specific feature of power relations in the family, whereby individual dignity and interpersonal intimacy are intertwined, creating tensions and requiring coordination among family members.

Scholars have discussed the dynamics between intimacy and power in the family. For instance, Wu (2009) points out that "family life is a combination of affection and politics." Familial love is the beginning and the end of family politics; however, the latter does not follow the logic of the former. The principle of family politics is that everyone seeks more power in family life, or at least seeks to be respected by other family members, thus creating a fundamental tension between affection and politics. Wu focuses on this tension in his examination of cases of suicide that end any family relations. In contrast, the present study looks into ongoing intergenerational collaboration, despite the existence of conflicts, thereby better illustrating the coordination of affection and power. I argue that in the process of intergenerational collaboration individuals may hesitate to seek more power in decision making and in the discourse on family affairs so as to maintain a desirable intimate relationship. Maintaining a satisfying intimate relationship constitutes an important goal of family life and to a certain extent compensates for the impairment of power.

A number of scholars have noted an "intimate turn" in intergenerational relationships in contemporary China. With the establishment of the urban pension and medical insurance systems, the elderly are demanding less financial support from their children but more communication, trust, and empathy (Evans 2010; Wang 2012). Norms of filial piety have been redefined by relinquishing unconditional obedience and submission from the junior to the senior generations, thus paving the way to intergenerational intimacy (Yan 2016). Parents are willing to offer financial assistance in order to develop "negotiatory intimacy" with their children (Zhong and Ho 2014), or to yield their authority or power in the process of childcare so as to maintain desirable and sustainable intimate intergenerational ties, as illustrated in this article.

By analyzing the dimension of power in the intergenerational parenting coalition, this study further elucidates the tendency for an inversion in the power hierarchy between the parent and an adult child in intergenerational collaboration. To some extent, the inversion is associated with the fact that the adult child has a higher socioeconomic status than his/her parents. However, the formation, development, and modification of patterns of power in the intergenerational parenting coalition largely depend on the cultivation of intimate bonds among the parents and the adult child. Highlighting these intimate bonds sheds light on the importance of bringing in individual agency regarding the conception and pursuit of family life in studies of intergenerational relations, and thus better informs the logic of practice in collaboration across generations. Future research is needed to unpack the ways in which intimate relations affect family members' pursuit of respect and justice in other forms of intergenerational exchanges and collaborations.

References

Bian, Fuqin, John R. Logan, and Yanjie Bian. 1998. "Intergenerational Relations in Urban China: Proximity, Contact, and Help to Parents." *Demography*, 35(1): 115–124.

Chen, Feinian, Guangya Liu, and Christine A. Mair. 2011. "Intergenerational Ties in Context: Grandparents Caring for Grandchildren in China." *Social Forces*, 90 (2): 571–594. Accessed August 13, 2020.

Chen, Jianxiang and Yufu Wang (eds.). 2005. 《他们影响了一亿家庭——中国当代最著名的十大家庭教育主张》 (They Have Influenced 100 Million Families: The Ten Most Popular Theories of Parenting in Contemporary China). Beijing: Beijing Press.

Cherlin, Andrew J., and Frank F. Furstenberg. 1986. *The New American Grandparent: A Place in the Family, A Life Apart*. New York: Basic Books.

Dong, Yige. 2014. "The Discovery of Parenthood: Science, Gender, and Class in Childrearing Literature during 1980's China." Paper presented at the Association for Asian Studies Annual Meeting, Philadelphia, PA, March 27–30.

Evans, Harriet. 2010. "The Gender of Communication: Changing Expectations of Mothers and Daughters in Urban China." *The China Quarterly*, no. 204: 980–1000.

Fei, Xiaotong. 1998. 《乡土中国 生育制度》 (From the Soil and Fertility System). Beijing: Peking University Press.

Fong, Vanessa L. 2004. *Only Hope: Coming of Age Under China's One-child Policy*. Stanford: Stanford University Press.

Gibson, Priscilla A. 2005. "Intergenerational Parenting From the Perspective of African American Grandmothers." *Family Relations*, 54(2): 280–297.

Goh, Esther C.L. and Leon Kuczynski. 2009. "Agency and Power of Single Children in Multi-Generational Families in Urban Xiamen, China." *Culture & Psychology*, 15(4): 506–532.

Goh, Esther C.L. 2010. "'Only Children' and Their Coalition of Parents: Considering Grandparents and Parents as Joint Caregivers in Urban Xiamen, China." *Asian Journal of Social Psychology*, 13(4): 221–231.

Goh, Esther C.L. 2012. "'She is Too Young for These Chores': Is Housework Taking a Back Seat in Urban Chinese Childhood?" *Children and Society*, 28(4): 280–291.

Guo, Yuhua. 2001. "代际关系中的公平逻辑及其变迁" (The Logic of Equality and Its Transformation in Intergenerational Relations: A Case Study of Elderly Support in Rural Hebei). 《中国学术》 (China Academics), no. 4: 221–254.

He, Xuefeng. 2009. "农村带机关系论:兼论代际关系的价值基础" (On Intergenerational Relationships in Rural China: The Ethical Foundation of Intergenerational Relations). 《社会科学研究》 (Social Science Research), no. 5: 84–92.

Hsiung, Ping-chen. 2005. *A Tender Voyage: Children and Childhood in Late Imperial China*. Stanford: Stanford University Press.

Kang, Lan. 2012. "代差与代同：新家庭主义价值的兴起" (Differences and Similarities between Generations: The Emergence of Values of New Familism). 《青年研究》 (Youth Studies), no. 3: 21–29.

Lamb, Michael E. 2000. "The History of Research on Father Involvement." *Marriage and Family Review*, 29 (2–3): 23–42.

Li, Xia. 2010. 《娘家与婆家：华北农村妇女的生活空间和后台权力》 (Ningjia and Pojia: Women's Living Space and Backstage Power in a North China Village). Beijing: Social Science Academic Press.

Lin, Guangjiang. 2009. 《国家、独生子女、儿童观：对北京市儿童生活的调查研究》 (Nation, Single Child, and the Views of Children: Survey Research on the Life of Children in Beijing Municipality). Beijing: Xinhua Press.

Liu, Guili. 2005. "眼泪为什么往下流？转型期家庭代际关系倾斜问题探析" (Why Are the Aged Suffering? Analysis of Changes in Family Generational Relations). 《南昌大学学报（人文社会科学版）》 (Journal of Nanchang University: Humanities and Social Sciences), no. 6: 1–8.

Liu, Wenrong. 2011. "家庭价值的变迁和延续——来自四个维度的经验证据" (Continuing and Changing Family Values: Empirical Evidence from Four Dimensions). 《社会科学》 (Journal of Social Sciences), no. 10: 78–89.

Liu, Wenrong. 2012. "孝道衰落？成年子女支持父母的观念、行为及其影响因素" (Has Filial Piety Declined? Attitudes, Behavior, and Factors Influencing the Support of Old Parents). 《青年研究》 (Youth Studies), no. 2: 22–32.

Liu, Wenrong. 2013. "当代家庭代际支持观念与群体差异——兼论反馈模式的文化基础变迁" (The Group Difference of Attitudes toward Intergenerational Support in Contemporary Families: Discussion on the Changes in the Cultural Basis of the Feedback Model). 《当代青年研究》 (Contemporary Youth Research), no. 3: 5–12.

Liu, Yan, and Yanping Song. 2013. "中国城市3–6岁儿童家庭学前教育消费支出水平调查" (Survey on Family Expenditures for the Pre-school Education of 3–6=Year-Old Children in Urban Families in Our Country). 《华中师范大学学报（人文社会科学版）》 (Journal of Huazhong Normal University: Humanities and Social Sciences), no. 1: 155–160.

Luan, Liyun. 2009. "变迁中的中国家庭与儿童看护的社会学考察" (A Sociological Investigation of Families and Childcare in Transitional China). 《湖北社会科学》 (Hubei Social Science), no. 8: 50–52.

Ma, Chunhua, Jinqun Shi, Yinhe Li, Zhenyu Wang, and Can Tang. 2011. "中国城市家庭变迁的趋势和最新发现" (Family Changes in Urban Areas of China: Main Trends and Latest Findings). 《社会学研究》 (Sociological Studies), no. 2: 182–216.

Mead, Margaret. 1970. *Culture and Commitment: A Study of the Generation Gap*. Garden City, NY: Natural History Press.

Shen, Conglin, Dongshan Li, and Feng Zhao. 2009. 《变迁中的城乡家庭》 (Urban and Rural Families in Transitional China). Chongqing: Chongqing University Press.

Shen, Yifei. 2013. 《个体家庭iFamily：中国城市现代化进程中的个体、家庭与国家》 (Individual Family (iFamily): Individual, Family and Nation in the Process of Modernization in Urban China). Shanghai: SDX Joint Publishing Company.

Tan, Tongxue. 2010. 《桥村有道：转型乡村的道德权力与社会结构》 (Qiao Cun You Dao: Moral Authority and Social Structure in Rural China during the Transition). Beijing: SDX Joint Publishing Company.

Wang, Xiangxian. 2014. "关于欧美建构新型父职的评述" (A Review of the Construction of New Fatherhood in Euro-American Countries). 《晋阳学刊》 (Academic Journal of Jinyang), no. 3: 77–81.

Wang, Yuesheng. 2009. "制度变革、社会转型与中国家庭变动———以农村经验为基础的分析" (Institutional Reform, Social Transition, and Family Change in China: An Analysis of Evidence from Rural Areas). 《开放时代》 (Open Times), no. 3: 97–114.

Wang, Yuesheng. 2010. "个体家庭、网络家庭和亲属圈家庭分析——历史与现实相结合的视角" (Individual Family, Network Family, and Kinship Circle Family: From the Combined Perspective of History and Reality). 《开放时代》 (Open Times), no. 4: 83–99.

Wang, Yuesheng. 2012. "城乡养老中的家庭代际关系研究——以2010年七省区调查数据为基础" (Intergenerational Relations in Elderly Support in Rural and Urban China: Evidence from a 2010 Survey of Seven Provinces). 《开放时代》 (Open Times), no. 2: 102–121.

Wu, Fei. 2009. 《浮生取义：对华北某县自杀现象的文化解读》 (For Justice: A Cultural Interpretation of Suicide in a North China County). Beijing: Renmin University of China Press.

Xiao, Dong. 2002. "最后一代传统婆婆？" (The Last Generation of Traditional Mothers-in-Law). 《社会学研究》 (Sociological Studies), no. 3: 79–91.

Xiong, Yuegen. 1998. "中国城市家庭的代际关系与老人照顾" (Intergenerational Relations and Elderly Care in Chinese Urban Families). 《中国人口科学》 (Chinese Journal of Population Science), no. 6: 15–21.

Xu, Anqi. 2004. "孩子的经济成本：转型期的结构变化和优化" (The Financial Cost of Childrearing: Structural Change and Optimization in the Social Transition). 《青年研究》 (Youth Studies), no. 12: 1–8, 35.

Xu, Qin. 2011. "农村老年人家庭代际交往调查" (A Study of Intergenerational Interactions Among Elderly People in Rural China). 《南京人口管理干部学院学报》 (Journal of Nanjing College for Population Programme Management), no. 1: 5–10.

Yan, Yunxiang. 2003. *Private Life under Socialism: Love, Intimacy, and Family Change in a Chinese Village*, 1949–1999. Stanford: Stanford University Press.

Yan, Yunxiang. 2012. 《中国社会的个体化》 (The Individualization of Chinese Society). Shanghai: Shanghai Translation Publishing House.

Yan, Yunxiang. 2016. "Intergenerational Intimacy and Descending Familism in Rural North China." *American Anthropologist*, 118 (2): 244–257.

Yang, Shanhua. 2011. "中国当代城市家庭变迁与家庭凝聚力" (Changes Among Urban Families in Contemporary China and Family Cohesion). 《北京大学学报（哲学社会科学版）》 (Journal of Peking University: Philosophy and Social Sciences), no. 2: 150–158.

Yang, Shanhua and Changmei He. 2004. "责任伦理与城市居民的家庭养老" (The Ethics of Responsibility and Family Support in Beijing: An Analysis Based on Data from a 1999 Survey on the Demands of the Aged in Beijing). 《北京大学学报（哲学社会科学版）》 (Journal of Peking University: Philosophy and Social Sciences), no. 1: 71–84.

Zheng, Dandan and Shanhua Yang. 2003. "夫妻关系定势与权力策略" (Marital Relations Formulary and Power Tactics). 《社会学研究》 (Sociological Studies), no. 4: 96–105.

Zhong, Xiaohui and Sik Ying Ho. 2014. "协商式亲密关系：独生子女父母对家庭关系和孝道的期待" (Negotiative Intimacy: Expectations of Family Relationships and Filial Piety Among Only-child Parents). 《开放时代》 (Open Times), no. 1: 155–175, 7, 8.

Zuo, Jiping and Yongping Jiang. 2010. 《社会转型中城镇妇女的工作与家庭》 (Work and Family of Urban Women during the Transitional Period). Beijing: Cotemporary China Press.

CHAPTER 8

Losing an Only Child

Parental Grief among China's Shidu *Parents*

Lihong Shi

Throughout Chinese history, parents always grieved over the loss of a beloved child when they encountered the fragility of a young life ended by illness, an accident or a disaster, or suicide. Mourning essays, memorial poems, and burial laments reveal the deep yearnings and profound sorrow experienced by such bereaved parents following the loss of a child (Hsiung 2005:196–97; Hung 1995). For example, a Han dynasty eulogy, inscribed beside a relief stone that portrays a young boy, tells the story of parental grief over the death of the five-year-old boy: "... Your spirit wanders alone/ In eternal darkness underground/ You have left your home forever/ How can we still hope to glimpse your dear face?/ Longing for you with all our hearts/ We came to pay an audience to our ancestors/ Three times we increased offerings and incense/ Mourning for our deceased kin. ..." (Hung 1995:80). Such parental grief is vividly encapsulated in the widely known Chinese saying "a gray-haired parent burying a dark-haired child" (*baifaren song heifaren*, 白发人送黑发人).

Although coping with the death of a beloved child has always been a psychologically and emotionally traumatic experience for many bereaved parents, in China today parental grief can be exacerbated because Chinese society is witnessing a rise of neo-familism (Yan 2018) that features a child-centered family ideal and practice (Fong 2004; Jankowiak 2009; Kipnis 2009; Shi 2017; Yan 2016). Further aggravating parental grief is an unintended consequence of China's one-child policy that was in force from 1979/80 to 2015). Many families may lose their only child, due to illness, accidents, suicide, or homicide. Referred to as *shidu* families (失独家庭), meaning literally losing an only child, in official documents, media reports, and by the bereaved parents themselves, a substantial number of these families are unable to have another child due to age (Han 2017; Shen et al. 2016). It is estimated that in 2010, one million Chinese women over the age of thirty-five who had previously given birth then became childless (Wang et al. 2013).

In this chapter, I discuss parental grief among China's *shidu* parents, focusing on the impact of the changing intergenerational relations and chil-drearing practices on the experience of parental grief. I employ the notion

© LIHONG SHI, 2021 | DOI:10.1163/9789004450233_009

of post-patriarchal intergenerationality proposed by Yunxiang Yan (see the Introduction to this volume) in my analysis. Yan argues that post-patriarchal intergenerationality highlights the subjective domain of Chinese family life and the significance of intergenerational interactions in the formation of personal identity and the construction of personhood. Yan points out that Chinese personhood is relationally constructed (see also Yan 2017) and the intergenerational relationship is the primary relational thread in the construction of Chinese personhood. "Individuals of different generations constitute each other: parents regard children as part of themselves and vice versa" (see the Introduction chapter to this volume). Yan conceptualizes such a construction of personhood as the "intergenerational integration of personhoods."

With the emergence of an increasingly child-centered parenting landscape in China, the intergenerational integration of personhood is intensified. Meanwhile, among families who have only one child, the intergenerational integration of personhood relies on the bonds between a parent and an only child. Thus, losing an only child not only severs the parent-child tie but also disrupts the formation and development of Chinese personhood. Consequently, child loss may present enormous psychological, cognitive, and existential challenges to the *shidu* parents. In the following sections, I first discuss how the parent-child integrated personhoods are developed and strengthened through the pursuit of shared life goals between the parents and their child. I argue that in their pursuit of shared life goals with their child, parents identify themselves by their child's successes or failures. I then delineate how the premature death of an only child can lead to a self-imposed identity of a failed parenthood. Meanwhile, as they have to continue to live in a child-centered environment, not being able to live up to the ideal of having an intact and happy family can result in a notion of failed personhood among the *shidu* parents. I also discuss how, in the process of coping with grief and the reconstruction of personhood, *shidu* parents try to identify new shared life goals and experiences with their child without the physical participation of their child. I conclude the chapter by discussing how the integration of personhood across generational lines will continue to present challenges for *shidu* parents along their journey of grief.

Data for the analysis in this chapter are based on in-depth interviews with fifty-three *shidu* parents (thirty-two women and twenty-one men) between 2016 and 2019 in urban areas of China. *Shidu* parents often find each other through introductions by mutual friends or in virtual communities via two social media platforms—Tencent QQ and WeChat. Many *shidu* parents have formed their own groups and have organized gatherings and interest-group activities, some with the support of a local government or a non-governmental organization. I thus recruited my informants through snowball sampling by asking my informants to introduce me to their *shidu* friends as potential interviewees.

The interviewees were between the ages of fifty-one and eighty at the time of my first interview, but the majority were between their mid-fifties and mid-sixties. All but six were retired. Among the retirees, the majority had worked for government agencies or state-owned factories and were receiving retirement pensions. All of my informants were longtime urban residents and owned at least one apartment. However, some of their pensions were relatively small and some owned an apartment situated on the outskirts of a metropolitan region. Sixteen of my informants had one or two grandchildren whom their own child had left behind (thirteen with one grandchild and three with two grandchildren).[1] None of my informants had another child after their loss, although some had attempted to have another child with or without assisted reproductive technologies or through adoption.

Due to the extremely traumatic pain experienced during the initial stage of grief, I purposefully recruited informants who had lost their child at least one year earlier. The majority of my informants had lost their child for more than three years at the time of my first interview. The age of their child at the time of his/her death ranged from eight to the mid-thirties. Some parents had spent many years caring for their child who was seriously ill, such as with cancer, whereas others had experienced the sudden death of their child due to an accident, sudden cardiac arrest, suicide, or homicide. Although each grief experience is unique depending on the variations in their parenting experiences, the circumstances surrounding the child's death, and the differences in the availability of economic resources and social support for the bereaved parents, they share a group identity as *shidu* parents because of their shared loss.

In addition to interviews, I conducted participant observations by attending their group gatherings, such as dinners and interest-group activities. I also stayed with six of the informants during my field trips and had the opportunity to observe their daily coping and grandparenting practices. In addition, in 2016 and 2019 I visited a cemetery located on the outskirts of a metropolitan region, where several of my informants had buried their child. Covering an area of over one hundred and fifty acres, this large cemetery had two sections reserved for small children, adolescents, and young adults. Through the gravesite arrangements, I collected data on how parent-child bonds were manifested and how parental grief was expressed. Moreover, from three WeChat public accounts

---

1 Their child was able to have a second child after the one-child policy was relaxed. In the early 2000s couples were allowed to have a second child if both spouses were singletons, and in the early 2010s couples were allowed to have a second child if one spouse was a singleton.

LOSING AN ONLY CHILD

(*weixin gongzhonghao,* 微信公众号), created and edited by *shidu* parents that published original essays written by *shidu* parents, I collected a large number of essays to understand how parental grief is experienced and expressed.

1 Pursuit of Shared Life Goals

During my interviews with *shidu* parents, many of them shared with me their cherished memories of their child, telling me about their child's personality and character, his/her hobbies and friendships, educational and career achievements, and unfulfilled dreams. Some also told me stories about their parenting experience as they were navigating the emerging landscape of intensive parenting. Their accounts revealed not only who their child was but also how their parenting experience had shaped who they had become. As their childrearing practices indicated, they had found purpose and meaning in life by pursuing shared life goals with their child and they identified themselves through their child's successes and failures, joy and sadness.

My informants' pursuit of shared life goals with their child is manifested during various stages of their child's life. Those who had lost their child before the child had graduated from high school, college, or graduate school often shared with me their child's educational pursuits and their own efforts to help their child achieve educational success. Like their peers who have high aspirations for their child's educational and career achievements, my informants had expected that their child would complete college or even graduate school and their educational attainments and skills would be translated into successful careers. They had tried to save family financial resources to provide their child with the best possible living conditions and educational opportunities. Some of my informants shared how they wholeheartedly supported their child's educational pursuits by paying large sums for their child's college education and graduate education. Two of them were among an increasing number of middle-class parents in urban China who paid high tuition fees for an overseas education that could provide the child with an opportunity for transnational upward mobility (Fong 2011); two others told me that their child had been accepted by overseas universities for graduate studies at the time of their child's death.

According to my informants, helping a child achieve educational success goes far beyond financial support. In China's highly competitive educational system, parents have to offer emotional support and practical guidance when the child encounters educational challenges or failures. Some of my informants shared with me intimate memories of comforting a child who experienced distress or anxieties from his/her studies. For example, like many of my informants who were devoted parents, Ms. Liu, a mother who had lost her daughter one year before I first met her, told me of her shared experience with her daughter the day before the daughter had taken the college-entrance examinations ten years earlier. Considered one of the most important life events for a high-school senior, the college-entrance examinations represent the ultimate challenge that a student must confront in his/her pursuit of a college education. The day before the first day of the examinations, Ms. Liu had accompanied her daughter to the site of the examination so her daughter would become familiar with the route to the location. Despite the fact that since elementary school her daughter had always been an outstanding student, later that night her daughter expressed feelings of extreme anxiety. Ms. Liu comforted her by reminding her of her excellent school record and the importance of focusing on her efforts instead of concentrating on the outcome of the examination. In an essay Ms. Liu wrote, she describes in detail this memorable experience, writing: "I was actually more nervous than my daughter." For parents like Ms. Liu, supporting a child's educational pursuits involves embarking on an emotional journey with the child as the child competes for the best possible educational opportunities.

Some parents also told me about their conscious efforts to help their child seeking intellectual nourishment, such as taking their child to bookstores or on regular museum visits. Similar to middle-class parents in Kunming in Southwest China who took their child to Beijing to "broaden his/her range of experience" (Kuan 2015:192), many of my informants had taken their child to historical and scenic sights in China during the summer or winter breaks. According to my informants, sightseeing was not only a break for a child from their rigorous educational programs but it was also an opportunity for the child to be exposed to China's natural beauty and to enrich his/her knowledge of Chinese history and culture.

Several of my informants had even made major career decisions to accommodate their child's educational pursuits, such as by giving up their own career advancement opportunities so they could place a priority on helping their child do well or by changing their job and relocating to another city with better educational resources for their child. For example, a father told me that his wife had been a high-achieving manager at her company and once had even been given the opportunity to be promoted, which would have required a commitment to a busier work schedule. However, she did not accept this opportunity so that she could spend more time with her daughter who was preparing to compete for admissions to one of China's top universities.

The shared life goals did not end with a child's completion of his/her educational pursuits. My informants with a child who had become financially

LOSING AN ONLY CHILD   181

independent through gainful employment continued to identify with their child's desires for career success, marriage, and parenthood. Urban Chinese parents devote their time to provide practical support to their adult children, living with their child and assuming responsibility for household chores so that their child can focus on their careers, enjoy their leisure time, or pursue friendships (see the chapter by Fong et al. in this volume), to help a child find a marriage partner and finance their wedding (see the chapter by Davis in this volume; Zhang and Sun 2014), or to provide care for a daughter during her pregnancy (Zhu 2010). Similarly, my informants whose child had reached marriage age continued their pursuit of shared goals with their child by providing financial and emotional support. Some of my informants owned two apartments, one of which they had purchased for their child's wedding or in preparation for their child's future wedding. Four parents whose child had experienced a difficult divorce shared with me their emotional and practical support to their child, such as comforting their child who was deeply distressed or moving into their child's apartment to take care of the grandchild.

With the birth of a grandchild, many Chinese parents offer extensive childcare assistance to relieve their child of the financial burden of having to hire a nanny and to support a child's career pursuits, forming "intergenerational parenting coalitions" (Goh 2011) or "intergenerational cooperation (see Xiao's chapter in this volume). Although urban retirees are not as confined to childcare duties as their rural counterparts, who often serve as surrogate parents for a grandchild while their own child migrates to an urban area for employment (Santos 2017; see Thompson's chapter in this volume) or who have to relocate to their migrant child's city to offer childcare support (see Qi's chapter in this volume), many urban parents still have to sacrifice the free time that they have after retirement and continue their support by helping their child with childcare (Chen et al. 2011). Some grandparents have even replaced the parents as caretakers and emotional guardians for their grandchild (see Jankowiak's chapter in this volume). Despite the tremendous amount of physical and affective labor involved in caring for a grandchild, involvement in their child's married life solidifies the intergenerational bonds and gives the parents a sense of fulfillment (Jankowiak and Moore 2017). Among sixteen of my informants who had one or two grandchildren, thirteen were providing extensive childcare assistance to their child at the time of their child's death, co-residing with or living close to their child's family.

In their active pursuit of shared life goals with their child, parents identify themselves through their child's successes and failures. Those whose child was considered successful, measured by the criteria shared among Chinese parents, i.e., going to one of China's most prestigious universities or a university overseas, receiving a master's degree or even a doctoral degree, or obtaining an extremely competitive position with a highly coveted employer, felt a particular sense of pride. These parents shared with me their child's achievements, some mentioning the competitiveness of the challenges that their child had overcome to reveal their child's outstanding performance vis-à-vis their peers. In the essays written by *shidu* parents, some parents also shared their child's accomplishments by mentioning their child's alma mater, usually a prestigious university, or the name of their child's employer and the position that their child had held. At the cemetery referred to above, I saw a few graves where the alma mater of the deceased was inscribed on the gravestone. A few informants used the well-known phrase *tiandu yingcai* (the great have a great hardship to contend with, 天妒英才) to describe their child's talents and outstanding achievements and the ways in which they had attempted to come to terms with their child's premature death.

Those whose child did not attend a prestigious university or had not achieved career success emphasized the outstanding characteristics of their child, conveying their pride in the child's cultivation of a moral personhood (Kuan 2015; Xu 2017). They frequently referred to the child's filial piety, a highly regarded virtue in Chinese society, sharing with me stories that revealed their child's consideration and sensitivity toward them even at a very young age. Several parents told me of an intimate bond that their child had with the child's grandparents, such as a child showing loving care to an aging grandparent. Other virtues that parents frequently mentioned were a child's compassion and kindheartedness, such as their child helping a friend in need. In addition, a few parents whose child had battled a serious illness expressed sincere respect for their child's emotional strength. After sharing with me cherished memories of her child, a mother, who lost her daughter three years earlier, said: "My child was not as outstanding (*youxiu* 优秀) as those of some of my *shidu* friends. She did not attend a good university, but she was a very good child. The children who died were all good children (*zoude doushi haohaizi*, 走的都是好孩子)."

2 Child Loss and Failed Personhood

An only child's premature death abruptly ends a parent's shared pursuit with that child and thus terminates the intergenerational integration of personhoods. Consequently, while coping with a new reality of a life without their beloved child, many *shidu* parents encounter challenges in forming a new identity as a parent without a child. First, while grieving over the loss of their child, *shidu* parents often hold strong feelings of guilt and self-blame, which may lead to a self-imposed identity of failed parenthood. Furthermore, as they continue to live in a child-centered society where having a happy family and maintaining a strong bond with a child plays an indispensable role in the formation of personal identity and the construction of personhood, child loss may also lead to a perceived sense of failed personhood.

Parental grief often involves feelings of regret, guilt, and self-blame. Among many of my informants, these feelings were first derived from their constant struggles with thoughts of things they could have done to save their child's life or to prevent their child from a fatal accident. Although some of them also expressed a sense of powerlessness for not being able to prevent their child's premature death, many parents had strong feelings of self-blame. Among my informants whose child had died of illness, some blamed themselves for not taking good care of their child. For example, several informants mentioned overlooking a child's complaints of physical discomfort, only to be informed later of a fatal diagnosis when the symptoms worsened. Among parents whose child had died by suicide, their feelings of guilt and self-blame were even more intense. Many of the children who had died by suicide suffered from clinically diagnosed depression. Some parents who knew about their child's condition had tried all possible means to find a cure to their child's suffering, such as traveling to a hospital in another city that specialized in treatment for depression and even preventing earlier suicide attempts. After the loss of their child, the parents blamed themselves for not being able to prevent their child's suicide, for not being patient enough as their child was battling depression, or for not being caring enough to be aware of their child's distress.

Parental guilt and self-blame often extend beyond the circumstances related to their child's death. My informants tended to reexamine their parenting experiences during various stages of their child's life and to identify their parenting mistakes. Some parents expressed their regret for not being patient or for not spending enough time with their child. For example, a mother, who lost her son to illness three years earlier, shared her regret, saying: "One time my son did something that made me really angry. I didn't speak to him for several days. Now, whenever I think about this, I have feelings of great regret." Some mentioned their regret for not being able to provide better living conditions for their child or for not raising their child to enjoy life to the fullest. For example, a mother, whose daughter had died at the age of sixteen, said: "My daughter was a very hardworking student. Had I known that she would have such a short life, I would have let her have more fun." While some parents also emphasized the selfless and wholehearted efforts that they had made for their child, self-perceived mistakes could become greatly magnified after the death of their child. For instance, a father told me that he could not forgive himself for not trying hard enough to help his daughter with her job search, saying that this had become the most difficult obstacle for him to overcome in his grief journey.

Such feelings of guilt and self-blame could lead to a strong sense of parental failure among my informants. In particular, many of the children who had passed away were unmarried and many of them were completing their education in graduate school, college, or even high school and middle school. They had not reached the stage when they could live independently by supporting themselves through employment. My informants felt a strong sense of responsibility to provide financial support to their child and to guide their child through the transition to gainful employment and marriage. When sharing with me their childrearing experiences, my informants often mentioned their active involvement in the decision-making process during their child's major life transitions, such as choosing the university that their child attended or offering critical suggestions about their child's career choices. Thus, according to my informants, child loss suddenly transformed them from proud parents who devoted their lives to supporting their child's life goals and enjoyed their child's achievements into parents who failed to protect their child from premature death and even failed in their parental responsibilities. Some parents who held intense feelings of parental failure tended to contrast their child's excellence with their perceived unforgivable parenting mistakes.

Although feelings of guilt and self-blame following child loss can result in a self-imposed identity of failed parenthood, the misfortune of losing an only child can lead to a notion of failed personhood among the *shidu* parents. Some informants told me that they felt like a loser (*shibai* 失败) when they compared themselves with others whose families remained intact. When I inquired about such feelings of failure, some explained that they felt that they had failed to live up to the ideal of having an intact and happy family (*jiating yuanman*家庭圆满). While coping with child loss, they had to continue to live in a child-centered environment where their acquaintances, friends, and relatives were all continuing to pursue shared life goals with their child. Some parents told me that they had reached the stage of life when their peers were celebrating a child's transition to marriage and parenthood. As proud grandparents, their peers often engaged in lively conversations about their grandchild, sharing the joy of grandparenting. Those who had not yet become grandparents enjoyed exchanging news about their child. Socialization with their peers constantly reminded the *shidu* parents of their loss and the reality of the collapse of an intact and happy family. If they had integrated their life goals with those of their child and had identified themselves with their child's achievements

LOSING AN ONLY CHILD   185

and cultivation of moral personhood, the premature death of their child ended both their shared pursuit with their child and their identity as a person who had achieved success and happiness. When I asked a mother who had already lost her son for over ten years about the strong feelings of failure among the *shidu* parents, she explained: "I guess we still care very much about the halo of having an intact and happy family."

Feelings of failure may lead to an internalized inferiority among many *shidu* parents. In interviews and group dinners, my informants often shared with me such feelings as they tried to describe their experiences as *shidu* parents, using phrases such as *diren yiding* (feeling inferior 低人一等) or *tai bu qi tou* (being unable to held their head high 抬不起头). For example, a father who lost his son eight years earlier explained his decision not to attend dinners with his friends, saying: "I used to enjoy having dinner with my former classmates. After my son died, I no longer wanted to attend those dinners. My son was a good child. He had a very good job. If my son had been alive, for sure my former classmates would have wanted their daughters to date him. I certainly would have been a grandfather already. Now how can I go to the dinners and hear them talking about their child and grandchild?" Similar to this father's experience, the drastic turn of life after child loss led to a strong sense of inferiority among many *shidu* parents when they encountered their peers who did not share such a loss.

Consequently, many of my informants tried to hide the loss of their child from others to avoid revealing their emotional pain or conveying to others their sense of failure. It became common practice among *shidu* parents not to engage in active socialization with strangers for fear that inquiries about their child would come up at a certain point during the socialization process. For example, some parents told me that when participating in group exercises in a park or when joining travel excursions, they tried not to become too close to others to avoid having to exchange information about their personal lives. Some shared with me that when they were asked about their child, they would lie about their child and try to end the conversation as fast as they could. Among the parents who had lost their child to suicide, some even tried to hide the cause of their child's death when they met with other *shidu* parents. In China, suicide is considered a loss of face for the entire family (Chow 2006) and parents whose child has died by suicide are found to have experienced greater feelings of shame than parents whose child has died in an accident (Séguin et al. 1995). A father whose son died by suicide told me that when asked he would say that his child died of illness or an accident, instead of admitting it had been suicide.

3 Continuation of the Parent-Child Bond

After surviving the initial stage of child loss when their grief consumed them and their daily functioning was compromised, *shidu* parents had to learn to rebuild their lives without their beloved child. Studies on bereavement reveal that a grieving individual can maintain continuing active bonds with a deceased loved one through a sense of presence of the deceased, belief in the deceased person's continuing influence on thoughts or events, or a conscious incorporation of the deceased's virtues or characters into oneself (Klass 1996; Klass and Steffen 2017). In the process of healing from their grief, many of my informants found new ways to maintain the parent-child bond despite the physical absence of their child and ways to reconstruct the integrated intergenerational personhoods. Some parents tried to fulfill their child's wishes, thus identifying new shared goals with their child. For example, some who took sightseeing trips tried to make the journey into a shared experience with their child. Those who had a grandchild helped their child's surviving spouse raise the grandchild, a way to continue the shared life pursuit with their child without the actual participation of the child. Finally, some parents prepared to share a grave with their child, thus continuing the parent-child bond in the afterlife.

Some parents who tried to fulfill their child's wishes identified such endeavors as new shared goals with their child. One example was the longtime effort by *shidu* mother Yi Jiefang to fulfill one of her son's final wishes expressed before his death. Well-known among my informants through media reports and their participation in tree-planting activities she had organized, Mother Yi had started to plant trees in the desert areas of Inner Mongolia province in 2002, two years after her son had died in an automobile accident in Japan. While grieving over the loss of her son, Mother Yi remembered that her son told her after graduation from college of his wish to plant trees in the desert to help prevent and control the sand storms that plagued northwest China (Liu 2017; Ma and Zeng 2018). She and her husband closed their clinic in Japan, returned to China, and founded an organization dedicated to planning trees in Inner Mongolia (Ma and Zeng 2018). During the next fifteen years, her organization planted five million trees in the desert (Ma and Zeng 2018). In an interview, Mother Yi told a journalist: "Had it not been for my son, planting trees was not something I would ever had considered" (Liu 2017).

While Mother's Yi's story is unique because of her strong determination and the financial resources required to engage in this endeavor (she and her husband had to fund their organization on their own) (Ma and Zeng 2018), several of my informants identified other achievable pursuits that allowed them to fulfill their child's wishes. For example, a father decided to study a foreign language that he had learned many years earlier as a way to honor his son who had majored in a foreign language in college and who had wished to work as an interpreter after graduation. The father told me that he had been following a plan to read a few pages in that foreign language daily and he had even attempted to translate them into Chinese. The father said: "My son was not able to fulfill his dream. I am doing it for him. Doing this makes me feel as if he is still alive." Some informants emphasized their child's kindheartedness and spirit of volunteerism when they extended a helping hand to others, such as comforting a newly bereaved parent or providing practical help to a *shidu* friend. While in an intensive parenting environment in which a child's success in the pursuit of his/her life goals is viewed as an extension of a parent's achievements, a *shidu* parent may extend a child's life pursuits by fulfilling the child's wishes on the child's behalf.

In addition to identifying a shared pursuit with their child, some parents tried to create a shared experience with their child to maintain the parent-child bond. One example is taking a trip as a shared experience with a child. After surviving the initial stage of child loss, many parents found traveling for sightseeing to be therapeutic as they could enjoy being a tourist and feel relaxed when away from an environment where they were constantly reminded of their loss. The majority of my informants were middle-class retirees who could afford at least one trip each year to a tourist destination. At the time when I met them, many parents had already traveled to the major tourist destinations in China and even a few foreign countries. Some of them shared with me that they made traveling a shared experience with their child. They mentioned that their child had not had the chance to see the outside world and thus they wanted to see the world on behalf of their child. One mother said to me: "We are our child's eyes to this world (*women shi haizi zai renjian de yan*, 我们是孩子在人间的眼)" as an explanation for the motivation behind her and her husband's regular sightseeing trips. When making decisions on travel destinations, they often avoided places that they had visited with their child in the past in order not to evoke painful memories of an earlier shared travel experience with their child. Instead, they tried to create new shared experiences by traveling to destinations that their child had never visited. Some told me that their decision to travel to a particular place was due to their child's earlier expressed wish to visit that destination. While on the trip, they kept a photo of their child with them. Some took a child's belongings with them, such as wearing their child's backpack or a child's shirt, symbolizing their child's presence in spirit. One mother in tears shared with me that on her trip to a foreign country, to which her daughter had expressed a strong interest in visiting, she sat by the ocean with her daughter's photo in her hand and in her heart she said a few words to her daughter.

The shared travel experience with a child was described by a mother in an essay written in the style of a letter to her daughter, published in one of the WeChat public accounts edited by *shidu* parents. The mother wrote to her daughter: "For the remainder of our lives, mom and dad will serve as your eyes in this world. Carrying with us love and longing for you, we will take you to the outside world to see the beautiful scenery that you did not have the chance to visit" (Hui 2919). She wrote about a "three-person trip" she had taken with her husband and her daughter several months earlier, describing the museums they visited, the shopping malls where they strolled, and the river they toured. She wrote: "Mom and dad decided to take you to this place because we knew that you would like it," and her daughter was thus present in spirit on the trip.

Among the *shidu* parents who have one or two grandchildren, helping to raise their grandchildren allows them to continue their shared pursuit with their child as well as to maintain the parent-child bond through the grandchildren. Among the sixteen informants who had one or two grandchildren, nine were primary caretakers of their grandchildren, raising their grandchildren alone or with their spouse or other family members; their grandchildren's surviving parent made regular or no visits to the grandchildren. Three informants were secondary caretakers of their grandchildren, often spending weekends with their grandchildren. The remaining four informants were not involved in raising their grandchildren due to the long distance from their grandchildren's place of residence or intense conflicts with their grandchildren's surviving parent, thus making it difficult to meet with their grandchildren on a regular basis.

Raising a grandchild when already in their fifties and sixties in a highly intensive parenting environment presents serious challenges, for instance, for paying for a grandchild's increasing education costs, helping a grandchild with schoolwork that required a high level of involvement by an adult family member, or communicating with a grandchild with whom there is a big generation gap. In addition, among my informants conflicts often arose over shared childrearing responsibilities between a *shidu* parent and a grandchild's surviving parent who had remarried and who placed a priority on his/her newly formed family. Despite the challenges, none of my informants told me that they wanted to relinquish the opportunity to raise their grandchildren.[2] Those who were primary caretakers of their grandchildren told me of their willingness to make

---

2   None of my informants were the legal guardians of their grandchildren because their grandchildren had a surviving parent.

LOSING AN ONLY CHILD

their best effort to support their grandchildren's educational and career pursuits. When I met Ms. Li in 2019, she was widowed and was the primary caretaker of her nine-year-old grandson whom her son had left behind four years earlier. Her grandson's mother had remarried and had recently given birth to another child. The mother had not been very involved in raising Ms. Li's grandchild after the death of Ms. Li's son, only making financial contributions for childrearing. Ms. Li's grandson was enrolled in one of the most highly ranked elementary schools in the city and thus his time after school was taken up with his very demanding schoolwork. Ms. Li had to supervise her grandson to do his schoolwork as well as to take part in extracurricular activities, as was required by her grandson's school. She shared with me that she had debated whether she should enroll her grandson in this school one year after her son's death when her grandson was ready to start elementary school. She told me that her son had moved his family to the area from a different part of the city so that the grandson could enroll in that particular elementary school. She thus considered it her duty to fulfill his son's wishes. Although not all of my informants made such great efforts for the sake of their grandchildren's education, they all shared a similar sense of responsibility and a willingness to raise their grandchildren on behalf of their deceased child. By raising their grandchildren, they were able to maintain a bond with their child by continuing to share his/her life goals through the grandchild.

Perhaps the ultimate manifestation of a lasting parent-child bond is the arrangements among some *shidu* parents for a shared grave with their child. China officially bans coffin burials but the ashes after cremation are commonly buried. Adult children often purchase plots for graves in a cemetery for their deceased parents and they visit the graves on Tomb-Sweeping Day (*qingming jie*, 清明节), when Chinese families honor and mourn deceased family members, as well as on other occasions such as the anniversary of a parent's death. Married couples are often buried in the same grave after death, symbolizing their reunion in the afterlife. The spouse who passes away first will have his/her ashes placed in an urn inside a grave with his/her name inscribed on one side of the gravestone. When the other spouse dies, the urn that contains the person's ashes will be placed next to those of his/her spouse and his/her name will be added to the gravestone.

Shidu parents make various arrangements for a final resting place for their child, usually purchasing a grave or scattering their child's ashes in the ocean. Among those who choose a grave burial, their child's grave becomes an intensely personal and emotionally charged space where the bereaved parents can express both their love and loss. In the cemetery that I visited, one of the two sections that were reserved for small children, adolescents, and young adults had forty-four custom-designed graves with epitaphs through which the bereaved parents expressed their respective interpretations of the personalities, virtues, and accomplishments of their child as well as their intense yearnings for their child. Epitaphs with phrases such as "We are together forever (*women yongyuan zai yiqi*, 我们永远在一起)," "We will meet again in heaven (*tiantang chongfeng*, 天堂重逢)," and "In this life, you are mom and dad's beloved child; in the next life, we will continue our destined ties (*jinshi ni shi baba mama zhiai, shiwai women ren xu ciyuan*, 今世你是爸爸妈妈挚爱, 世外我们仍续此缘)" were inscribed to convey their strong longings for their child and their desire to continue the parent-child tie in the afterlife.

While strolling in this section of the cemetery, I found that twenty-five of these graves were designated for a parent-child burial. The granite stone covering this type of grave was divided into three equal parts or into two parts with one part larger than the other, indicating a three-person grave. Typically, the name of the child was inscribed in the middle or on one side of the gravestone along with the years of the child's birth and death, while the remaining space was reserved for the names of the parents, although on several of these gravestones the names and birth years of the parents were already inscribed. As I was walking through other sections of the cemetery, I found additional same style parent-child graves. A father who had buried his daughter in one of the parent-child graves in the cemetery explained his and his wife's choice for a parent-child burial, saying that they wished to keep their daughter company in the afterlife (*pei zhe ta* 陪着她). A mother, who was divorced after her son's death and whose husband remarried and had another child, told me of her wish to have a shared grave with her son, saying that, "I didn't get to spend enough years with my son and I want to be with him after I die." Except for a few parents who said that they were believers in religion, the majority of my informants either denied the existence of an afterlife or were ambivalent about such an existence. Nevertheless, the arrangements for a parent-child burial revealed their desire for a continuation of the parent-child bond in the afterlife.

4 Conclusion

The changing intergenerational relations that highlight the intergenerational integration of personhood present particular challenges for *shidu* parents as they learn to cope with child loss. With the death of an only child, and thus the disruption of the construction of personhood, such parents either have to establish an individual identity that is separate from their identity as parents or to find new ways to continue their integrated personhood with their child. Claiming a separate identity is a difficult task for the majority of the *shidu* parents who had incorporated their life goals, their sense of meaning in life, and their identity into their child's life pursuits and their child's achievements and failures. Several informants focused on their own career successes, defined by their positions and their income-earning capacity, in an attempt to refute the notion of a failed personhood. For example, one father, a highly successful and wealthy businessman who had already lost his child for over ten years, said to me: "When others ask me about my child, I tell them the truth and say my child died. So what? I live a very good life. No one can look down upon me." Nevertheless, the majority of my informants, who were retirees and had not achieved such a level of career success, resorted to new ways to identify a shared life pursuit, and even a shared experience, with their child in an effort to reconstruct an integrated personhood with their child.

All of my informants told me that they never will get over the pain from losing their beloved child. Therefore, parental grief is a journey that they will have to take for the rest of their lives. As Chinese society is becoming increasingly child-centered and as *shidu* parents are approaching old age, when support and companionship from a child are highly valued, parental grief will remain a challenging experience for *shidu* parents. Thus, as they continue to cope with child loss they will have to look for ways to redefine their identity and reconstruct their personhood.

Acknowledgements

Funding for field research was provided by the Wenner-Gren Foundation for Anthropological Research and the College of Arts and Sciences at Case Western Reserve University.

References

Chen, Feinian, Guangya Liu, and Christine A. Mair. 2011. "Intergenerational Ties in Context: Grandparents Caring for Grandchildren in China." *Social Forces* 90 (2): 571–594.

Chow, Amy Yin Man. 2006. "The Day After: Experiences of Bereaved Suicide Survivors." In *Death, Dying and Bereavement: A Hong Kong Chinese Experience*, ed. Cecilia Lai Wan Chan and Amy Yin Man Chow, 293–310. Hong Kong: Hong Kong University Press.

Fong, Vanessa L. 2004. *Only Hope: Coming of Age under China's One-Child Policy*. Stanford: Stanford University Press.

Fong, Vanessa L. 2011. *Paradise Redefined: Transnational Chinese Students and the Quest for Flexible Citizenship in the Developed World*. Stanford: Stanford University Press.

Goh, Esther C. L. 2011. *China's One-Child Policy and Multiple Caregiving: Raising Little Suns in Xiamen*. London: Routledge.

Han, Shengxue. 2017. 中国失独家庭调查 [A Study of China's *Shidu* Families]. Beijing: Qunzhong Press.

Hsiung, Ping-chen. 2005. *A Tender Voyage: Children and Childhood in Late Imperial China*. Stanford: Stanford University Press.

Hui. 2019. 带着思念去旅行: 思儿的味道 [Traveling with My Longing: The Scent of Longing for My Child]. 爱在蓝天之家 [Love under the Blue Sky], March 21.

Hung, Wu. 1995. "Private Love and Public Duty: Images of Children in Early Chinese Art." In *Chinese Views of Childhood*, ed. Anne Kinney, 79–110. Honolulu: University of Hawai'i Press.

Jankowiak, William. 2009. "Practicing Connectiveness as Kinship in Urban China." In *Chinese Kinship: Contemporary Anthropological Perspectives*, ed. Susanne Brandtstädter and Gonçalo D. Santos, 67–92. London: Routledge.

Jankowiak, William and Robert Moore. 2017. *Family Life in China*. Malden, MA: Polity Press.

Kipnis, Andrew. 2009. "Education and the Governing of Child-Centered Relatedness." In *Chinese Kinship: Contemporary Anthropological Perspectives*, ed. Susanne Brandtstädter and Gonçalo D. Santos, 204–222. London: Routledge.

Klass, Dennis. 1996. The Deceased Child in the Psychic and Social Worlds of Bereaved Parents during the Resolution of Grief. In *Continuing Bonds: New Understandings of Grief*, ed. Dennis Klass, Phyllis R. Silverman, and Steven L. Nickman, 199–215. New York: Routledge.

Klass, Dennis and Edith Maria Steffen. 2017. Introduction: Continuing Bonds---20 Years On. In *Continuing Bonds in Bereavement: New Directions for Research and Practice*, ed. Dennis Klass and Edith Maria Steffen, 1–14. New York: Routledge.

Kuan, Teresa. 2015. *Love's Uncertainty: The Politics and Ethics of Child Rearing in Contemporary China.* Berkeley: University of California Press.

Liu, Shangjun. 2017. "大地妈妈"易解放和她的五百万棵"绿色生命树" ["Mother of Earth" Yi Jiefang and Her Five Million "Green Trees of Life"]. *Zhongguo qingnian wang* [China Youth Net], December 1. http://qclz.youth.cn/znl/201712/t20171201_11091092.htm, retrieved October 8, 2019.

Ma, Mingyue, and Hong Zeng. 2018. "大地妈妈"易解放的十五年"生死承诺" [Fifteen Years of the Life-and-Death Promise of "Mother of Earth" Yi Jiefang]. *Fenghuang wang* [Fenghuang Net], March 8. https://gongyi.ifeng.com/a/20180308/44899816_0.shtml, retrieved October 8, 2019.

Santos, Gonçalo D. 2017. "Multiple Mothering and Labor Migration in Rural South China." In *Transforming Patriarchy: Chinese Families in the Twenty-First Century*, ed. Gonçalo D. Santos and Stevan Harrell, 91–110. Seattle: University of Washington Press.

Séguin, Monique, Alain Lesage, and Margaret C. Kiely. 1995. "Parental Bereavement after Suicide and Accident: A Comparative Study." *Suicide and Life-Threatening Behavior* 25 (4): 489–498.

Shen, Changyue, Long Xia, Bingying Shi, Pingju Li, and Qi Tan. 2016. 失独家庭救助与社会支 持网络体系研究 [A Study of Social Support Networks for *Shidu* Families]. Shanghai: East China University of Science and Technology Press.

Shi, Lihong. 2017. *Choosing Daughters: Family Change in Rural China*. Stanford: Stanford University Press.

Wang, Guangzhou, Yaoling Hu, and Liping Zhang. 2013. 中国生育政策调整 [Adjustment of the Family Planning Policy in China]. Beijing: Social Sciences Academic Press.

Xu, Jing. 2017. *The Good Child: Moral Development in a Chinese Preschool*. Stanford: Stanford University Press.

Yan, Yunxiang. 2016. "Intergenerational Intimacy and Descending Familism in Rural North China." *American Anthropologist* 118 (2): 244–257.

Yan, Yunxiang. 2017. "Doing Personhood in Chinese Culture: The Desiring Individual, Moralist Self and Relational Person." *Cambridge Anthropology* 35 (2): 1–17.

Yan, Yunxiang. 2018. "Neo-Familism and the State in Contemporary China." *Urban Anthropology and Studies of Cultural Systems and World Economic Development* 47 (3/4): 188–224.

Zhang, Jun and Peidong Sun. 2014. " 'When Are You Going to Get Married?' Parental Matchmaking and Middle-Class Women in Contemporary Urban China." In *Wives, Husbands, and Lovers: Marriage and Sexuality in Hong Kong, Taiwan, and Urban China*, ed. Deborah S. Davis and Sara L. Friedman, 118–146. Stanford: Stanford University Press.

Zhu, Jianfeng. 2010. "Mothering Expectant Mothers: Consumption, Production, and Two Motherhoods in Contemporary China." *Ethos* 38 (4): 406–421.

CHAPTER 9

The Chinese Proto Neo-Family Configuration

A Historical Ethnography

William Jankowiak

1   Introduction

Chinese kinship patterns are being reformulated as individuals respond emotionally and pragmatically to the formation and management of the family. As a result, new patterns of kinship are emerging. Although some researchers report a continued preference in some regions to follow the patrilineal decent principal and the patrilocal resident norm, that is, a form of cultural continuity (Eklund 2018), there remains strong agreement that in other regions Chinese kinship and family organization no longer routinely adhere to the patrilineal decent and patrilocal resident norms (Harrell and Santos 2016). Instead, there is a more fluid and open (kin) relationship that "now unites both sides of the couple's family" (Zang and Jankowiak 2017:341). The new family configuration, which involves active participation by the paternal and maternal grandparents, has been described in various ways, with each author looking to establish a clear perspective on the new phenomenon: the bilateral multi-generational family (Jankowiak 2009), the only-hope phenomenon (Fong 2004), intimacy through inter-generational negotiations (Zhong and Ho 2014), child-centered relatedness (Kipnis 2009), or the neo-family (Yan 2016:253–54).

In a series of pioneering publications, Yan (2003; 2016) notes the behavioral traits of the neo-family, or the inverted family, as conjugal intimacy, a warmer parent-child relationship, inter-generational intimacy, and a striving for self-fulfillment and success. Although Yan does not discuss when the neo-family first crystalized into its present form, the neo-liberal perspective argues that it is relatively recent phenomenon, arriving in the mid-1990s when China's economic reforms reshaped societal values and introduced new norms. A cultural historical perspective would stress the critical importance of focusing on the parents' values, attitudes, and actions to establish a base line so as to identify which behaviors persist across generations and which behaviors have been transformed. I am in solid agreement with the core traits that Yan identifies as typical of the neo-family. In support, I offer a correction to the dating that the neo-liberal perspective (Anagnost 1997; Greenhalgh and Winckler 2005;

© WILLIAM JANKOWIAK, 2021 | DOI:10.1163/9789004450233_010

THE CHINESE PROTO NEO-FAMILY CONFIGURATION 195

Rofel 2007; Hairong Yan 2008) ascribes to the first appearance of neo-family–behavioral traits.

Earlier archival research (Diamant 2000), combined with my own field research in the 1980s, finds that many of the traits were already present, though in a more muted form, during the pre-market, or *danwei*, era. I contend that this earlier proto–neo-family configuration set the stage for what would later become the neo-family.

To illustrate the gradual rather than sudden transformation of the Chinese family into its present-day form, I will focus on five areas representative of the neo-family configuration: a good marriage, the parent-offspring relationship, the relationship with the in-laws, individual expression and achievement, and a residence preference (e.g., patrilocal, matrilocal, neolocal, or multi-generational local). My premise is that prior to the reform era (which began in the mid-1990s when the work-units were abolished or they adopted a more limited scope), the desire for mutual love as well as changes in parenting behavior were already present in northern Chinese cities. So, too, was the new value of individual happiness—underscored by heightened self-awareness and personal reflection—and changes in the visiting patterns between parents and children. In the 1980s adult offspring visited their parents, whereas beginning in the twenty-first century parents and children now visit each other.

2 Family Organization: A Brief Overview

China is an agrarian civilization in the gradual process of becoming an urbanized society. During different eras and in different regions, the Chinese family has displayed a variety of forms, functions, and relationship dynamics (Hsu 1971). The pre-1949 Chinese family was an economic, political, and jural unit. It was organized around patrilocal residence and a patrilineal descent ideology and it was grounded in a patriarchal kinship authority. Elderly males, especially fathers, held authority over the entire family (Watson and Watson 2004).

The transformation of the family as a common-property–holding unit expanded rapidly under Chinese socialist policies throughout the Maoist era (1951–1979) (Diamant 2000). Government policies were the determining factor in the reconfiguration of the urban family that reshaped the social landscape through the introduction of "new features or possibilities (e.g., high age of marriage, elimination of polygamy and concubinage, reduced dowries, and weakened corporate kin groups)" (Davis and Harrell 1993:19; Croll 1994; 2002). Without this sweeping sociological transformation, the neo-family as we know it today would not have appeared.

3   The Neo-Family: Attitudes Toward Love and Marriage in the 1980s and the 2000s

For much of Chinese history, families attempted to inhibit the development of deep-seated marital intimacy. Because a large family was deemed to be more important than its individual members, personal sacrifice was expected for the sake of the well-being of a larger family (Salaff 1981; Schneider 2014; Whyte 2005). "Spouses' personal feelings toward each other were comparatively unimportant when it came to loyalty, cooperation, and harmony within the larger kinship unit" (Salaff 1981:42). This ethics of sacrifice made an individual marriage something larger than merely the interests of two individuals. The interests and welfare of others, including not only the child but also the grandparents on both sides had to also be taken into consideration. Previous generations defined a "good marriage" according to an individual's ability to effectively perform his or her respective family roles (Watson and Watson 2004). For women, the roles were child-bearing and responsibility for management of the household; for men, it was the commitment and ability to provide for the family (Croll 2002; Fan and Huang 1998; Watson and Ebrey 1991). The collective will, as opposed to that of the couple, was deemed to be most important, thus making it an essential value (Jankowiak 2013; Yu and Liu 2014; Watson and Watson 2004).

The 1950 Chinese Marriage Law provided women with a new source of power. Government approval to obtain a divorce effectively undermined the ability of many families to enforce their collective will (Diamant 2000). A woman could reject such a collective will through divorce. The new freedom for the woman to pursue her own interests contributed to the transformation of the family reconfiguration into a hybrid, neo-local/bilateral descent arrangement. This is not a recent phenomenon. Archival research by Diamant (2000) has uncovered rich evidence that the Marriage Law enabled women, through calculated divorce and rapid remarriage, to realize their own interests. The result was the refusal of many women, at times in open defiance, to obey their mothers-in law.

Throughout the 1980s, as in the 2000s, there was a wide range of responses by residents of Hohhot to the meaning of marriage and family life. During both eras, if a couple loved each other, they expected to be considerate of each other. For example, a good marriage, in the words of one woman, should be "a bond between equals who do not keep secrets from each other and who enjoy each other's company. They should prefer to do everything together." A younger 24-year-old female said: "In a good marriage, men and women should help each other." Another female asserted that in a good marriage "there should not be any secrets between a husband and a wife." For the most part, men and women shared similar expectations from the marriage. Spouses and outsiders considered mutual consideration and respect to be important values with which to assess the quality and the success of a marriage. These are not gender-specific values. However, the wishes of the wife carried much weight in how a husband would spend his free time, though not every man responded with similar sensitivity. In any case, sacrifice and compromise were not constitutionally foreign to either spouse (Jankowiak 1993:228–29).

The assumption of the single-child generation about what constitutes a good marriage has not deviated from the assumption of their parents in the 1980s. At the beginning of the twenty-first century, Chinese youth continue to marry for a variety of reasons, ranging from a desire to amass material resources, fulfil social expectations, or achieve mutual love. The overall concept of love as articulated by singleton youth is strikingly similar to that of their parents' generation. For example, a 2008 focus group of Shanghai residents described the same attributes of romantic love as did residents of Hohhot in a 1987 focus group, best summarized in the following comment: "It is maddening, a hot, crazy, and amazing feeling; it makes us happy; it makes us worried; it makes us excited, and it is one that we do not want to share with others."

The Hohhotian focus group was asked: "How do you know you are in love? The responses elicited the following comments: "You feel a hurt in your heart when he is not around." "He is my only, and without him I cannot live." "Love is determined. I will obey this arrangement until I die." "I cannot sleep without her." "I miss her, I think about her constantly" (Jankowiak 2013).

A question asking how one should behave in love, yielded the following responses: "You show you care." "You do everything for the person." "You help one another." "You want your lover to be happy." A 22-year-old, not part of the focus group, added: "When I am in love, I want a lot of affection and I also want to give a lot of affection. Being in love involves simple things like holding hands, sitting close together, snuggling up on the sofa to watch a late-night movie. It also means speaking and acting kindly and having respect for one another." In both 1987 and 2008, love was conceptualized as an idealization of the beloved (Jankowiak et al. 2015).

However, there are generational and social-class differences. Most single children participated in a dating culture rather than in the semi-formalistic courtship culture of their parents and, unlike those of their parents' generation, for the most part they tended to fall in love before marriage rather than after agreeing to marry (Jankowiak 2013; 2018). In the 1980s there was a difference between those who were and were not college-educated: the former put a greater priority on the spousal relationship. In the 2000s there appears to be less of a class difference. According to a 2006 national survey including80,000 participants, both the college-educated and the non-college–educated agreed that it is important to place a priority on the spousal relationship while at the same time to respect each other's autonomy (Zang and Jankowiak 2017:351)

A belief in the viability of a loving marriage gave rise to a related expectation of an egalitarian marital relationship. In this way, urban China renegotiated the meaning of the marriage contract, in a similar way that British society did in the 1830s, to include a rational practicality concerned with material realities along with a newer assumption that a good marriage should also be based on perfect harmony or true love (Hays 2015:21). This expanded definition of a "good" Chinese marriage has become intertwined with a new, albeit evolving, moral code (Davis 2014; Davis and Friedman 2014). In Chinese society, the generations continue to be in dialogue with each other and among themselves about what should, and should not, constitute an appropriate standard to assess a good marriage. The resultant assessment is linked to the meaning of life satisfaction. This is consistent with the findings of Jieyu Liu (2006) in her study of marriage in Nanjing. Liu found that a good marriage is defined less by the fulfillment of complementary sex roles and more by the degree of shared empathy and mutual respect. In this way, the single-child generation has been influenced by their parents' conviction that love and marriage do not exist in inevitable tension, even if in the parents' experience harmony between love and marriage had to be worked for and maintained.

4 The Neo-Family and Parent-Child Involvement: The 1980s vs. the 2000s

Historically, Chinese sex-linked parenting roles were sustained, if not developed, because men and women occupied different positions within the social structure. By controlling the distribution of the family inheritance, a father could create a special, if not psychological, dependency on the part of the child. A mother's parenting style was seen as much as a result of being considered an "outsider" as it was of a "natural" attachment fostered through childbirth and early childcare. Given her lower status in her husband's family, the mother needed a friend and an ally, and there was no better candidate than her own child (Stafford 2000; Wolf 1972). In this way, the different access to, and use of, economic and psychological "resources" contributed to the reinforcement and elaboration of the two complementary parenting styles: the father as disciplinarian provider and the mother as intimate nurturer (Jankowiak 1993).

THE CHINESE PROTO NEO-FAMILY CONFIGURATION 199

Although this sex-linked pattern was present throughout the 1980s, many youth voiced complaints about it. Some rejected the aloof and reserved position of their father. Others vowed that they would interact with their only child differently after he/she married. This shift in emotional orientation is similar to the one found among youth wanting to establish a warmer, closer relationship with their spouse. Among the 1980s' generation, both spouses preferred this kind of "ideal" relationship, though few achieved it. However, there was a correspondence in the way they interacted with their children An interest in, if not an idealization of, a warmer spousal relationship had a corresponding impact on the transformation of the interactions between parents and their offspring. Although they were not clear how best to achieve such a relationship, most were emotionally awakened to its possibility, even if they felt it was not for them. In this way, the 1980s' generation, compared to the marital/parenting orientation of the single-child generation, was muted and less-clearly defined. Still, urban youth in the 1980s, rather than believing in the detachment of their fathers and the obligational duty that grounded it, thought it desirable to interact with their spouse and offspring based on authentic feelings.

The desire to form a more affectionate parent-child bond is a salient feature of the neo-family configuration (Kim, Brown, and Fong 2017). During the preceding decades there was a gradual shift as the parent-child relationship deepened and expanded. For example, unlike their parents' generation, fathers of the single-child generation become more involved with their child at a younger age (Li and Lamb 2015). An observational survey of parenting found that the sex of the child did not affect the frequency that the child was taken on a public outing. Daughters (n = 31) were taken out as frequently as sons (n = 30). But this was the case only among fathers. Mothers took out their sons (n = 86) compared to their daughters (n = 44), a discrepancy of almost 50 percent. I suspect the difference arises from the fact that boys are more physically active in their homes. It is a wholly positive and supportive motivation meant to encourage sons to engage in physical activity. Getting out of the house is simply faster and cheaper than going on an outing. As one mother stated: "Sometimes I just need to get my son out of the house." Mothers did not feel the need to do the same with their daughters. There were no external or inner pressures to do so. It is telling that the majority of children accompany both parents on public outings, further demonstrating the value married men place on the development of closer family bonds (Jankowiak 2011).

Perhaps one of the more surprising changes has been the reversal in family roles whereby fathers are more involved and more nurturing and mothers have become the family disciplinarian and are responsible for the time management of their only child (Li and Lamb 2015). In this way, what began in the

1980s as a generalized wish to become more engaged, twenty years later had become a new family dynamic that was no longer based on role performance but rather on a warmer and kinder child-parent bond.

The increased value attached to gender equality and conjugal affection has further enhanced a woman's social standing within the family. Unlike women in Beijing during the 1940s, urban women during both the 1980s and the 2000s are no longer hesitant to voice their opinions and they readily do so in their roles both as wife and mother. As noted above, today it is the mother, not the father, who is the family disciplinarian. Moreover, there is an increased frequency of fathers attempting to forge closer, warmer bonds with their child (Li 2018).

The shift in parenting style had a corresponding impact on reshaping the mother-daughter relationship in the single-child generation. Throughout the 1980s when the work-units still existed, daughters maintained close and intimate relationships with their mothers. The special attachment of younger wives to their mothers was reflected in the frequency of their contacts with their mothers.

Margery Wolf, finding a similar pattern in Beijing, described her surprise at "how often women were taking care of their daughter's children, not their son's children" (1985:210). Wolf reported that: "Married daughters are closer to their mothers than married sons are" (1985:210). This is not to say mothers were distant from their married sons but rather that they felt closer and more intertwined with their daughters. Harriet Evans's 2008 study of urban mother-daughter relationships also found a strong generational shift from a mild emotional parent-child connection to a more intense, intimate, and enduring mother-daughter relationship. However, Jankowiak, working in Hohhot during 1980s, did not characterize the mother-offspring relationship as "mild." For most, especially for daughters, it was more accurate to characterize such a relationship as lovingly intimate. Evans's other finding that mothers preferred a daughter represents a marked departure from the earlier era that attached more value to the mother-son bond (Fong 2002).

Another departure from the 1980s is the parental, especially the mothers', interference with a daughter's mate selection. Parents made suggestions and daughters and sons sometimes sought advice, but if a parent insisted on the rejection of a potential mate, most children refused to comply. In 1983, a 22-year-old college student speaking about her own unique circumstance noted: "They [my parents] only have one child, so they have to take me back." By the early 2000s single-child youth, especially daughters, were actually beginning to listen to their mothers and they would drop a potential boyfriend based on their parents' advice, even if they had strong feelings for him. Daughters consistently assert that they can trust their mother more than they can trust themselves. The more open, liminal dating culture has heightened a woman's anxiety about making a mistake in mate selection and this has translated into the single-child generation having more faith in their mothers' opinion of possible mates. This is particularly true for daughters (Jankowiak and Li 2017). It is a relatively new and remarkable phenomenon that is consistent with the neo-family configuration.

5 The Neo-Family: The Daughter-In-Law and the Mother-In-Law Relationship

To fully appreciate the degree to which the Chinese inter-generational family organization has changed, or has been inverted, it is essential to examine the transformation in the mother-in law and daughter-in-law relationship. Similar to changes in marital and parental expectations, mother-in-law and daughter-in-law relationships were redefined away from a hierarchical command response to mutual respect. This transformation—parallel with the change in the definition of a good marriage—was well under way before the reform era.

For much of Chinese history, the mother-in-law was the custodian of the patrilineal family line and a determining force in managing (one can accurately describe it as micro-managing) her beloved son's wife, which indirectly affected her son's emotional orientation (Wolf 1972). The old family script held that a daughter-in-law would work closely with her husband's family. As a matter of domestic routine, she was constantly tested to see if she placed the interests of her new family above all else. If she did not pass this test, she was thought to be unreliable and disloyal. In both the earlier and later eras, a mother's greatest fear was that she would lose her son to his wife (Wolf 1972).

The introduction of land reform and open market policies weakened family organization, enabling the daughter-in law to renegotiate the relationship with her mother-in-law to one of mutual respect, if not primacy (Croll 2002; Diamant 2000). Other factors that helped to weaken the husband's relationship with his mother, at least in the early years of the marriage, were the absence of a patrilocal residence norm as well two new developments: the financial independence of women and the husband's increasing emotional dependency on his wife.

The role of the wife's mother is an indicator of the newly gained power of the wife within the family. It also highlights the continuing importance that mothers exert on their daughters' lives. Childbirth often fundamentally alters family social roles, reshaping the nuclear family and transforming it into a stem family. For example, a young wife in 1983 who had dutifully followed the patrilineal custom of regularly visiting her husband's family after the birth of her child looked to her own mother for advice, emotional support, and child-care. Childbirth typically reactivates the mother-daughter bond and justifies the wife's decision to visit her mother more often than she visits her mother-in-law. Furthermore, husbands accepted this new visiting pattern.

In an effort to prevent the potential loss of their sons, mothers in Hohhot, in a dramatic break with patriarchal norms, during visits tend to cater to their daughters-in-law as honored guests. In 1982 a 54-year-old mother pointedly told me that she treated her daughter-in-law with special attention because she did not want to lose her son and become a forgotten mother (*hou ma*). She explained: "Whenever she [the daughter-in-law] drops over, I give her special things and if she wants to help out, I always praise her and thank her. You see, China has changed. I am afraid that if she does not feel comfortable in her husband's home, she will no longer accompany him on visits and, in time, I will lose my son to her family. Do you know that daughters in China follow their mothers and husbands follow their wives?"

Other mothers-in-law, to their own dismay, were not so enlightened. A 73-year-old woman shouted: "When I was young, I obeyed my mother-in-law. Not so today. Everything has changed. My daughter-in-law is not afraid of me. In fact, she rarely listens to me. She worries more about her own mother than she does about me, her husband's mother!" Another elderly woman con-stantly bitterly complained that her son loved his wife more than he loved his own mother because "men love sex more than they love their own mothers" (Jankowiak 1993:240–41). This rearguard reaction is not representative. By the 2000s, this pattern of mothers' assisting their daughters-in-law has become even more pronounced. They are aware that the wife plays a central role in shaping family interactions and she will react with anger if she feels that she no longer is respected. As a result, both the husband and the wife's parents work to maintain respectful interactions.

The awareness among urbanites of the importance of routine politeness has extended to the countryside, where research reports that village mothers-in law are acutely aware of the importance of maintaining a polite, respectful discourse with their daughters-in-law (Qi 2018; Yan 2015). Still, no matter how polite a mother-in law attempts to be, several daughters in Hohhot resent the presence of their mothers-in–law and actively lobby their husbands to visit their mothers less frequently or to visit their mother on their own (Wang, a sociologist at Inner Mongolia University, oral communication). Although this action appears to contradict neo-family behavioral patterns, it is the exception that proves the rule. The few wives who reject the presence of their mothers-in-law prefer a closer, more totalizing bond with their husbands.

THE CHINESE PROTO NEO-FAMILY CONFIGURATION 203

Throughout the 1980s and the 2000s, sons were caught between two conflicting cultural expectations. On the one hand, they were expected to support their parents both emotionally and financially, and most wanted to do so. On the other hand, they desired a smooth, happy, cooperative household and a warm relationship with their wife's parents. Wives had the same desire and herein one finds the conflict. Both spouses, on a small budget, attempted to please three different households, with the household of the in-laws last in terms of priority. In the 1980s, it was expected that the son would regularly every month present his parents with a small monetary gift. I found, however, that daughters preferred to send money to their own parents.

A major source of conflict among married couples stems from the continued conflicting cultural expectations and demands to meet their traditional parental obligations. In one way, this conflict can be viewed simply as an economic problem but, in another way, it also portrays the already persistent conflict between husband and wife over which set of relatives, if indeed either, should be favored. The question of special or favored treatment is a matter of serious disagreement. It rests on the fundamental question of fairness, which boils down to an ethical question. Regardless of what issue is involved, a conflict of cultural norms is inevitable.

In the 1980s more than 86 percent of all urban women between the ages of 26 and 40 held jobs. The increased household income enabled a number of women to send money home to their parents. Significantly, among seventy households surveyed in the 1980s, 29 percent gave money to both the wife's and the husband's parents (Jankowiak 1993). But the arrival of children—a deciding factor—often changed this pattern. Many married urbanities insisted that once they had children their own immediate families were in need of larger incomes than their parents who did not have serious financial needs. In the 1980s, most parents, especially among elite families, supported their children's priorities. Other families understood their children's reasoning but still felt that the change was further evidence of a reduction in their children's love. In 1982, a 57-year-old mother of three children summed up the issue: "We saved and gave our eldest son an expensive wedding; now he no longer wants to give us any money."

In the 1980s, the woman's ability to shift her family's Sunday visiting schedule to her own natal family and away from her husband's family was representative of the wife's new-found confidence as well as her ability and power within the domestic sphere to be more assertive. The current politics of the family cuts across every social class. In this way, family politics is grounded in the rhetoric of folk axioms, socialist ideology, as well as pragmatic necessity. Although some researchers (Hong Fincher 2014; Zurndorfer 2015; 2018) insist that the reform era resulted in a reduction in women's power resources and this has led to a heightened dependency on their husbands who are thus able to reshape the family in their own interests, my research has not found evidence that the shift weakened or diminished the domestic authority or power of women in their roles as wives within the family.

To summarize: the appeal of a loving marriage among the single-child generation did not reduce the quality of the mother-daughter bond nor did it change the daughter-in law/mother-in-law pattern of respectful tolerance that was prevalent in the 1980s. Both the parent-offspring interactions and the in-law relationships, two of the core features of the neo-family configuration, reveal a remarkable cultural continuity in both eras (Whyte 2005). There has been a more pronounced shift in the way fathers, as opposed to mothers, interact with their offspring, often resulting in more active involvement by the father with their only child. In the process, in this century mothers have transformed the parent-child bond into a more-nuanced, emotional bond of co-dependency, as opposed to independence (an often-stated parenting goal). This especially pertains to daughters who adamantly insist on maintaining a close and warm mother-daughter relationship.

6   The Neo-Family: Individual Introspection, the 1980s vs. the 2000s

The redefinition of the work-unit as the primary means to organize society, along with the state's retreat from actively monitoring citizen behavior, provided an opportunity for greater individual experimentation. No longer constrained within a web of social surveillance, individuals found that the market economy provided greater anonymity. Late-night restaurants, entertainment clubs, and dance halls made for a zone of privacy in which individuals could engage in behavior that previously had been deemed inappropriate. For example, the singleton generation adopted a more open attitude and increased tolerance of all of the following: bodily decoration (e.g., tattoos), career mobility, foreign travel, casual dating, spontaneous sexual trysts, active pursuit of true love, divorce, cohabitation, the distribution of pornography, conjugal intimacy, and hands-on parenting.

In spite of the sociological transformation, it is not clear whether singletons are more introspective than the generation of the parents, who often bemoaned their lack of choice, expressing regret at not having a chance to pursue their dreams or life goals. Members of the 1980s' generation were acutely aware that social organization during the work-unit era blocked individual achievement and they resented government rules restricting choice and opportunity. In every way, the social structure of the work-unit in the 1980s restricted employment opportunities. It blocked upward mobility, which undermined the value that Chinese society placed on personal achievement (i.e., norms and values that celebrated achievement or individual success). The disjuncture between the value of achievement and the limited options contributed to feelings of existential anxiety. For example, a young woman felt that her life was a failure because she had never been able to choose her own job: "I was told to be a clerk. I never had a choice to do anything else."

The unmistakable yearning among youth to engage the full range of their abilities is evident in a 1980 letter to the editor of a popular magazine, *Zhongguo qingnian* (China Youth). It reads in part: "Dear Editors: I am 23 this year, I should say that I am just beginning life, but already all of life's mysteries and charms are no longer available to me. I feel as if I have reached the end. Looking back on the road I have traveled; I see that I was on a journey from crimson to gray—from hope to disappointment and despair. I used to have beautiful illusions about life. ... Now they are all gone" (Xu 2002:52–53).

During this period, many Chinese suffered from a kind of spiritual malaise arising from the perception that they had no way to change their life circumstances. A 23-year-old male summarized the feeling: "I lost my dreams; I had wanted to study Mongolian history. But I can never leave the country. The government is afraid of the brain drain. Thus, I cannot go abroad. I must change my plans and become a small businessman." During my family visits, I found that residents of Hohhot, regardless of age-cohort or gender, spoke in a voice of one experience—a general dislike, at times, bitterness, about the lack of choice. The emotional impact is obvious in the words of a 26-year-old man who, talking about his life's disappointments, harshly criticized low-level government officials who "just want to hurt you by denying everything you want to do." He added: "Life is boring." For most, life appears to be a dead end. The 1980s' generation burned with ambition and a strong desire for advancement, but it was eventually stifled by the prevailing social organization.

Throughout the 1980s, residents of Hohhot regularly talked about the meaning of happiness and their feelings about not having any opportunities to find an appropriate mate based on strong and loving connections. They also talked about their expectations for happiness in marriage, improved relationships with their in-laws, and their yearning for a better life. Contrary to the neoliberal perspective (Anagnost 1997; Greenhalgh and Winckler 2005; Rofel 2007; Hairong Yan 2008), the shift from a command economy to a market economy did not stimulate or promote an increase in personal introspection. It did, however, allow for an easier and often more public articulation of personal desires.

In the 1980s the Chinese spoke of their lost dreams; two decades later, the youth of the single-child generation spoke of dreams they thought could be realized. A 1998 survey of the attitudes of Chinese urbanites about the future identified a new ethos, described in its simplest form as "the best is yet to come" (Tang and Parish 2000). For most, the future held an array of choices and possibilities. This new attitude is captured by a 20-year-old migrant cook who said his dream for the future was to "have my own restaurant, [so] that I will be able to travel and go places and learn about the world and become successful in life and marriage. I know that with hard work and dedication I can make it." His dream is not unlike the Horatio Alger stories popular in the United States at the turn of the twentieth century. Alger's heroes were poor boys who faced many challenges, but through hard work, underscored by their character development and personal diligence, were rewarded with success (Jankowiak 2008: 228).

Like the 1980s' college-educated youth, the single-child generation believes it is necessary to be committed to a personal goal and through self-mastery to create a more satisfying life. A 23-year-old youth who moved from a small town to Hohhot put it this way: "I struggle for a better life. It is this struggle to improve that makes life worth living. I have a kind of faith that I can make it and this makes my life worth living." For him and for most of his friends, he told me, success is not only about obtaining greater material benefits; it is also about the fulfillment of personal goals that are based on a mastery of the self. This same desire for personal improvement was expressed by a 31-year-old female salesclerk who reported: "There are days when I wonder why I cannot make a sale. I get depressed. I work very hard. I always wonder how I might improve." Similar feelings are expressed in the hopes of a 35-year-old mother has for the future of her ten-year-old: "I want my child to travel and see the world. I never had the opportunity to travel. I want my child to have such an opportunity." There is a thrill of involvement that can arise from hope and expectations, as echoed by a 20-year-old woman who said: "I was so excited and felt so fulfilled the day I opened my hairdressing salon. ... I knew I was going to learn a lot and improve my social position."

The ambition to improve oneself, to learn new skills, to be tested in a competitive arena, and to succeed is obvious in the response of 24-year-old male who described it in this way: "I could get a good job in Inner Mongolia. ... But in Beijing life is fast. ... I think I can make my fortune in Beijing. I can earn enough to do things and find a wife." To top it off, he added, "I want a challenge. Money isn't everything, but it is important these days." For this young man, like so many men and women with whom I spoke, money was not the driving force but rather the challenge to test one's mettle in a major cosmopolitan arena,

THE CHINESE PROTO NEO-FAMILY CONFIGURATION 207

which, for people from Hohhot, is Beijing. This orientation led some to migrate from Hohhot to Beijing and other major Chinese cities, such as Shenzhen. The pursuit of self-improvement is also found in a 25-year-old man's explanation for why he quit his job at a foreign-operated hotel and took a pay cut for a job that offered better opportunities to learn new tasks and, perhaps, to accelerate his personal growth and attain happiness. "Before, I thought that money was everything. I now realize that there is more to life than consumption and the drive to obtain more and more material things or to find the most beautiful girl" (Jankowiak 2008: 229–300). Significantly, the 1980s' generation college-educated youth held similar outlooks and ambitions and retained comparable desires for personal fulfillment. That generation differed less in terms of their life orientations than in their opportunities to realize their life goals.

Throughout the 2000s, rural migrants in Hohhot readily acknowledged that one reason they wanted to live in the city was to undergo training by enduring challenging circumstances (*duanlian ziji*) in order "to open my eyes" (*kaikuo yanjing*), or "to change myself" (*gaibian ziji*) (Zheng 2008:453). Tamara Jacka's research (2006:148) among rural migrants living in Beijing found that they too enjoyed "a sense of expanded horizons and freedom and autonomy in the city." In contrast, those who remained in the rural areas or returned to the villages after a stint in a city often felt confined and frustrated over their life circumstances.

The 1980s' generation did differ from the single-child generation in its normative understanding of the appropriate time to marry and start a family. In the 1980s, there was a cultural consensus about the stages of life and the accomplishments to be achieved at each stage. Perhaps most pressing was the stage of life marked for marriage and the stage soon thereafter to produce a child. In general, members of China's younger generation no longer hold to this life course schedule, and in cases when they do, their commitment and adherence are not as strong as it was for those of their parents' generation. Cultural norms have shifted to allow for greater individual discretion, not the least of which is in terms of the criteria for mate selection. A description of the ideal mate for a 20-year-old woman is representative of public acceptance of the replacement of instrumental considerations (e.g., income, connections) by those that value personality, compatibility, and character development. This woman yearned for "a man with whom I can explore and share feelings and experience the beauty of life. I want to accept him as himself and for us to learn to appreciate one another and what we have to offer one another." Both men and women emphasized their development as unique individuals and their freedom from customary obligations. This emphasis reverberated in a 24-year-old man's explanation about why he broke up with his girlfriend: "She was so forceful, and I felt I could not develop myself; I could not express myself." The criteria of a 23-year-old woman for her ideal husband or boyfriend is based as much on psychological attributes as it is on material possessions: "I want a man who is committed to a cause, something larger than himself. I want a man who is internally motivated" (Jankowiak 2008: 227–300).

The more intense personalization of one's life goals can account for why an increasing number of professional women are reluctant to enter into a marriage that fails to meet their definition of a good marriage (Chow 2018; To 2015). A generational bias is revealed in the once commonly used term "left-over women." The rejection by the senior generation of its youths' choice to delay marriage is openly critical (Steinfeld 2015:28). The senior generation is acutely aware of their differences in views, harboring misgivings about the youths' redefinition of conventional morality.

In the 1980s there were gender differences in terms of perceptions of what constituted life satisfaction. Women continued to stress the importance of their natal family, their child, and, if not married, their boyfriend, while most men stressed career development and the ability to support their family. Upon becoming a mother, most women placed more emphasis on and paid more close attention to the parent-child relationship than to the relationship with their husband. A 33-year-old married woman expressed this succinctly: "I worry about my children. Will they be able to eat well? If my business is not good, I will not be able to afford tuition and related expenses. I am less concerned about myself, but I am very concerned about my children." Many women felt empowered by their decision to seek fulfillment in the conventional role of motherhood. Twenty years later, many young women are now engaged in an existential dialogue with themselves over whether or not to have a child.

Perhaps one of the clearest expression of the change in the way society has come to value a more autonomous self, and its tacit power to redefine cultural norms, is through young women freely admitting they may not want a child and their openly "admitting" this. I think that in the past they felt constrained, if not afraid, to straightforwardly admit this. As is the case in other Asian and European countries, it is clear that some women want to delay marriage and to forgo having children (Song and Ji 2020a). Such an open admission was unheard of in the 1980s. The existential dialogue that women are having internally and with others is increasingly becoming a public conversation, or at least a conversation that is not inhibited—a clear expression of the new dynamic of the younger generation. In the 1980s there may have been women who did not want to marry or to have a child, but they did not admit so out loud. Such was the force of the prevailing normative order at that time. The dramatic change is evident in a 2018 a survey of the attitudes of Mongolian and Shanghai women toward pregnancy. In response to the question "Do you plan to have children in the future?" 102 respondents responded in the affirmative, but 40 responded negatively, and 42 were unsure. In all, 45 percent of the respondents were not committed to childbirth (Volsche and Jankowiak 2020). Given the strong traditions of duty and cultural conformity, the significance here is not whether this 45 percent will ultimately become parents, but rather it is notable that parenthood as a cultural "given" is no longer operative as so many women are considering all their options.

Despite this open change, Chinese mothers continue to attempt to persuade their children to become parents. As one 21-year-old male spoke of parental pressures to have a child and hence the likelihood of doing so at some point: "I think it is impossible for me to have no children in the future. Because my parents will not agree with me." In some cases, respondents also acknowledged there may be a conflict between the desires of their parents and those of their future spouse. One 19-year-old male, in response to the question about having a child in the future, said, "yes" but he qualified it, adding: "It depends. Having a child may be a happy occasion for my parents. However, it may be an unhappy experience for my wife." His uncertain response speaks to the awareness of conflicting expectations and the ongoing need to negotiate multiple relationships around the choice of whether or not to have a child. It seems that the main difference between China, and Europe and the United States, is that in the latter the parents accept the real possibility that their children may choose not to have children.

The open affirmation of the importance of self-development has an uneasy side: some are deeply conflicted over what they often see as dual responsibilities in their marriage—to their parents and to themselves (Song and Lai. 2020a). One 24-year-old man admitted he wanted to help his parents but he felt he was not as involved with his family and young son as he wanted to be. Compounding the dilemma, he told me that he wanted to achieve something beyond merely being a family man. But then, lowering his voice and looking downward, he admitted: "A family man has a good status and is recognized as a success outside of the family." Accepting the cultural value of having a large happy family does not always reconcile with his conflicting obligations and personal life goals. Such tensions intensify over the course of time rather than abating.

Respondents, regardless of gender, the university they are attending, or whether they intend to have children, agreed with the statement, "Having children is a personal choice." The fact that nearly all our respondents agreed with this statement is significant; it highlights a fundamental shift among the single-child generation to a wider view of possibilities and what makes life worth living. Though many may be open to accepting their parents' assertion about the central importance of parenthood, most Chinese youth regard the final choice to be their one of their own.

It is significant that most of the respondents who had no intention of having children were women. It is clear that women feel freer and more confident to assert and expand their autonomy within the family. It is also possible that Chinese women are identifying their position at the intersection of domestic and public space as the proper setting to assert their personal autonomy in the family and in the conjugal bond. It is equally clear that the inter-generational bonds of the Chinese singleton are in flux, with a growing emphasis on autonomy and desires to assume a more prominent role in Chinese society. The increase in female autonomy within the Chinese family is a sign that women are more willing not only to challenge inter-generational gender roles but also to alter them. This presents a potential conundrum: it is difficult to create and sustain a child-centered relatedness, or a neo-family, without offspring.

7 Reconfiguring the Inter-Generational Family

The grandparent-child relationship has always occupied an esteemed position in Chinese society. This was especially the case for grandfathers who had grandsons. Funerals that involved a deceased male who had one or more grandsons were called "red happiness" as it was a time of grief and celebration as the man had died knowing his line would continue. It is common for a father who had assumed a more aloof posture toward his offspring to demonstrate public affection toward his grandson. This selective pattern of behavior is consistent with the logic of patrilineal descent. Because only males will remain in their home village and thus potentially reproduce themselves as well as work the farm, sons, not daughters, were celebrated and honored as the more worthy gender. This preferential sex bias changed with the institution of the single child. In time, urban Chinese came to value daughters as much as sons. What is less known and thus less appreciated is how the structural reality of having an only child is reshaping the way maternal and paternal grandparents are relating to each other through their efforts to see their only grandchild.

In Hohhot, the contemporary urban family consists of an amalgamation of shapes and forms. Some families are conjugal units, while others continue to function as extended or stem families. Given the new-found wealth as well as the parents' desire to live independent of their offspring, it is not clear if every

THE CHINESE PROTO NEO-FAMILY CONFIGURATION   211

conjugal unit will eventually become a stem family. For example, over 65 percent of the parents (45 out of 67) whom I interviewed admitted they would prefer, if health permitted, to live separately from their offspring. Even if the senior generation prefers residential independence from their offspring, this does not mean they do not want to be closely connected with their child or grandchild. I found a strong interdependency between a singleton and his or her parents. The strength of this emotional bond is evident in the way parents are embracing their role as grandparents.

Because the patrilineal ideal is no longer critical to achieve material gain or social success, urban Chinese live in a de facto bilateral universe organized around sentiment and negotiated ethical obligations. This means that paternal and maternal grandparents can claim rights to their only grandchild. In the pursuit of their own interests, a new situation has emerged—the inverted or multi-generational family that is organized around the sharing of responsibilities toward the rearing of the grandchild. As an emerging institution, there are no formal norms and thus this institution requires frequent negotiation over issues of parenting rights, responsibilities, and future obligations.

As in the case of Hohhot, Helen Siu (1989) found that parents in the Pearl River Delta continued to promote inter-generational dependency based more on personalized affection rather than on fear of the parents' authority or possible negative economic sanctions. The continuation of emotional interdependency continues to be embraced by the junior generation. Taken together, these highly individualistic negotiations and habitual patterns are reshaping what was once a patrilineally grounded extended family into something that resembles a vertical orientation that links the paternal and maternal generations together into a quasi-bilateral multi-generational family. The bilateral multi-generational family, as in the case of friendship between neighbors and ethnic associates, is not automatic but rather is based entirely on sentiment and personal commitment.

The Chinese multi-generational family, however, is a fragile institution. The relationship between the paternal and maternal grandparents is seldom strong. There is, therefore, an uneasy alliance among all interested parties who are also potential rivals in their efforts to gain greater access to a valued, albeit scarce, resource, that is their only grandchild. The arena in which most negotiations take place is often is the home of their adult offspring. If one set of grandparents is perceived as being unreasonable, the other set of grandparents will appeal to their offspring (i.e., their son or daughter) for support.

The emergent institution's representativeness is illustrated in my grandparent-child coresidence survey in 2000 that found 213 out of 261, or 82 percent, of the people sampled had lived for a period of time with a grandparent. Moreover, there is no evidence of a patrilateral bias. Of the 261 respondents, 111 lived for a period of time with their paternal grandparents, whereas 102 had lived with their maternal grandparents, and 48 had not lived with any grandparent. The length of time living with a grandparent ranged from between one and sixteen years, with the average time being 8.16 years. However, there is a regional variation. In Chengdu, the capital of Sichuan province in southwest China, on average a grandchild stayed with a grandparent for 33 months, whereas in Hohhot the average was about 62 months. Clearly, Chengdu parents are reclaiming their child earlier, while people in Hohhot tend to wait until their child is old enough to attend first grade. This may be a reflection of urban scale. In Hohhot, a smaller city, it is easier for parents to regularly interact with their child even when they do not live together (Jankowiak 2008). But in both cities, grandparents have replaced parents as caretakers and emotional guardians. This pattern appears to be representative throughout China. For example, a 22-year-old noted that she had lived with her grandmother for the first two years of her life, but that she "had lunch with my [paternal] grandmother once she started middle school, and then every day for the next ten years." She added: "I feel so close and warm around her." In this way, what was once a traditional patrilineal restricted social universe has been transformed into something resembling an egocentric pattern based on personal preference. The survey by Susan Short (2001:920) of family life in central China found one-third of those sampled had lived with a grandmother or grandfather.

The shift in the way the generations now interact is not unique to China. There is a new world-wide pattern in the way inter-generational bonds have been reorganized so that economic and non-economic resources have shifted from offspring giving to a parent to something like the reverse: resources shifting from the parent to the children. This pattern, with only a few modifications, is typical of inter-generational relations in most complex societies throughout the world. Contrary to William Goode's (1963) conjugal loyalty thesis, grandparents devote a large amount of time to contact their grandchild (Attias-Domfort and Segalen 2002:284). In this way, behavior in Hohhot is consistent with behavior found in research on Western Europe where a new inter-generational trend has emerged in which grandparents are making a "massive investments in their grandchild(ren)" (Attias-Domfort and Segalen 2002:285). This pattern is also typical of Taiwan, where children have retained a deep-seated responsibility for their parents' well-being. Robert Marsh found the inter-generational flow of help and resources from offspring to their parents was greater in 1991 than it was in 1963 (Marsh

1998:305). In Hohhot, such a resource exchange between generations is somewhat mixed.

The extensive involvement of Chinese grandparents with their grandchild is consistent with studies of kinship and family interactions in the United States (Lawton et al. 1994). Although the dual multi-generational family is common in other parts of the world, it had no official existence in Chinese society where the patrilineal descent system legally elevated the rights of the father's kin over those of the mother's kin. In this milieu, official inter-generational ties were primarily, but not entirely, unilineal (Watson and Watson 2004). This changed, however, under socialist China's policies designed to create a new society. The party's expectations and policies that required that younger women had to work made childcare, especially infant care, a pressing issue. As in many Eastern European countries (e.g., the Czech Republic and Hungary), grandparents from either side of the family have stepped into the void to perform the necessary child-care duties. Parents remain vigilant and often complain about the quality of grandparenting (e.g., providing inferior traditional foods) (Short 2001: 926). From their child's perspective, this is a minor concern compared with their emotional involvement with their grandparent(s). It is the strength of the emotional entanglement that has resulted in the creation of a strong, vibrant, and psychologically pleasing child-parent relationship. For example, a 22-year-old man in Hohhot told me that he never gave money to his parents, as he "needs money to buy things and improve my life." He also knew that his parents did not need money. His response was representative of more well-off youth. The only exception to this pattern was among some youth, especially unmarried females, who give a small sum of money to their parents, but this was more as a symbolic statement of affection than because of their parents' financial need.

Given the city's newfound affluence, there is less need for parents to receive financial support from their offspring. I found that only teenagers from families with laid-off parents (*xiagang*) or who were recent migrants regularly gave money to their parents. This sociological fact has not diminished the intensity of the affective bonds between child and parent, which has not changed from the 1980s and, in some cases, has intensified in depth of feeling and commitment.

I initially thought there was no sex bias—a grandparent's involvement did not shift with sex of the grandchild. However, a 2008 survey of 108 singletons did reveal a sex bias: If the child was a female, the child's maternal grandmother (*laolao*) would be the more intimate and emotionally connected grandparent Sixty percent of the female respondents (n= 65) reported feeling emotionally closer to the grandparent on their mother's side. In contrast, 50 percent of the males reported closer contact and being more emotionally intimate with their paternal grandmother (*nainai*). This pattern highlights another significant shift that was evident by the early 1980s—the power of the wife. Woman feel closer and more intimate with their natal mother and now that they are no longer living with their mother-in law, they are able to follow their own feelings, which allows them to maintain closer bonds with their natal family. This preference enables the maternal grandparent to forge closer and more long-lasting bonds with their grandchild. In contrast, if the child is a male, paternal grandparents make a stronger and more sustained effort to remain involved with their only grandson. Still, efforts by paternal grandparents are only successful 50 percent of the time. This speaks loudly and forcefully to the emotional salience of mother-daughter bonds in transforming cultural customs (Jankowiak 2008).

Grandparents can also view their offspring's expectations of child-care assistance as either a blessing or a burden. Chinese parents understand the importance of staying connected to their roots. For most, grandchild care generally provides a sense of fulfillment rather than being onerous. When asked what a 66-year-old grandmother got from spending so much time with her granddaughter, she replied: "I enjoy taking care of her [my granddaughter]." Another 64-year-old grandmother added: "She is me." This is a point echoed by a 72-year-old grandfather who acknowledged, while he hugged his 3-year-old grandson, "he is my life." Such sentiments are consistent with Yan's findings (2016), albeit in a different urban setting.

There is a variation in the willingness of grandparents in Hohhot to reorganize their lives to care for their only grandchild. Wang's 2017 survey of families in Hohhot found a variety of factors influencing the degree to which parents agreed to assist their offspring with childcare. Wang's investigation found pragmatic, especially financial, factors to be more significant than adherence to moral norms of filial piety in determining the level of a grandparent's involvement with their grandchild. For some grandparents, age is a factor. If they or their offspring believe they are too old (post-1970s) to help care for their grandchild, they will not become involved. Other parents enjoy their jobs and/or relationships with long-term friends and do not want to abandon their township life for a new life in a larger city. Still others who had multiple offspring do not know which offspring they should assist. This usually results in the mother choosing to support her "favorite" child. Finally, when a daughter-in law does not like, appreciate, or want any involvement with her mother-in law, she will insist that the mother-in law leave. Wang's research did find strong support, however, that Yan's inverted family is the more representative

THE CHINESE PROTO NEO-FAMILY CONFIGURATION

family unit, with around 60 percent of her sample already establishing, or planning to establish, an inverted family arrangement (Wang 2018, personal communication).

It is the grandparents' involvement in the rearing of their only grandchild that has reshaped the urban Chinese family. How the grandparents are incorporated into caring for their only grandchild is critical for shaping the degree of emotional intimacy between parents and their offspring. Societies around the world engage in alloparental care whereby non-related adults contribute to caring for a family's children. China's incorporation of the grandparents into an inverted family organization is similar to the alloparental care found in other societies. A less typical type of alloparental care is the "farming out" of children to be raised by grandparents who raise their grandchild(ren) on their own for several years, only to return the grandchild(ren) to their parents at a later date. Whenever this occurs, the parent-child emotional bond is fragmented, with the child(ren) having ambivalent feelings toward their parents, while retaining a deeply felt emotional attachment to their grandparents. For example, a 34-year-old woman confided that: "I feel more comfortable with my grandmother than I do with my mother. I did not listen to her [i.e., her grandmother] as I know what she had to tell me about the contemporary world was nonsense. Her ideas were old. But I simply enjoyed being around her." Another 29-year-old woman acknowledged: "My mother [who had not raised her] is always ordering me to do this or that. She makes lists. I still resist her. We are NOT close." However, she added: "This is not the case when I am with my grandmother. I just want to sit next to her."

In short, there are both continuities and changes between the 1980s and the 2000s, which are summarized in the table below:

1980s and 2000s Cultural Change and Continuity in Attitude and Behavior

	1980s	2000s
Good Marriage	Similar social status but love feelings not essential Before marriage. Mate selection was conducted as part of a semi-formal courtship process.	Similar social status but love feeling essential before agreeing to marry. Mate selection was conducted through dating process that allowed for more casual interaction.

1980s and 2000s Cultural Change and Continuity in Attitude and Behavior

Parent-Offspring Relationship	Close but independent. Complementary parenting styles: the father as disciplinarian and the mother as intimate nurturer. Mothers' have multiple children which makes it difficult to forge a deep-seated emotional bond with every child. Offspring actively resist parental suggestion as to whom to marry.	Both parents want to form a more affectionate parent-child bond. Mothers are the more disciplinarian, while fathers are the more nurturant parent. Mothers' have an only child which allows for a more intense closer bonding. Parents are more effective in influencing their offspring marital choice.
Relationship With In-laws	Daughter-in-law and mother-in-law interaction is characterized by mutual politeness. Few living together as everyone has their own apartment.	Daughter-in-law and mother-in-law interaction is characterized by mutual politeness. Daughter-in-law often needs mother-in-law financial assistance and childcare support.
Individual Expression	Individuals readily express desire to develop their abilities, mastery of self, and achieve personal fulfillment. Social adulthood is measure through marriage and parenthood. Few individuals had the opportunity to do so.	Individuals readily express desire to develop their abilities, mastery of self, and achieve personal fulfillment. Social adulthood is no longer determined by marriage or parenthood. Many individuals have the opportunity to do so.
Residence Preference	Government work unit assigned apartment which meant most married couples lived in separate location, but regularly visited their parents. The work-unit also provided in expensive childcare. The inter-generational exchange of resources was symbolic with offspring giving a token cash amount to their parents who did not require financial support.	The preference is to live separate but near parents. The arrival of child activates need for parental support which can bring a parent(s) to live with their married son or daughter. There is an inter-generational exchange whereby parents give much needed financial resources to their offspring.

8   Conclusion

Yan (2003, 2009) has aptly conceptualized the way the Chinese family is being transformed from an economic social unit into a unit centered on an emotional/psychological axis that provides its members with a variety of personal and social supports (Fong 2004; Xu 2017). Since 1949, the transformation of the family has consisted of a gradual shift away from its preference for patrilineal descent and patrilocal resident principles in favor of a less normative and more pragmatic response to life's challenges (Xiao 2016). In the process, new forms of cooperation and interfamilial alliances are being formulated. The new family configuration is also being shaped by an independent, albeit coterminous, process: a heightened respect for the self as a cognitive and emotional entity. The expansion of the ethics of the self has reinforced support for valuing autonomy and self-expression, but not for the complete independence or self-sufficiency that is typically found in the United States. In this setting, emotional connections between spouses or parents are no longer denied or rejected; rather, to a large extent they are more publicly affirmed, even though they are resisted by some or cause inner conflicts for others. This new emotional orientation is an essential feature of the neo-family configuration.

The Hohhot data provide a baseline from which to examine the factors that have, and are continuing to, shape the neo-family configuration. However, I disagree with those researchers who take a neo-liberal perspective to argue that there has been a psychological reorientation from the work-unit era to the reform era. The 1980s' generation sought to raise and socialize their only child somewhat differently from the way they themselves were raised. They encouraged their offspring to be more open and pragmatic in how they responded to changes in government policies and economic opportunities, taking a closer interest socio-economic changes. The data from Hohhot are consistent with Yan's core thesis: the patriarchal family organization has been transformed into a more open society, one that is publicly tolerant of the values of individual emotional development and personal achievement while also continuing to maintain a strong identification with the natal family.

If "every age contains the seeds of its heirs" (Rabb 1975:99), then youth in the 1980s had already begun to re-imagine their lives as consisting of more opportunities than their parents had. In many ways, it was the desire of the 1980s' youth to expand their horizons that contributed the embrace of parenthood and the increased tolerance of individual expression. The positive attitudes of individual parents to life's uncertainties, including the uncertainties of opportunities, opened the way for the creation of fresh new ideas about what makes for a good marriage, more effective parenting, an appropriately balanced kinship relationship, and a focused yearning for self-fulfillment. Taken together, an affirmative response to these fresh ideas and the resultant sense of a real entry into other aspects of life makes life worth living.

But the new ethical code surrounding individual choice, self-fulfillment, and behavioral preference has presented something of a paradox. In its current form, the neo-family configuration relies on the early retirement of parents, a lack of affordable daycare, a parental life-orientation devoid of any personal interest other than to care for the children, and an intimate mother-daughter codependency that binds daughters with their natal family. This raises an intriguing question: what will happen if government policies change or economic realities prevent support or parents develop other interests and no longer want to dedicate themselves to childcare? This leads to yet another question: Is the neo-family configuration, as masterfully identified by Yan, a temporary interlude which once again will be transformed into something else? Or does it represent a new enduring type of family formation that will be replicated in the next generation? Only time, and the necessary follow-up by renewed scholarly investigations, can provide the answers.

References

Anagnost, Anne.1997.National Past-Times: Narrative, Representation, and Power in Modern China. Raleigh: Duke University Press.

Attias-Donfut, Claudine and Martine Segalen. 2002. "The Construction of Grandparenthood." Current Sociology. 50(2): 281–294.

Chow, Yiu Fai. 2018. How Caring in Times of Precarity: A Study of Single Women Doing Creative Work in Shanghai. New York: Palgrave Press.

Croll, Elisabeth. 1994. 2002. *From Heaven to Earth: Images and Experiences of Development in China.* London: Routledge.

Davis, Deborah, S.. 2014. "Privatization of Marriage in Post-Socialist China." *Modern China* 40, 6: 551–77.

Davis, Deborah S. and Stevan Harrell. (1993). "Introduction." In *Chinese Family*, D. Davis and S. Harrell, eds, 1–12. Berkeley: University of California Press.

Davis, Deborah S. and Sara K. Friedman. 2014. *Wives, Husbands, and Lovers: Marriage and Sexuality in Hong Kong, Taiwan, and Urban China.* Stanford: Stanford University Press.

Diamant, Neil J. 2000. *Revolutionizing the Family: Politics, Love, and Divorce in Urban and Rural China, 1949–1968.* Berkeley: University of California Press.

Eklund, Lisa. 2018. "Filial Daughter? Filial Son? How China's Young Urban Elite Negotiate Intergenerational Obligations." NORA – Nordic Journal of Feminist and Gender Research 26, 4, 295–312.

THE CHINESE PROTO NEO-FAMILY CONFIGURATION 219

Evans, Harriet. 2008. *The Subject of Gender: Daughters and Mothers in Urban China.* Lanham, Md.: Rowman & Littlefield.

Fan, C. Cindy and Youqin Huang. 1998. "Waves of Rural Brides: Female Marriage Migration in China." *Annals of the Association of American Geographers* 88, 2: 227–51.

Fong, Vanessa L. 2002. "China's One-Child Policy and the Empowerment of Urban Daughters." *American Anthropologist* 104, 4: 1098–1109.

Fong, Vanessa L. 2004. *Only Hope: Coming of Age Under China's One-Child Policy.* Stanford: Standard University Press.

Goode, William. 1963. *World Revolution and Family Patterns.* New York: Free Press.

Greenhalgh, S. and E., Winckler. 2005. *Governing China's Population: From Leninist to Neoliberal Biopolitics.* Stanford: Stanford University Press.

Harrell, Stevan and Gonçalo Santos. 2016. "Introduction." In *Transforming Chinese Patriarchy: Chinese Families in the Twenty-first Century,* ed. Gonçalo Santos and Stevan Harrell, 3–36. Seattle: University of Washington Press.

Hays, Daisy. 2015. *Mr. and Mrs. Disraeli: A Strange Romance.* London: Chatto and Windus.

Hong Fincher, Leta. 2014. *Left Over Women: The Resurgence of Gender Inequality in China.* London: Zed Books.

Hsu, Francis L. K. 1971. *Kinship & Culture.* Chicago: Aldine.

Jacka, Tamara. 2006. *Rural Women in Urban China: Gender: Migration and Social Change.* Armonk, New York: M. E. Sharpe.

Jankowiak, William R. 1993. *Sex, Death, and Hierarchy in a Chinese City.* New York: Columbia University Press.

Jankowiak, William R. 2008. "Well Being, Cultural Pathology, and Personal Rejuvenation in a Chinese City: 1981–2005." In *The Good Life: Well Being in Anthropological Perspective,* ed. Gordon Matthews and Carolina Izquierdo, 147–66. Oxford: Berghahn Publishers.

Jankowiak, William R. 2009. "Practicing Connectiveness as Kinship in Urban China." In *Chinese Kinship and Relatedness: Some Contemporary Anthropological Perspectives,* ed. Susanne Brandstäder and Gonçalo D. Santos, 67–92. London: Routledge.

Jankowiak, William R. 2011. "The Han Chinese Family: The Realignment of Parenting Ideals, Sentiments, and Practices." In *Women and Gender in Contemporary Chinese Societies: Beyond Han Patriarchy,* ed. Shanshan Du and Ya-chen Chen, 109–32. Lanham, Md.: Lexington Books.

Jankowiak, William R. 2013. "From Courtship to Dating Culture: China's Emergent Youth." In *Restless China,* ed. Perry Link, Richard P. Madsen, and Paul G. Pickowicz, 191–212. Lanham, Md.: Rowman & Littlefield.

Jankowiak, William R. 2018. "An Anthropologist Goes Looking for Love in All the Old Places: A Personal Account." In *The New Psychology of Love,*" 2nd ed., ed. Robert J. Steinberg and Karin Sternberg, 240–58. Cambridge: Cambridge University Press.

Jankowiak, William and Xuan Li. 2017. "Emergent Conjugal Love, Mutual Affection, Female Marital Power." In *Transforming Patriarchy: Chinese Families in the Twenty-first Century*, ed. Gonçalo Santos and Stevan Harrell, 146–62. Seattle: University of Washington Press.

Jankowiak, William, Yifei Shen, Shiyu Yao, Cancan Wang, and Shelly Volsche. 2015. "Investigating Love's Universal Attributes: A Research Report from China." *Cross-Cultural Research* 49, 4: 422–36.

Kim, Sung Won, Kari-Elle Brown, and Vanessa L. Fong. 2017. "Chinese Individualisms: Childrearing Aspirations for the Next Generation of Middle-Class Chinese Citizens." *Ethnos* 45, 3: 342–66.

Kipnis, Andrew. 2009. "Education and the Governing of Child-Centered Relatedness." In *Chinese Kinship and Relatedness: Some Contemporary Anthropological Perspectives*, ed. Susanne Brandstäder and Gonçalo D. Santos, 204–22. London: Routledge.

Lang, Olga. 1946. *Chinese Family and Society*. New Haven: Yale University Press.

Lawton, Vern., Silverstein, Michael., & Bengtson, Vern. 1994. Solidarity Between Generations In Families. In Vern Bengtson and Robert Harootyan (Eds.), *Intergenerational Linkages: Hidden Connections in American Society,* 19–42. New York: Springer Publishing Co.

Levy, Marion J., Jr. 1968. *The Family Revolution in Modern China*. New York: Atheneum.

Li, Xuan. 2018. "Chinese Fathers in the Twentieth Century: Changing Roles as Parents and as Men." *NORA – Nordic Journal of Feminist and Gender Research* 26, 4: 331–50.

Li Xuan and Michael Lamb. 2015. "Fathers in Chinese Culture: From Stern Disciplinarians to Involved Parents." In *Fathers in Chinese Culture*, ed. David W. Shwalb, Barbara J. Shwalb, and Michael E. Lamb, 15–41. London: Routledge.

Liu, Jieyu. 2017. *Gender, Sexuality and Power in Chinese Companies: Beauties at Work.* London: Palgrave Macmillan.

Marsh, Robert. 1998. *The Great Transformation: Social Change in Taibei*. Armonk, N.Y: M.E. Sharpe.

Qi, Xiaoying. 2018. "Floating Grandparents: Rethinking Family Obligation and Intergenerational Support." *International Sociology* 33, 6: 761–77.

Rabb, Theodore K. 1975. *Struggle for Stability in Early Modern Europe*. Oxford: Oxford University Press.

Rofel, Lisa. 2007. *Desiring China: Experiments in Neoliberalism, Sexuality, and Public Culture.* Raleigh: Duke University Press.

Siu, Helen. 1989. *Agents and Victims in South China: Accomplices in Rural Revolution. New Haven:* Yale University Press.

Short, Susan, Zhai Fengying, Xu Siyuan and Yang Mingliang. 2001. "China's One-Child Policy and the Care of Children: An Analysis of Qualitative and Quantitative Data." *Social Forces* 79.3:913–943.

Salaff, Janet W. 1981. *Working Daughters of Hong Kong: Filial Piety or Power in the Family?* New York: Columbia University Press.

Schneider, Melissa Margaret. 2014. *The Ugly Wife is a Treasure at Home: True Stories of Love and Marriage in Communist China.* n.p.: Potomac Books.

Song, Jing and Weiwen Lai. 2020a.Cohabitation and Gender Equality: Ideal and Real Division of Household Labor among Chinese Youth. *The China Review* 20, 2: 53–80.

Song, Jing and Yingchun Ji. 2020b. Complexity of Chinese Family Life: Individualism, Familism, and Gender. *The China Review* 20, 2: 1–17.

Stafford, Charles. 2000. "Chinese Patriliny and the Cycles of Yang and Laiwang." In *Cultures of Relatedness: New Approaches to the Study of Kinship*, ed. Janet Carsten, 35–54. Cambridge: Cambridge University Press.

Steinfeld, Jemimah. 2015. *Little Emperors and Material Girls: Youth and Sex in Modern China.* London: I. B. Tauris.

Tang, Wenfang and William L. Parish. 2000. *Chinese Urban Life Under Reform.* Cambridge: Cambridge University Press.

To, Sandy. 2015. *China's Leftover Women: Late Marriage Among Professional Women and its Consequences.* London: Routledge.

Volsche, Shelly and William Jankowiak. 2020. "Chinese Women's Autonomy and Personal Choice." *Psychoanalysis and Psychotherapy in China.*

Wang, Hongyan.2019. Personal Communication, June 2018.

Watson, James L. and Rubie S. Watson. 2004. *Village Life in Hong Kong: Politics, Gender, and Ritual in the New Territories.* Hong Kong: Chinese University Press.

Watson, Rubie S., and Patricia Buckley Ebrey, eds. 1991. *Marriage and Inequality in Chinese Society.* Berkeley: University of California Press.

Whyte, Martin King. 2005. "Continuity and Change in Urban Chinese Family Life." *China Journal* 53: 9–33.

Wolf, Margery. 1972. *Women and the Family in Rural Taiwan.* Stanford: Stanford University Press.

Wolf, Margery. 1985. *Revolution Postponed: Women in Contemporary China.* Stanford: Stanford University Press.

Xiao, Suowei. 2016. "Intimate Power: The Intergenerational Cooperation and Conflicts in Childrearing among Urban Families in Contemporary China." *Journal of Chinese Sociology* 3, 1: 1–24.

Xu, Jing. 2017. *The Good Child: Moral Development in a Chinese Preschool.* Stanford: Stanford University Press.

Xu, Luo. 2002. *Searching for Life's Meaning: Changes and Tensions in the Worldviews of Chinese Youth in the 1980s.* Ann Arbor: University of Michigan Press.

Yan, Hairong. 2008. *New Master, New Servants: Migration, Development, and Women Workers in China.* Raleigh: Duke University Press.

Yan, Yunxiang. 2003. *Private Life under Socialism: Love Intimacy, and Family Change in a Chinese Village, 1949–1999*. Stanford: Stanford University Press.

Yan, Yunxiang. 2009. *The Individualization of Chinese Society*. London School of Economics Monographs on Social Anthropology. Oxford: Berg Publishers.

Yan, Yunxiang. 2015. "Parent-Driven Divorce and Individualisation among Chinese Youth." *International Social Science Journal*, Issues 213/214, pp. 317-330.

Yan, Yunxiang. 2016. "Intergenerational Intimacy and Descending Familism in Rural North China." *American Anthropologist* 118, 2: 244–57.

Yu, Ruoh-yong and Yu-Sheng Liu. 2014. "Change and Continuity in the Experience of Marriage in Taiwan." In *Wives, Husbands, and Lovers: Marriage and Sexuality in Hong Kong, Taiwan, and Urban China*, ed. Deborah S. Davis and Sara K. Friedman, 239–61. Stanford: Stanford University Press.

Zang, Xiaowei and William Jankowiak. 2017. "Review Essay: Family and Sexuality." In *Understanding Contemporary China*, 7th ed., ed. Robert E. Gamer and Stanley Toops, 337–66. Boulder, Colo.: Lynne Rienner.

Zheng, Tiantian. 2008. "Commodifying Romance and Searching for Love: Rural Migrant Bar Hostesses' Moral Vision in Post-Mao Dalian." *Modern China* 34, 4: 442–76.

Zhong, X. and S.Y. Ho. 2014. "Negotiating Intimate Relationships: The Expectations of Family Relations and Filial Piety Among Only Child Parents." *Open Times* 1, 155–75.

Zurndorfer, Harriet. 2015. "Men, Women, Money, and Morality: The Development of China's Sexual Economy." *Feminist Economics* 22, 2: 1–23.

Zurndorfer, Harriet. 2018. "Escape from the Country: The Gender Politics of Chinese Women in Pursuit of Transnational Romance." *Gender, Place & Culture* 25, 4: 489–506.

CHAPTER 10

The Statist Model of Family Policy Making

Yunxiang Yan

In this chapter I examine how the party-state uses family policies to reform the family institution for its national agenda from 1949 to the present. My central argument is that in numerous ways and during different periods, the party-state took a statist approach in the making of family policies and in the reshaping of the Chinese family, and this statist model generated complex, inconsistent, and sometimes even conflicting policy results affecting family wellbeing. This statist model of family policy making originated with the early attempts to reform the family for the purpose of nation-state building at the turn of the twentieth century, most particularly during the May Fourth New Culture Movement. Eventually, and unexpectedly to a great extent, the convergence of these historical and contemporary policy results contributed to the rise of neo-familism in the early twenty-first century.

In contemporary Western societies, family policies arguably constitute the most important administrative mechanism by which governments can promote the wellbeing of the family institution though the provision of welfare and the protection of the rights of individuals (especially the rights of in vulnerable groups—to be discussed below in the section on the "harmonious society") by way of domestic legislation and government intervention. Therefore, the interests and happiness of the individual, therefore, can be regarded, at least at the level of ideology and the social contract, as the ultimate goal of family policy making. Logically, the family should be the end of family policy making instead of a means to serve higher ends. However, family policies in China were formulated and implemented for the interests and wellbeing of the nation-state, which is ultimately represented by the leadership of the Chinese Communist Party to modernize the nation-state. According to this logic, the family and individuals can be, and indeed have been, the beneficiaries of many family policies, but this is the case because they serve as a necessary means to a higher end represented by the party-state instead of being an end in and of themselves. This stands out as a firm statist model of family policy making by which the family first and foremost has been constantly recalibrated to enhance the power, prestige, and wellbeing of the nation-state.

In existing scholarship, family policies are defined and studied in both a broad and a narrow sense. Narrowly defined, family policies refer to the laws,

© YUNXIANG YAN, 2021 | DOI:10.1163/9789004450233_011

policies, and other forms of government interventions that directly or indirectly affect the family institution. However, this definition can be extended to include "a perspective for understanding and thinking about policy in relation to families" (Zimmerman 1992). The former helps to make studies of family policies feasible and operational, whereas the latter opens up the possibility of perceiving and conceiving of family policy making as a dynamic process whereby ordinary people, communities, family scholars, and professionals in the social-service sector all have a certain role to influence the formulation and implementation of family policies. However, the statist model of family policy making, presents a challenge to both perspectives because in making any kinds of policies the party-state rarely shares its power with any other entities, and most of its family policies are not explicitly made to affect the family even though they may have important, and in some cases even determining, impacts on the family. Furthermore, for a large period of time during the Maoist era, the will of the state was expressed mainly by way of the propaganda apparatus such as newspaper editorials and political campaigns, which had an equally important impact on the family (Whyte 2005). Therefore, below I will attempt to integrate both the narrow and the broad definitions of family policy making and to consider both the direct and indirect policies, with a focus on the actual agenda and impact of statism on the Chinese family.

As will be shown in the following pages, the interplay among familism, individualism, and statism constitutes a clear thread in Chinese family policy making and family change that links the radicalism of the family revolution at the turn of the twentieth century, the individual-centered family idealism of the New Culture Movement, the statist family policies of both the KMT (Nationalist Party) government and the CCP (Chinese Communist Party) in the 1930s and the 1940s, and the party-state's changing family policies from 1949 to the present. Familism refers to a familial mode of ethical values and social practices in many traditional societies. It emphasizes the primacy of family interests over those of its individual members and of loyalty to the family over allegiances to any outside social organizations (Garzón 2000). As a social practice, familism is manifested as a cooperative organization in the family dedicated to the survival and flourishing of the family and as a building block in a given society that plays crucial economic, socio-cultural, and political functions. For both ideological and practical reasons, familism relies on a hierarchal arrangement of gender and generational relations and it opposes equality and intimacy in family life. The commonly recognized shortcomings of familism include its indifference toward society and national politics (see Banfield 1958 for his study of the Italian case) and its oppression of youth and women.

THE STATIST MODEL OF FAMILY POLICY MAKING 225

In many respects, modern Western individualism stands out as the antithesis of familism. Unlike familism, which is constructed through a discourse of obligations and self-sacrifice and that defines the individual as a means to the higher end of the continuity and prosperity of the family group, modern individualism centers on the inalienable rights and entitlements of the individual as an end in and of her/himself. It places the individual at the center of the universe, with innate qualities of autonomy, freedom, dignity, and self-development and, through notions of the social contract and the sovereignty of the people, it obligates the individual to be a citizen contributing to the nation-state (see Dumont 1986; Lukes 1973; Taylor 2003).

Statism refers to the ideological claim that the state is entitled to control the economic and social lives of its people, and the interest of the nation-state is superior to that of the society, communities, families, and individuals. Statism is closely related to nationalism and arguably the strongest version of collectivism (Barry 1999). In the Chinese case, although for a brief time in the 1910s individualism was invoked by the early reformers to overcome the political indifference of familism so that the family could be mobilized to serve the nation-state, it was statism that has dominated the ideology and practice of family policy making and that has determined the orientation of family change during the last one hundred years.

There are five sections in the following pages. The first briefly reviews the historical background of the statist model in family policies, tracing its origins to the radicalism of the family revolution in the New Culture Movement during the first two decades of the twentieth century. This model was, intriguingly, established and applied to actual family reforms through laws and policies implemented by both the ruling Nationalist Party in Republican China and the revolutionary CCP in its base areas during the 1930s to the 1940s, despite the fact that they were political foes and most of the time they attempted to decimate one another. Statism seemed to have transcended the party political differences to make both familism and individualism the enemies of the nation-state.

In the subsequent three sections, I examine the development of family policies during three phases, each of which is marked by the chief agenda of the party-state. The first phase, which falls neatly into the Maoist era (1949–76) and occurred in the context of the full-blown planned economy and the radical ideology of the CCP, the core mission of major family policies was to revolutionize the family for the purpose of establishing the party-state's political legitimacy and for carrying out socialist transformation. Next, I move to the second phase, during which the party-state regulated the family through various pragmatic policies in order to carry out the national project of the four modernizations. Chief among these policies was the one-child policy that aimed to radically reduce the national birth rate. But the challenge of urban unemployment and social mobility also compelled the party-state to invoke family policies for the interests of the nation-state when dealing with pressing issues such as the return of the sent-down youth (see Chen 2015) or the influx of rural-urban migration. This phase, which began in 1980, gradually faded out by the late 1990s when a new type of family policies occupied central stage. The third phase took a shape when the Hu-Wen leadership pushed for China's global ascent in the early twenty-first century, and accordingly the focus of family policy making shifted to strengthening the family for the construction of a harmonious society, as first stated first by CCP General Secretary Hu Jintao and then elaborated and expanded upon by China's current leader Xi Jinping.[1]

I conclude the chapter by recapping the main features of the statist model of family policies and its contribution to the rise of neo-familism.

1 The Triumph of Statism over Familism and Individualism, 1900–1949

The call for a radical family revolution emerged at the beginning of the twentieth century and, intriguingly, was first introduced by the pioneers of the women's liberation movement. Jiu Qin, the famous anti-Qing heroine, for example, stated that "revolution must start with the family." At about the same time, an influential essay called for the rise of female revolutionaries: "Revolution! Revolution! Family revolution first!" (cited in Zhao 2018). In an essay entitled "On Family Revolution," the author argues that family revolution is a precondition for political revolution because it was familism that prevented the Chinese people from achieving citizenship and therefore destroying the family is necessary for building the modern nation-state (see Deng 1994: 39). Yang Du (1986), a leading intellectual figure who played an important role in early Republican politics, noted that in the era when nation-states were competing with one another, familism had become the obstacle to statism and the key mission of revolution was to turn familial persons into citizens (出于家人登于国民). As

---

1 At the twenty-eighth study meeting of the central party Politburo, Hu Jintao called for policies of family development to build a harmonious society (see Zhu and Chen 2013). In his speech to the participants at the first National Conference of Civilized Family Representatives, Xi Jinping asserted that the fate and future of the family are closely linked to the fate and future of the nation-state. The family is the basis for state development, national progress, and social harmony (Xi 2016).

THE STATIST MODEL OF FAMILY POLICY MAKING 227

David Faure (2007) acutely observes, the emergent modern notions of state and citizen constituted the largest challenge to kinship and familism. Most noticeably, throughout the discourse on the family revolution in the 1910s, statism, as a symbol of modernity, gained moral supremacy over familism, which was condemned as a root cause of China's backwardness and stagnation in modern times (Deng 1994; Zhao 2018).

Radical reformers in the late Qing and early Republican periods also believed that in order to build a strong nation-state it was necessary to recast the Chinese people into strong and modern citizens who are willing to serve the nation-state and to contribute to the common good of the society. Western individualism, which was widely regarded as the secret recipe to accomplish this, was thus enthusiastically introduced into China. The Western notion of individualism, which was embraced without any reservation, focused on two particular traits of individualism—freedom and equality—and it also emphasized the power of individual will. A large number of educated youth found individualism extremely attractive and applied it to their pursuit of freedom in spouse selection. Unlike the middle-aged radical reformers who promoted the family revolution for a political agenda but never practiced it in their own private lives, the youth put their ideals into action and turned the family revolution in a more individualistic direction of personal happiness and reform in private life. Individualism, therefore, achieved a short-lived primacy over statism in the fight against familism during the peak of the New Culture Movement from 1915 to 1919 (Zhao 2019).

The family revolution was, however, meant to serve the purpose of building the nation-state and thus could not be diverted by individualism. Beginning with Liang Qichao, who was a leading enlightenment figure in modern China, intellectuals increasingly began to place the individual in the larger context of the individual-society relationship. They hoped to recast the individual into a new type of responsible and competitive citizen who devotes her/himself to the greater goal of building a strong and modern nation-state. This was both part of the modernization dream and at the same time a key strategy for modernizing (Schwarcz 1986). Liang was arguably the first to call for the making of a new Chinese citizen (新民), maintaining that the self is divided into two parts—the small self (小我) that is embedded in individual interests and the great self (大我) that only can be realized by serving society or the nation-state. Intriguingly and symbolically important, both Hu Shi, who was a strong advocate of political liberalism and served as Republican China's ambassador to the United States in the 1940s, and Chen Duxiu, who was a major Communist thinker and founding general secretary of the CCP, played major roles in promoting Liang's idea of the small self versus the great self from the right and the left respectively. As Duan Lian insightfully notes, although some young intellectuals and educated youth embraced and advocated an individualism that defines the individual as an end in and of her/himself, the majority of the leading political and cultural elite in the 1910s–20s regarded individualism as a means to a higher end, as is vividly captured by the notion of the small self versus the great self (Duan 2012: 165–192).

Soon after taking national power in 1927, the KMT government promulgated the first modern law regarding marriage and the family in its 1930 Civil Code and promoted the May Fourth ideal of a small nuclear family. The new law made monogamy the only legal form of marriage and it regulated family relations, rights and obligations, and property inheritance (Ocko 1991; Watson 1984). Meanwhile the government also launched social campaigns to change traditional customs related to the family, such as group weddings or placing symbols of the state at family rituals. The goal of the government-led family reform, however, was clearly to promote nationalism and patriotism and to solidify the political legitimacy of the KMT, making the state both its leading agent and its major beneficiary (Glosser 2003: 81–133). The political contestation over national power between the KMT and the CCP and later the pressing task of resisting the Japanese occupation rendered the task of nation-building more urgent and demanding. Statism, along with nationalism and patriotism, was eventually adopted as the sole political doctrine and it was used to justify all sorts of authoritarian policies of the Republican government, as illustrated in the infamous KMT slogan "one party, one leader, and one ideology (一个政党，一个领袖，一个主义).[2] As far as family policies are concerned, by the end of the 1930s the triumph of statism over familism and individualism was ratified at the level of the ideology, law, and elite discourse of family life.

There was, however, also a more liberal and individualistic push for family change because the KMT government was competing with the CCP to reform the family to meet the demands of the younger generations that had been awakened by the ideas of the New Culture Movement. In its base areas, the CCP launched more radical campaigns of family reform. In 1931, the CCP promulgated its first marriage law, the "Marriage Regulations of the Chinese Soviet

---

2 The idea of unifying China with one party, one leader, and one ideology originally came from Sun Yat-sen's effort to reorganize the KMT in 1924 and it was firmly believed and practiced by Chiang Kai-shek in subsequent years, including during the 1927 mass killing of the Communists. On February 10, 1938, a hardline anti-Communist mouthpiece of the KMT, *Saodang bao* (扫荡报), elaborated on it again in an editorial. This was regarded as a new attempt by the KMT to incorporate the CCP by appealing to the ideology of statism in the context of the Japanese invasion.

THE STATIST MODEL OF FAMILY POLICY MAKING

Republic," establishing the freedom of marriage and divorce (Hu 1974). The accompanying "Decree Regarding Marriage," which was undersigned by Mao Zedong himself, declared: "In the Soviet districts, marriages now are contracted on a free basis. Free choice must be the basic principle of every marriage. The whole feudal system of marriage, including the power of parents to arrange marriages for their children, to exercise compulsion, and all purchases and sale in marriage contracts shall henceforth be abolished" (Diamant 2000: 341). After the CCP moved to northwest China due to its defeat by the KMT, it continued to carry out family reforms throughout the late 1930s and early 1940s (Zhou 2017). The top priority of the CCP governments in both the Jiangxi liberated area in the early 1930s and the northern China base areas during the anti-Japanese occupation period was to destroy the dominant influence of lineage organizations and the ideology of familism. In both places and during both periods, however, the CCP had to retreat from its initial radical attack on familism and patriarchal power in order to win back the support of male peasants who had lost power and privileges to women and youth. This makes an interesting contrast to the KMT case in which the state had to radicalize its family reform in order to win the support of youth and women (Ouyang 2003). Therefore, balancing the different demands and interests across age and gender lines was an important issue in the state-led family reforms of the 1930s and 1940s, and it remained so from 1949 to the present.

2   Revolutionizing the Family for Socialist Transformation, 1950s–1970s

The KMT's statist model of family policies and its efforts to promote state-led family reform largely stopped at the level of policy making on paper and it rarely made significant changes to family life among ordinary people in cities, and much less among the vast majority of the population—the peasants in the countryside. In sharp contrast, the CCP was the master of mobilizing and organizing the masses, accumulating much experience during its experiments with family reform in the 1930s and 1940s (Hu 1974; Zhou 2017). More importantly, when the CCP promulgated its 1950 Marriage Law and launched a full-scale offensive to implement the new law and related family-reform policies, it did so as part of its much larger project of land reform, which in turn was supported by a number of political campaigns, including the violent Suppression of Counterrevolutionaries Campaign that resulted in many executions and the ideological attacks on ancestral worship and lineage organizations that shattered the power base of patrilineal kinship and patriarchal authority in the family. Family policies during this period were politically charged, aimed at uprooting familism and shifting individual loyalty from the family to the state.

The single most important family policy is certainly the 1950 Marriage Law, which is widely known for banning parental arranged marriages, concubines, and child marriage, and in their stead, promoting and legalizing a new marriage and a new family form that is based on freedom in spouse selection, gender equality in conjugal relationships, and women's rights to own and inherit family property as well as rights to divorce. However, Western scholars have different assessments about the effects of the radical marriage and family reform of the 1950s. Whereas feminist scholars measure the state-claimed agenda of women's liberation against the reality and regard it as a failed attempt due to the continuity of patriarchal power and gender inequality in family life (Johnson 1983; and Stacy 1983), others find that women's agency played a central role among working-class people in both urban and rural China and thus carried out the marriage revolution to a much greater extent than scholars generally observe based on intellectual accounts (Diamant 2000; Ocko 1991). More importantly, the party-state was able to replace values of familism with values of statism through the implementation of the 1950 Marriage Law and to transfer the authority and power over marriage from the family to the state (Glosser 2003; Chen 2010).

For example, the new legal requirement of civic registration of marriage effectively undermined, if not immediately eliminated, parental authority and power in arranging their adult children's marriage, and thus it has widely been regarded as a progressive outcome of the 1950 Marriage Law. Yet, the same requirement also empowers the state to be the sole authority to legitimize a marriage, giving the party-state a new power to exercise policies of political discrimination by disapproving of marriage proposals that did not fit the correct political line, such as those between an individual with a good class background and her/his partner with a bad class background. In a similar vein, the 1950 Marriage Law required mediation by the local government for contested divorces, and how liberal the local government approached divorce depended almost entirely on the party-state's strategic decisions to serve state interests at any given time; hence, the rise of the divorce rate in the early 1950s and its sharp fall in subsequent years until the early 1980s. On both accounts, the 1950 Marriage Law took a much more hardline approach to increase state power over the family in comparison to the 1930 Civil Code under the KMT government (Glosser 2003: 171–174).

In retrospect, we can see clearly that a number of new socialist institutions and policies of the 1950s had more of an impact in changing the Chinese family than the legal text of the 1950 Marriage Law. Chief among them are rural

THE STATIST MODEL OF FAMILY POLICY MAKING 231

collectivization and the urban work-unit, household registration, the class-label system, and associated policies that integrated the family into these new socialist institutions and dissolved the authority and power of familism in practical details of social daily life. Let me reiterate here that the party-state regarded familism as its enemy, but not the family institution per se. Therefore, the party-state integrated the family into the socialist institutions by formulating specific policies to incorporate and even empower the family so that it could serve as an instrument to realize state interests and the ultimate goals of the state.

Familial ownership of private property and the family mode of social organization were the main pillars sustaining patriarchal power and values of familism in traditional Chinese culture (Cohen 1976; Greenhalgh 1994; Wolf 1972). In studies of family change, particular attention should be paid to the "transformation of the family mode of organization by the proliferation of social structures outside the family that have come to perform or direct many of the activities formerly carried out by family units" (Thornton and Fricke 1987: 749). The socialist transformation of ownership of the means of production began in 1953 and was completed in 1956 with the nationwide establishment of the rural collectives and the nationalization of industry and commerce in the cities. Familial ownership of the means of production was by and large replaced by state/collective ownership, and most of the economic, political, and social functions of the family were transferred to the jurisdiction of the party-state. Consequently, parental authority and power, along with values of familism, were seriously undermined. Through the urban work-unit system and the rural collective system, the state controlled economic production, product circulation, resource distribution, and income allocation, effectively playing the role of the ultimate family head of the entire country, known as the "big socialist family" in its propaganda campaigns (for a detailed description and penetrating analysis, see Davis-Friedmann 1991; Parish and Whyte 1978; Whyte and Parish 1984).

Later, during the radical years of the Cultural Revolution, the attack on familism advanced to a new and irrational high, whereby even emotional attachments among family members were condemned as corrupt bourgeois thoughts to be eliminated (see a case analysis in Meng 2008: 136–138). Individuals were mobilized to report on suspect family members to the state authority if they believed the interests of the state were at risk. In a published confession, Mr. Zhang recalls how, at the age of 15 in 1970, he had beaten up his mother and reported to the government when his mother went insane and denounced Chairman Mao during a family conversation. His mother was soon found guilty and executed, leaving Zhang in endless remorse and sorrow in subsequent years (Hannon 2013). By the late 1960s, the party-state had nearly destroyed familism, seriously weakening parental power and to a great extent redirecting individual loyalty from the family to the state through a combination of direct and indirect Maoist family policies.

At the level of everyday practice, however, the party-state was also limited by its own capacity and thus had to rely on the family institution for the operation of many of the new socialist institutions, effectively retaining the family as a key unit to receive distributed resources and provisions of public goods as well as to support individuals in family life. The household, for example, continued to be the unit of accounting and redistribution in the rural collectives. The urban work-unit system provided its employees with many benefits in addition to secure employment, but housing, arguably the most important resource next to wages, was allocated by either the work-unit system or the local government based on family need, which was measured by family size and structure. More importantly, the household registration system, established in 1958, defined the identity of Chinese individuals in terms of their family of origin (i.e., urban vs. rural residents) and they were subjected to differentiated social rights and family policies, such as pensions, medical care, childcare, education, travel privileges, and quantity and quality of consumer goods through the rations of the supply system. The class label system that divided people into politically good and bad classes was based mainly on the political and economic standing of the family head at the time of the victory of the revolution, but it also classified other members of a given family into the same class. During the subsequent three decades, various types of institutionalized discrimination were imposed on families of bad classes and they were even expanded to the second generation of bad-class families, as the political outcast label was hereditary through the patrilineal line (while household registration status was hereditary through the matrilineal line). These policies created inequality in spouse selection whereby rural women married less desirable urban husbands and bad class families married their daughters up into good class families (see Davis-Friedmann 1991). In these cases, the family became the inescapable "iron cage" that to a great extent defined and determined an individual's life chances; yet, this seeming return of familial authority/power was actually part of the statist model of family policies.

However, the same social institution could have produced a diametrically opposite impact on the family. Take the household registration system and state-controlled employment as an example. While fixing Chinese individuals to, or at least close to, their family of origin, the combination of these two systems also separated numerous couples from each other and from their family of origin for prolonged periods of time because the work-relocation of one

THE STATIST MODEL OF FAMILY POLICY MAKING   233

spouse, urban workers marrying rural wives, or professionals and cadres being sent to the May 7 Cadre Schools, was all carried out through the work-unit system, yet their spouses and children were fixed by the household registration system to the original place of birth or initial work assignment. This is known as the problem of a living-apart-family (两地分居家庭问题) that involved more than 10 million people by the end of the 1970s (see Chen 2015: 177). Again, this was done in the name of the interest of the state, and individuals and families were taught to accept the state determination of their fates without any complaints or critical opinions. For example, my co-author and I closely examined 264 letters between a couple who had to live and work apart for sixteen out of the twenty-five-year span of writing these letters. In a few letters, they did complain about the hardships of a living-apart-family, especially missing their children, but they also constantly criticized themselves for having incorrect thoughts of putting the interest of the family above that of the state (Li and Yan 2019). Intriguingly, when the party-state decided to help families reunite in the early 1980s, it cast the new policy as a great favor to families in need and demanded gratitude from the latter, which in turn reinforced the supremacy of statism instead of discrediting it.[3]

The party-state also made implicit policies to make the family an important bearer of state responsibility and financial burdens. For example, about 17 million youth were sent to the countryside in the late 1960s and early 1970s when the state tried to resolve the unemployment problem in the cities, thus affecting about one-third of the urban families by separating parents and their adult children. However, family ties were also strengthened by the same state policies in an unexpected way. A large number of these sent-down youth relied on parental support to survive the harsh life in the impoverished countryside, and the parents were asked to decide which one of their adult children could stay in the city while the others were sent to the countryside to meet the policy requirements. In the late 1970s, the state began to change its policy by allowing the sent-down youth to return to the cities, but the precondition was the provision of housing by their families. When the state could not provide

---

3 On January 21, 1980, the central party Organization Department teamed up with several ministries to issue an official notice aiming to resolve family-separation problems. The document was introduced in detail in *Labor Issues* (劳动工作), no. 3 (1980): 11–12. The State Council issued another document on December 8, 1989, stating that although more than 1,000,000 cases of family separation had been resolved during the past decade, more efforts were needed to resolve the remaining cases, especially cases involving intellectuals and professionals. See "State Council Notice on Further Resolving the Problem of Family Separation Among Cadres" (国务院关于进一步解决干部夫妻两地分居问题的通知), http://www.gov.cn/gongbao/content/2000/content_60018.htm (accessed January 22, 2020).

enough employment opportunities to the returnees, a new policy, known as the "replacement policy" (顶替政策), forced the parents to retire and to pass on their employment to their adult children returning from the countryside. These policies tied together the parents and their adult children and even made employment in a work-unit a hereditary resource passed down through the family institution (for an excellent study, see Chen 2010 and 2015).

Overall, family policies during this period were formulated mainly based on the party-state's political needs of state-building and they were also driven by the ideological commitment to eliminate familism and the family mode of social organization as well as to shift the political loyalty of Chinese individuals from the family to the state. Some policies, however, ended up strengthening family ties or seemingly empowering the family as an agent of the state. Yet, we must bear in mind that these specific policies still served the statist agenda and prioritized state interests over those of the family, thus constituting an integral part of the statist model of family policies. This model remained intact during the subsequent four decades, but it took different forms due to the changing focus of the party-state's national agenda.

3 Regulating and Privatizing the Family for the Four Modernizations, 1980 to the mid-1990s

By the late 1970s, the CCP had begun to shift its top priority from the radical Maoist project of revolutionizing China to the pragmatic pursuit of the Four Modernizations (i.e., modernizations of industry, agriculture, national defense, and science and technology). The strategic goal of four modernizations was first formulated by Mao Zedong in 1959 but in subsequent years, until Mao's death in 1976, it was overshadowed by the political line of radical Maoism. On December 22, 1978, the CCP announced to the world in the "Communiqué of the Third Plenary Session of the Eleventh Central Committee of the Chinese Communist Party" that beginning in 1979 the focus of the CCP work would shift from political campaigns to the construction of socialist modernization (CCP 1978). The significance and impact of this CCP document can hardly be overstated as it effectively opened up a new era in which economic growth gradually replaced Communist ideology as the ultimate criterion to guide and measure the party-state's national agenda and policy making, including policy making related to family policies.[4]

---

4   It was by no means accidental that in 1978 a nationwide debate on the criterion of truth was launched under the party-state's sponsorship, which included specific directives from Hu

THE STATIST MODEL OF FAMILY POLICY MAKING   235

It is in this context of the shifting focus to the four modernizations that family policy making changed its priority from revolutionizing the family as the building block of socialist society to regularizing the family as the agent of economic growth. The first and also the most radical step toward this new goal was one-child policy that was supposed to boost economic growth by creating a more rational ratio between population size and economic resources. Intriguingly, the CCP, not the government, took the lead in formulating and implementing the one-child policy. It was first clearly stated as a mandatory policy in the CCP's open letter to all members of the CCP and the Communist Youth League on September 25, 1980, and subsequently it was confirmed as China's primary national policy (基本国策) at the CCP's Twelfth Party Congress in September 1982. Three months later, the policy was written into the revised Constitution of the People's Republic of China. In the 1980 open letter, the CCP stated that the one-child policy is an important action that "determines the speed and future of the construction of the four modernizations, is related to the health and happiness of our descendants and fits the long-term and short-term interests of the Chinese people." The open letter stressed the benefits of the one-child policy for the country and for every family, clearly stating: "The Party requires that all members of the Communist Party and Communist Youth League, especially cadres at various levels, must care about the future of the state, be responsible for the people's interest and for the happiness of our descendants, thoroughly understand the meaning and necessity of this important and major action, lead [the masses] to follow your good example" (CCP 1980).

The impact and implications of the one-child policy is the most-studied topic in the existing literature on Chinese family policies and thus need not be explored here. But actual implementation of statist family policies is another story, in which urban and rural families had differing experiences. Strong resistance from rural China, for example, forced the party-state to retreat and rectify the radical assault on natalism, one of the core elements in traditional familism (see Greenhalgh 1993). I will omit this and focus on the 1980 open letter because it, together with the initial steps of making it a primary national policy, vividly demonstrates the determining role of the party-state, and the party-state's statist ideology in making family policies and the party-state's

---

Yaobang, the general secretary of the CCP at that time. The campaign-like debate ended with the conclusion that practice is sole the criterion for measuring truth, thus paving the way for the CCP's shift from Maoism to Deng Xiaoping's pragmatic line of modernization at the CCP Central Committee meeting in December 1978.

power to carry out its statist agenda regardless of the specific content of the family policies (or for that matter of any policy in the country).

Unlike the unfriendly one-child policy that regulated the most intimate part of family life—child bearing and the size and structure of the family—the party-state issued a number of family-friendly policies and regulations between 1977 and 1986 aimed to undo the Maoist policies of incorporating the family into the state and to normalize family life, such as uniting couples who had long been separated by work assignments, restoring the policy of annual family visits with full pay, and allowing overseas Chinese to visit their relatives. Chinese sociologist Chen Yingfang has collected a total of forty-six such policies to examine how the party-state used this cluster of policies to normalize family life, to bring the individual back to the family, and, at the same time, to emphasize the responsibilities of the family to build the four modernizations (Chen 2015: 174–183). In a similar vein, in the early 1980s Deborah Davis noted that, despite the reform policies of the 1980s that changed certain constraining parameters in the development of the family under Maoism, the urban family remains "a supplicant to a socialist state" (Davis 1993: 76).

Since the mid-1980s, an enduring thread in family policy making has been to expose the family to the emerging market competition so that it may become a productive agent for the nation-state. Such a new direction derives from the party-state's new national agenda to promote economic growth and to realize the goal of *xiaokang shehui* (小康社会), which compels the party-state to shift more responsibilities and financial burdens to Chinese individuals and their respective families, encouraging them to realize their full potential in economic activities. This change has been characterized as a neo-liberalist invasion of China (Rofel 2007) or "privatization and neo-liberalism without political liberty" (Ong and Zhang 2008). My approach to understanding this new trend in the 1980s and 1990s is to adopt Ulrich Beck's individualization theory, but with important modifications in accordance with Chinese social practices (Yan 2009 and 2010).

As in Western Europe (Beck and Beck-Gernsheim, 2002; Bauman, 2001), detraditionalization, disembeddedment, the creation of a life of one's own by a do-it-yourself approach, and the pressure to be more independent and individualistic have all been experienced in China.[5] In Western Europe, the

---

5 Ulrich Beck's individualization thesis highlights five basic features of the categorical shift in individual-society relations. The first is detraditionalization, referring to the loss of traditional security with respect to practical knowledge, faith, and guiding norms. Yet, this does not mean tradition no longer plays a role in contemporary society; instead, tradition may still be important as long as it serves as a usable resource for the individual. The second feature captures the removal of the individual from historically prescribed social forms and

THE STATIST MODEL OF FAMILY POLICY MAKING 237

individualization process has relied on what Beck calls "cultural democratization," meaning that democracy was widely accepted as a principle in everyday life and social relations for so long that it became part of the culture rather than merely a part of the political regime. Individualization also relies on the systems of education, social security, medical care, and employment and unemployment benefits that are backed up by a welfare state (Beck and Beck-Gernsheim, 2002, 22–29 and 204–205). In China the absence of cultural democracy and the provision of comprehensive welfare has resulted in major differences in the Chinese path to individualization (Yan 2010).

Chief among the differences is that the party-state, to a great extent, has been promoting the process of individualization by sponsoring institutional changes and directing the interplay among the players—the individuals, the market, social groups, institutions, and global capitalism—to maintain its monopoly of power, to modernize the country, and then to improve the living standards of the people. During the peak of the individualization process (1995–2005), the state promoted economic liberalization in order to stimulate individual initiative, creativity, and efficiency. At the macro level of economic reform, during the 1980s the family institution regained certain functions in agricultural and light industrial production through the household responsibility system of the rural reforms and the private household business system (个体户) of the urban reforms.

The party-state continued to shift more responsibilities to the family institution and Chinese individuals throughout the 1990s. During the restructuring

---

commitments in the sense of traditional contexts of dominance and support, such as the family, kinship, community, gender, and social class; this is called disembedding, or the "liberating dimension" in Beck's terms. Third, the disembedded or liberated individuals eventually strive to find new ways of committing themselves to a new type of social institutions, for example, by forming various forms of free associations, NGO s, and social movements, which is called "re-embedding" or the "reintegration dimension" (for a precise statement on these three dimensions, see Beck 1992: 128). The fourth feature is a paradoxical phenomenon known as "compulsive and obligatory self-determination" (Bauman 2001: 32). This is done through a set of new social institutions, such as the education system, the labor market, and state regulations. The fifth characteristic of individualization is the pursuit of a life of one's own through conformity, meaning that the promotion of choice, freedom, and individuality does not necessarily make every individual unique. These distinctions are made primarily to prevent the misunderstanding that individualization is a manifestation of the values of individualism or simply the rise of individuality; instead, individualization under the second modernity often presents itself as the antithesis of individualism. To better understand the individualization thesis, one must be aware of the differences between individualization and individualism, institutional changes at the macro level of society, biographical changes at the micro level of the individual, and finally the objective and subjective dimensions of the individualization process (see Yan 2009 and 2010).

of state-owned enterprises between 1993 and 2002, more than 63 million jobs were cut, and workers who were laid off received little or no severance pay (Hurst 2009: 16). Chinese official data recognize that between 1998 and 2003 more than 30 million workers were laid off from state-owned enterprises, and when they lost their jobs and incomes, by default the family became their safety net. Meanwhile, the state also withdrew from the provision of social welfare to reduce its own financial burdens, thus making the family the major provider for elderly care, psychological care, and disability care, known as the familialization of social welfare provision (Tang 2013; Wu 2015). Other major institutional changes that directly impacted the family included the marketization and commercialization of urban housing, medical-care provision, and the education system. The immediate impact was that, all of a sudden, tens of millions of urban residents found themselves at the mercy of the market and they had to pull together family resources to pay for medical care and the education of their children, and to buy their own apartment unit, all of which formerly were generally paid for by the party-state through its all-encompassing work-unit system. To meet these new challenges and to manage the new risks, Chinese individuals and families had to make extra efforts to accumulate wealth, which certainly contributed to the economic miracle at the national level but also resulted in what I call the phenomenon of the "striving individual" and eventually the rise of neo-familism in the twenty-first 21st century (Yan 2013, 2017/2018).

Concurrently, the individualization process also increased the freedom of individuals in the private-life sphere and resulted in some liberal and individualistic changes in family policy making. The best examples of such policy making include the 1980 Marriage Law, the 2001 Revised Marriage Law, and a number of official interpretations by the Supreme People's Court. Sociologist Deborah Davis generalizes that these new developments represented a "triple turn" by the party-state: a "turn toward" marriage as a voluntary contract between individuals rather than between family groups, a "turn away" from the previous close surveillance of sexual behavior, and a "turn away" from the notion of communal property in marriage (Davis 2014). Among others, the 1980 Marriage Law made a breakthrough by allowing no-fault divorce, and the 2001 Revised Marriage Law recognized both individual and communal property within a marriage, and defined the former as not only property owned by an individual before marriage but also gifts or an inheritance received by just one spouse after the marriage. This new legislation was understood by Chinese scholars as taking a Western individualistic approach to marital property. In a similar vein, Margaret Woo views these changes as a shift toward a "more individualized concept of citizenship" (2003). In response to vigorous criticism from defenders of a more traditional Chinese familial approach and to the confusion generated during the debates, the Supreme People's Court issued three "interpretations" between 2001 and 2010, clarifying while still upholding the provisions of the 2001 Revised Marriage Law. As Philip C.C. Huang sharply notes, the interpretations are essentially a reflection of the tensions between the individualized market economy and the continuing household economy, and between the imported individualistic legal principles and the traditional moral values of familism (Huang 2011). As Deborah Davis points out, viewed from another perspective this new provision defending individual property in a marriage actually underscores the bond between parents and their married adult children as well as the parents' investments in their children's marriages (Davis 2014: 570). More importantly, we must also keep in mind that the party-state, along with the well-established statist ideology, firmly stood above all of these tensions and made strategic choices between familial and individualistic preferences to maximize state interests.

Again, take the 1980 Marriage Law as an example. In addition to almost entirely withdrawing from its formal control over sexuality, marriage, and divorce of Chinese citizens, in the chapter on family relations the law also made important changes with respect to familism. Article 28 prescribes that paternal and maternal grandparents who have the financial ability have a legal obligation to raise their grandchildren in the case that the parents pass away or are incapable of raising the children; adult grandchildren have the same legal obligation toward their paternal and maternal grandparents in their old age. In a similar vein, Article 29 prescribes the mutual obligations of older and younger siblings. From an individualistic perspective, these legal changes actually marked a step backwards by blurring the boundaries of the family and the obligations of the family members because measured by the definition of the conjugal/nuclear family, grandparents and adult siblings are not family members. Yet, in traditional familism the boundary of the family group is almost unlimited, and it most certainly includes grandparents and siblings. In this connection, the statist model of family policies regarding family relations is obviously working against the trend toward individualization and liberalization with respect to marriage and divorce. This is because the practical need to shift more of the welfare burden to the family, as indicated above, is more important to the party-state than is the liberation of the individual from the constraints of familism. In the same legal text, the state chooses alternatively to make an alliance either with individualism or with familism depending on the situation in order to serve its national agenda, thus reminding us that we must read the legal text in its entirety so that we may completely understand the role of statism.

4 Recalibrating the Family for the China Dream in the Twenty-First Century

In September 2004, the CCP announced its new goal of building a socialist harmonious society. This was primarily a strategic response to the looming social crisis caused by the rapidly expanding income gap, the striking social inequalities, the widespread official corruption, and the various forms of social injustice. Despite the rapidly growing economy and the improved standards of living since the 1980s, there was a threat that these social problems would result in large-scale social unrest. As expected, family policy making had to be rectified to serve the purpose of building a harmonious society, and indeed, an entire new set of new family policies was implemented to alleviate the newly added burdens of the family and to assist the vulnerable groups in their family life. To do this, the party-state invoked some traditional values and even made friendly gestures to certain elements of traditional familism.

A major concern since the late 1990s has been how to meet the needs of the elderly when the proportion of younger, working-aged people has been shrinking. In 1996, the government adopted a law on the "Protection of the Rights and Interests of the Elderly," which emphasizes that "the elderly shall be provided for mainly by their families." The law enables parents over the age of 60 to sue their adult children if the latter fail to provide support. In the countryside, local authorities also ask villagers to sign "family support agreements." About 13 million rural families were reported to have signed such contracts by the end of 2005 (Chou 2010). In response to reports of a rise in suicides among the rural elderly who suffered both illness and depression as well as poverty in the 1990s, the government established the New Rural Co-operative Medical System in 2003 and the New Rural Old-Age Insurance program in 2005 in an attempt to establish a minimum social-security system. The Minimum Living Standard Guarantee Scheme was widely implemented in urban China in 1999 and in rural China in 2007, aiming to alleviate poverty among China's poorest families and to reduce the inequality gap. Although the actual effectiveness of these new laws and policies vary greatly (Gao and Zhai 2012), they do indicate that after leaving families at the mercy of market competition for decades, the party-state has turned to helping the family, especially vulnerable families, to regain strength and to develop.

At the end of 2012, the government amended the 1996 law on the rights of the elderly to require adult children to regularly visit their parents. The Chinese government has clearly been energetic in addressing the looming crisis of elderly welfare, yet nearly all of its policies and laws have emphasized that prime responsibility for the elderly remains with the family, not with the state. As Claudia Chang Huang (2019) explains so well, the state also vigorously promotes the idea of active aging and self-reliance as another new policy to address the issue of elderly support.

The second most noteworthy event was the new two-child policy in late 2015. Suffering from the negative consequences of the one-child policy, the party-state had been dealing with the problems of a rapidly aging society and the contraction of the labor force during the previous decade. In 2011, the one-child policy was modified to allow any couples where both spouses were single children to have a second child. Two years later, the policy was extended to couples where only one spouse was a single child. Under a law that took effect on January 1, 2016, all Chinese couples are now permitted to have two children. Despite these measures, however, the overall fertility rate continues to decline. Although the rate of second births has increased slightly since 2014, the first-born rate has dropped, leading to a looming risk of a sharp population shrinkage in the near future (Shen and Jiang, 2018).

Local governments appear to be bolder in addressing this problem. For example, in September 2016, the Department of Health and Birth Planning in Yichang city, Hubei province, posted an open letter on its website, calling on all municipal members of the CCP and the Communist Youth League to have a second child. Literally imitating the party-state's 1980 open letter but replacing the call for "one-child" with a call for "two-children," on the surface this open letter may seem hilarious, but a subsequent media interview with the department leader reveals that the local government was politically serious in promoting this as the best way to serve the nation-state (Wang 2016). Taking more pragmatic measures, Liaoning province has proposed income-tax breaks and education subsidies to encourage more births; Jiangxi province has taken measures to discourage abortions; and other provinces have tightened the requirements for couples to divorce, justifying the changes to keep alive the possibility of new offspring (Myers and Ryan 2018). The state media have also embraced this new great cause for the nation-state. The Communist Party's flagship newspaper, *People's Daily* (*Overseas Edition*), published a lengthy article on August 4, 2018, exhorting people to have more babies. The accompanying editorial proclaimed in unmistakably Maoist tones: "To put it bluntly, having a baby is not only a family matter, but a state affair" (Peng 2018).

A family matter as a state affair is indeed an important message delivered from the party-state leaders, who seem to have assigned a more important role to the family institution for governance, as a vehicle for the new national agenda of the Chinese dream and the harbinger of a happy life. The best spokesperson for the recalibration of the statist model is perhaps Xi Jinping, general secretary of the CCP. On numerous occasions since 2012, he has talked about the importance of the family and family life, the necessity of establishing healthy family ethics, and the party-state's commitment to family development (more on this in Chapter 11) As expected, Xi's various speeches on the importance of the family were quickly adopted by government leaders at all levels, thereby increasing the number of new surveys and the amount of research on family policy and family life. One of the immediate effects is that for the first time the central government established a Bureau of Family Development at the national level, which is housed with the National Health and Family Planning Commission. This bureau has published annual reports on the development of the Chinese family since 2014.[6]

With regard to actual family policies, the number of new laws and policies has been consistently growing since the 1990s, marking a sharp contrast with the first three decades under Maoism. In their sketch of Chinese family policies, Xia and her co-authors list only one policy, the 1950 Marriage Law, for the entire Maoist era, four policies for the "recovery and progress" period of the 1980s, and nine policies during the "rapid development and institutionalization" period since 1990 (Xia et al. 2014). Similarly, Liu Jitong records only two noteworthy family policies (the 1950 Marriage Law and the 1958 Regulations on Household Registration) for the entire Maoist era, two policies for the 1980s (the 1980 one-child open letter and the 1985 Inheritance Law), and twenty-one major policies in the years between 1990 and 2016 (Liu 2018: 106). These numbers should not be taken literally because none of the authors conducted a systematic survey of family policies; yet, they may still be indicative of a trend toward institutionalization, professionalization, and specification in family policy making during the last two decades. It is in this connection that the 2015 Anti–Domestic Violence Law is widely applauded as the victory of persistent collective efforts by advocates for the rights of women and children, social-work professionals, family-policy researchers, legal scholars, and sympathetic government officials.

A related new development is that, in light of the CCP's more favorable view toward the family institution, some Chinese scholars have taken a more proactive approach to push for more family-friendly policies and to call on the government to take more responsibility in the provision of social welfare so that the family can be relieved of its heavy burdens that were added in the 1980s and

---

6   In March 2018, the National Health and Family Planning Commission was renamed the National Health Commission, dropping the term "family planning." Interestingly, the Bureau of Family Development was renamed the Bureau of Population Monitoring and Family Development. These changes are obvious indicators of the changing state agenda and the focus on family policy making.

early 1990s. Despite differences in approaches and suggested solutions, most of these scholars advocate the idea of "family problems, government responsibilities" (Tang 2013), asking that the party-state reflect on its inconsistent and family-unfriendly policies in the past, slow down promotion of familialization of elderly support, and provide more public goods to support individuals and families. The core message voiced by many scholars is that the state bears a huge responsibility for the Chinese family and more proactive family policies are urgently needed (Li and Wang 2016; Peng and Hu 2015; Wu 2015).

Once again, when looking at these family-friendly policies we must keep in mind there is another side of the statist model that can be unfriendly, or can be friendly and unfriendly at the same time. Take the *shidu* (失独) families (those who lose their singleton child) as an example. According to the official and likely the most conservative estimation (National Statistics Bureau 2015), 660,000 families had lost their singleton child by 2010, but a higher estimation is as many as two million families. In comparison to other officially recognized types of "vulnerable families," such as childless elderly families or families with disabled or mentally ill members, *shidu* families have received more attention and actual help from the party-state. According to Kong's study, from 2006 to early 2018 the central government implemented a total of forty-four policies specifically for *shidu* families; the chief method of help is to provide financial aid (Kong 2018). The latest policy concerns management of a national database of *shidu* families, issued by the National Health Commission (2018). Yet, the tensions between *shidu* families and local governments have accelerated over the years, and some parents had taken collective actions to issue appeals to the central government in Beijing. At least three local commissions of health and family planning (the government agency in charge of family affairs and policy implementation) were discovered classifying *shidu* families, along with families of mentally ill people, as one of the targeted criminal groups in the recent campaign to strike down on criminal society (扫黑除恶). This incident shows that *shidu* families, while receiving policy support, are seen as a threat to political stability and thus part of the criminal sector of society, again reminding us of the two sides of the statist model of family policies.

The reason why *shidu* families were seen as politically dangerous is that most *shidu* parents refuse to accept the official classification that they are merely another group of vulnerable families. Instead, they insist that they have made a huge contribution to the nation-state by answering the call to have only one child and then they suffered after losing their only child. They want the state to recognize their heroic contribution and to compensate them accordingly (Kong 2018: 105).

In a way, their logic resembles the argument of the Shanghai sent-down youth when they initially tried to claim their right to be compensated by the state with relocation back to the city and urban employment. The state could not accept such a claim because, in accordance with the logic of statism, individuals and social groups must yield their interests to the supremacy of the interests of the state. Doing what the state needs them to do is their obligation, and there is no heroic or virtuous sacrifice involved. To challenge such a logic can be compared to challenging the authority of the state, and, conversely, acceptance of such a challenge implies that the party-state admits its previous wrongdoing and its weakness by conceding to the demands of individuals or families. Neither is acceptable in terms of the logic of statism. This is precisely why the sent-down youth initially failed in their collective action, but eventually succeeded when they pleaded that the party-state give them the chance to fulfill their filial piety duty to their aging parents (Chen 2015).

The *shidu* parents seem to make the same mistake as the Shanghai sent-down youth made in the late 1970s, but they have yet to change their way of dealing with the statist logic. Intriguingly, almost concurrently, during the last decade a grassroots organization of straight parents of gay children in urban China have been successful in negotiating with the state authorities and advocating the social rights of their gay children. This is because they have highlighted the moral capital of parenthood, the virtues of neo-familism, and the incorporation of homosexuality into the normal family structure, none of which can be seen as a threat to political stability or to the authority of statism (Wei and Yan n.d.). These examples illustrate the bottom line of the statist model of family policies, that is, no family policy or familial action that challenges the fundamental interests and ultimate goals of the party-state will be allowed.

5 Conclusions: The Statist Model of Family Policy Making

Three subthemes of the statist model emerge from the preceding sections. First, the party-state did not create its statist approach toward the family and family policy making from scratch. Instead, the party-state inherited it from the radicalism of the family revolution promoted by Chinese elite and educated youth in the 1910s and the 1920s, carried it out to near-perfection through the radical social-engineering projects of the Maoist era, and then recalibrated it in terms of laws, regulations, and policies during the era of post-Mao reforms that is characterized by a diametrically opposite orientation. On the surface, family policies during the past seven decades were made in different, and sometimes

THE STATIST MODEL OF FAMILY POLICY MAKING 245

conflicting, directions. Some policies were more radical and politically charged than others, whereas others, especially in recent years, were made to protect vulnerable families and to generally strengthen the capacity of the family institution. Although there has been a radical shift from destroying the family for the nation-state (Zhao 2018) to building the family for the nation-state (Yan 2018), the priority of state interests over family interests in policy making has remained intact from 1949 to the present.

Second, a closer look at the discourse on and the practice of the family revolution and family policies during the last century reveals that it was traditional familism and the patriarchal extended family, instead of the family institution per se, that was targeted during both the New Culture Movement of the 1910s and the1920s and the party-state–sponsored family reform from the 1950s to the 1970s. The party-state, however, differs from the radical advocates of the New Culture Movement in one critically important aspect, that is, while the early elite reformers invoked individualism to fight against familism, the CCP has regarded individualism as its enemy from its founding years to the present. Yet, to build a strong state and to pursue its modernization goals through economic development, the party-state has had to make use of the family institution and to tackle individual agency. Therefore, the second abiding theme in the operation of the statist model of family policy making has been how to fight against both familism and individualism on the one hand and to encourage and rely on contributions from the family and individuals on the other hand. This also explains the coexistence of the processes of individualization and familialization under state sponsorship (Yan 2010 and 2018).

Third, the construction of a new type of small nuclear family, known as *xiao jiating* (小家庭) that is based on free-choice marriage and that functions mainly as a private haven of the personal lives of couples with children was long proposed as both an ideal of modern family life and a pragmatic solution to end the tyranny of familism by the radical advocates of the family revolution during the New Culture Movement. This ideal was subsequently put into practice by the KMT and the Republican state in the 1930s and the 1940s because a small nuclear family would not be the breeding ground for the traditional and oppressive familism and thus could be a positive asset to the nation-state (see Glosser 2003). The CCP accepted the small family ideal and, unlike the KMT which was unable to carry it out in real life beyond the educated urban elite, actually made it part and parcel of everyday life among ordinary people in waves of both radical and modest family policies (Yan 2003, 2011). Chief among these is the radical one-child policy in the 1980s that drastically limited the size of the family and consequently simplified the family structure. The rise of neo-familism, which is a hybrid of traditional familism and modern individualism, however, twists the party-state's original agenda of limiting the family on behalf of the nation-state by reconstructing a new type of multi-generational family organization featuring intergenerational intimacy and a malleable ad hoc family structure (Yan 2016, 2017/2018). Yet, the party-state has shown the flexibility to incorporate neo-familism into its latest agenda of strengthening the family for the nation-state by readjusting family policy making and implementing a set of new family-friendly policies. The resilience of both the Chinese family and the party-state constitutes the third subtheme sustaining the statist model of family policies.

In the present study, I have used the concept of the statist model in two ways. At the level of ideology and value orientation, I examine the interplay among individualism, familism, and statism, noting that the party-state has been hostile toward both individualism and familism but for different reasons. From the statist perspective, familism is an obstacle to building a strong nation-state because of its emphasis on family loyalty, political apathy, and suppression of the creativity of youth. Yet, the primacy of the family interests over those of the individual, the principal value of familism, can be incorporated into statism. Indeed, by way of the ethical discourse on the division between the small self and the great self, the state eventually replaced the family to become the representative of the great self whereby individuals could find their belongingness and true identity. This is why the party-state began to show more tolerance toward values of traditional familism, such as filial piety, in the twenty-first century and seems at least to be sympathetic to the rise of neo-familism. Individualism, however, offers no commonality to statism and thus it must be harshly suppressed and stigmatized as an unhealthy, selfish, and anti-social value system. In short, as value systems, statism dominates familism and individualism in family policy making, suppressing both familism and individualism on most occasions but on some occasions making an alliance individualism.

The second way I use the statist model of family policies is to explore how the party-state makes pragmatic concessions and arrangements when dealing with the family institution and the individual at the level of social practice. The family institution has always been used by the party-state as a strategically important medium to link the individual and the state and, on many occasions, to provide protection and welfare to the individual so that the state can relieve itself of its responsibilities. Yet, the party-state has also sponsored institutional changes to encourage the individualization of the social structure and has rewarded individual creativity and capacity for competition (Yan 2010, 2013), which are also reflected in family policy making.

THE STATIST MODEL OF FAMILY POLICY MAKING 247

The statist model enables us to better understand the complexity and flexibility of family policy making from the statist perspective and thus make sense of the seemingly self-contradictory, inconsistent, and vacillating family policies over the last seventy years. Focusing on the most important interest and ultimate goal of the party-state, we will not be easily misled by its rhetoric or strategic policy changes. The radical start and conservative end of the marriage revolution in the 1950s actually served well the party-state's ultimate goal of solidifying political legitimacy and building a strong state, instead of half-failing due to resistance by male cadres at the grassroots level. The obvious evidence is that the approach of radicalism-to-revisionism in the marriage revolution was experimented with twice in the CCP-controlled areas during the 1930s and 1940s, and the party-state certainly knew what it was doing in the 1950s. The state, in other words, was firmly in the driver's seat all along throughout the Maoist era.

The introduction of the market economy and the influence of global capitalism, however, have begun to break the monopoly of the statist model of family policy making to a certain extent. Domestic migration, social mobility, a consumerist culture, and the individual pursuit of happiness have all had profound impacts on the previous hegemony of statism at the level of ideology and have affected the implementation of state policies at the level of practice. Professionalism and a more developed division of labor to address the new social needs in an open and mobile society, such as the rise of social work as a profession, also cracked open the statist model of family policy making. More calls for family-friendly policies, family-centered approaches, and individual-based welfare policies are signs of these new waves of change. Yet, it remains unclear how far this trend toward diversity can develop because, to date, no one has been able to successfully challenge the statist model of family policy making.

References

Barry, Brian. 1999. "Statism and Nationalism: A Cosmopolitan Critique." *Nomos* 41: 12–66.

Bauman, Zygmunt. 2001. *The Individualized Society*. Cambridge: Polity Press.

Beck, Ulrich. 1992. *Risk Society: Towards a New Modernity*, tr. Mark Ritter. London: Sage.

Beck, Ulrich and Elisabeth Beck-Gernsheim. 2002. *Individualization: Institutionalized Individualism and its Social and Political Consequences*. London and Thousand Oaks, CA: Sage Publications.

Banfield, Edward C. 1958. *The Moral Basis of a Backward Society*. New York: The Free Press.

CDIC (Central Discipline Inspection Commission, CCP). 2017. "注重家庭、注重家教、注重家风，习近平总书记这样说" (Focus on the Family, Family Education, and Family Ethics, General Secretary Xi Jinping Advises). February 10. http://www.ccdi.gov.cn/toutiao/201702/t20170209_125355.html (accessed November 2, 2017).

CCP (Chinese Communist Party).1978."中国共产党十一届中央委员会第三次全体公报" (Communiqué of the Third Plenary Session of the Eleventh Central Committee of the Chinese Communist Party). December 22. http://cpc.people.com.cn/GB/64162/64168/64563/65371/4441902.html (accessed March 6, 2019).

CCP (Chinese Communist Party). 1980. "关于控制我国人口增长问题致全体共产党员共青团员的公开信" (An Open Letter to all Members of the Communist Party and the Communist Youth League Regarding the Problem of Controlling Population Growth in China), www.wenshubang.com/gongkaixin/290852/html (accessed March 6, 2019).

Chen, Yingfang. 2010. "国家与家庭，个人—城市中国的家庭制度, 1949–1979" (State, Family and the Individual: Family Policies in Urban China, 1949–1979). http://ww2.usc.cuhk.edu.hk/PaperCollection/Details.aspx?id=8037 (accessed January 23, 2020).

Chen, Yingfang. 2015. "社会生活正常化：历史转折中的家庭化" (The Normalization of Social Life: Familization in the Turning Point of History). 社会科学研究, no. 5: 164–188.

Chou, Rita Jing-Ann. 2010. "Filial Piety by Contract? The Emergence, Implementation, and Implications of the 'Family Support Agreement' in China." *The Gerontologist* 51 (1): 3–16.

Cohen, Myron. 1976. *House United, House Divided: The Chinese Family in Taiwan.* New York: Columbia University Press.

Davis, Deborah. 1993. "Urban Households: Supplicants to a Socialist State." In Deborah Davis and Stevan Harrell (eds.), *Chinese Families in the Post-Mao Era*, pp. 50–76. Berkeley: University of California Press.

Davis, Deborah. 2014. "Privatization of Marriage in Post-Socialist China." *Modern China* 40(6): 551–577.

Davis-Friedmann, Deborah. 1991. *Long Lives: Chinese Elderly and the Communist Revolution* (expanded edition). Stanford: Stanford University Press.

Deng, Weizhi. 1994. 近代中国家庭的变革 (*Family Change in Modern China*). Shanghai: Shanghai renmin chubanshe.

Diamant, Neil J. 2000. *Revolutionizing the Family: Politics, Love, and Divorce in Urban and Rural China, 1949–1968*. Berkeley: University of California Press.

Duan, Lian. 2012. 世俗时代的意义探询：五四启蒙思想中的新道德观研究 (*Exploring Meanings in the Era of Secularization: A Study of New Moral Values during the May Fourth Enlightenment*). Taipei: Xiuwei zixun keji chuban.

Dumont, Louis. 1986. *Essays on Individualism: Modern Ideology in Anthropological Perspective*. Chicago: University of Chicago Press.

Faure, David. 2007. *Emperor and Ancestor: State and Lineage in South China*. Stanford: Stanford University Press.

Gao, Qin and Fuhua Zhai. 2012. "Anti-Poverty Family Policies in China: A Critical Evaluation." *Asian Social Work and Policy Reviews* 6(2): 122–135.

Garzón, Adela. 2000. "Cultural Change and Familism." *Psicothema* 12(suppl.): 45–54.

Glosser, Susan. 2003. *Chinese Versions of Family and State, 1915–1953*. Berkeley: University of California Press.

Greenhalgh, Susan. 1993. "The Peasantization of the One-Child Policy in Shaanxi." In Deborah Davis and Stevan Harrell (eds.). *Chinese Families in the Post-Mao Era*, pp. 219–250. Berkeley: University of California Press.

Greenhalgh, Susan. 1994. "De-Orentalizing the Chinese Family Firm." *American Ethnologist* 21(4): 746–775.

Hannon, John. 2013. "In China, A Son: Haunted by the Cultural Revolution." *Los Angeles Times*, March 30. https://www.latimes.com/world/la-xpm-2013-mar-30-la-fg-china-mother-revolution-20130331-story.html (accessed January 23, 2020).

Hu, Chi-hsi. 1974. "The Sexual Revolution in the Kiangsi Soviet." *China Quarterly*, no. 59: 477–490.

Huang, Chang (Claudia). 2019. *Self-cultivation and Sociality Among Retired Women in Urban China*. Ph.D. Dissertation, Department of Anthropology, University of California, Los Angeles.

Huang, Philip C. C. 2011. "The Modern Chinese Family: In Light of Economic and Legal History." *Modern China* 37(5): 459–497.

Hurst, William. 2009. *The Chinese Worker After Socialism*. Cambridge: Cambridge University Press.

Johnson, Kay Ann. 1983. *Women, the Family and Peasant Revolution in China*. Chicago: University of Chicago Press.

Kong, Xiangli. 2018. "风险社会视角下失独家庭的政策支持机制" (The Mechanism of Policy Support to the *Shidu* Families From the Perspective of Risk Society). 北京行政学院学报 (Bulletin of Beijing Administration College), no. 5: 101–109.

Li, Shuzhuo, and Wang Huan. 2016. "家庭变迁家庭政策演进与中国家庭家庭政策构建" (Family Changes, Family Policy Evolution, and Family Policy Formation in China), 人口与经济 (Population and Economy), no. 6: 1–9.

Li, Tian and Yunxiang Yan. 2019. "The Self-Cultivation of Politically Committed Lives in Maoist China: New Evidence from a Family's Private Letters, 1961–1986." *The China Journal*, no. 82: 88–110.

Liu, Jitong. 2018. "当代中国婚姻家庭政策历史经验、结构特征、严峻挑战与发展方向" (Marriage and family policies in contemporary China: historical lessons, structural features, challenges and future directions), 人文杂志 (Journal of Humanities), no. 4, pp. 100–114.

Lukes, Steven. 1973. *Individualism*. Oxford: Basil Blackwell.

Meng, Xianfan. 2008. "家庭：百年来的三次冲击及我们的选择" (Family: the three impacts in the last century and our choices). 清华大学学报(Journal of Tsinghua University) 23(3): 133–145.

Myers, Steven Lee and Olivia Mitchell Ryan. 2018. "Burying 'One Child' Limits, China Pushes Women to Have More Babies." *New York Times*, August 11. https://www.nytimes.com/2018/08/11/world/asia/china-one-child-policy-birthrate.html (accessed August 12, 2018).

National Statistics Bureau. 2015. "中国失独妇女及其家庭状况研究" (A study of women and their family conditions after losing their single child). http://www.stats.gov.cn/tjzs/tjsj/tjcb/dysj/201505/t20150528_1111157.html (accessed March 20, 2019).

National Health Commission. 2018. "计划生育特殊家庭服务信息管理标准和规范" (Information standards and guidance on the management of special families of population control). http://www.nhc.gov.cn/rkjcyjtfzs/zcwj2/201805/0491d75f2d064a048d6c80e66fe541b5.shtml (accessed April 2, 2019).

Ocko, Jonathan K. 1991. "Women, Property, and Law in the People's Republic of China." In Rubie S. Watson and Patricia Buckley Ebrey (eds.), *Marriage and Inequality in Chinese Society*, pp. 313–346. Berkeley: University of California Press.

Ong, Aihwa and Li Zhang. 2008. "Introduction: Privatizing China: Powers of the Self, Socialism from Afar." In Li Zhang and Aihwa Ong (eds.), *Privatizing China: Socialism from Afar*, pp. 1–19. Ithaca: Cornell University Press.

Ouyang, Shu.2003. "南京国民政府与革命根据地婚姻家庭法制比较研究" (A comparison of marriage and family institutions under the Nanjing government and in the revolutionary base areas). 二十一世纪 (The 21st Century), internet edition, no. 4. http://www.cuhk.edu.hk/ics/21c/media/online/0210085.pdf (accessed March 27, 2019).

Parish, William and Martin King Whyte. 1978. *Village and Family in Contemporary China.* Chicago: University of Chicago Press.

Peng, Xizhe, and Hu Zhan. 2015. "当代中国家庭变迁与家庭政策重构" (The contemporary transition of the Chinese family and the reconstruction of family policy), 中国社会科学 （China Social Sciences）, no. 12: 113–132.

Peng, Xunwen. 2018. "让人们敢生愿生二孩" (Let people have the courage and motivation to have a second child), 人民日报海外版 (*People's Daily*, overseas edition), August 5. http://www.wenxuecity.com/news/2018/08/05/7503101.html (accessed August 7, 2018).

Rofel, Lisa. 2007. *Desiring China: Experiments in Neoliberalism, Sexuality, and Public Culture.* Durham, NC: Duke University Press.

Schwarcz, Vera. 1986. *The Chinese Enlightenment: Intellectuals and the Legacy of the May Fourth Movement of 1919.* Berkeley: University of California Press.

Shen, Yang and Jiang Lai. 2018. "提高生育率，需要政府和社会为女性提供育儿支持" (To increasing fertility rate, child-rearing support for women are needed from government and society). 城市治理研究 (*Urban Governance Studies*), Issue 3, pp. 27–33.

Stacey, Judith. 1983. *Patriarchy and Socialist Revolution in China*. Berkeley: University of California Press.

Tang, Can. 2013. "家庭问题与政府责任" (Family Problematics and Government Responsibilities). In Tang Can and Zhang Jiang (eds.), 家庭问题与政府责任: 促进家庭发展的国内外比较研究 (*Family Problematics and Government Responsibilities: Comparative Studies in Promoting Family Development*), pp. 1–12. Beijing: Shehui kexue wenxian chubanshe.

Taylor, Charles. 2003. *Modern Social Imaginaries*. Durham, NC: Duke University Press.

Thornton, Arland and Thomas Fricke. 1987. "Social Change and the Family: Comparative Perspectives from the West, China, and South Asia." *Sociological Forum* 2(4): 746–779.

Wang, Xiuning. 2016. "两封计生公开信: 一样逻辑, 两种目的" (Two open letters on birth-planning: The same logic, two different goals). September 22. http://star.news.sohu.com/20160922/n468916629.shtml (accessed March 28, 2019).

Watson, Rubie S. 1984. "Women's Property in Republican China: Rights and Practice." *Republican China* 10(1): 1–12.

Wei, Wei and Yunxiang Yan. n.d. "Rainbow Parents and the Familial Model of *Tongzhi* (LGBT) Activism in Contemporary China." Unpublished manuscript in progress.

Whyte, Martin King. 2005. "Continuity and Change in Urban Chinese Family Life." *The China Journal*, no. 53: 9–33.

Whyte, Martin King and William L. Parish. 1984. *Urban Life in Contemporary China*. Chicago: University of Chicago Press.

Wolf, Margery. 1972. *Women and the Family in Rural Taiwan*. Stanford: Stanford University Press.

Woo, Margret. 2003. "Shaping Citizenship: Chinese Family Law and Women." *Yale Journal of Law and Feminism* 15: 99–134.

Wu, Xiaoying. 2015. "家庭政策背后的主义之争" (Ideological debates behind family policies). 妇女研究论丛 (Journal of Women's Studies), no. 2: 17–25.

Xi, Jingping. 2016. "在会见第一届全国文明家庭代表时的讲话" (speech at the first national conference of representatives of civilized family), December 12, 2019. http://www.ccpph.com.cn/sxllrdyd/qggbxxpxjc/qggbxxpxje/201901/t20190110_256815.htm (accessed January 6, 2020).

Xia, Yan Ruth, Haiping Wang, Anh Do, and Shen Qin. 2014. "Family Policy in China: A Snapshot of 1950–2010." In Mihaela Robila (ed.), *Handbook of Family Policies Across the Globe*, pp. 257–272. Berlin: Springer Science+ Business Media.

Yan, Yunxiang. 2003. *Private Life under Socialism: Love, Intimacy, and Family Change in a Chinese Village, 1949–1999*. Stanford: Stanford University Press.

Yan, Yunxiang. 2009. *The Individualization of Chinese Society*. Oxford: Berg.

Yan, Yunxiang. 2010. "The Chinese Path to Individualization." *British Journal of Sociology* 61(3): 489–512.

Yan, Yunxiang. 2011. "The Individualization of the Family in Rural China." *boundary 2* 38(1): 203–229.

Yan, Yunxiang. 2013. "Of the Individual and Individualization: The Striving Individual in China and the Theoretical Implications." In Michael Heinlein, Cordula Kropp, Judith Neumer, Angelika Poferl and Regina Romhild (eds.), *Futures of Modernity: Challenges for Cosmopolitical Thought and Practice,* pp. 177–194. Bielefeld, Germany: Transcript Publishers.

Yan, Yunxiang. 2016. "Intergenerational Intimacy and Descending Familism in Rural North China." *American Anthropologist* 118(2): 244–257.

Yan, Yunxiang. 2018. "Neo-Familism and the State in Contemporary China." *Urban Anthropology and Studies of Cultural Systems and World Economic Development* 47(3/4): 181–224.

Yang, Du. 1986. "论国家主义与家族主义之区别" (On differences between statism and familism). In Liu Qingbo (ed.), 杨度集 (*Collected Works of Yang Du*) pp. 530–532. Changsha: Hunan renmin chubanshe.

Zhao, Yanjie. 2018. "为国破家：近代中国家庭革命论反思" (Destroying the Family for the Nation-state: Reflections on the Family Revolution in Modern China). 近代史研究，no. 3: 74–86.

Zhao, Yanjie. 2019. "为了人生幸福：五四时期家庭革命的个体诉求" (In pursuit of happiness: the individualistic purpose of the family revolution during the May Fourth movement), 华东师范大学学报 (Journal of East China Normal University), 58(1): 128–141.

Zhou, Lei. 2017. "冲突与融合：抗战时期中国共产党家庭政策的变革" (Conflicts and compromises: the changing family policies of the Chinese Communist Party during the anti-Japanese war period" 妇女研究论丛 (Journal of Women's Studies), no. 3: 40–48.

Zhu Xibing and Youhua Chen. 2013. "中国家庭政策研究：回顾与相关探讨" (Studies of family policy in China: A review and a further discussion), 社会科学研究(Social Science Research), no. 4: 111–119.

Zimmerman, Shirley L. 1992. *Family Policies and Family Well-being: The Role of Political Culture.* Newbury Park, CA: Sage.

CHAPTER 11

Three Discourses on Neo-Familism

Yunxiang Yan

The preceding chapters superseded the conventional model of filial piety in studies of intergenerational relations to capture novel and nuanced features under neo-familism that often appear to be multi-directional or even self-contradictory. Despite the surge in national wealth during the last three decades, Chinese youth still heavily rely on parental support for marriage (Chapter 2 by Davis and Chapter 3 by Fong *et al*), and cannot afford to marry someone of whom their parents disapprove (Chapter 3 and Chapter 9 by Jankowiak). Young couples cannot raise their children without critical assistance—in many cases full-time work—from their parents (Chapter 4 by Thomason and Chapter 5 by Qi) who, in turn, must make radical adjustments to adapt to their new role as floating grandparents if they migrate to the cities to take care of their grandchildren (Chapter 5). Yet, it is equally noteworthy that parents and grandparents also increasingly rely on the younger generations for emotional and spiritual support rather than for financial or labor assistance (Chapters 4 and 5). Parents whose only child has died face an identity crisis because, both literally and spiritually, they had regarded their only child as part of themselves (Chapter 8 by Shi). Yet the aging urban parents or grandparents also feel an urgency to live a life of their own, and thus, they regard their grand-parenting obligation as a burden (Chapter 6 by Huang). The ambiguity, ambivalence, and in some cases even antagonism across generational lines are intensified in the caring, rearing, and education of the precious child of the third generation, which is the most important and most challenging familial project, requiring intergenerational collaboration and increasing the density and intensity of mutual dependence and solidarity among three or even four generations (Chapters 4, 5, 6, and Chapter 7 by Xiao).

Against the background of all these family-life actions and dramas, there is a new shared family ideal of prosperity, happiness, and self-development for all members of the domestic group. This ideal can only be partially realized by the self-sacrifice of some members for the betterment of other members (Chapters 4 and 5). Although a number of contemporary features of urban family life seem to have emerged under Maoism (Chapter 9), they have been reinterpreted and recalibrated in the early twenty-first century as part and partial of the ongoing trend of neo-familism. The complexity of neo-familism is

© YUNXIANG YAN, 2021 | DOI:10.1163/9789004450233_012

also explored from some oblique angles, such as the individualistic inspirations among grandparents, the ambivalent dynamics in intergenerational intimacy, and the integration of personal identities between parents and their lost child (Chapters 6, 7 and 8).

Elsewhere, I examine the contours of Chinese neo-familism as social practice (2016, 2018 and Chapter 1) and took a close look at the decisive role of the party-state in shaping the Chinese family through family policy making (Chapter 10). In the present chapter I shift my focus to neo-familism in three distinct types of social discourse—the popular, official, and intellectual.

By discourses on neo-familism I refer to what is said about family values, behavioral norms, an ideal family life, and the conceived relationship among the individual, family, society, and the state. These discourses invoke traditional familism to a certain degree, but in one way or another, they also are engaged in tensions or conflicts with traditional familism as well as with one another. Like the social practices of neo-familism, the discourses on neo-familism are essentially a reworking of traditional familism, but with new agendas, values, and ethical norms. Admittedly, all of these are the ought-to-be conditions in people's minds and are reflected in dialogues instead of in actual social actions. Yet, they may guide or even change social actions to a certain degree, and thus they constitute a kind of discursive reality. This is particularly the case with respect to the official discourse that is sponsored and promoted by the powerful party-state and that is meant to be a tool of governance.

1 The Popular Discourse on Neo-Familism

The popular discourse on neo-familism represents family values, life attitudes and self-evaluations with respect to family life among Chinese individuals, which can be easily found in social surveys and scholarly research. A number of recent studies on family values have found that a large majority of Chinese regard the interests of the family as a whole as more important than the interests of the individual family members. Based on her collection of data gathered from nearly all major survey studies of family values since 2000, family sociologist Xu Anqi, who is arguably the leading Chinese authority on family values, concludes: "More people tend to agree that the overall interests of the family are above their personal interest; that intergenerational interdependence is more important than the intimacy of the husband and wife; and that family values are more important than the values of personal development" (Xu 2017: 6). Data from the 2006 China General Social Survey and from a 2008 survey in Shanghai and Lanzhou demonstrate that the primacy of family interests over individual interests is supported by 84 percent of the respondents to these two surveys (N=4215). More than 50 percent identified family happiness as happiness in one's life, and nearly 80 percent considered one's greatest responsibility to be to create a good life for the family members (Liu 2011). A 2010 survey on the family conducted by a group of sociologists at Peking University finds that the top-ranked value for an individual life lies in achieving a harmonious family, and the meaning of the family lies in raising children and enabling them to succeed in life. Of secondary importance is individual happiness (Qiu 2011). Consequently, the notion that one ought to conduct one's life for the benefit of the family repeatedly appears in surveys as a widely shared value. Another survey study investigates respondents' subjective evaluations of filial piety, the primacy of the family, and male power—the three core values in traditional familism. The results show that 75 percent of the respondents strongly agreed with the value of filial piety, 55 percent agreed with the primacy of family interests over individual interests, and 52 percent agreed with male power (Peng 2014).

Confucian familism emphasizes the divide between the family/kinship group and the outside world of unrelated people. A moral relativism is employed in dealing with in-group and out-group relations as well as in dealing with in-group members who are differentiated in terms of their relational closeness to the ego, identified by Fei Xiaotong (Fei 1992 [1948]) as the "differentiated mode of association" (差序格局). Turning outwardly, the unreserved devotion to one's family and the value of self-sacrifice for one's immediate family members translate into a lower degree of social trust in strangers and in social institutions as well as a degree of political apathy. Political scientist Edward Banfield (1958) refers to this as amoral familism. Recent survey research shows that values of Confucian familism continue to play the role of reducing social trust in public life. The newly emerging elements of social risks and the precarious labor market have resulted in lower social trust among urban families, as opposed to the social trust among their counterparts in the countryside, despite that fact that the former are more frequently and deeply embedded in interactions with unrelated people (Lian and Xiong 2016).

Nevertheless, younger respondents in the above-mentioned surveys display weaker altruism toward family members than do their parents (see, e.g., Liu 2011). Another generational difference is that younger Chinese have begun to make a distinction between family happiness and individual happiness, and they are reluctant to sacrifice their personal interests for the sake of the interests of their extended family (Kang 2012; Wang 2017). Through fieldwork and survey research, sociologist Becky Hsu has observed that young and old Chinese both make sense of life and define the notion of happiness in the context of the family. People evaluate their lives in reference to an ideal happy family (Hsu 2019). There is a differentiation but also an entanglement between the family and the individual, as shown in ethnographic studies of young villagers who leave their parents and home communities to pursue freedom and new experiences in the cities, hoping to carve out lives of their own. They do not mind precarious employment experiences and many rural migrants choose not to sign protective labor contracts so that they can maintain their mobility. However, these free-spirited youths do not brush aside their families as a source of meaning in life. Many follow their parents' advice in terms of selecting a spouse and nearly all them rely on parental support for the costs of marriage and for assistance in child-rearing (Hansen and Pang 2008). Because of their marginal status in the cities, young migrant workers throughout China tend to be indifferent to politics and official organizations, and instead they regard the family as their own "imagined community" of pragmatic, symbolic, and emotional importance (Johnston 2013).

In the village community where I have conducted longitudinal field research since the late 1980s, both young and old villagers since the late 1990s have referred to the family as the only reliable safety net; this is in clear contrast to the consensus from the 1950s to the late 1980s among village youth who wanted to break away from the constraints of the patriarchal family and kinship. Under rural collectivization during the Maoist era, one's livelihood and life chances primarily depended on the success or failure of the rural collective, which directly contributed to the sharp decline in parental authority, the rise of youth autonomy, an early family division, and the widespread trend to form of nuclear families (Yan 2003). After decollectivization in 1983 and the combined impact of the market economy and the process of individualization in the 1990s, villagers found themselves struggling in the highly competitive and precarious society without the former safety net of the rural collectives and other provisions of public goods from the state. By default, they returned to the family, especially for intergenerational support and solidarity, as the only means to deal with the risks and challenges they faced. As Mr. Wang noted: "I am sure you will find a lot of problems in each household, all kinds of problems. How do these problems get resolved? The family! Family problems, family solutions (家庭问题，家庭解决). That's it. No one outside the family can help you" (quoted in Yan 2018: 182–183). The gist of his comment is that the family is of prime importance because it is the only source of assistance to deal with the many difficulties that villagers face, and this is why people continue to think and act in terms of the family. "Family problems, family solutions" was a motto widely shared among the villagers whom I interviewed, and they

THREE DISCOURSES ON NEO-FAMILISM

also often added that the family was "all we've got" (Yan 2016, 2018; see also Jankowiak 2009; Kipnis 2011; Mu and Yuan 2016).

The family solution approach, however, is by no means a preferred choice, at least among young villagers, who, in most cases, are forced into a new kind of dependence on their parents. When I first interviewed six young couples in Xiajia village (my field site since 1989) in 2006, they were trying to maintain what they considered an urban lifestyle in their rural community— dressing fashionably, following trendy pop singers, and regularly partying even after they had married and had children. They claimed that their happiness made their parents happy and therefore in this way they were also performing their filial piety duties (Yan 2011: 203–205). When I gathered them together for a group interview in 2015, however, they had all become hard-working, caring, responsible—even a tad old-fashioned—people diligently playing their respective roles as husband/wife, father/mother, or son/daughter-in-law (Yan 2016: 250). Several of them were holding two jobs and they all agreed that the happiest thing they could imagine was to enjoy a worry-free long rest. As Mr. Guan, a reserved, stocky 34-year-old, with a slight stoop and shallow wrinkles on his forehead, told me:

> My son is attending a very good primary school, and my little girl was just accepted into a prestigious pre-school. Our regular income doesn't even cover their education, so we have to have second jobs and we also have to ask for additional help from my parents. I swore to myself that my children would not grow up like me—you know, poorly educated and only fit for manual labor. They are attending the best schools in our city and they are doing well. ... My wife and I are already working two jobs and we have no time to take care of our kids, so we need my mother's help. We don't earn enough money to pay all our bills so we also need help from my father's income. My parents never complain, but I know they're exhausted. You have to believe me. We want to be filial children, but we have to keep exploiting our parents!
>
> Cited in YAN 2018: 188

Mr. Guan's testimony confirms the above-mentioned major findings from survey research, but it includes as well the additional dimension of anxiety, stress, and guilt. Mr. Guan had been an ambitious and self-driven youth who worked hard to break away from the traditional life trajectory that his parents had followed, but only ten years later he was forced back onto a very similar track. He was very disappointed with his own life, but he shifted his dreams to the imagined bright future of his children, for which he had to seek parental support and return to the traditional values of familism. This case shows that the popular discourse on neo-familism might be much more complex and nuanced than what is captured in general surveys.

2 The Official Discourse on Neo-Familism

The second type of discourse consists of official views on the national project of family construction that are delineated through the top leadership of the CCP and through all sorts of government propaganda, including a surge in quasi-scholarly publications. In the official ideology, the Chinese party-state once took a rather hostile stand toward traditional familism and carried out political campaigns attacking belief in ancestor worship and traditional values such as filial piety. Admittedly, this highly critical discourse against familism has never been fully translated into social practice. As I note in the preceding chapter, the party-state took a pragmatic statist approach in dealing with the family institution and, through laws and government policies, it radically changed the traditional family in some respects but also preserved some of its functions in other respects, all depending on what would best serve the party-state's national agenda of political stability and economic development during any given period. The early twenty-first century was the first time, however, that the party-state ended its critique of traditional familism and took a sharp turn to openly promote some key elements of traditional familism. This is what I refer to as the official discourse on neo-familism, which so far has developed in two distinct phases.

The first phase is highlighted by the term "harmonious family" (和谐家庭) which can be seen as a byproduct of the CCP's push to build a harmonious socialist society, a strategic goal that was first put forward at the Fourth Plenary Session of the Sixteenth Central Committee of the CPC in September 2004. Hu Jintao, general secretary of the CCP at that time, mandated that a harmonious society and a scientific view of development would be the two key concepts of governance defining his leadership. To build a harmonious society, one had to begin by building a harmonious family. This point was most clearly stated by Hu Jintao in a 2007 speech to the Seventeenth Party Congress and thereafter in a 2011 speech to the twenty-eighth study meeting of the Politburo of the CCP Central Committee, when he called for new family construction policies to build a harmonious society (Zhu and Chen 2013). Meanwhile, the idea of a harmonious family was widely advocated through the official propaganda and in politically motivated scholarly accounts, with a focus on conflicts in family

THREE DISCOURSES ON NEO-FAMILISM

life (Yao 2010). A title-search of the National Social Science Data Base finds 148 articles on a "harmonious family," starting with 4 articles in 2005 and suddenly jumping to 31 articles in 2007 in response to Hu's speech at the Seventeenth Party Congress. The citations dropped from 16 articles in 2013 to 4 articles in 2014, and then to 2 articles in 2019 because, as will be shown below, by that time Xi Jinping had already launched his own family-construction campaign.

Under Hu Jintao, the party-state began to promote the Confucian value of filial piety, the centerpiece of traditional familism, through government-sponsored media and education channels, including numerous posters in public spaces. In 2004, the central government launched a filial-piety emulation campaign, honoring ten people as national exemplars of filial piety and bestowing various titles on another 2,000 people as filial models; this annual campaign continued in subsequent years. In 2010, October was designated by the National Committee on Aging as the "Month to Respect Elders" and instructions were issued that volunteers and ordinary citizens were to perform acts of filial piety. In 2012, the All-China Federation of Women joined with several government agencies to publish the "The 24 New Paragons of Filial Piety," an updated version of a fourteenth-century collection of parables on filial devotion. By the end of 2012, the government had amended the 1996 Law on the Rights of the Elderly to require that adult children regularly visit their parents (for an insightful analysis of state efforts to promote filial piety, see Zhang 2017). Public service advertising (PSA) is a new official tool of propaganda and it has been widely used in promoting filial piety and the notion of harmonious family, which are presented in the ubiquitous PSA boards on urban streets and embedded in television programs including the China Central Television's Spring Festival Gala (Landsberger 2009; and Puppin 2018).

The official discourse on neo-familism entered the second phrase soon after Xi Jinping took over the top leadership position in 2012 as he began to proactively use the family as a tool of governance. Xi first called on party and government leaders to enforce disciplinary control over their family members through a family ethos to solve the problem that many officials had become corrupt due to the influence of family members (Xi 2013). In subsequent years, Xi began to emphasize the importance of traditional familial virtues for the construction of a healthy, civilized, and socialist family (2014, 2015). He delivered a systematically developed version of these ideas at the first national convention of civilized families in 2016. In this speech, Xi defined the goal of building a civilized family to make "thousands and tens of thousands of families into important basic units to work for the development of the state, the progress of the nation, and the harmony of society." Xi also further developed the framework of "three emphases" (三个注重) that he had first put forward in early 2015 (Xi 2015), that is, to emphasize the family, family education, and a family ethos. A close reading of Xi's 2016 speech shows that the first emphasis is placed on the close link between the family and the state, the symbiotic relationship between family prosperity and state prosperity, and the unity of familism and patriotism. In Xi's own words: "All families must combine love of family and love of the country and assimilate realization of the family dream into realization of the national dream." The second emphasis, placed on family education, refers to the transmission of family values through moral teachings, with the goal of "cultivating and practicing core socialist values in the family, guiding family members, especially the young generation, to love the party, love the motherland, love the people, and love the Chinese nation." The third emphasis on family ethos continued Xi's early idea of preventing official corruption through a good family spirit, but here he extended its application to all families and expanded its function to the provision of a spiritual home for the soul (Xi 2016).

In Xi's 2016 speech, the incorporation of familism into patriotism, and by way of this, the incorporation of the family into the state, clearly emerged as the central theme in the official discourse on neo-familism. Thereafter, this theme of submitting the family to the state was amplified and elaborated upon in hundreds of official, semi-official, and semi-scholarly publications as well as in the mainstream media and academic outlets.

In his Chinese New Year speech on February 3, 2019, Xi developed this theme of the family-under-the state by adding two elements. The first is about the dialectical relationship between family prosperity and state development. In all previous speeches Xi first claimed that only when all families became prosperous can the state develop, and he stressed that only when the state is strong and rich can the family be prosperous. In his 2019 speech, however, the order was reversed. Xi stated: "It is in the precious tradition of our nation to fulfill the duty of filial piety in the family and of loyalty to the state. Without the prosperity and development of the state, there will be no happiness and harmony in the family. In a similar vein, without the happiness and harmony of thousands and tens of thousands families, there will be no prosperity and development of the state." The reversal of the order in these two clauses indicates the state has finally surpassed the family in the official discourse on neo-familism.

Immediately after stating this new formula of putting the state ahead of the family, Xi continued: "We want to make a great effort to advocate the "sentimental disposition of the family-state" (*jiaguo qinghuai*, 家国情怀) in the entire society, to cultivate and practice core socialist values, and to advocate patriotism, collectivism, and a socialist spirit, thus promoting the integration of loving the family and loving the state and enabling everyone and every

THREE DISCOURSES ON NEO-FAMILISM

family to contribute to the large family of the Chinese nation" (Xi 2019). To the best of my knowledge, this is the first time that Xi directly invoked the Confucian notion of a family-state in an open speech, indicating the latest development in the official discourse on neo-familism.

The Confucian notion of the family-state (家国) has long stood out as a powerful social imaginary among the Chinese elite, and, through the trickle-down effect of Confucian education, to a great extent it has been shared by ordinary people. Its origins can be traced back to the feudalist political regime of the Western Zhou dynasty, but its widespread ethical power was formulated during the Han dynasty and continuously reinforced in subsequent dynasties until the turn of the twentieth century (Xu 2015; Jiang 2011). The social imaginary of the family-state is sustained by three more specific notions. The first is the sentimental disposition of the family-state that Xi used in his 2019 speech. It stands for a special inner quality of Confucian literati that highlights both the ethical and the political as well as the emotional connections among the individual, the family, and the state. The second term is the "isomorphism of the family and the state" (家国同构), which literally depicts the sameness of the structural and operational principles of the family and the state. The third term "家国一体" is simple and straightforward, meaning the integration of the family and the state. Working together, these three Confucian notions serve to support and reinforce the social imaginary of the family-state, which in the final analysis places the state above the family.

There is, however, a tension within the notion of the sentimental disposition of the family-state: when the interests of the family conflict with those of the state, should one ethically and emotionally prioritize the family over the state or the other way around? This has long been known as the ethical incompatibility of filial piety to one's parents/family and loyalty to the emperor/state. From the state perspective, such a tension also speaks to traditional familism as an obstacle to state power. The issue was partially addressed in Confucian ethics in terms of the compromise of "移孝作忠", which means to appropriate the moral duty of filial piety and to transform it into the political duty of loyalty.

It is noteworthy that in his 2019 speech Xi Jinping also invoked this Confucian solution by stating that Chinese citizens practice filial piety at home but should devote loyalty to the state in public life. Meanwhile, Xi provided a new interpretation of a sentimental disposition of the family-state as patriotism, collectivism, and the socialist spirit. By so doing, Xi, and quickly the entire official discourse on neo-familism (see, e.g., Anhui Daily Commentary Department 2019; People's Daily Commentator 2019; Guangdong Provincial Center for Xi Jinping Thought 2019), replaced the core value of traditional familism, i.e., loyalty to the family, with Communist morality that prioritizes loyalty to the party-state. In this connection, the official discourse on neo-familism conflicts with both traditional familism that promotes political apathy and the modern trend in family change that defines the family as the private haven of one's personal life instead of the site of governance or an instrument of state power.

Indeed, how to reconstruct the family as a site of governance is a central issue in the official discourse on neo-familism. Wang Liming, a leading authority on Chinese civil law and also a party leader at one of the top Chinese universities, clearly states in the title of his widely reprinted essay that the isomorphism of the family and the state is a mode of governance. He argues that the sentimental disposition of the family and the state requires the isomorphism of the family and the state in practice and he emphasizes the sameness or the integration of family love and state love. Wang contends that such a family-state mode of governance means that when the interests of the state and the nation conflict with those of the family and the individual, then one must sacrifice family and individual interests for the sake of state interests (2017). The most straightforward and clear interpretation was offered by Lu Shizhen, a high-ranking party official in the Communist Youth League and a professor in the field of youth and family education. Focusing on Xi's 2016 call for all party-state agencies to engage in the family construction project, Lu states that Xi's idea of "constructing and sharing [by the family and the state]" provides a basic blueprint and perspective, that is, of "under the leadership of the party to form a mechanism of family construction that consists of the party, the government, and social organizations [here she is referring to the organizations led by the party-state, such as the Communist Youth League, the All-China Women's Association, and the All-China Federation of Trade Unions], in which the party provides the leadership, the government takes the initiative, and the social organizations participate. The result is to be shared by the entire society" (Lu 2019). It should be noted that Wang Liming's article was published by *Beijing Daily*, the mouthpiece of the Beijing Municipal Committee of the CCP, and Lu Shizhen's article was published by *China Women's News*, the official newspaper of the All-China Women's Association, which is the leading state agency in charge of the family-construction campaign.

A large number of official interpretations of Xi's views on the Chinese family were published by mainstream media outlets, such as a co-authored article by the Guangdong Provincial Center of Xi Jinping Thought (2019), and the articles by *People's Daily* Commentator (2019), and from the *Anhui Daily* Commentary Department (2019). At another level and covering a much larger scope, hundreds of articles were published to propagate Xi's family theory (see, e.g., Gong 2019; Ying 2017; Zhu 2018). A title-search of the National Social Science Data

Base finds 1,419 articles that discuss the social imaginary of the family-state, 524 of which are about the sentimental disposition of the family-state. Other related keywords include the isomorphism of the family and state, Xi Jinping's views on the family and the state (习近平家国观), and the integration of the family and state. In addition to the research focusing on Xi Jinping thought that mushroomed nationwide, universities devoted many research resources to study Xi Jinping's published works and speeches, and at least two dissertations on Xi Jinping's family-state theory were published in 2019.

In other words, the official discourse on neo-familism originated at the very top and has been propagated nationwide at multiple levels of interpretation and dissimilation to serve the party-state's national agenda of using the family institution as both a site of political governance and a major provider of social welfare services (see Chapter 10 by Yan).

3   The Intellectual Discourse on Neo-Familism

The third type of discourse is advocacy for familism among a group of intellectuals who regard familial ethics and behavioral patterns as an integrated part of the valuable cultural assets that will enable China to define its own unique path to modernity. This is part of the larger intellectual movement of Confucian Revival. To a great extent, this movement fits well with the official discourse on the rejuvenation of China and the China Dream under Xi Jinping.

Whereas the official discourse subsumes familism under patriotism, the intellectual discourse on neo-familism has been carried out on a different trajectory, that is, invoking familism as an indigenous cultural resource to resist individualism and to revitalize traditional (primarily Confucian) culture in Chinese society. One of the earliest attempts was made by Sheng Hong, a political economist, in his 2008 essay "On Familism." Sheng argues that, in contrast to individualism that is based on the rationality of the individual, familism "thinks" and "acts" in terms of the family as a collective entity. The family as a "thinking subject" has the advantage of transcending the limitations of the individual in two respects: its life goes beyond the life span of an individual and its interests benefit all members of the family instead of only one individual. Sheng Hong provides a real life story to illustrate the advantages of familism. In this case, a family that includes a husband, wife, and two children emigrated from China to the United States and in order to maximize the family's interests, one member of this particular family had to work so as to support the other three to attend school. The wife chose to work so that her husband could complete his Ph.D. degree at a university and so the two children would also receive a good education. In the end, the careers of the husband and the two children took off, and the wife was content for having made her own critical contribution. Sheng argues that if the husband and wife were both to have insisted on their individual rights instead of collaborating as a collective, the family would not have been able to pursue its American dream. This shows the advantage of familism over individualism (Sheng 2007).

What Sheng advocated was by and large a simple return to traditional familism in the sense that the family is defined as a thinking and acting subject in economic activities and thus it demands submission of loyalty from its members, and the family consists of the necessary hierarchical relations in which the wife is expected to subordinate her individual interests to those of her husband and her children. While noting that in the real-life story that he cites, the wife voluntarily made the decision to work, Sheng completely ignores the institutional impacts of gender-and-generation hierarchy on the female and the junior members in the family group, and he openly expresses a favorable view of the traditional patriarchal family. Such a radical turn to conservatism encountered sharp criticism from Chen Zhiwu, a Yale-based economist, who attempts to debunk Sheng's economic familism in light of modern individualism (Chen 2008). Other commentaries by Chinese scholars focus on the unprogressive potential of invoking traditional familism (Tianze Institute 2007).

Sheng's economic familism emerged from the larger intellectual Confucian Revival trend, which began as a scholarly discourse on New Confucianism in the 1990s but thereafter, in the early twenty-first century, developed into a cultural nationalist movement. The overarching theme of this movement is to imagine and to discover China's unique path to modernity, or, more specifically, China's path to its rejuvenation as a global power and to the establishment of Chinese subjectivity outside of the Western discourse on political liberalism and individualism. Such a quest for Chinese exceptionalism led its promoters to invoke Confucianism as a new leading ideology in social life— cultural, social, political and economic—practically turning the Confucian Revival into a movement of cultural nationalism and secular religion (Deng and Smith 2018; Kubat 2018). Traditional familism became a perfect fit with the rise of Confucianism as a secular religion.

There are also important differences among Chinese intellectuals who view familism and Confucian ethics in favorable terms. For those who are deeply concerned about the spiritual life of the Chinese people and the perceived moral crises in public opinion since the 1980s (Yan 2021), the restoration of Confucian social imaginary of the individual-family-state-universe (家国天下) is viewed as the only way to regain meaning in life for the individual struggling in a secularized world. Their primary concern is how to establish an individual identity in a Chinese way that will be protected from excessive individualism and statism (Jiang 2011; Xu 2015). The family and its moral-teachings may function as a moral castle against the invasion of the immoral market and its instrumental individualism, and the revitalization of familism will help to restore balance and peace in Chinese spiritual life (Chen 2015). As familism prioritizes the spiritual, emotional, and material interests of all members, instead of the interests of any one individual, it is necessary to employ familism to offset the negative impacts of individualism that arouse too many personal desires and put too much of an emphasis on individual rights. "On the basis of familism, Chinese cultural tradition established a set of values about the family, ethics, state, and the universe. This system of traditional values contains a strong historical rationality. To negate this pillar of values is nothing less than destroying the foundation of Chinese culture" (Sun 2015:68). Unlike Sheng Hong who is opposed to individualism (2008), other intellectuals recognize individualism as part of modernity and thus they try to strike a balance between familism and individualism. Yet, like Sheng Hong, they also downplay the oppressive and patriarchal nature of Chinese familism, especially the dual oppression of women by patriarchy and male-centrism (Sanghwa 1999). Some scholars argue that dominance and oppression are not necessarily an integral part of Confucian familism, and the ideal family in Confucianism is asymmetrical; it is a mistake to conflate asymmetry into hierarchy and domination (Sun 2019: 178–179).

Another group of Chinese scholars attempt to define the uniqueness of Chinese society in terms of familism, and by way of Chinese exceptionalism to elaborate on the unfitness of Western values in China. According to Feng Longfei, Western bioethics faces a crisis because it is rooted in the values of individualism and liberalism; by contrast, Confucian familism defines the family as the basic ethical entity and thus it can resolve the ethical problems found in Western bioethics. The key to the advantages of Confucian familism lies in the priority of the interests and the good of the family community over the interests and the good of the individual. In the case of a patient's right to know, Confucian familism encapsulates all personal relations into the family and, in the case of curing and caring for a patient, it asks all family members to make a collective decision on behalf of the patient. It emphasizes the values of harmony, solidarity, and the wholeness of the family, a decision-making mechanism that is superior to the Western value of a patient's right to know (Feng 2018). The Chinese notion of the isomorphism of the family and the state has the advantage of avoiding the opposition between state and society in the modern West and represents a more effective mode of governance as well as a different structure of society. Familism as the Chinese mode of governance promotes core values such as unity, harmony, responsibility, sacrifice, and submission of individual interests to collective interests, all of which prioritize the livelihood of the people instead of the interests of politicians and the affluent classes, as is the case in the modern West (Wan 2017).

Such a favorable view of familism as the basis of the Chinese mode of governance has been pushed to an extreme, in contrast to the British mode of governance that is based on the notion of a social contract. As the Chinese state is in essence the extended family of its people, state leaders are bound by the two major responsibilities of the family head: to ethically educate and cultivate its citizens and to create happiness for its citizens. In return, the citizens are obligated to obey the state leaders and to contribute to the prosperity of the big family of the Chinese state. As the Hong Kong SAR is part of this family-state, the people of Hong Kong do not have a Western type of social contract with the CCP and the central government; what they have, like people in other parts of China, is a relationship between the members and the leader of the big family (Bian 2019: 196). The Chinese family provides a protective umbrella for its members in numerous ways and thus enables the self-development of the individuals. Legal reforms during the reform era have been unduly influenced by Western individualism, creating contradictions between familial practices in real life and individualistic norms in the legal codes, such as the confusions and conflicts caused by the individualization of property rights regarding family and conjugal properties. There would be no conflicts between individual development and family interests if a familial perspective were the basis of the legal reforms (Xia 2016).

Equally noteworthy is that traditional familism, especially its key notion of the isomorphism of the family and the state, had long been the target of intellectual critiques for being part of a patriarchal cultural and political despotism that existed in imperial China and throughout the twentieth century (Deng 1994; Glosser 2003; and Zhao 2018; for a recent example, see Xie and Li 2003). The intellectual movement of cultural nationalism and the Confucian Revival completely reversed such critiques, effectively making familism the reborn phoenix of the early twenty-first century. Despite isolated attempts by liberal intellectuals to reiterate the negative impact of familism on public life due to its inherent political apathy (Zhang 2011), the dominant voice is to praise familism for providing a foundational identity for the China Dream (Wang 2016) and cultural capital for a moral reconstruction among the citizenry (Cheng 2015, Wang 2017).

4 Concluding Remarks

To summarize, the three types of neo-familism discourse share a favorable view of the collective power of the family group and the collectivist values of familism, but they also differ from each other in some important respects. In the popular discourse of neo-familism, the family is valued as the only reliable resource for ordinary people to cope with the increasingly competitive, risky, and precarious workplace in particular and social life in general. The motto "family problems, family solution" reflects the pragmatic resort by default that ordinary people may invoke to solve problems in real life instead of a proactive choice to return to tradition. This ambivalence is best illustrated in the tensions between individualistic and familial values that are revealed in social surveys and individual testimonies in ethnographic research (see also Chapter 6 by Huang and Chapter 7 by Xiao).

In sharp contrast to the discourse on neo-familism among ordinary people, the official and intellectual discourses have a clearly defined political agenda. While the party-state views the family as a site of governance, the intellectual advocates of familism seek to find the cultural resources for and to define the Chinese alternative to modernity and global power. Whereas the official discourse incorporates familism into patriotism, the intellectual discourse invokes familism to resist Western individualism. In both cases, the individual is defined as the instrument or the means by which to reach a higher goal, be it the China Dream or the rejuvenation of Confucian culture. The two discourses are merged into a united force through their shared preference for traditional familism and they support each other with their shared advocacy on behalf of some key Confucian notions, such as the family-state, the sentimental disposition of the family-state, and the isomorphism of the family and the state. Together, they fight against individualism, liberalism, and feminism as misleading Western values that will hinder the rise of China, and, by way of restoring and recalibrating traditional familism, they attempt to reestablish the benevolent image of patriarchy in the family and the paternalist polity in the state.

There is a visible gap between the values of Confucian familism promoted by the party-state and conservative intellectuals on the one hand and the pragmatic neo-familism discourse among ordinary people on the other. Yet, as the party-state has drastically expanded its social welfare programs in the new century in order to mitigate the surge in inequality of the 1990s (Shen, Wang, and Cai 2018), a new image of a paternalist state has been created. For example, the party-state's policy decision to abolish agricultural taxes and levies in 2005 and the establishment of the New Rural Old Age Insurance Program in

2009, which pays a monthly pension to rural residents who are sixty-years-old or older, have won the wholehearted support of most rural people, especially the elderly. During my recent returns to the field site that I have been visiting for thirty years, nearly all the villagers spoke of Xi Jinping as a benevolent emperor with the mandate of heaven (真命天子). They also agreed with Xi's calling: "All families must combine love of the family and love of the country and assimilate realization of the family dream with realization of the national dream," reasoning that their living standards had indeed been improved by the increasingly richer and stronger Chinese state.

Consequently, the elite Confucian concepts of the sentimental disposition of the family-state and the isomorphism of the family and the state have regained their ground in popular culture, gradually affecting the mentality of ordinary people. A good example is the song "*Guojia*" (国家, the State) that was first sung by Hong Kong movie star Jacky Chan in 2009 in commemoration of the sixtieth anniversary of the People's Republic of China. Its lyrics skillfully depict a symbiotic relationship between the family and the state, with a reiterated central message: "The family is the smallest state, the state is made of numerous families" and concluding that having a strong state is a precondition for having a rich family. This song has been hugely influential as it has been performed in all major shows in the official media during the past decade, so much so that even commentators at several major newspapers have cited the lyrics of "the family is the smallest state ..." in essays amplifying Xi Jinping's 2019 speech on the sentimental disposition of the family-state (*Anhui Daily* Commentary Department 2019; *People's Daily* Commentator 2019; Guangdong Provincial Center for Xi Jinping Thought 2019).

In the contemporary world, it is common to view and define the family as the smallest cell in a society, but by no means the smallest cell in the state. The lyrics in the 2009 song "Guojia" about the family being the smallest state and the later official adaptations of the expression effectively denied the boundaries between the family, as a private haven of the individual, and the state, as the public entity of political, legal, and military power, and by so doing, society was pushed out of the relationship between the family and the state.

This new imagery of the family as the smallest state encounters little difficulty in its journey of dissemination because it derives from the Confucian notion of the isomorphism of the family and the state. It is therefore logical that familism should be incorporated into patriotism, and, as Xi Jinping clearly states, one's family ideals can only be realized when the national China Dream is realized. It is plausible that, as time goes by, and more importantly, as the party-state promotes its image as a benevolent and paternalist head of the big family of the Chinese nation by way of a newly recalibrated official moral framework (Yan 2021), the current gap between the popular discourse on neo-familism on the one hand and the official and intellectual discourses on the other hand might shrink or even vanish. But until then, we must still make the critical distinction between what ordinary people say about their family and their family ideals and the values of familism that are promoted by the party-state and cultural-nationalist intellectuals.

Yet, I cannot help but wonder what will happen to the public-private divide in Chinese society if the three discourses converge into a more or less unified version. The same question applies to the family and the Chinese individual as well. I have observed a dual transformation of private life by the early 1990s, that is, the family became a private haven for individuals and individuals also gained their own private space within the family institution (Yan 2003). If "the family is the smallest state" (or more logically, the smallest cell of the state), will the private life sphere of the Chinese people again be transformed? Is it possible that the inverted family might be re-inverted and the post-patriarchal intergenerationality we explore in this volume be reversed back to the old patriarchal order in the name of classic filial piety? These are big and unanswerable questions at the present time. But given the radical and deep changes in family ethics and practices, especially the shift in the foci of family life from ancestors to children/grandchildren and the rising awareness of individual rights among both the senior and junior generations (see the preceding chapters, and Yan 2015, 2016, 2017/18), the return of Confucian familism and patriarchy in real social practice seems to be unlikely. But, the tensions between what can be said in ideology and what can be done in social practices are acute and will likely be intensified in the perceivable future. This is another reason I refer to the ongoing trend of family change as neo-familism.

References

Anhui Daily Commentary Department. 2019. "弘扬家国情怀，创造美好未来" (Promoting a sentimental disposition of the family-state, creating a beautiful future), *Anhui Daily*, February 12. https://www.hubpd.com/c/2019-02-12/790881.shtml (accessed January 10, 2020).

Banfield, Edward C. 1958. *The Moral Basis of a Backward Society*. New York: The Free Press.

Bian Hengqin. 2019. "社会契约与家国同构：大英帝国与中国的立国之道辨析" (Social contract vs. *jiaguo tonggou*: The differences in state theory between the British empire and China), 中央社会主义学院学报 (*Journal of the Central College of Socialism*), no. 1: 180–186.

Chen Yun. 2015. "'去家化' 与 '再家化': 当代中国人精神生活的内在张力" (Defamilization and re-familization: The inner tension of spiritual life among contemporary Chinese people), 探索与争鸣 (*Exploration and Debate*), no. 1: 80–84.

Chen Zhiwu. 2008. "关于盛洪的 '论家庭主义' 的批评" (A critique of Sheng Hong's essay on familism). 新政治经济学评论 (*New Political Economy Review*), 4 (2): 98–104.

Cheng Wen. 2015. "儒家 '家国同构' 思想对社会转型期公民道德建设的借鉴意义" (The contribution of the Confucian isomorphism of the family and the state to the construction of citizen morality during the social transition period), 遵义师范学院学报 (*Journal of Zunyi Normal College*), no. 6: 24–26, 31.

Deng, Jun and Craig A. Smith. 2018. "The Rise of Confucianism and the Return of Spirituality to Politics in Mainland China," *China Information*, 32(2): 294–314.

Deng Weizhi. 1994. 近代中国的家庭变革 (*Family Change in Modern China*). Shanghai: Shanghai Renmin Chubanshe.

Fei Xiaotong. 1992 [1948]. *From the Soil: The Foundations of Chinese Society*, trans. by Gary G. Hamilton and Wang Zheng. Berkeley: University of California Press.

Feng Longfei. 2018. "儒家家庭主义的母性角色: 以医疗实践为视角" (The motherly role of Confucian familism: The perspective from medical practice), 江西社会科学 (*Jiangxi Social Sciences*), no. 8: 35–41.

Garzón, Adela Pérez. 2000. "Cultural Change and Familism," *Psicothema*, 12(suppl.): 45–54.

Glosser, Susan L. 2003. *Chinese Versions of Family and State, 1915–1953*. Berkeley: University of California Press.

Gong Jintao. 2019. "习近平家国观: 实现中华民族伟大复兴的价值遵循" (Xi Jinping's view on the family-state: the value guide for the realization of the great rejuvenation of the Chinese nation), 厦门广播电视大学学报 (*Journal of Xiamen Radio and Television University*), no. 3: 1–6.

Guangdong Provincial Center for Xi Jinping Thought. 2019. "弘扬家国情怀, 践行核心价值观" (Promoting the sentimental disposition of the family-state, practicing [socialist] core values), 光明日报 (*Guangming Daily*), May 22. http://www.71.cn/2019/0522/1044553.shtml (accessed January 10, 2020).

Hansen, Mette Halskov and Cuiming Pang. 2008. "Me and My Family: Perceptions of Individual and Collective Among Young Rural Chinese," *European Journal of East Asian Studies*, 7 (1): 75–99.

Hsu, Becky. 2019. "Having It All: Filial Piety Moral Weighting, and Anxiety among Young Adults." In Becky Yang Hsu and Richard Madsen (eds.), *The Chinese Pursuit of Happiness: Anxieties, Hopes, and Moral Tensions in Everyday Life,* pp. 42–65. Berkeley: University of California Press.

Jankowiak, William. 2009. "Practicing Connectiveness as Kinship in Urban China." In Susanne Brandtstädter and Gonçalo D. Santos (eds.), *Chinese Kinship: Contemporary Anthropological Perspectives*, pp. 67–91. New York: Routledge.

Jiang Yihua. 2011. "中国传统家国共同体及其现代嬗变" (The family-state entity in traditional China and its modern changes), part 1 and 2, 河北学刊 (*Hebei Academic Journal*), no. 2: 48–54 and no. 3: 53–58.

Johnston, James. 2013. "Filial Paths and the Ordinary Ethics of Movement." In Charles Stafford (ed.), *Ordinary Ethics in China*, pp. 45–65. London: Bloomsbury.

Kang Lan. 2012. "代差与代同: 新家庭主义价值观的兴起" (Generational differences and similarities: The rise of new familism values), 青年研究 (*Youth Studies*), no. 3: 21–29.

Kipnis, Andrew B. 2011. *Governing Educational Desire: Culture, Politics, and Schooling in China*. Chicago: University of Chicago Press.

Kubat, Aleksandra. 2018. "Morality as Legitimacy under Xi Jinping: The Political Functionality of Traditional Culture for the Chinese Communist Party," *Journal of Current Chinese Affairs*, 47(3): 47–86.

Landsberger, Stefan R. 2009. "Harmony, Olympic Manners and Morals—Chinese Television and the 'New Propoganda' of Public Service Adversising." *European Journal of East Asian Studies* 8 (2): 331–355.

Lian Tengfei and Xiong Zhongkui. 2016. "个人家庭因素对普遍信任的影响作用" (The influence of personal family background on social trust), 社会 (Society), no. 1: 124–125.

Liu Wenrong. 2011. "家庭价值的变迁与延续" (Change and continuity in family values), 社会科学 (*Social Sciences*), no. 10: 78–89.

Lu Shizhen. 2019. "共建共享: 建设中国特色社会主义新家庭" (Constructing and benefiting together: Building the new Chinese family with socialist characteristics), 中国妇女报 (*China Women's Daily*), June 15. http://paper.cnwomen.com.cn/content/2019-06/15/060713.html (accessed January 11, 2020).

Mu Yingtan and Xin Yuan. 2016. "代际支持的家庭主义基础: 独生子女改变了什么? 基于内蒙古调查数据的实证研究" (The foundation of familism for intergenerational support: What has the only child changed into? An empirical study based on survey data from Inner Mongolia), 西北人口 (*Northwest Population Studies*), no. 1: 32–37.

Peng Dasong. 2014. "家庭价值观结构、代际变迁及其影响因素" (The structure of family values, generational changes, and their impact), 当代青年研究 (*Contemporary Youth Research*), no. 4: 75–82.

People's Daily Commentator. 2019. "在全社会大力弘扬家国情怀" (Greatly promoting the sentimental disposition of the family-state in the entire society), 人民日报 (*People's Daily*), February 5. http://www.cac.gov.cn/2019-02/05/c_1124087111.htm (accessed January 10, 2020).

Puppin, Giovanna. 2018. "Happiness 'with a Chinese Taste': An Interpretive Analysis of CCTV's 2014 Spring Fesstival Gala's Public Service Announcement (PSA) 'Chopsticks'

(Kuaizi pian)." In Gerda Wielander and Derek Hird (eds.), *Chinese Discourses on Happiness*, pp. 64–85. Hong Kong: University of Hong Kong Press.

Qiu Zeqi. 2011. "家庭主义价值共识与民营企业发展" (The shared values of familism and the development of private enterprises), 人民论坛 (*People's Tribune*), no. 2: 239–241.

Sanghwa, Lee. 1999. "The Patriarchy in China: An Investigation of Public and Private Spheres," *Asian Journal of Women's Studies*, 5(1): 9–49.

Shen, Ke, Feng Wang, and Yong Cai. 2018. "A Benevolent State Against an Unjust Society? Inequalities in Public Transfers in China," *Chinese Sociological Review* 50(2): 137–162.

Sheng Hong. 2007. "论家庭主义" (On familism), public lecture at Tianze Institute, December 7, http://www.unirule.cloud/index.php?c=article&id=2338&q=1 (accessed July 23, 2017).

Sun Xiangchen. 2015. "个体主义与家庭主义: 新文化运动百年再反思" (Individualism and familism: Reflections on the new cultural movement on its 100th anniversary), 复旦学报：社会科学版 (*Fudan Journal: Social Science Edition*), no. 4: 62–69.

Sun Xiangchen. 2019. "重建 '家'在现代世界的意义" (Reconstructing the meaning of the "family" in the contemporary world). 文史哲 (*Literature, History, and Philosophy*), no. 4: 5–14, 165.

Tianze Institute. 2007. "盛洪论家庭主义讲座问答部分" (The Q & A section of Sheng Hong's speech on familism," the 350th Tianze Seminar. http://www.unirule.cloud/index.php?c=article&id=2338&q=1 (accessed July 23, 2017).

Wan Junbao. 2017. "中国人的家国情怀怎样异于西方" (How the Chinese notion of the emotional disposition of the family-state differs from the West). 解放日报 (*Liberation Daily*), September 7, p. 2. https://www.gmw.cn/xueshu/2017-09/07/content_26060701.htm (accessed January 26, 2020).

Wang Liming. 2017. "家国同构是一种治理模式" (The isomorphism of the family and the state is a mode of governance), 北京日报 (*Beijing Daily*), March 6. http://theory.people.com.cn/n1/2017/0306/c40531-29125060.html (accessed December 12, 2019).

Wang Zengyi. 2016. "家国同构: 中国梦的民族精神认同基础" (The isomorphism of the family and the state: The national spiritual foundation of the China dream), 河南师范大学学报-社会科学版 (*Journal of Hainan Normal University-Social Science Edition*), no. 9: 103–110.

Xi, Jinping. 2013. "同全国妇联新一届领导班子的谈话" (Conversation with the new leadership of All China Women's Association), October 31. http://www.xinhuanet.com//politics/2013-10/31/c_117956150.htm (accessed January 8, 2020).

Xi, Jinping. 2014. "从小积极培育和践行社会主义核心价值观" (Cultivating and practicing socialist core values from childhood), May 30. http://www.xinhuanet.com//politics/2014-05/30/c_1110944180.htm (accessed January 8, 2020).

THREE DISCOURSES ON NEO-FAMILISM

Xi, Jinping. 2015. "在2015春节团拜会上的讲话" (speech on the 2015 celebration of Chinese spring festival), February 17. http://www.xinhuanet.com//politics/2015-02/17/c_1114401712.htm (accessed January 8, 2020).

Xi, Jinping. 2016. "在会见第一届全国文明家庭代表时的讲话" (speech at the first national conference of representatives of civilized family), December 12, http://www.xinhuanet.com//politics/2016-12/15/c_1120127183.htm. (accessed November 29, 2020).

Xi, Jinping. 2019. "在2019春节团拜会上的讲话" (speech on the 2019 celebration of Chinese spring festival), February 3, 2019. Renmin Ribao (People's Daily), February 4, http://cpc.people.com.cn/n1/2019/0204/c64094-30613956.html (accessed January 6, 2020).

Xia Yongmei. 2016. "论个人发展观如何在家庭中实现: 以新发展理念为指引" (On how to realize the individual's right of development within the family: guided by new development concepts), 学术交流 (*Academic Exchange*), no. 12: 85–90.

Xie Changzheng and Min Li. 2003. "论中国古代家国同构与腐败的关系" (On the link between corruption and the isomorphism of the family and the state in ancient China). 广西社会科学 (*Guangxi Social Sciences*), no. 11: 154–156.

Xu, Anqi. 2017. "Introduction." In Xu Anqi, John DeFrain, and Liu Wenrong (eds.), *The Chinese Family Today*, pp. 1–13. London: Routledge.

Xu Jilin. 2015. "现代中国的家国天下与自我认同" (The notion of family-state-world and individual identity in modern China), 复旦学报: 社会科学版 (*Fudan Journal: Social Science Edition*), no. 5: 46–53.

Yan, Yunxiang. 2003. *Private Life under Socialism: Love, Intimacy, and Family Change in a Chinese Village, 1949–1999*. Stanford: Stanford University Press.

Yan, Yunxiang. 2011. "The Individualization of the Family in Rural China." *boundary 2*, 38 (1): 203–229.

Yan, Yunxiang. 2015. "Parent-driven Divorce and Individualization among Urban Chinese Youth," *International Social Science Journal*, 64(213/214): 317–330.

Yan, Yunxiang. 2016. "Intergenerational Intimacy and Descending Familism in Rural North China," *American Anthropologist*, 118(2): 244–257.

Yan, Yunxiang. 2018. "Neo-Familism and the State in Contemporary China," *Urban Anthropology and Studies of Cultural Systems and World Economic Development*, 47(3/4): 181–224.

Yan, Yunxiang. 2021. "The Politics of Moral Crisis in Contemporary China." *The China Journal*, no. 85 (forthcoming).

Yao Haitao. 2010. "论和谐家庭的内涵及其构建" (On the content of the harmonious family and its construction), 学术论坛 (*Academic Forum*), no. 8: 51–54.

Ying Zongying. 2017. "习近平家庭建设核心理念及其时代价值初探" (On the core concepts of Xi Jinping's thought on family construction and their timely values), 湖湘论坛(*Huxiang Forum*), no. 3: 25–30.

Zhang, Hong. 2017. "Recalibrating Filial Piety: Realigning the State, Family, and Market Interests in China." In Gonçalo D. Santos and Stevan Harrell (eds.), *Transforming Patriarchy: Chinese Families in the Twenty-First Century*, pp. 234–250. Seattle: University of Washington Press.

Zhang Jing. 2011. "公共性与家庭主义: 社会建设基础性原则辨析" (The public and familism: analysis of the fundamental principle of social building), 北京工业大学学报: 社会科学版 (*Journal of Beijing University of Technology: Social Science Edition*), no. 3: 1–4, 10.

Zhao Yanjie. 2018. "为国破家: 近代中国家庭革命论反思" (Destroying the family for the nation-state: Reflections on the family revolution in modern China), 近代史研究 (*Journal of Modern History*), no. 3: 74–86.

Zhu Xibing and Youhua Chen. 2013. "中国家庭政策研究: 回顾与相关探讨" (Studies of family policy in China: A review and a further discussion), 社会科学研究 (*Social Science Research*), no. 4: 111–119.

Zhu Yi. 2018. "习近平家庭建设思想的基本内容" (The essentials of Xi Jinping's thought on family construction), 江苏师范大学学报 (*Journal of Jiangsu Normal University*), no 2: 93–99.

Index

aged parents 103, 105, 113–115, 117–119
aging xii, 64, 67, 80, 83, 109, 182, 241, 244, 253
alloparental 215
ambivalence 28, 67, 71–72, 84, 94, 96, 100,
  111–112, 121, 123, 129, 140, 253, 267
ancestors 4, 6, 16, 149, 176, 269

bare branches 20, 55

caregiving 86, 88, 136, 143, 146, 149
child loss 177, 183–187, 190–191
childbearing 2–3, 35, 55, 59, 62–63, 65–67,
  69–70, 72–73
childcare 8, 50, 63–64, 72, 80–82, 90, 94,
  103–117, 119, 129, 136n2, 135–138, 140–141,
  143–145, 149, 151–152, 155–157, 159, 161n6,
  161–163, 168, 170–171, 181, 198, 202,
  213–214, 216, 218, 232
childrearing 5, 13–14, 20–23, 55, 62–66, 70,
  111, 112, 137, 140, 143–145, 150n2, 148–152,
  157n4, 155–159, 161, 165, 170, 176, 179, 184,
  188, 250, 256
Chinese state 9, 55, 266, 268
conflict 8, 12, 78, 94, 97, 106, 111–112, 136–137,
  166, 203, 209, 261–262
Confucian familism 255, 265
Confucian Revival 263–264, 266
conjugal affection 32, 200

dance group 123, 127, 129, 132, 134–135,
  137–140
daughter-in-law 31, 80, 89–90, 92–94,
  109–112, 114, 117, 127–130, 135, 137–138,
  160, 163, 166–167, 201–202, 257
daughters 20, 31, 71, 76–77, 81, 83–84, 90, 93,
  95, 98, 105, 109–112, 114–115, 117, 152, 185,
  199–204, 210, 218, 232
demographic 2, 7, 33, 51, 56, 78–79,
  93–94, 141
dependency 87, 97, 198, 201, 204, 211
dispute 133, 137
divorce xi, 2, 5, 20, 33, 33n1, 40, 50f 49–51, 59–60,
  71–72, 92, 143, 181, 196, 204, 229–230,
  238–239, 241

education xii, 17–18, 22, 32, 35, 48–49, 55,
  60, 63–66, 69, 71–72, 81–83, 85, 87, 97,
  144n1, 149, 150n2, 152–153, 155–160,
  179–180, 184, 188, 232, 237n5, 237–238,
  241, 253, 257, 259–262, 264
elderly care 14, 106, 146, 238, 241, 243
emotional attachments and support 16, 21,
  84, 90–91, 116, 165, 179, 181, 202, 231
emotions 16, 37–38, 47, 91, 104, 116, 129, 136

face 34, 70, 76, 81, 87, 89, 117, 139, 143, 153–154,
  156, 164, 176, 185, 253, 256
familism ix, 3–4, 6, 9–10, 12, 15–19, 23–25,
  32, 58, 72, 112, 124, 145, 147, 176, 223–231,
  234–235, 238–240, 244–246, 252–255,
  258–272, 274
  Descending Familism 29, 54, 75, 122, 142,
  175, 193, 222, 252, 273
family
  ethics 146, 242, 269
  harmony 78, 80, 137, 139
  interests 15, 17, 21, 147, 224, 245–246,
  255, 266
  obligation 104, 112, 116, 118–119
  strategy 3, 94, 170
  unity 84, 97
  values 24, 254
  property 105, 230
  prosperity 9, 15–16, 260
family Law 53, 251
family planning 193, 242n6, 242–243
family policies 9, 24, 223–226, 228–229,
  232, 234–235, 239–240, 242–247, 249,
  251–252
family revolution 15, 29, 224–227, 244–245,
  252, 274
family-state 16, 24, 260–264, 266–273
fathers 35–39, 41–42, 48, 144–145, 149, 157n4,
  157n5, 156–158, 195, 199–200, 204, 216
feminism 2, 267
fertility rate 2, 6, 241, 250
filial piety 3–4, 11–12, 14, 16–18, 31, 35, 104,
  107, 112, 128–129, 132, 137, 140, 163, 171,
  182, 214, 244, 246, 253, 255, 257–261, 269

floating grandparents 8, 21, 94, 103, 105, 107,
    110–113, 115, 117, 120, 253
friendship 66, 124–125, 133–134, 138, 179,
    181, 211

gender xiii, xiv–1, 5, 11, 15–16, 22, 37, 60, 77,
    81–82, 106, 109–110, 147, 149, 157, 170,
    197, 200, 205, 208–210, 224, 229–230,
    237n5, 264
governance 16, 24, 125, 241, 254, 258–259,
    262–263, 265–267, 272
grandparenting xiv–3, 13, 78, 93–94, 96, 119,
    139–140, 178, 184, 213
grave 186, 189–190

happiness 12, 16–17, 22, 25, 31, 35, 66–67, 78,
    88, 92, 126, 185, 205, 207, 210, 223, 227,
    235, 247, 252–253, 255, 257, 260, 266
harmonious family 91, 255, 258–259, 273
health insurance 106, 113, 171
hierarchy 4–7, 10, 12, 14, 17–20, 32, 78, 95,
    125, 127–128, 132, 147, 171, 264–265
horizontal tie 2, 15, 31, 50, 94
household registration 7, 82, 97, 113, 231–232
housing 5, 48–49, 61, 64–65, 72, 148,
    232–233, 238

idleness 86, 97
individual
    autonomy 2–3, 22–23
    desire 13
    happiness 9, 15, 21, 23, 195, 255
interests 15, 17, 118, 126, 227, 255, 262, 264, 266
    strategies 21
individualism 1, 3, 12, 15, 24, 58, 146,
    224–225, 227–228, 237n5, 239, 245–246,
    263–267
individualization xiv, 4, 9, 104, 107, 236n5,
    236–239, 245–246, 256, 266
inheritance 31, 105, 198, 228, 238
intergenerational
    cooperation 95–96, 144–147, 162, 181
    dependence ix–2, 9, 14, 19–21
    dynamics xii, 4, 11, 13, 17–19, 21, 23
    intimacy 16, 22
    solidarity 2, 6, 10, 12, 137
intergenerational parenting coalition 144,
    147–148, 151, 157, 159, 161, 165, 167,
    170–171

intergenerational relations xiv, 4, 7–15, 18,
    26, 104, 111–112, 144–145, 147, 163–164,
    169, 170, 172, 176–177, 253
intergenerationality 4, 11–14, 20–21, 78,
    95, 177
intimacy 1–2, 4, 9, 13, 15–16, 22, 97, 144, 148,
    161, 163, 169, 169n9, 171, 194, 196, 204,
    215, 224, 246, 254
intimate power 22, 148, 171
intimate relations 22, 148, 161, 167, 169, 172
inverted family 5–6, 8–10, 124, 128, 139–140,
    194, 214–215, 269
isomorphism of the family and the
    state 261–262, 265–268, 270, 272–273

jobs 8, 39, 43, 55, 63–66, 71–72, 80, 85–86,
    107, 144, 144n1, 203, 214, 238, 257

leftover women 20, 55, 69, 208
longitudinal study xii, 3, 23, 55–56, 256
loyalty 15, 31–32, 131, 196, 212, 224, 230, 232,
    234, 246, 260–261, 264

marriage 2–3, 5, 7, 9, 19–20, 23, 31–32, 34–35,
    37–38, 38n3, 40n4, 40–43, 47, 49–52, 55,
    57–62, 64–73, 79, 85, 89–90, 92, 105, 181,
    184, 195–198, 201, 204–209, 215–217, 228,
    230, 238–239, 245, 247, 250, 253, 256
marriage Law 9, 32, 38, 49, 52–53, 118, 196,
    229–230, 238–239, 242
matchmaking 33n1, 33–36, 39, 54, 69–71, 193
maternal power 164, 171
migrant parents 78, 83–84, 103, 107
migrants 8, 10, 21, 43, 78, 85, 104–105, 117,
    207, 213, 256
migration 5, 7, 21, 79, 82–83, 94, 103, 113, 119,
    226, 247
morality 78–79, 90, 208, 262, 270
moral code 97, 198
moral framework 96, 269
moral meaning 98
mother-daughter bond 202, 204
motherhood 18, 208
mothers-in-law 83, 90, 93, 112, 202
multigenerational family 3, 4, 11, 21, 84, 111,
    194, 211, 213, 246

natal family 31, 145, 203, 208, 214, 217–218
nationalism 96, 225, 228, 264, 266

INDEX

nation-state   9, 24, 29, 223, 226n1, 225–227, 236, 241, 243, 245–246, 274

negotiation   22, 113, 148, 151, 161, 165, 171, 211

neo-familism   ix, 3, 5, 9, 15–17, 19, 24–25, 245–246, 253–254, 258, 260, 262–263, 267, 269
   intellectual discourse of   24, 263, 267
   official discourse of 24, 132, 254, 258–263, 267
   popular discourse of   24, 55, 254, 258, 267, 269

neo-liberal perspective   194, 205, 217

one-child policy   xii, 7, 9–10, 38, 48, 51, 58, 64, 110, 139, 150, 176, 178n1, 226, 235–236, 241, 245

parentalauthority   1, 5, 9, 20, 230–231, 256
   commitment   1 grief 23, 176, 178, 191
   guilt   183

power   5, 15, 23, 32, 232

parental support   5, 20, 216, 233, 253, 256, 258

parent-child bonds   23, 177, 178, 190, 195

parent-child burial   190

parenting style   198, 200
   scientific parenting   150, 157, 159, 170
   intensive parenting 59, 179, 187–188

party-state   4, 9, 16, 24, 96, 223–225, 234n4, 230–241, 243–247, 254, 258–259, 262–263, 267–268

patriarchal family   2, 5, 7, 11, 95, 147, 217, 256, 264

patrilineal decent   194

patrilocal residence   9, 11, 195, 201

patriotism   16, 24, 228, 260–261, 263, 267–268

personhood   14, 22, 81, 91, 96, 177, 182–184, 190–191
   failed personhood   177, 183, 191

parent-child integrated personhoods   14, 177

polite but distant   168–169

post-marital residence   10–11, 23, 17–18, 28, 195

post-patriarchal intergenerationality   4, 10–12, 14, 17, 19, 32, 177, 269

power relations   4, 10, 22, 144, 147–148, 151, 159, 161, 170

qinqing   116

reciprocity   96, 104, 145–146, 162

relocation   106–108, 115, 232, 244

remittances   87, 94

respect   11, 23, 68, 90, 118, 124, 128, 131, 147–148, 167, 172, 182, 197–198, 201, 217, 236n5, 239, 254

retirement   xii, 6, 67, 81, 115, 129, 178, 181, 218

sacrifice   15–16, 60, 72, 80, 82, 96–97, 115, 181, 196–197, 225, 244, 253, 255, 262, 266

sandwich generation   21–22, 83, 93, 123–124, 139

self-development   6, 13–14, 22–23, 125, 207, 209, 225, 253, 266

self-interest   118, 123, 126, 132, 138

sentimental disposition of the family-state   25, 260–263, 267–268

shidu parents   23, 176–179, 182, 184–186, 188–191, 243–244

singletons   7, 17, 22, 26, 55, 146, 178n1, 204, 210, 213, 241, 250

statism   224–228, 228n2, 230, 233, 239, 244, 246–247, 252, 265

statist model of family policy-making   9–10, 24, 223–226, 229, 232, 234, 239, 241, 243–247

suffering   55, 77–78, 80, 84, 86, 88, 90–91, 95–98, 124, 173, 183, 241

suicide   171, 176, 178, 183, 185

surveys   24, 55–58, 143, 150n2, 242, 254–255, 258, 267

tolerance   112, 163–164, 204, 217, 246

values   6, 10, 15, 17–18, 20–21, 36, 78, 97, 111, 118, 120, 139, 194, 197, 205, 217, 224, 230–231, 237n5, 239–240, 246, 254–255, 258, 260, 265, 267, 269–273

vertical tie   2, 14–15, 31, 48, 50, 94, 211

weddings   19, 32n1, 40–42, 48, 56, 228

welfare   4, 10, 48, 82, 94, 115, 118–119, 196, 223, 237–240, 242, 246–247, 263, 267

wellbeing   24, 117, 223

youth   5, 7, 10, 19–20, 39, 68, 81, 192, 197, 199–200, 205–207, 210, 213, 217, 224, 226–229, 233, 244, 246, 253, 256–257, 262

Printed in the United States
by Baker & Taylor Publisher Services